In Memory of
Leopold N. Judah

FOUNDING FIGHTERS

FOUNDING FIGHTERS

*The Battlefield Leaders Who Made
American Independence*

ALAN C. CATE

PRAEGER SECURITY INTERNATIONAL
Westport, Connecticut • London

Library of Congress Cataloging-in-Publication Data

Cate, Alan C., 1957–
    Founding fighters : the battlefield leaders who made American independence / Alan C. Cate.
      p.   cm.
    Includes bibliographical references and index.
    ISBN 0–275–98707–8 (alk. paper)
    1. United States—History—Revolution, 1775–1783—Biography.   2. United States.
Continental Army—Officers—Biography.   3. Generals—United States—Biography.
4. Soldiers—United States—Biography.   5. United States—History—Revolution,
1775–1783—Campaigns.   6. Command of troops—History—18th century.   I. Title.
    E206.C38   2006
    973.3′30922–dc22   2006021000
    [B]

British Library Cataloguing in Publication Data is available

Library of Congress Catalog Card Number: 2006021000
ISBN: 0–275–98707–8

First published in 2006

Praeger Security International, 88 Post Road West, Westport, CT 06881
An imprint of Greenwood Publishing Group, Inc.
www.praeger.com

Printed in the United States of America

The paper used in this book complies with the
Permanent Paper Standard issued by the National
Information Standards Organization (Z39.48–1984).

10 9 8 7 6 5 4 3 2 1

Contents

Preface

AMERICANS have always displayed toward the Founding Fathers a fascination that borders on ancestor worship. Indeed, and somewhat perversely, the only modern states that have ever approached our zeal in this regard have been twentieth-century totalitarian dictatorships with their leader-centered cults of personality. The exemplar was the late, unlamented Soviet Union with its enshrinement of Lenin and Marx. Other democracies nod to their ancestral leaders and seminal political thinkers, but we Americans positively venerate ours. Jefferson, Madison, and the rest still speak timelessly to us and our concerns in ways that, say, Locke and Burke or Montesquieu and Voltaire do not resonate for the British and French. More than two centuries after they were written, we continue to cite the Declaration of Independence and the Constitution, and pore over the Federalist Papers, as if they were holy writ. Recent bestseller lists provide another indication that this reverence remains strong. Major new biographies of George Washington, John Adams, Benjamin Franklin, and Alexander Hamilton have all earned critical acclaim and achieved commercial success. Additionally, a cursory search on the web reveals scores of titles collectively treating the "Founding Brothers," "Founding Mothers"—even "Founding Mothers and Fathers"—and many more of a similar nature.

This is as it should be. The Founders' vision and brilliance were central to gaining independence and forging a republic. But while necessary, their idealism and intellect were hardly sufficient. History is littered with failed rebellions. Americans won independence not just with lofty ideas and stirring words, but also through force of arms. For some time now, historians of the Revolutionary period (as well as many other eras of American history) have largely ignored this blunt fact. There are many reasons for this. One is a belief that the Revolutionary

War is a well-plowed furrow; this leads to the conclusion that there exists nothing fresh to say about the colonists' armed struggle. Another reason is the sense that the warfare of that distant time seems somewhat arcane and antiquated—almost quaint and baroque—compared to the visceral, immediate horror and violence of more recent conflicts. Further, many of us, if we think at all of the armed contest for independence, carry images of a rag-tag, frequently beaten force that Washington somehow managed to hold together until a succession of miracles turned the world upside down at Yorktown. Then there is the generally liberal worldview of most academic historians practicing today, whose opposition to war in general (exceeded in fervor only by practicing soldiers who have experienced it first hand) frequently leads to a disdain for studying or writing about it. A final factor relates to what for more than a generation has been the dominant trend in scholarly writing, which concerns itself more with social and cultural history "from the bottom up"—that is, the everyday lives of common folk, especially hitherto voiceless women and minorities. This approach, while it has often enriched our understanding of the past, takes a dim view of "great events" such as battles, and an even more jaundiced stance toward the notion of "great men" such as military commanders (for instance, all the above mentioned bestsellers are by so-called "popular historians"). Nevertheless, to have recourse to the communists one last time here, as Trotsky put it, "you may not be interested in war, but war is interested in you." His meaning, of course, was that whether one likes it or not, wars have decisive and far-reaching effects.

The American War of Independence was first and foremost a *war*. And this particular war had enormous human, economic, and political costs and consequences. Between 1775–1783, something like a quarter of a million Americans (out of a total of fewer than three million inhabitants in the 13 colonies), along with French allies, took up arms against British soldiers and their American Loyalist, German, and Native American auxiliaries. At least 4,500 patriots died in battle (as a percentage of the population that would equate to more than 400,000 American battlefield deaths today) and thousands more were wounded or succumbed to sickness and other non-battle causes. Reckoned in current dollars, the conflict destroyed millions worth of property. It created tens of thousands of refugees, particularly among those Americans who remained loyal to the British crown— a significant minority estimated to have comprised 20 percent of the colonists. Ultimately, more than 100,000 of them fled to Canada or the British isles. Most profoundly, of course, the War of Independence resulted in the birth of a new nation.

Founding Fighters explicitly recognizes the decisive role that military victory played in creating the United States. And integral to this battlefield success was the combat leadership provided by a relatively small number of hard-fighting warriors who held commands at the regimental, brigade, and division echelons or their naval equivalents. This book highlights selected members of this fierce list and tells their stories, while examining who they were, what they believed, and why they fought. Tracing their exploits and personalities permits us to explore several important aspects of American military and cultural history. First and most obviously, these narratives provide a means of analyzing the War of Independence at all levels, from strategic to tactical. Second, they offer a superb window for investigating two of the major continuing themes of the American military experience, civil–military relations, and the respective roles and worth of professional and citizen soldiers. Third, while these officers resembled each other in displaying martial virtues such as personal courage, professional skill, and ability to lead others in battle, they also varied greatly in vital ways. Collectively they represent—and allow the study of—a large sample of that diverse American *pluribus* that would eventually become *unum*.

Taken as a group, the leaders examined in *Founding Fighters* participated in virtually all of the war's significant battles and campaigns from 1775 onwards. They helped win stunning, legendary victories such as Trenton, Princeton, Saratoga, and Cowpens. They knew bitter defeats, including Quebec, Long Island, Brandywine, and Camden. And they suffered physical and spiritual privation through "times that try men's souls," when ultimate victory and independence appeared impossibly remote. Their service encompassed war in the northern, middle, and southern theaters, and shifts between a defensively oriented "war of posts" and an offensive war of maneuver. They practiced the traditional, eighteenth century European style of warfare, as well as the more irregular tactics that had taken root in North America during nearly two centuries of colonial Indian fighting. These men experienced the War of Independence in all its variants: conventional contest between opposing armies, savage guerilla struggle between partisans and regulars, and pitiless civil war pitting neighbors, and even family members, against each other. Therefore, reviewing the combat records of *Founding Fighters'* protagonists readily permits an understanding of how the war was fought, to include the evolution of American and British strategies, the operational problems both sides faced, and how they were (or were not) solved. Additionally, the accounts in this book furnish notable and frequently inspiring examples of command and leadership.

Besides allowing us to survey the particulars of the War of Independence, *Founding Fighters* also illuminates two fundamental issues surrounding America's military heritage. The first of these, military subordination to civilian authority, has long been firmly embedded in American military culture, but it did not necessarily have to turn out that way. Washington, his principal lieutenants—that is, the men chronicled here—and the Continental Congress worked out the contours of this civil–military tradition during the war. The profiles in these pages aid us in gaining purchase on the establishment of this crucial relationship between soldier-servants and civilian masters in our society. The second major issue is also an enduring part of our military experience—the tension between fielding a professional or regular force and relying upon an armed citizenry or militia. The majority of Americans during the colonial and revolutionary years harbored longstanding fear and hatred of "standing armies"—indeed, the presence of British forces in America was one of the precipitating causes of colonial rebellion and cited as such in the Declaration of Independence. Yet, many American military leaders—including, most notably,

Washington—despaired of ever gaining victory with amateur soldiers. The warrior leaders described here represented both sides of this schism. Several first gained military seasoning as militia officers, and some employed militia or led partisans with great effect, while others shared Washington's contempt for their lack of discipline and training.

Finally, these founding fighters all were products of a time and place quite distant from our own. They were different from us in many ways—and also from each other. They hailed from various parts of the eighteenth-century English world. Some were born in the British Isles; the others came from the very different sections of the American colonies—New England merchants, southern tidewater planters, middle colony men of affairs, and backcountry woodsmen. Their lives and peregrinations vividly illustrate the remarkable—in an age when travel was slow and laborious—geographic mobility possible in this world, as well as its great economic and social fluidity, with its attendant potential for dramatic rise and fall. Some grew up in poverty or were of the "middling class," while others knew relative ease and affluence. A few owned slaves. Their ranks included those from leveling democratic and communitarian backgrounds, and those of aloof patrician disposition. Several had impressive formal educations and others were unschooled or self-taught. Among them were veteran soldiers, as well as men who had never seen battle before the Revolution. They represented a variety of religious traditions and varying degrees of devoutness. They were Congregationalists, Anglicans, Presbyterians, Quakers and deists; virtually all had a belief in Providence or a higher power of some sort that took an interest in the destinies of men and nations.

Their motivations were equally mixed. The ideals of what scholars have labeled classical republicanism inspired most of them. This ideology, rooted equally in the history of the ancient Roman republic and more recent memories of the English revolution, emphasized distrust of power and loathing for its corruptions. Adherents to republicanism saw in the actions of the English parliament and king a conspiracy to deprive free men of their liberties. The only safeguard lay in a virtuous, public-spirited citizenry willing to defend itself and its rights. Conceptions of personal honor and reputation spurred these founding fighters as well. Honor was extremely important to gentlemen of this era; recall that the signers of the Declaration of Independence pledged their "sacred honor," as well as their lives and fortunes, in endorsing the document. This prideful coveting of honor in some instances made gentlemen prickly, swift to take offense, and hot-tempered, as we shall see in tracing the careers of several of the officers in this book. Finally, burning ambition for fame and glory, along with—more prosaically—an eye for the main chance, also fired more than one of these warriors.

Founding Fighters elaborates these topics of Revolutionary War combat, American military tradition, and cultural diversity by examining 15 important and colorful American military figures of the Revolution. Following an introduction that traces the war's outlines to establish context, the book devotes succeeding chapters to thematically linked pairs and trios of these officers. Contemporaries generally recognized them as capable, and in some cases even extraordinary, leaders, although to be sure most of them had bitter enemies too and became embroiled in controversy at one time or another. Likewise, posterity has rendered largely favorable—with a couple notable exceptions—appraisals as well.

When the fighting commenced, patriot leaders were especially eager to procure experienced, professional soldiers to command American troops. Three former British officers living in America, each of whom had also seen active service in North America during the French and Indian War, answered the call. In effect, each of them chose to go from redcoat to rebel. Nevertheless, despite their similarities, their Revolutionary War careers were quite different and, in a sense, disappointing. One died before fulfilling his immense promise and two were controversial in the extreme. Richard Montgomery, a son of Ireland, came to New York after leaving the British Army and became a prosperous landowner. At the war's outset he somewhat reluctantly accepted a brigadier general's commission in the Continental Army. He was among the patriots' first heroes, gaining early success in the ultimately abortive Canada campaign, before falling gallantly at the head of his troops in the doomed assault at Quebec on the last day of 1775.

Charles Lee issued from an aristocratic family in England. Well educated and deeply read in history and political philosophy, Lee was an ardent opponent of George III's corrupt court and policies. For this reason, he immigrated to America and involved himself in republican politics on these shores. In 1775, his military experience and political activity obtained him a major general's commission in the Continental Army and the post of Washington's second in command. He rendered good initial service during the siege of Boston and served as a troubleshooter for the commander in chief by assisting with American defensive dispositions in New York City, Rhode Island, Virginia, and Charleston, South Carolina. By the end of 1776 however, just before his capture by the British, Lee's personal irascibility, disobedience, and radical strategic views caused him to fall out with Washington. His advocacy of a "peoples' war" approach to the struggle based largely upon the militia especially horrified the politically and militarily conservative Washington. There even exists reason to believe that Lee collaborated to some degree with his captors before being exchanged back to the Continental Army in 1778. His final act was to enrage Washington with his handling of his troops at the battle of Monmouth, resulting in a court-martial that ended Lee's career in disgrace.

Horatio Gates was born in England and after serving the crown as an officer became an energetic republican and advocate of the colonists' position in their dispute with the mother country. A colonial with whom he had become friendly during the French and Indian War, George Washington, persuaded Gates to move to Virginia, where he bought a plantation. With considerable enthusiasm, he too accepted a brigadier general's rank in the Continental Army when war broke out. Like his friend Charles Lee, his wartime record was mixed and contentious. He displayed superior administrative talent on several occasions and was the senior American commander at Saratoga. He may be said to have set the conditions for this crucial victory, though other generals actually led the fighting. Gates's name became associated with shadowy cabals aimed at Washington and the Continental

Congress both before and after the British humiliated an army under his command at Camden, South Carolina in 1780. Relieved following this defeat, he was subsequently restored to active duty and finished the war as Washington's deputy.

Henry Knox and Nathanael Greene were not professional soldiers, but rather self-taught amateurs who proved to be two of Washington's most able lieutenants. Consequently, they ranked among the most trusted and long serving. Indeed, and somewhat ironically, their battle records were far superior to those of the much more professionally experienced Charles Lee and Horatio Gates. Knox received a very limited formal education in his native Boston. He joined the militia, and pursued his avid interest in military art and science by extensive reading in the bookshop he owned. When war came, he volunteered and soon became chief of the Continental Army's artillery. He handled his guns brilliantly throughout the war, from the opening siege of Boston to the finale at Yorktown. Greene was a Rhode Island Quaker and, like Knox, compensated for a smattering of schooling with voracious reading. He too participated in the local militia and the Rhode Island assembly appointed him commander of the colony's forces in 1775. He subsequently rendered superb service as a combat leader directly under Washington, winning laurels at Trenton and Princeton. He also acted for a stint as the Army's quartermaster general from 1778–1780, where he performed effectively, though not without running afoul of Congress. Greene's greatest contribution to the patriot cause came after he returned to field command in the Carolinas, replacing Gates in the wake of the rout at Camden. His orchestration of the southern campaign of 1780–1782, combining regular and partisan forces, remains one of the most remarkable feats in American military history and set the stage for Yorktown.

Benedict Arnold and John Paul Jones make for an especially intriguing comparison with each other. Arnold's name has, of course, become a by-word for treason, while Jones is revered as the "Father of the American Navy." Yet their lives and careers reveal some fascinating parallels. If nothing else, to those only casually acquainted with the Revolutionary War, their names are probably the most familiar of all the founding fighters covered in this book. More significant was their shared combativeness and hunger for recognition. Arnold, a Connecticut merchant, was a firebrand for independence and took the field immediately following Lexington and Concord. He ranked among the bravest and most hard fighting of all the American generals before his fall from grace. His honors include an arduous trek through the wilderness during the Quebec expedition; he was severely wounded in the failed assault—the same action that killed Montgomery—on that citadel. He fought two naval engagements against the British on Lake Champlain and was one of the heroes of Saratoga, where he again suffered serious wounds. Nevertheless, Arnold continually chafed under slights, real and imagined, from Congress and his fellow generals. This sense of injury to his *amour propre*, combined with serious financial problems, led to his traitorous attempt to hand over West Point and Washington to the British in 1780. John Paul was a Scotsman who went to sea at 13 and rose to command merchant vessels plying the trade routes between England and the Americas. A scrape with the law forced him to seek refuge in Virginia and create a new identity by adding "Jones" to his name. He offered his services to the Revolutionary cause as a naval officer and led several successful prize-taking forays before his apotheosis during the epic fight between his *Bonhomme Richard* and *HMS Serapis* in 1779. Yet, as with Arnold, Congress repeatedly passed Jones over for promotion in favor of less competent and aggressive officers. Jones deeply resented these indignities, but unlike Arnold remained loyal to cause and country.

Three South Carolinians carved out impressive reputations as partisan chieftains in the bitter struggle against the British and their Loyalist supporters in the south. Andrew Pickens was a backcountry settler who possessed considerable experience combating frontier Indians. A quiet Presbyterian Church elder, he was a natural leader and a tactically adroit fighter. He displayed a commendable willingness to cooperate and synchronize his men's actions with other forces, most successfully at Cowpens in 1781. Thomas Sumter, the "Gamecock," was a well-off planter and another old Indian fighter. As a militiaman in his native Virginia, he gained some campaigning experience in the French and Indian War, and served in the Continental Army in the war's early days before withdrawing to his estate. When marauding British forces burned his plantation, he returned to the fray with a vengeance. He generally fought ferociously, although not always successfully. His practice of paying his band in plunder taken from Loyalists was reviled even by some patriots, as was an independent streak that led him to coordinate only sporadically with Continental Army generals. The final and most famous member of this triumvirate was Francis Marion, also a prosperous planter, whom we remember today as the "Swamp Fox." He initially saw service as a field grade officer, first in a South Carolina regiment, then in the Continental line. After the debacle at Charleston in 1780 that saw the city surrendered to the British, Marion began his legendary career as a daring partisan leader whose incessant raids and ambushes, along with the intelligence he gathered, contributed substantially to Greene's southern campaign.

A trio of fighting frontiersmen finds a place in this book as well. Ethan Allen was a profane giant of a man. Originally from Connecticut, Allen settled in what is present-day Vermont, but in the colonial period was territory much disputed between New Hampshire and New York. He raised an armed body of followers known as the Green Mountain Boys to defend his claims. In 1775, he led his private army to seize the important stronghold of Fort Ticonderoga on Lake Champlain for the patriots. The British subsequently captured him when he tried to storm Montreal later that year and he spent over two and a half years as their prisoner before being exchanged. In recognition of his fortitude, he was made a brevet colonel in the Continental Army. George Rogers Clark was a Virginian. In 1777 his state approved the 25-year-old woodsman's audacious plan to defend its westernmost settlements against attacks by the British and their Indian allies. Acting upon the tenet that the best defense is a good offense, Clark led an expedition into the Illinois country between the Ohio and Mississippi Rivers, and conquered half a continent. Daniel Morgan, an especially ferocious and skilled battlefield leader from the Virginia backcountry, joined the patriot cause at its inception. He distinguished himself at the head of his corps of riflemen at Quebec and Saratoga. Like several other founding fighters, however, chagrin at Congress's failure to recognize his sacrifices and achievements enraged Morgan, and drove him to leave the army temporarily in 1779. He returned to the struggle a year later and won the Americans' most impressive tactical success of the war at Cowpens.

Finally, a pair of dashing and ambitious young leaders completes the set of portraits offered in *Founding Fighters*. Henry "Light-Horse Harry" Lee was another Virginian, though from a much more genteel and privileged background than the rough and ready Morgan and Clark. He joined a cavalry regiment in 1776. Here he displayed the boldness and ability that earned him his nickname in many raids and skirmishes, most notably under Greene during the latter's masterful southern campaign. Before the war, Anthony Wayne was the scion of a well-to-do Pennsylvania family. Active in anti-imperial politics from the start, he was commissioned in the Continental Army in 1776 and quickly rose to flag rank. His fearlessness and hot temper made the soubriquet of "Mad Anthony" a fitting one. Wayne built his formidable reputation as a brigade and division commander in many Revolutionary battles, most memorably with a nighttime bayonet assault against a British outpost at Stony Point, New York in 1779.

In addition to the many insights into history, heritage, and culture contained in these tales of combat leadership, one further lesson shines through. Each of these stories illustrates what historians call the power of contingency. Events now embedded in a seemingly long-dead past were once simply future possibilities. Concerning the American Revolution, although we can now look back and find reasons for the outcome, this does not mean that the results were inevitable or foreordained. The combat careers recounted in *Founding Fighters* demonstrate that individual choices and actions, more so than mere accidents or vast, impersonal historical forces, make a difference. These men made war and in so doing helped make a nation.

Introduction

The Founding Fighters' War, 1775–1783

THIS BOOK RECOUNTS the stories of 15 important American combat leaders during the War of Independence. Understanding them and their times offers us a means to gain greater insight into their war and its meaning. But conversely, to explore their careers, it is first necessary to know something about the war's overall scope and character. This introduction establishes that required context by sketching out the strategies attempted by both sides, tracing the war's major outlines, and indicating where the various founding fighters participated. Of course, in reading the subsequent chapters, readers will note that, fairly often, they find themselves revisiting familiar scenes. An early nineteenth-century writer commented on this phenomenon while composing a similar collective biography. In his preface to *Washington and His Generals* (1847), J. T. Headley wrote "I have avoided repetition, as much as possible, but yet have chosen in some places to let this fault remain, in order to secure an object I could not reach without it . . . It seems to me, that a series of sketches ought not to be judged by the same rules as a connected history."[1] In a book of this sort, and given the often remarkable ties among several of the protagonists, some repetition is inescapable. Ideally, this necessity will even prove a virtue, in permitting exploration of key events from different perspectives.

The American Revolution defies simple or easy description. It was a political and social phenomenon as much as a military one though, as in all conflicts, these three strands were closely related. It was a complex, wide-ranging, and long-lasting affair (our longest war until Vietnam) that changed shape several times. Over a span of 8.5 years, it involved multiple forms of combat: traditional European, irregular "Indian style," naval, partisan, and civil war. In North America alone it stretched from Canada to Georgia and the Atlantic seaboard to the Mississippi. Contending over this vast expanse of territory were Americans, both patriots battling for independence and Loyalists still true to the crown; British regular troops, assisted by hired German mercenaries (most from the province of Hesse, hence known to us as "Hessians"); French forces sent to aid the embattled Americans; and assorted Indian allies on both sides. Great Britain ultimately found herself embroiled in a world war, as several European nations in addition to France supported the infant United States and the fighting spread to the West Indies, the Indian subcontinent, and other spots around the globe.

In addition to these complicating factors, the war's remoteness in time further hinders our efforts to reconstruct it. For one thing, it is simply not as well documented as our more recent conflicts. Records are spotty and, since it occurred half a century before the advent of photography, there is no Revolutionary War equivalent of Matthew Brady to help us with envisioning what the soldiers and battlefields looked like. Further, as the war that created our nation, the War of Independence is especially encrusted in myth, due primarily to the pietistic work of its earliest chroniclers, writing long before historical scholarship became a profession.

Nevertheless, scholars have done some truly extraordinary historical work on the Revolution. At the microlevel, imaginatively using existing sources such as letters, diaries, and even postwar pension requests, they have been able to help us enter the worldviews of this era's men and women. And at the macrolevel, scholars have imposed a number of different frameworks upon the war. These organizing structures are of course somewhat arbitrary, based primarily upon chronology, geography, and events. Of necessity, like all models, they are a bit oversimplified in order to aid in clarity. What follows is such a construct based upon time, space, and purpose, intended here to illuminate American and British strategies, as well as the war's major phases, in order to set the stage for relating the founding fighters' exploits.

AMERICAN STRATEGIES

As the historian Dave R. Palmer has observed, "strategy" was not a familiar word to George Washington or his contemporaries. It would take another half century, the Napoleonic wars, and a Prussian genius named Clausewitz to popularize the concept in something like the modern sense.[2] Nevertheless, Washington, and other Americans too, clearly thought in terms of the relationship of ends, ways, and means—the essence of strategy as we think of it today.

So what was the American strategy? This is not a question that permits a facile answer. Scholars have discerned a number of different American strategies and disagreed among themselves over them. This is not surprising; after all, history has been famously described as "an argument without end." Those responsible for actually conducting the war—Washington, the Continental Congress above him, and his principal subordinates below—not infrequently found themselves at odds as to which course to follow as well. Again, this is perfectly understandable to any student of the annals of war or of human nature. Additionally, the conditions of the struggle changed over time. Objectives, resource constraints, enemy actions—all of these shifted at various points and drove strategic choices.

For instance, in the war's early stages the Americans' ultimate objective of political independence from England had not yet crystallized. The first 14 months of conflict—April 1775 to June 1776—took place before the Continental Congress made the momentous decision to sever permanently the relationship with the mother country. During this first phase, while Americans mulled reconciliation or independence, the goal was to assert and protect American rights against British reprisal. Further, as the struggle progressed, it became clear that beyond independence, Americans also wanted security, expressed most tangibly in terms of territorial expansion. This is clear from any number of sources and actions. Thomas Paine's *Common Sense* enthused over an empire of liberty and the Declaration of Independence in its bill of particulars against the Crown included British efforts to stymie western settlement. Likewise, the American invasion of Canada in pursuit of a "fourteenth colony," the war's frontier campaigns, and the negotiating instructions given by the Congress to American diplomats abroad also furnish evidence of this impulse. American strategy reflected these changing and multiple goals.

Regarding resources, the Americans were sorely inferior to the British in terms of trained soldiers, naval supremacy, and finances. This obviously shaped American strategic options. When France joined the war on the American side in 1778, and with Spain and Holland also providing assistance, the resource situation changed and so did the strategic landscape. Besides adding men, ships, and money to the American cause, each of these allies and partners brought their own strategic imperatives to the struggle. But, in addition to bolstering the patriot undertaking, this also complicated the strategic equation. While one might say that Washington was, with forces from 13 states, a coalition commander from the start, the European entry further required Americans to harmonize competing national interests as an integral part of forging strategy.

Finally, as an old military aphorism has it, "the enemy gets a vote too." For much of the war, due to their superior resources, as well their requirement to quell a colonial rebellion, the British took the initiative. Thus American strategy was frequently reactive in response to British moves. Given all of this, it is perhaps best then to speak not of American strategy, but rather American strategies.

Fundamentally, throughout the war, one of Washington's overriding goals was to preserve his army as a viable symbol of resistance and independence. As long as the Continental Army remained in being, so did the Revolution. At one point Washington described his strategy to Congress as a "war of posts," where he concentrated on keeping the army together and avoiding a major engagement with the main British force, which would have risked a crushing American defeat. For this reason, historians have often described Washington as a "Fabian general" (after the Roman, Fabius, who avoided decisive battle and instead sought to wear down and frustrate his adversary, Hannibal). American strategy has therefore been characterized by most scholars as essentially defensive and one of attrition or "erosion." Other, more romantic and less historically informed renderings, have incorrectly (and somewhat anachronistically, since like "strategy," "guerilla war" was another term that came into use after the Revolution) portrayed the Americans as primarily waging a guerilla campaign against the British.[3]

Nevertheless, overall American strategy was not nearly as one dimensional or simplistic as any of this. In their initial Revolutionary fervor the patriots exhibited notable offensive spirit, seizing numerous key points throughout the colonies and invading Canada. Later on, they launched strikes against the British and their Indian allies along the Mississippi, as well as in the Susquehanna, Mohawk, and Allegheny valleys. Washington himself possessed a naturally aggressive temperament. He longed to go over to the attack, as demonstrated at Trenton, Princeton, Monmouth, and elsewhere. On other occasions, it required councils of war to dissuade him from offensive action. For instance, during the siege of Boston, he proposed an ill-advised attack to sweep away the British forces barricaded inside the city. Most auspiciously, of course, Washington grasped the initiative in the fall of 1781, and led a combined Franco-American force from New York to Yorktown to trap a British army and win the war's climactic battle.

And while the Americans practiced irregular and partisan warfare (as did the British with their Loyalist and Indian allies) on occasion, especially in the south, most of the war's battles were fought according to established eighteenth-century European custom. To be sure, by the time of the Revolution, this style of battle included the use of light infantry, skirmishers, and riflemen who fought in open order. Decision was still achieved, however, by serried ranks of infantry drawn up in opposition to each other in open terrain exchanging musket volleys at close range until one side broke and the other could close with fixed bayonets. Field artillery would blast holes in enemy formations, while cavalry searched for an assailable flank or rode down the fleeing foe as part of a pursuit. Indeed, one of Washington's most cherished desires was to build the Continental Army into a professional, regular force on par with the British redcoats and their Hessian allies. He frequently despaired about the caliber of amateur soldiers and militia under his command. Washington also clashed with one of his ranking subordinates, the former British officer General Charles Lee, on the issue of fielding regular forces as opposed to Lee's advocacy of what we would today call "peoples'" or "unconventional" warfare. Washington won this dispute. Nevertheless, he and some of his more gifted subordinates, notably Nathanael Greene in his brilliant southern campaign, made adroit use of colonial militia and irregular forces when required to harass the enemy and garner intelligence.

At bottom, American strategy was remarkably sophisticated. As embodied by Washington it was at times even paradoxical. The American commander in chief was a conservative aristocrat who found himself leading a revolutionary struggle. And though he possessed an aggressive disposition, he in fact had to rely regularly upon evasion and the defense. Overall, the Americans blended defense and offense, regular and irregular tactics, as the situation dictated. Washington and the other founding fighters exhibited patience when necessary, yet were generally quick to grasp opportunities when they presented themselves. In waging war, the Americans passed the basic test of strategy: they effectively matched available ways and means to their desired ends.

BRITISH STRATEGIES

One of the questions that perpetually exercises historians is whether the Americans won the War of Independence or the British simply lost it. Certainly, especially at the war's outset, the British possessed considerable advantages. London was the seat of the world's richest, most powerful empire. Although she had jealous rivals in Europe, England was at peace and had been unchallenged since a series of victorious wars—including much North American combat—in the first half of the eighteenth century. Her ability to project power with a potent army and a magnificent navy was unmatched, and she had the 13 colonies strategically surrounded with outposts on the western frontier, as well as in Canada to the north and her Caribbean colonies to the south. England had suppressed rebellions before (admittedly closer to home, in Ireland) and successfully made war in North America. A considerable percentage of the American population—estimated at about 20 percent—remained loyal to the crown and at least a similar number were neutral.

Stacked against these favorable conditions were disadvantages. The British had to contend with a 3,000-mile lifeline across the stormy north Atlantic, upon which imperial forces depended for reinforcements, some logistical sustainment, and strategic direction. Internal lines of communication in America were no less fraught. While there were a handful of excellent ports, a paucity of good roads into the interior made the countryside poorly suited for maneuver and worse for logistics. As the war progressed, the British faced an increasingly aroused American populace, as well as the patriots' European allies in what became a global struggle. In part, these last two developments reflected inept British political and diplomatic efforts, as well as the Americans' more effective work in these spheres. Yet what hindered British more than any of these was the lack of a coherent strategy.

The objective was clear enough—end the colonial uprising and restore imperial rule throughout the 13 colonies. Yet British leaders were divided to some degree as to whether the best method to achieve this was through conciliation or coercion. In London, policymaking responsibility lay in the hands of three individuals: King George III; his prime minister, Sir Frederick North; and the secretary of state for colonies, Lord George Germain, a former Army officer cashiered for misconduct. Historians have given all three exceedingly low marks for leadership ability and strategic insight. While a number of eloquent and influential British politicians—the best known being Edmund Burke and William Pitt—argued for a conciliatory policy and against the folly of violent repression, the three men at the top resolved on the latter.

While that would seem to have settled the matter, senior British officers in America had their own views. Both General Sir William Howe, who became the British commander in chief in America in October 1775, and his brother Lord Richard Howe, who assumed command of the British fleet in American waters in 1776, strongly favored conciliation. They remained at their respective posts until the middle of 1778 and their joint conduct of military operations reflected their ambivalence about prosecuting the war.

British command problems extended beyond the mixed feelings of the brothers Howe; indeed the entire chain of command was highly dysfunctional. The British violated the principle of unity of command in the American theater for much of the war by retaining a separate commander in chief for Canada, Sir Guy Carleton. General Howe's deputy and eventual successor, General Sir Henry Clinton, while displaying flashes of professional talent, was congenitally incapable of taking risk or cooperating with either superiors or peers. Significant shortcomings in temperament and skill afflicted the other two senior British generals in America, John Burgoyne and Charles Lord Cornwallis, as well. Compounding the friction created by the collision of these bumptious egos, Germain back in London frequently bypassed the commander in chief to correspond directly with generals in the field. This fractured system led to considerable confusion and disastrously poor coordination, most significantly in the Saratoga and Yorktown campaigns.

Essentially, the British had two broad military schemas open to them. One was to be force oriented, that is to focus on the destruction of the main American armies, especially the one personally led by Washington. The other was to be terrain oriented—to seek to snuff out the rebellion through the control of key geographical points.[4]

The first of these, in theory, offered the best hope to the British. In practice, destroying the enemy proved difficult to bring about for a number of reasons. For one thing, the Napoleonic battle of annihilation was alien to the Age of Reason and the eighteenth century way of war, which tended to be limited in scope and purpose. Then, during the war's first half, General Howe was reluctant to essay a strategy of destruction due to his hopes for Anglo-American conciliation. For instance, in the fall of 1776 he routed Washington out of New York, but eschewed the opportunities afforded by his greater, seaborne mobility to cut the Americans off. Howe subsequently pushed the reeling patriots out of New Jersey, but again neglected to strike a death blow. But only part of this failure can be attributed to Howe's personal disposition. Washington deserves at least as much credit for his skillful withdrawals.

As a result, the British ended up attempting, or at least considering, a variety of terrain-oriented schemes. The most basic was a naval blockade of American ports. Though seconded by a number of British strategists, it never got much purchase for a couple of reasons. First, despite its status as the world's premier fleet, even the Royal Navy lacked the assets to close off completely America's lengthy Atlantic seaboard. Further, strangling America would take time and could prove as costly to British merchants as to colonial traders, especially unpalatable for a war that was far from universally popular at home in England. Finally, in this preindustrial age, there really was not any necessary commodity that the Americans could not produce—or smuggle—in sufficient quantities to sustain the struggle.

Another tack, which the British pursued for the first part of the war, can be called the northern strategy. Here the British used the operational mobility afforded by their fleet to capture New York City as a base of operations. From there they rapidly conquered New Jersey and also Rhode Island, securing another naval bastion at Newport. A year later, they seized the rebel capital in Philadelphia, forcing the Congress into headlong and undignified flight. Almost simultaneously, though in totally uncoordinated fashion, they mounted a drive down from Canada with the goal of controlling the Hudson River valley and effectively severing the cradle of rebellion, New England, from the rest of the colonies. Successful in taking large cities, thwarted at Saratoga in the effort to command the line of the Hudson, this northern strategy ultimately failed to achieve the strategic goal of ending the rebellion. Indeed there is good reason to believe that even had the British achieved their aims in the Hudson Valley, they would have had insufficient resources to control all the key terrain necessary to cut off the colonies completely from each other.

The final terrain-centered strategy tried by the British came in the war's concluding act, an invasion of the American south. In essence, the south always seemed like low-hanging fruit to some British strategists. Loyalist sentiment appeared stronger in the south, farther from the New England cockpit, and additionally the British could perhaps hope that southerners' fear of hostile Indians and slave uprisings might keep them in check. Again British naval supremacy brought them swift control of coastal cities such as Savannah and Charleston. But though they won a string of tactical victories in the Carolinas and Virginia, none were strategically decisive. Meanwhile, rebellion thrived in the north and the British army in the south wore itself down chasing rebels until it became trapped itself at Yorktown.

The preceding catalog of British shortcomings and miscalculations might seem to indicate, in answer to the question posed at the beginning of this section, that the British lost the war more than the Americans won it. They certainly failed to break either the patriots' army or their will. And they found it much easier to conquer territory than to control it. Such a conclusion, however, overlooks how American leaders and soldiers capitalized on the opportunities presented to them, and overcame their own deficiencies and errors in judgment. War is a dynamic contest of wills. The Americans proved eminently worthy of the victory they won.

TO ARMS: APRIL 1775–JUNE 1776

The newly appointed commander in chief of the Continental Army rode into Cambridge, Massachusetts, on July 2, 1775. General George Washington's mission was to assume command of the heterogeneous collection of forces engaged in a tense stand off with a British army in Boston. The previous weeks and months had witnessed an explosion of passion and violence following years of long-simmering discord between England and 13 of her American colonies. In April at Lexington and Concord, enraged patriot militia had fiercely resisted a British attempt to disarm them and capture their leaders. In the immediate aftermath, the harried British under General Thomas Gage holed up in Boston as thousands of farmers, mechanics, and laborers flocked to Cambridge from New England and the other colonies to join what had become a siege against the redcoats. Scarcely 2 weeks prior to Washington's arrival, on June 17, Gage had sent his scarlet-clad regiments to dislodge dug-in rebel positions on Charlestown peninsula, which dominated the British lodgment from the north. The result was a pyrrhic British victory and the creation of an enduring symbol of American resolve and valor, the battle of Bunker Hill.

Patriotic enthusiasm and activity were not limited to Massachusetts. Fort Ticonderoga, on New York's Lake Champlain, had been key terrain during the French and Indian War, and American eyes turned to it again after the outbreak of fighting. Patriots coveted the fort both to block any British expedition launched southward from Canada over the old colonial wars invasion route—St. Lawrence and Richelieu Rivers, Lakes Champlain and George, and thence the Hudson River valley—and for the decade-old stockpile of artillery pieces and mortars emplaced there. An enterprising group of Connecticut men of affairs enlisted a harum-scarum frontiersman named Ethan Allen to seize Ticonderoga. Allen and his followers, known as the Green Mountain Boys, set forth in early May and gathered an assault force just below Ticonderoga. Much to his surprise and chagrin, he was joined there by Colonel Benedict Arnold of Connecticut, who had convinced Massachusetts officials that he was just the man to capture the prize. Despite having no troops of his own, the energetic Arnold proclaimed himself overall commander. These two strong-willed men predictably bickered, but nevertheless somehow managed to mount a surprise dawn attack against the lightly garrisoned fort. On May 10 the Americans surprised Ticonderoga's hapless British commander in his bedchamber and took control of the place. Part bold stroke, part comic opera, here was another patriot victory.

This and similar spontaneous and uncoordinated actions had led, in part, to Washington's appointment. The second Continental Congress, containing representatives from all the colonies except Georgia, had convened in Philadelphia the very day of Allen's and Arnold's joint *coup de main* and immediately found itself confronting myriad headaches. War fever raged throughout the land. British government in the colonies had effectively ceased with royal governors increasingly isolated, ignored, and in some cases decamping from their previous seats of power to less hostile surroundings. Holding the reins in their stead were various provisional assemblies and revolutionary councils. These bodies now importuned Congress, seeking guidance and assistance. New Yorkers wanted to know how to respond to an anticipated British descent upon the colony. Massachusetts requested the creation and rapid dispatch of troops to Boston to succor the motley patriot assemblage facing off with Gage's redcoats. Dozens of other questions, great and small, of policy, strategy, and administration, perplexed Congress. Composed of what were, in some cases, mutually suspicious colonies and high-strung individuals of differing views, the Congress attempted to proceed deliberately. What it could not be put off, however, was the question of an army. Even though they were still undecided whether their ultimate objective was reconciliation with England or independence, there was no question that America was at war. And war demanded an army.

Accordingly, Congress took the appropriate steps, among them instructing the colonies to arm themselves, appointing a committee to obtain military supplies, and borrowing money to buy gunpowder. On June 14, 1775, still celebrated as the birthday of the United States Army, the nation's oldest military service, Congress began to raise a Continental Army. It accomplished this by adopting forces already in the field in Massachusetts and New York, and by authorizing the recruitment of ten companies of riflemen from Pennsylvania, Maryland, and Virginia to augment them. Subsequently Congress, which zealously retained the prerogative of appointing general officers throughout the war, appointed the first slate of Continental Army generals. These numbered 13 officers—four major generals and nine brigadiers—chosen with equal regard for military abilities, sectional balance, and presumed subordination to congressional control.[5]

Just as everyone recognized that an army was required, most agreed that the man best fitted to command it was a delegate from Virginia, George Washington. The Mount Vernon planter-aristocrat looked every bit the part, and not only because he had chosen to wear his Virginia militia colonel's uniform to Philadelphia. Tall, imposing, reserved yet charismatic, Washington had inspired confidence through his bearing and conduct in the Congress's early days, tendering sound advice on the many pressing military questions. Although he had never commanded a large body of troops, and several other members also held militia commissions, Washington possessed the most extensive military background of any of the Congressmen. He had served honorably on the Virginia frontier and with imperial forces during the French and Indian War. In addition to his sterling character and professional qualifications, Washington's Virginia origins furnished a good political reason for selecting him. Virginia was the largest and most populous of all the colonies, and some delegates feared that Massachusetts had already attained too much power in national councils. Naming Washington to head the Continental Army on June 15 was thus perhaps the first instance of sectional balancing in the emerging nation.

As he took up his duties, Washington faced a bewildering array of issues and questions. He had to organize, administer, and hold together a new army composed for the most part of indifferently disciplined colonial militias and independent-minded recruits. He needed to maintain close and constant liaison with his political masters in Philadelphia who, despite their expressed confidence in him, retained a healthy suspicion of "men on horseback" and standing armies, and entertained their own ideas about conducting the war. His civil–military responsibilities ranged from winning over the local Cambridge citizenry to conducting an extensive correspondence with the different provincial governments on a broad palette of issues ranging from supplying troops to proposed military operations. Over time, Washington proved equal to each of these challenges. But the immediate tactical and operational problem at hand was that of ejecting the British from Boston.

Washington began a simultaneous process of digging in and training his forces, which for the siege of Boston ultimately numbered about 16,000 men, divided almost equally between militia and elements of the new Continental Army. The British, at peak strength about 10,000 soldiers and supported by a fleet, likewise erected fortifications to barricade themselves within the city. Among the American officers on the scene were Arnold, fresh from his Ticonderoga triumph, and the commander of a company of Virginia riflemen, Captain Daniel Morgan. Also on hand were two former British Army officers, Major General Charles Lee and Brigadier General Horatio Gates; Rhode Island's Nathanael Greene, a newly appointed Continental brigadier; and young Henry Knox, a 25-year-old Bostonian. The latter held the impressive sounding post of the army's artillery chief, although somewhat inconveniently, Washington's host possessed no artillery to speak of.

While Washington coped with the situation in Boston, Congress decided to add Canada to the rebellious fold. The Canadians resisted friendly blandishments, so in late June that body ordered Major General Philip Schuyler (like Washington, a member of the Continental Congress—a further illustration of Congress's ardent desire to maintain control of the military), to mount an expedition from New York to capture Montreal. Supporting the Congressional intent, Washington designated Colonel Arnold to lead a separate column up through the Maine wilderness to attack Quebec. Arnold in turn selected the impressive Captain Morgan's outfit to join him. By November 1775, the western or Montreal aspect of this twin-pronged invasion succeeded, thanks primarily to the energy and leadership of Brigadier General Richard Montgomery, an Irish-born former British Army officer now from New York, who had replaced the ailing Schuyler. To the east, Arnold's bedraggled men had completed a heroic 6-week tramp through trackless wastes to arrive at the gates of Quebec by mid-November. Here they waited until Montgomery arrived in early December to assume overall command. Outnumbered by the British and loyal Canadians inside the heavily fortified town, lacking the necessary heavy artillery and engineer assets to conduct a siege, and facing the imminent dissolution of their force upon the expiration of enlistments at year's end, Montgomery and Arnold resolved upon a desperate assault. This gallant but doomed attempt, undertaken in a blizzard in the predawn hours of December 31, 1775, ended with Montgomery dead, Arnold wounded, and Morgan a prisoner.

Events unfolded considerably better for the patriots in the American south. Cooped up in hostile Boston, the British eyed the southland as an area that seemed to harbor considerable Loyalist sentiment and thus suitable for a foray. Accordingly, late in 1775 the British devised a scheme to launch a fleet from England to the Carolinas, ferrying several regiments of redcoats and a considerable number of small arms to equip the crown's supposedly avid supporters. General Howe dispatched a smaller detachment under General Clinton by sea to link up with this element and jointly foment counterrevolution. Bad weather and worse luck delayed the rendezvous between the two forces until May 1776. Meanwhile patriot militia handed Loyalist forces some stinging setbacks and established political dominance throughout much of the region. Seeking to retrieve something from a failed campaign, Clinton attempted an attack on Charleston harbor. South Carolina militia under the overall command of Charles Lee, and aided by tricky tides and winds, handily repelled this effort and forced the British to abandon their southern strategy—at least for several years. The June 28, 1776, defense of Fort Sullivan became part of the Palmetto State's military heritage; marked the Revolutionary debut of Major Francis Marion, a low country planter who commanded a portion of the American artillery in the battle; and added another victory to the patriot cause.

The denouement in Boston was equally glorious. In an epic of endurance and ingenuity to match Arnold's trek to Quebec, Colonel Knox led a wintertime march to Fort Ticonderoga to secure the artillery stored there and drag it over 300 snow and ice-covered miles to Cambridge. His most glaring deficiency thus redressed, by early March 1776 Washington had secured the critical terrain on Dorchester Heights, whence he poised to blast the British out of the city. With memories of Bunker Hill still fresh, General Howe, who had relieved Gage, declined to attack and try to drive off the Americans. Given the required latitude from London to quit Boston if he saw fit, and heartily sick of the place, he embarked his command and left the city on March 17, 1776, a date nowadays overshadowed by celebrations of Erin's patron saint, but still formally recognized by the Commonwealth of Massachusetts as Evacuation Day. The British sailed for Halifax, Nova Scotia, to refit themselves for their next move while Washington pondered his own options. Meanwhile Congress moved toward a momentous decision.

DEFENDING INDEPENDENCE: JULY 1776–DECEMBER 1777

On July 3, 1776, John Adams, one of Massachusetts's Congressional delegates wrote, "Yesterday the greatest Question was decided, which ever was debated in America, and a greater perhaps, never was or will be decided among Men."[6] The previous day Congress had unanimously adopted a resolution of independence and the following day would approve a formal Declaration to that effect. But even as independence was being proclaimed, a powerful British armada appeared off New York City and began landing troops on Staten Island. This was Howe's contingent from Halifax. Soon additional reinforcements arrived from England. By late August 1776, Howe disposed of a combined force of over 30,000 British regulars and German mercenaries, supported by more than 70 warships, positioned to threaten New York. An additional 13,000 British troops had been dispatched to Canada. The British had fixed on a campaign plan to crush the rebellion. Using New York City, with its excellent harbor and sizable Loyalist population, as a base, British strategy envisioned an advance up the Hudson River in conjunction with a supporting attack from Canada down the river. Defeating any Continental forces, should they offer battle, the two thrusts would meet, cut New England off from the rest of the colonies, then turn east to wipe out that nest of rebellion.

Anticipating a British move on New York, Washington had arrived there to take personal command less than a month after General Howe had departed Boston. By midsummer, as the British continued their buildup on Staten Island, Washington reinforced a series of positions established on Long Island, and in lower and upper Manhattan by his alter ego and troubleshooter Charles Lee. Defending the city presented a tactician's nightmare, although political considerations demanded that Washington make the effort. In addition to the Americans facing a larger, better trained and provisioned force, the city itself was surrounded by water. This circumstance gave the British, with their complete mastery of the waves, the capability to envelop and trap Washington's army at any juncture. This the Howe brothers chose not to do. Rather, the British merely pushed the American army out of New York. The campaign opened in earnest with late August landings on Long Island by a sizable British force. The ensuing battle on August 27, 1776, resulted in an American defeat that could have been catastrophic had the British acted with the necessary alacrity to cut off the American withdrawal from Brooklyn Heights across the East River to Manhattan. As it was, the Americans were routed with heavy losses.

Operations continued their leisurely development when the British and Hessians conducted another amphibious landing 2 weeks later. This time they descended on the east side of Manhattan at Kips's Bay, at about the same level as present-day midtown. The Connecticut militia charged with securing this approach panicked and deserted their positions, causing a furious Washington to throw his hat on the ground and exclaim, "Good God, have I got such troops as those!"[7] This was another American fiasco, partly redeemed only by the British failure once again to press their advantage to the fullest. The landing force moved inland, but refrained from blocking the withdrawal of large numbers of American troops, who escaped to the north. Washington repaired to fixed positions along Harlem Heights and his men gave a better account of themselves in a fight there on September 16. General Howe then attempted to flank Washington with two more landings. The Americans beat back the first of these at Throg's Neck and they managed to delay the second at Pell's Point long enough for Washington to retrograde his main force farther north to the village of White Plains. There Washington's men stubbornly resisted a British attack on October 28, before retiring in good order, ultimately to cross the Hudson over to New Jersey. There remained one last American garrison on Manhattan, Fort Washington, which guarded the Hudson on the island's northern extremity. General Howe had bypassed it earlier; now he turned on it and took it by storm on November 16 as a helpless Washington watched from the Jersey shore. The New York campaign was over.

Washington withdrew his army through New Jersey, crippled by battle losses, desertion, and the familiar bane of expiring enlistments. Howe stayed content to nudge Washington along, rather than vigorously pursue and destroy him or attempt a lunge at Philadelphia. The British and Hessians spread throughout the state, establishing winter outposts in scattered towns. Washington eventually slipped across the Delaware into the temporary sanctuary of Pennsylvania. As 1776 drew to a close, patriots could reflect on a bitter 6 months since the heady summer proclamation of independence. The British were snug in New York City, occupied all of New Jersey, and had also seized another base at Newport, Rhode Island. Strategically, about all that had gone right for the Americans was the action of the indomitable Benedict Arnold in stymieing Carleton's attempt to advance southward from Canada. Recovered from the wound he received at Quebec, Arnold, acting under the command of Horatio Gates, had remained vigilant against the northern threat. In October he met the British in a battle of makeshift flotillas on Lake Champlain. Two engagements led to the destruction of the American craft, but the resistance and delay, combined with the lateness of the season, persuaded Carleton to withdraw to Canada until the following spring. It was at this grim moment for American fortunes in December that the patriot pamphleteer Tom Paine published *The American Crisis*, with its stirring opening, "These are the times that try men's souls. The summer soldier and sunshine patriot will, in this crisis, shrink from the service of his country; but he that stands it NOW deserves the love and thanks of man and woman."[8]

In this dramatic setting, Washington rose to the full heights of greatness. His army badly beaten and on the verge of disintegration, the Virginian took the offensive, executing a masterful campaign in New Jersey during the winter of 1776–1777, one of the war's pivotal moments. He prevailed upon his shattered regiments to extend their enlistments and, keeping his doubts to himself, inspired all around him with his fortitude and courage. What posterity remembers best from this period is the Christmas night crossing of the Delaware, immortalized in Emmanuel Leutze's iconic painting, and the stunning raid against the Hessian garrison at Trenton. Washington also made a second, larger sortie against Trenton a week later and fought a successful defensive battle against British reinforcements. Then, pressed hard by the enemy, instead of withdrawal Washington chose to make a daring night march to the British rear and won another victory at Princeton on January 3, 1777. Especially distinguishing themselves were Knox with his handling of the American guns and Greene as the commander of one of the army's wings. Washington then withdrew to winter quarters at Morristown, New Jersey. This performance lifted patriot morale and dampened the enemy's—both in the field and back in England. More tangibly, in conjunction with a relentless follow on partisan campaign by New Jersey militias that Washington adroitly leveraged, it inflicted heavy losses on British and Hessian forces, and caused Howe to withdraw most of his troops from New Jersey. This in turn unbalanced the Loyalist position in the countryside and gave the Continental Army breathing space.

The campaign of 1777 might be called a tale of two British generals; it was in a sense also the best and worst of times for the imperial cause. One general, Howe, gained victories; the other, Burgoyne, suffered a shattering defeat. Both, as a result of the year's developments, would find their reputations ruined and themselves relieved of their commands—back in England and never to return to America. The first of these was Howe who, after broaching several different schemes to Germain back in London, chose to make the capture of Philadelphia his objective. At various times—it is not perfectly clear based upon the imprecision of his correspondence—his other aims included securing his base in New York, bringing Washington to battle, and supporting another attempt from Canada to drive down the Hudson. Once more, Howe proceeded diffidently, wasting precious weeks and months in making up his mind and preparing to move. He eventually departed New York with his main force embarked upon his brother's vessels in late July. Incredibly, he then spent a month sailing up and down the coast before landing at the northern end of Chesapeake Bay and approaching Philadelphia from the southwest.

Washington and the Congress kept a watchful eye on the fully expected British move from Canada, but focused more intently on the threat to the rebel capital. As was the case throughout the war, warm spring weather swelled the army's ranks with recruits, just as the fall harvests and winter's blasts diminished them. Additionally, secret French logistical aid, arranged by American agents in Paris, further strengthened the patriots. Thus bolstered, Washington drew up his forces in line of battle to meet Howe along Brandywine Creek, approximately 25 miles west of Philadelphia. The engagement took place on September 11, 1777. As during the previous year's fighting on Long Island and Manhattan, Howe and his subordinates exhibited superior tactical skill in winkling the Americans out of their positions. Again, British and Hessian regulars relentlessly flooded gaps in the patriot dispositions. And, once more, though in possession of the field at battle's end, Howe disdained to follow up and annihilate the retreating Continentals. Rather he let them slip away and contented himself with occupying Philadelphia, as Congress unceremoniously fled, on September 26.

Washington's offensive spirit, especially unquenchable in adversity, led him to prepare a riposte against the bulk of Howe's army, based just north of Philadelphia at Germantown, on the night of October 3–4. Once again indulging his penchant for bold, nighttime maneuver, Washington this time devised a scheme that would have taxed even the best-trained troops and proved too ambitious for his own men. A 16-mile approach march by four separate columns became badly unsynchronized and a thick morning fog blanketed the battlefield, leading to a "friendly fire" incident where one American division fired upon another. Realizing the hopelessness of the situation, Washington withdrew in good order. He hoped to lure Howe into another fight, but the British commander was satisfied to have attained his campaign objective. Howe had won tactical victories, though it was evident even then that these conferred no appreciable strategic advantage on the British cause.

For their part, despite being beaten in two battles and losing Philadelphia, Washington's men had fought well. Knox and Greene further distinguished themselves as battle leaders, as had a newly commissioned Continental brigadier from Pennsylvania, Anthony Wayne. The army, numbering about 6,000, moved into winter quarters northwest of the city at Valley Forge. Here it suffered a legendary ordeal of privation, but also developed further into a professional force under the tutelage of a Prussian drill master, Washington's inspector general, Baron Friedrich von Steuben. These men could draw encouragement not only from their own performance in facing the redcoats, but also from the spectacular results achieved by their countrymen in a series of battles far to the north.

The second British general who figured so prominently in the 1777 campaign was John Burgoyne. Nominally Carleton's subordinate in Canada, "Gentleman Johnny," so nicknamed for his lavish ways on and off active service, had taken leave in London the previous winter. Through court intrigue, he convinced Germain that he was the man to succeed, where Carleton had failed the previous year, in leading an offensive down the Hudson toward Albany to link up with Howe approaching from the south. Of course, Howe had abandoned any thought of such a scheme early in his own planning, but there was a complete absence of coordination, either between Burgoyne and Howe directly, or imposed by Germain from above.

Unaware that Howe would not be joining him in a pincer movement, Burgoyne initiated his plans by launching a supporting column of about 2,000 men from Montreal in late June. Comprised mostly of Indians, Canadians, and American Loyalists, its task was to attack from the west toward Albany along the Mohawk River valley. New York militia intercepted them and blunted their efforts in sharp, bloody August fights at Fort Stanwix and Oriskany. The ubiquitous Arnold, now a major general, played a role by leading forces to relieve the militia, before returning to join the main American body, which was moving toward the New York village of Saratoga to block Burgoyne.

Meanwhile, Burgoyne's procession southward was ponderous in the extreme. A large artillery and supply train hampered his 8,000-man army, accompanied by a considerable body of camp followers that included women and children, as it tried to cut its way through the wild north country. The desertion of most of his Indian scouts, his eyes and ears, further impeded him. Fort Ticonderoga fell to the British without a shot in early July, but otherwise the situation looked unpromising. Burgoyne began to experience severe supply problems, expected Loyalist support failed to materialize, and most ominously, local militia swarmed angrily around the invaders. Burgoyne suffered his first major setback at the battle of Bennington on August 16, when a combined force of New Hampshire and Vermont militia destroyed a large detachment sent out to forage for provisions. The aroused patriot militia then proceeded to cut Burgoyne's line of communications from Ticonderoga back to Canada. Burgoyne persisted in moving ahead. In mid-September, he crossed over to the west bank of the Hudson and continued south toward Saratoga.

General Gates, who had recently replaced Schuyler in command of the Americans' northern department, headed the forces waiting for him there. Gates emplaced the bulk of his 7,000-strong army in good positions on Bemis Heights, south of Saratoga. On September 19, the first of two engagements collectively known as the battles of Saratoga took place. American riflemen and light infantry met the advancing British in front of Bemis Heights at a spot called Freeman's

Farm. This vicious, day-long fight only ended at darkness with the British owning the field, but having sustained heavy casualties that Burgoyne, unlike Gates who had men streaming in daily, could not replace. By this point, Burgoyne's only remote hope of salvation lay in relief from a British force pushing northward up the Hudson from New York City. General Clinton, commanding the rump of the British army there, sent a sortie upriver in early October, but halted it below the American fortress of West Point, some 50 miles north of the city and well short of Burgoyne. Abysmal command and control again hindered the imperial cause. Clinton had only the dimmest picture of Burgoyne's situation, to say nothing of Howe's or Washington's dispositions. Under these circumstances and lacking any direction, he withdrew his forces back into Manhattan.

The doomed Burgoyne renewed the attack on October 7 by flailing at the Americans on Bemis Heights. The patriots counterattacked and routed their opponents in this second battle of Saratoga. The remnants of Burgoyne's command, badly beaten up and outnumbered, then endured more than a week of hellish rebel sniping and shelling before surrendering on October 17. Gates had set the operational conditions for this signal victory by realizing that time and the terrain favored him. Arnold and Morgan once more displayed extraordinary battlefield leadership and tactical acumen.

During the 18 months following the Declaration of Independence, the patriots had successfully defended their bid for freedom. Despite the loss of New York and Philadelphia, along with the accompanying tactical reverses, 1777 ended on a note of high promise for the Americans. Washington's skill and tenacity in handling his army, in victory at Trenton and Princeton, and even in defeat at Brandywine and Germantown, inspired his countrymen. The overwhelming triumph at Saratoga stunned friend and foe alike. Crucially, these developments encouraged France, which had been courted assiduously by American diplomats, to declare openly its support for, and enter into a formal alliance with, the infant United States. The war would expand widely over the next 4 years. Americans would again experience the depths of despair, perhaps even more bitter and perilous than that prompting Paine's *American Crisis*, before gaining ultimate victory.

WIDER WAR, DESPAIR, AND VICTORY: JANUARY 1778–OCTOBER 1781

Conscious of his failure to subdue the rebellious colonists, General Howe offered his resignation as England's overall commander in America and Clinton replaced him in May 1778. By then the strategic situation had altered considerably. French entry into the war caused London to take a wider view. Clinton received instructions to evacuate Philadelphia and fall back on his bases at New York and Newport. Additionally, he was ordered to send a substantial portion of his forces to reinforce British possessions in Florida and the West Indies to defend against anticipated French attacks. The last major battle in the Revolution's northern theater occurred June 28, 1778, at Monmouth, New Jersey. Here Washington's forces engaged Clinton's rear guard covering the withdrawal from Philadelphia. After wavering initially, the Continentals, personally rallied by Washington and displaying the professionalism instilled by Steuben, fought the British to a draw. For the remainder of the war, the north witnessed only general skirmishing, though two notable American passages of arms stand out. Wayne stormed a British outpost with a daring nighttime bayonet attack at Stony Point, New York in July 1779. A month later Henry Lee, a dashing Virginia cavalryman who would make his reputation as "Light Horse Harry" in the southern theater, conducted a successful raid at Paulus Hook, New Jersey (modern Jersey City).

While the northern theater slipped into a kind of stalemate, with Washington and Clinton warily eying each other around New York, relatively small scale but savage combat raged on the western frontier. Following the French and Indian War, the British had maintained a handful of forts along the Great Lakes, as well as on the upper Mississippi and in the lower Mississippi-Gulf region. With the onset of the Revolution, the British used these as launching points for attacks on American settlers. These forays normally consisted of mixed Indian-Loyalist forces led by British officers. Congress was largely powerless to counter these incursions, so responsibility to meet them devolved upon the states. Virginia mounted the most ambitious of these efforts in June 1778, by dispatching an expedition under the frontiersman George Rogers Clark. Clark cleansed much of the expanse between the Ohio and Mississippi Rivers—territory claimed by Virginia—of British influence, thus neutralizing for a time Indian incursions into Kentucky. More significantly, his conquest of the Old Northwest set the stage for postwar American expansion. Washington ordered the largest—and best-conducted—Continental frontier campaign in the spring of 1779. He sent a sizeable force against the Iroquois Confederacy and by August these British allies had been temporarily "pacified" in the Susquehanna, Mohawk and Allegheny Valleys. Despite these two American successes, warfare flared up repeatedly along the New York–Pennsylvania frontier and in Kentucky in the familiar pattern of raid and reprisal. Not until the Revolution's successful conclusion were the Americans able to secure fully the frontier.

The high seas represented another frontier of sorts. The 13 rebellious colonies hugged the Atlantic and most Americans lived within reach of the ocean. Maritime affairs represented an important sector of the economy, particularly in the northeast. Foreign and intercolonial trade, as well as fishing, and the nascent whaling and shipbuilding industries all depended upon the sea. From the American standpoint, there was never any question of building a navy to challenge directly the Royal Navy. The patriots concerned themselves principally with coastal defense and commerce-raiding, outfitting a few frigates for the latter purpose. As with the frontier war, a combination of Continental and state-sanctioned forces conducted the fighting. Both the Congress and various state naval boards and agents issued letters of marque (essentially licenses to prey on enemy shipping) to entrepreneurial privateers. In many ways this inefficiently led to competition between skippers for crews and other scarce assets. Nepotism and localism were additional plagues; most commanders of newly commissioned warships resided in the city or state whence the vessels came. John Paul Jones, America's most famous sea dog, especially suffered repeated slights due to these sorts of machinations.

During the war, American privateers, ranging from the waters off Newfoundland to the Caribbean, took about 600 prizes. Jones raided the English and Scottish coasts in the spring of 1778, causing little real damage but much alarm and consternation to the British Admiralty. And of course, Jones won the most celebrated ship-to-ship duel in naval history when his *Bonhomme Richard* bested *HMS Serapis* in September 1779. Yet despite the individual glory achieved by Jones and a handful of other brave captains, the war at sea was hardly decisive for either the Americans or the British. As noted earlier, the British never were able to bottle up completely the American ports with an effective blockade and though they generally roamed at will along the American coastline for most of the war, this conferred no strategic advantage on them. After France entered the war in 1778, the British and French fleets fought some desultory engagements in the West Indies. The sole exception to the otherwise inconclusive naval struggle was the French fleet's role in trapping the besieged British army at Yorktown, thus sealing American victory there in 1781.

For the Americans, even more so than the two winters of discontent—the "crisis" season of 1776 and the Calvary of Valley Forge in 1777–1778–1780 witnessed the nadir of the patriot cause. The American economy was in shambles. Inflation ran rampant, as the Congress and the individual states issued reams of worthless paper money in order to finance the war. Many suffered while, as always in such circumstances, a few profited obscenely in speculation and profiteering. The Continental army frequently went unpaid and wanted badly for weapons and supplies. Several mutinies, centered on disputes over pay or enlistment expirations, took place involving regiments from Massachusetts, Connecticut, and New York. All were suppressed, sometimes ruthlessly. More serious mutinies occurred among the Pennsylvania line under Wayne and in three New Jersey regiments in January 1781. It required governmental negotiation with the disgruntled soldiers to quell the first, while a heavier hand settled the second. The year 1780 was also the year that Benedict Arnold's name became forever synonymous with treason. Emblematic of this dismal period, this heretofore courageous fighter had been under investigation for fiscal corruption when he offered his services to the British. Given command of the key fortress of West Point, Arnold plotted to hand it over to the British. Only timely patriot discovery of the scheme foiled Arnold, who escaped to British lines. Finally, the Americans endured two of their most painful military defeats in 1780, both in South Carolina. In May, the British successfully concluded a siege of Charleston, accepting the surrender of 5,000 troops—the largest bag of patriots taken during the entire war—plus a huge store of supplies. Three months later the British won a smashing victory at Camden over an army led by Gates, killing 800 and capturing another 1,000 Americans. Few on either side during this year could have imagined the shift in fortunes that would occur over the next 12 months.

Stalemated in the north, the British once again contemplated shifting the focus of action to the south. By late 1778 they had reconquered Georgia and a year later Clinton led a sizeable, joint army–navy force from New York to Savannah, where he established a southern base of operations. From there Clinton mounted the siege of Charleston. Once the city fell, he returned north to face a feared French-American threat and turned over command in the south to Cornwallis, who won the one-sided battle at Camden. After the twin disasters in South Carolina, the Americans were reduced to conducting a partisan struggle against the occupying British and their Loyalist allies. Foremost in waging this savage backcountry fight of surprise raid and ambush were a trio of partisan chieftains—Andrew Pickens, Thomas Sumter, and Francis Marion. Seeking to retrieve the military situation, the Congress, acting on Washington's recommendation, named Nathanael Greene to relieve Gates in command of the southern department in October 1780.

Taking the reins at the head of a badly beaten and demoralized army huddled in Charlotte, North Carolina, Greene commenced perhaps the most unique campaign in American military history. With more dexterity than shown by any commander on either side during the war, Greene coordinated conventional military operations with those of the roving partisan bands. He dispatched mobile columns into South Carolina under Daniel Morgan—now a brigadier general—and Henry Lee to reinforce the resistance effort there. This initiative paid off almost immediately when the British challenged Morgan's combined militia-Continental force in northwestern South Carolina in January 1781. Morgan fashioned a tactical masterpiece at the resulting battle of Cowpens, utterly destroying the attacking British. An enraged Cornwallis resolved to hunt down and destroy the patriot forces, falling into the cunning trap Greene had laid for him. Greene led Cornwallis on a frustrating and debilitating winter chase through North Carolina. When Greene crossed into Virginia, Cornwallis fell back. Greene then reentered North Carolina and the armies clashed at Guilford Court House in March 1781. At battle's end, the British held the field, but had suffered heavy losses that they could not replace. Cornwallis abandoned the deep south and ultimately took refuge at Yorktown, Virginia. Meanwhile Greene, working in conjunction with the partisans, created more misery for the British by overrunning their isolated outposts and ultimately liberated the Carolinas and Georgia.

For more than 3 years after its inauguration, the French alliance had been a source of frustration and disappointment as well as hope to the patriots. In July 1778 a powerful French fleet under the Comte d'Estaing arrived in American waters. Washington keenly wished to employ this armada and its embarked marines as part of a combined Franco-American assault upon New York City, but d'Estaing demurred. The two military chiefs then agreed to fall upon the British base at Newport, Rhode Island. The expedition began promisingly with French forces landed to join with American troops already in Rhode Island to menace Newport.

But when Admiral Richard Howe's numerically inferior British fleet sortied out of New York to challenge the French, d'Estaing broke off the operation and, after a violent storm whipped both fleets, decided to quit North America for the remainder of the year and retire to French bases in the West Indies. D'Estaing returned in September 1779, but displayed no interest in New York or Newport as objectives. Rather he elected to support American forces laying siege to British-held Savannah. An allied land and sea attack badly miscarried and the French admiral himself was severely wounded. This ended D'Estaing's career in America and also a second fruitless year of military collaboration.

The only good these otherwise ineffectual French efforts accomplished was to convince a worried Clinton to return to New York after his triumph at Charleston and to evacuate his exposed garrison at Newport. The French returned to North America in July 1780. This time the expeditionary force was an army led by the comte de Rochambeau; however, to Washington's consternation, his French counterpart limited his operations for the remainder of the year to establishing a base at recently vacated Newport. Throughout 1781 Washington, while admiringly watching his protégé Greene's southern campaign, burned to conduct a decisive offensive. He proposed a number of alternative stratagems to Rochambeau that included combined attacks on New York or against the British someplace—Charleston, Savannah, or Virginia—in the south. Finally, by late summer, events coalesced that led to the Yorktown campaign. Washington had sent a portion of the army south to his native Virginia to fight Cornwallis. The young Marquis de Lafayette commanded these forces. The Frenchman's subordinates included "Mad Anthony" Wayne. One of his opponents was none other than Benedict Arnold, now serving with the British. In the face of this pressure, Cornwallis buttoned himself and his Army up in Yorktown, hoping for reinforcement, resupply, or evacuation by sea. Here the dreadful British command and control system reared its dysfunctional head again. Cornwallis was bombarded with contradictory instructions from his superior Clinton, telling him to send men to New York, and from Germain in London absolutely forbidding him to denude the south of troops. Most significantly, Washington received assurances that a powerful French fleet under a fighting admiral, the comte de Grasse, would be on station at the Chesapeake by late August. Washington and Rochambeau resolved to strike their blow in the south and trap Cornwallis.

In a complicated movement that would be impressive even in our own age of communication and transportation marvels, the combined armies covered more than 400 miles to link up with the Continental forces already in Virginia and then effected a rendezvous with de Grasse's fleet. In early September Washington began to invest Yorktown while French ships sealed off any possibility of British escape by sea. Relentlessly French and American sappers worked to dig closer to the British works as Knox's artillery hammered Cornwallis's desperate troops at will. On October 17 Cornwallis asked for terms. Two days later he surrendered with more than 8,000 of his men as a British band played a tune entitled "The World Turned Upside Down."

PRESERVING VICTORY: NOVEMBER 1781–DECEMBER 1783

In London, upon learning of the Yorktown debacle, the Prime Minister, Lord North, is supposed to have cried "Oh God! It is all over!"[9] Although Yorktown was indeed decisive, hostilities dragged on for another 2 years and serious dangers still attended the American cause. While many Americans, after 6 years of fighting, gave in to euphoria, Washington reacted with a professional soldier's innate caution. In his correspondence he repeatedly echoed the ancient Roman maxim about the paradoxical and perverse relationship between peace and war, noting on one occasion that "Nothing will hasten peace more than to be in a condition for war."[10] As had been the case throughout the conflict, the Continental Army represented a vital American center of gravity. Washington recognized the need to preserve it not only as a force in readiness to deal with a still-potent British presence in New York, but also as an instrument responsive to civilian control.

Following Yorktown, the British government fell; both North and Germain were turned out. George III now found himself with a parliament and ministers disposed to cut England's losses in America while concentrating on the ancient French enemy in other far flung corners of the world. In May 1782 the British relieved Clinton and called Carleton down from Canada to replace him as their last commander in chief in America. Unknown to Washington, Carlton had orders to avoid all conflict with the Americans while Anglo-American peace talks took place in Paris. Washington gathered the Continental Army in the vicinity of the Hudson Highlands above New York City, which along with Charleston was the only remaining British enclave in the 13 colonies, to monitor his opposite number. Meanwhile, sporadic, small scale but nonetheless violent combat still flared against the Indians on the frontier as well as between Loyalists and patriots in the southern and middle states.

Besides remaining vigilant against any renewed British activity, maintaining a battle-ready army was important to back up the American negotiating posture in Paris. The biggest threat to that army, and the infant American republic, was internal dissent in the ranks and among the officers. As previously noted, elements of the Continental line had mutinied during the war; some historians have observed that the question is not why they did so, as much as why there were so few instances of mutiny. Certainly the soldiers had been ill-used by the Congress and had some legitimate grievances, mostly centering on arrears pay and promised pensions. Late in 1782, a delegation of officers petitioned the Congress, but to no avail. Subsequently, in the early months of 1783 at Newburgh, New York, a faction in the officer corps attempted to bring further pressure upon the Congress by issuing vaguely worded threats in a pair of "addresses" to that body. The facts of the "Newburgh Conspiracy" are shrouded in mystery. It appears that some members of the Congress, who favored a stronger central government than existed under the Articles of Confederation, encouraged the disgruntled officers. Their evident hope was that the prospect of an army uprising might force greater centralization of national authority, such as levying taxes, in order to satisfy the army's demands. While most of the grumbling officers were field-grade level, General Gates, recently reinstated as Washington's deputy after his earlier disgrace at Camden, was at least sympathetic to the malcontents' activities. Getting wind of all this, Washington brilliantly disarmed any incipient cabal in a March 15 meeting, where by sheer force of his personal example he shamed any would-be protesters from dishonorable action. The possibility of intemperate military revolt against civilian authority evaporated and the officers resolved to accept whatever relief the Congress decided.

England recognized American independence in the Treaty of Paris, concluded on September 3, 1783, and the last British contingent sailed away from New York in late November. Washington bid an emotional farewell to his officers at Fraunces Tavern in that city on December 4, before riding on to Annapolis where the Congress sat in order to surrender his commission. But that his active service had been so extraordinary, one is tempted to say that nothing became Washington's tenure as commander in chief more than his leaving of it. He could have been Caesar or Cromwell or Bonaparte—successful generals all—who seized civil power. Instead he was Cincinnatus, humbly returning to private life.

Near the beginning of the great contest—in fact, on the day the Congress had voted for independence—Washington had written that "The fate of unborn millions will now depend, under God, on the Courage and Conduct of this Army."[11] The courage and conduct of those founding fighters who led Americans to victory, though not always undaunted and unsullied, on the whole magnificently upheld that immense charge. Their stories serve as inspiration, and reminder that individual strengths and weaknesses matter in the destiny of peoples and nations.

Redcoats to Rebel Fighters

Richard Montgomery, Charles Lee, and Horatio Gates

THE NEW AMERICAN ARMY desperately needed experienced, trained officers, especially in its senior positions. While a number of colonials had served in middle grades with the British army during the French and Indian War or had fought Indians on the frontier, few possessed the credentials or cachet of professional soldiers. For this reason, and perhaps also reflecting something of a provincial inferiority complex, throughout the Revolution Congress would look hopefully to various European volunteers and adventurers who claimed military backgrounds and offer them commands. Indeed, this seeming preference for foreigners over native-born Americans proved to be one of several sore spots that developed between Continental officers and Congress during the war. As events proved, some of these foreigners went on to inscribe their names in American history—Lafayette, Steuben, Kosciuszko, Pulaski among them—while others showed themselves to be little more than charlatans.

In June 1775, Congress in its search for military talent turned its eyes upon three former British officers living in America who were sympathetic to the cause. All had served creditably in North America years earlier at the company or field grade level, then left the king's service and immigrated to the 13 colonies. Richard Montgomery and Horatio Gates were peacefully settled with their families in New York and Virginia respectively, while a recently arrived and single Charles Lee traveled extensively throughout the colonies on the eve of the Revolution. Gates and Lee avidly sought and accepted the general officer commissions proffered to them, while Montgomery was a more reluctant warrior. All rendered valuable service in the war's early days. Montgomery became a venerated martyr, while disgrace and controversy enmeshed Lee and Gates.

RICHARD MONTGOMERY

Richard Montgomery lived in his adopted American homeland barely 3 years and his military service in behalf of American liberty lasted only 7 months. He met crushing defeat as well as death in his last battle. Despite this, Montgomery, the first—and also most senior—Revolutionary American general killed in action became a patriotic icon during the war and the first years of the republic. Universally respected for his character and ability, he was eulogized in both the Continental Congress and British Parliament. Although early or tragic death often confers exaggerated romantic virtue on individuals, to all appearances Montgomery indeed was a leader of immense promise.

He was born on December 2, 1738, to a comfortable family of Irish gentry in County Dublin. He received a decent liberal education, including 2 years at Dublin's Trinity College, before emulating an older brother at age 18 and choosing a military career. Montgomery's father, himself a former officer, purchased an ensign's commission for his son in the 17th Regiment of Foot. The young subaltern had relatively little garrison experience when in February 1757 his unit received orders to ready itself for deployment to North America.

Like Charles Lee and Horatio Gates, as well as colonials such as George Washington and many of the British generals who would oppose them two decades later, Montgomery's baptism of fire occurred in America as part of England's great eighteenth-century duel for empire with France. Both kingdoms had New World possessions whose inhabitants repeatedly rubbed up against each other with violent results. Global in scale, previous eruptions were known in the 13 colonies as Queen Anne's War (1702–1713) and King George's War (1744–1748). The third outbreak of this intermittent imperial struggle—the French and Indian War (1754–1763) to Americans—came in western Pennsylvania after a clash over disputed territory between Virginia militia, commanded by young Colonel Washington, and French troops. Upon learning of this, authorities in London resolved to settle conclusively their French problem in America. They dispatched immense forces and augmented them with colonial troops. After many setbacks, 1758 and especially 1759— "the year of miracles"—witnessed decisive British victories at Louisbourg, Fort Ticonderoga, and Quebec. The issue had been decided, though more fighting followed before the war formally concluded in 1763. Britain expelled France and won an empire. And Montgomery, along with the other young officers who were to be Revolutionary War generals, had learned his profession in the harsh school of the Canadian wilderness, the American frontier, and the sweltering West Indies.

The 17th Foot arrived in Halifax, Nova Scotia in July 1757, but experienced no action for the remainder of the year as the British buildup continued. In the spring of 1758, having assembled a powerful striking force, the British mounted a seaborne attack on the French fortress of Louisbourg on Cape Breton in the Gulf of St. Lawrence. Montgomery and his regiment embarked as part of the invasion fleet and conducted an amphibious assault under enemy fire—among the most hazardous of all military operations—on June 8, 1758. Montgomery performed coolly here and during the subsequent siege, winning battlefield advancement to lieutenant as casualties thinned the 17th's ranks. Louisbourg fell in late July and Montgomery's unit was one of several redeployed to New York to bolster British forces that had experienced a bloody repulse at Fort Ticonderoga in New York. The 1758 campaigning season drew to a close with Montgomery seeing no further combat, however.

Montgomery participated in one of the two signal British expeditions of 1759. While General James Wolfe earned immortality with his victory over the French General Louis Montcalm at Quebec, Montgomery was part of Sir Jeffrey Amherst's conquest of Ticonderoga, which the French abandoned in the face of overwhelming odds on July 26, exactly a year to the day after Louisbourg's surrender. Amherst's pursuit of the French was desultory and his command ended up wintering at Crown Point, about a dozen miles north of Ticonderoga. Montgomery continued to win the approbation of his superiors and in May 1760 became the regimental adjutant, a post typically assigned to the unit's most outstanding lieutenant. As the weather improved, Amherst resumed his drive north. Montgomery traversed ground that he would revisit 15 years later as the British seized French posts at Isle aux Noix and Chambly en route to taking Montreal in September 1760, thus securing all of Canada. Montgomery's regiment then took station in New York's Mohawk Valley for the winter while British strategists contemplated offensives far to the south.

In 1761 the British resolved to seize the French-held island of Martinique in the West Indies. The 17th and the rest of the 14,000-man invasion force assembled in New York City and departed to its staging area in Barbados in November, landing on Martinique on January 16, 1762. A siege of Fort-Royal, the island's capital, ensued. Montgomery saw some heavy fighting in the city's outer works before the French surrendered in early February. Neither the British nor Montgomery were finished with amphibious landings or assaults on fortified cities. Spain had entered the war on France's side and in the spring of 1762 the British took aim on the Spanish colony of Cuba. On June 6, British forces, including the newly promoted Captain Montgomery in command of one of the 17th's companies, stormed ashore at Havana. They encountered not only staunch defenses but also appalling tropical conditions. Heat and disease killed scores of British soldiers, many more than the number who perished in 2 months of bitter fighting before the Spanish capitulation in August. Like virtually all the British survivors of this grueling ordeal, Montgomery's health was broken. Years later his wife would recall "that the heat and severity of this climate made him lose a fine head of hair."[1]

So much had its troopers suffered that the 17th, along with other regiments, was redeployed back to the more salubrious climate of New York before the campaign ended. In Manhattan, Montgomery convalesced and socialized for a season before being deployed once more to the Mohawk Valley in June 1763. On his way up the Hudson Montgomery made his most significant American acquaintance when he stopped briefly at the estate of one of New York's leading citizens, Judge Robert Livingston. Here he encountered Livingston's pretty

20-year-old daughter, Janet, who 10 years later would become his wife. Montgomery spent one more year in America, highlighted by his participation in a punitive expedition against hostile Indians that took him as far west as Detroit, before returning to England on a well-deserved leave of absence in late 1764. Seven years in America had given him extensive practical experience in leadership and seigecraft, exposure to the type of American troops he would one day command, and detailed knowledge of the terrain over which he would again fight.

Back in England, Montgomery came into a decent inheritance from his deceased parents. His military duties were light and his political attitudes began to manifest themselves, particularly as he associated with English opposition thinkers such as his Irish compatriot Edmund Burke. Although never as radical as his fellow redcoats-turned-rebels Lee or Gates, Montgomery shared many of their liberal or Whig political views. These included disdain for the corrupt practices of King George III's courtiers and concern over the erosion of traditional English liberties, not only in England and his native Ireland, but in the American colonies as well. He combined this with an innate pessimism about human nature. He was hardly a leveling democrat; he believed in noblesse oblige and the superiority of gentlemen to the common herd. He is probably best described as an aristocratic Whig.

Disillusioned with the English political scene, army life lost its attractions for him as well. He briefly rejoined his regiment in America in 1767, only almost immediately to accompany it on its rotation back to England after 10 years abroad. With England at peace, the army was cut back; promotion opportunities decreased accordingly and Montgomery was thwarted in his efforts to purchase a major's commission. His thoughts began to turn to the fertile land and opportunities he had spied in New York. By 1772 he determined to immigrate and become a gentleman farmer. He arrived late that year in New York City and renewed his connections with members of the city's commercial elite he had met during his wartime sojourn. With their assistance he got on his feet and obtained a small farm at Kingsbridge just north of town. Though balding and with a face pocked from earlier disease, the 34-year-old Montgomery nevertheless cut an attractive figure with his tall, slender build and commanding presence. He soon courted Janet Livingston, who had remained unmarried, in part because no suitable mates had presented themselves to her and her family, and also because she was something of a "black widow"— at least three previous suitors had died in falls or drowned. Despite these grim portents, Janet assented to his marriage proposal and the powerful Livingston clan welcomed the newcomer. They married in July 1773 and settled down to a peaceful, happy existence in Rhinebeck, New York, on land that belonged to Janet.

Public events soon intruded on Montgomery's private life. Since the conclusion of the great war for empire, England and her American colonies had disputed the terms of their relationship. British ministers' attempts to reassert political and economic control over the colonies met opposition from many Americans. Their resistance took the form of petitions, boycotts, and mob violence before ultimately exploding into armed conflict at Lexington and Concord in April

1775. New York was not immune from this ferment; indeed politics there were especially complicated. Not only did powerful Loyalist factions contend with patriots, opponents of imperial policies also divided among themselves into radical and more moderate elements. Montgomery was among those moderates who disapproved British policies, but hoped for some sort of reconciliation with the crown. His sympathy for American liberty and attachment to his new family—leading patriots—competed with his reluctance to give up his domestic tranquility by plunging into the maelstrom. Nevertheless, when in May 1775 his neighboring Dutchess County worthies elected him as a delegate to New York's Provincial Congress—one of the many provisional governing bodies that sprouted in that revolutionary American spring—Montgomery felt compelled to answer duty's summons.

This convocation quickly became New York's de facto government. Montgomery served on a number of committees, most of which leveraged his military experience in such areas as equipping troops and defending key points. His innate modesty—and wisdom—surfaced when, concerning the construction of fortifications, he confessed "I know only enough to be afraid of undertaking what I never had any practice in."[2] Events continued at their dizzying pace and by June the Continental Congress in Philadelphia was raising a national or Continental Army. It selected Washington as commander in chief, along with an initial slate of four major generals and nine brigadiers from six different colonies. Montgomery was chosen the second most senior brigadier. Eighteenth-century gentlemen routinely expressed formulaic reservations about their fitness upon accepting public office. Montgomery's declaration fit that mold: "I would most willingly decline any military command from a consciousness of want of talents. Nevertheless, I shall sacrifice my own inclination . . . if our Congress . . . cannot find a more capable servant."[3] Nonetheless, unlike many, his misgivings were likely quite sincere. Once engaged he set himself to his duty. As his wife recollected, he declared to her, "You shall never blush for your Montgomery."[4]

Montgomery was assigned duties in New York underneath Major General Philip Schuyler, a wealthy landowner with extensive holdings in the northern part of the colony. Their initial charge was to look to the defense of New York City and the security of the western frontier against hostile Indians, but that focus soon changed. Congress wished to add Canada to the revolutionary fold—partly from expansionist impulses and partly to preempt any British attempt on the colonies from the north. That General Guy Carleton, the capable British commander in Canada, appeared to be gathering forces for exactly this purpose added urgency to this latter rationale. Therefore, Congress ordered Schuyler and Montgomery north to prepare an expedition.

Just as it had during England's struggle against France for control in America, geography dictated the outlines of the campaign. The traditional invasion route, which ran both ways between New York and Canada, began in the south by following the Hudson River north up to Lake Champlain. Champlain was the liquid highway into Canada, stretching for just over 100 miles before connecting with Canada's Sorel River, which in turn fed into the St. Lawrence River. Key terrain along this route included Fort Ticonderoga and Crown Point at the southern tip of Lake Champlain, Valcour Island in the center of the Lake and Ile aux Noix in the Sorel, and the outposts of St. Johns and Chambly on that river. The two major prizes in Canada, of course, were Montreal and Quebec on the St. Lawrence.

By August 1775 both Schuyler and Montgomery were established at Fort Ticonderoga, which had been seized by the patriots 3 months earlier. Their troops were a motley combination of newly recruited Continentals and raw militia from several New England colonies as well as New York. While not exactly a rabble in arms, they represented a far cry from the crack regulars Montgomery had known in his majesty's service. Compounding the leadership challenge, not only were these troops untrained and loosely disciplined, they were also prone to suspicion of and animosity toward men from colonies or regions other than their own. Montgomery, already a reluctant warrior and homesick for Janet and his farm, would frequently despair over their martial worth in the months ahead. Another headache for Montgomery concerned Schuyler. Although the two got on tolerably well, Schuyler was much the amateur compared to his subordinate. Further, as was to prove the case throughout his Revolutionary career, Schuyler was prone to frequent bouts of ill health and prolonged absences from the scene of action. As Montgomery wrote to Janet, "I wish sincerely he [Schuyler] was able to do his duty, if that can't be, I wish him at home."[5]

Schuyler had departed for meetings, leaving Montgomery in command when intelligence of new activity on Carleton's part arrived. The British at St. Johns were constructing naval vessels that could give them control of the vital Champlain–Sorel corridor. Displaying keen initiative and decisiveness, Montgomery decided to initiate the American invasion of Canada in Schuyler's absence. Like a good subordinate, however, he also informed Schuyler of what he was doing and why, "I think it absolutely necessary to move down the lake with the utmost dispatch. Should the Enemy get their vessels into the lake 'tis over with us for this summer."[6] To Schuyler's credit, he subsequently approved Montgomery's action and rushed troops forward to support him, while hurrying north from Albany himself. The Americans moved in a makeshift flotilla and struck at St. Johns on September 6. Montgomery personally led the assault, which the British beat off with little difficulty. After an anxious night outside the enemy works, the American force reembarked and retreated to Ile aux Noix. A second try, on the evening of September 10, proved a fiasco. American columns sent against St. Johns ran into each other in the dark and spooked themselves into headlong retreat back to their boats. Montgomery regrouped them, but another advance also ended ignominiously when the troops stumbled across some enemy pickets and fled. To Montgomery's immense disgust, his junior officers demanded a council of war to determine what to do next. Further, they also polled the men. Ultimately, Montgomery elected to put an end to the farce and retired the force once again to Ile aux Noix. Shortly after he described the troops to Janet as "a set of pusillanimous wretches..." and added "Could I with decency leave the army in it's present Situation, I would not serve an hour longer."[7] With Schuyler now so sick as to have to quit the campaign altogether, Montgomery could not in good conscience act on his desire. Instead, he was now in full command of the Canadian expedition.

Montgomery returned to St. Johns on September 17 and began a siege that lasted 7 weeks. Six hundred soldiers with 48 cannon, plus a smattering of women and children, inhabited this key British post on the west bank of the Sorel River. It was a formidable position. Two large, earthen redoubts about 200 yards apart protected various buildings within. A deep ditch, reinforced with obstacles, surrounded the redoubts and a communications trench connected them. A palisade to the west and the river to the east further shielded the fortress, as did an armed schooner anchored in mid-stream. Montgomery quickly cut St. Johns's communications with Chambly to the north and Montreal to the west. His men constructed batteries on both sides of the river to shell the British. Several patriot detachments, more or less under his command, roamed the countryside, harassing the enemy and attempting to recruit Canadians to the American cause. One of those "less" under his command was led by the irrepressible Ethan Allen. The Vermonter took it into his head to make an unsupported attempt to capture Montreal, assumed to be full of sympathetic French-Canadians, with 80 men. Instead, on September 25 a combined British-Loyalist force routed them and took Allen prisoner.

This setback was one of many travails that consumed Montgomery. The early October weather was atrocious and he likened his troops to "half-drowned rats crawling thro' the Swamps."[8] Even more trying was the continued behavior of the officers and men—"It would take a Volume to describe . . . the badness of the troops."[9] Drunkenness, shirking, and having his orders debated as mere suggestions all exasperated Montgomery. Nevertheless, while complaining in his private correspondence, the young general persevered, mixing firmness and tact in a textbook display of how to transform indifferent troops into high-performing units. The seizure by his men of Chambly to the north—along with a considerable store of badly needed gunpowder—in mid-October essentially sealed St. Johns's fate. The 2,700-man patriot force mercilessly shelled the fortress and on November 3 its garrison surrendered. The year was far advanced, however, and winter's onset near. Montreal and Quebec remained in British hands.

Montgomery rapidly turned his forces west and made for Montreal. Simultaneously, he pushed troops north to positions along the St. Lawrence River, isolating Montreal from any possible succor from Quebec. Given the city's indefensibility, Carleton and his men attempted a breakout to the northeast along the St. Lawrence. The Americans in their blocking positions bagged most of them, along with a store of badly needed supplies. The British commander, however, managed to slip through and began to organize the bastion at Quebec. Left to their own devices, Montreal's municipal leaders allowed the Americans to enter the city on November 13. Recognizing that "until Quebec is taken, Canada is unconquered," Montgomery was eager to press on and link up with Colonel Benedict Arnold, whose detachment had recently completed an arduous march to Quebec's outskirts.[10]

Once more, however, Montgomery had to deal with querulous subordinates. The enlistments of many of his New England units were due to expire in early December. Most of these men felt that they had accomplished more than enough for a season's campaigning and wanted no part of a winter offensive. Montgomery cajoled and pleaded, but to little avail. Even before the enlistments ran out, large numbers of them began to stream south—most as "sick" ranks, some as deserters. Montgomery's correspondence reflects his disgust with these "sunshine patriots," though he was no less homesick than they were. Fed up, he communicated to Schuyler his desire to hand over his command and suggested that Charles Lee might be a suitable replacement. Schuyler duly forwarded Montgomery's concerns to Congress and for good measure announced his own desire to step down. A worried Congress begged both to reconsider, especially since Montgomery's recent string of triumphs had made him a patriotic hero. In recognition of these accomplishments, and perhaps also to sway him to stay on, Congress promoted him to major general on December 9, though Montgomery would not live to learn of this. Eventually, it took Washington to persuade the northern army's two leaders not to resign. Citing his own, similar problems with balky troops, he dramatically asked, "When is the Time for brave Men to exert themselves in the Cause of Liberty and their Country, if this is not?"[11] Determined now to see the Canadian venture through to the end, in late November Montgomery and approximately 300 of his most stalwart adherents advanced on Quebec.

On December 2, 1775, Montgomery's and Arnold's commands joined at Point aux Trembles, about 20 miles southwest of Quebec. Combined, they numbered about 1,000 effectives. As previously agreed, Montgomery assumed overall command. Despite some trepidation on Montgomery's part over the fractious Arnold's reputation, the two men respected each other and worked well together. Montgomery also favorably impressed Arnold's men, one of whom confided to his journal that the general had "an air and manner that designated the real soldier."[12] This small band of Americans, hundreds of miles from home and exposed to the brutal Canadian winter, would need all the skill, courage and luck they could muster, for Quebec presented a daunting military challenge.

Quebec lay at the confluence of two rivers, the St. Charles and the St. Lawrence, and consisted of an upper and a lower town. The upper town sat atop a plateau and contained most of Quebec's important structures. Thick, high walls surrounded the upper town on its western and northern sides, while steep cliffs rising from the St. Lawrence protected the east and south. The lower town hugged the river below the cliffs, and consisted mostly of warehouses and shops. Three gates provided entry to the upper town from north and west, while a stairway accessed it from the lower town. Carleton's garrison of about 1,800 manned batteries and redoubts within the upper town, and had emplaced a series of barricades along the main approaches through the lower town.

Essentially two courses of action were available to Montgomery. The first was to attempt a siege, as he had done at St. Johns and was prepared to execute at Montreal before it surrendered. This option carried serious disadvantages, however.

The Americans were not equipped for a siege. Their limited artillery was too light to make an impression on Quebec's walls and was vulnerable to the counter battery fire of the heavier British guns. The Americans also lacked the engineer expertise to supervise the required sapping or digging of approach trenches. Even had it existed, they were without adequate tools and, in any event, the frozen ground was too hard for digging. Climate and time also worked against the Americans. While the defenders were reasonably snug inside the city, the besiegers outside faced exposure to the brutal elements of cold, wind, and snow. Carleton had enough provisions to last him until spring—especially after he expelled those *Quebecois* whom he deemed insufficiently loyal—when he could reasonably expect the arrival of a relief expedition. The British General Wolfe had won a legendary victory at Quebec in 1759, when the French foolishly elected to sortie out of their fortifications onto the Plains of Abraham to the city's west. Carleton, who was with Wolfe that day, had no intention of gratifying Montgomery by repeating this error. Finally, the specter of expired enlistments manifested itself once more. Most of Arnold's men—about two thirds of the entire force—were due for release on January 1. Therefore, Montgomery adopted the second possible course of action—an assault into the city as soon as practicable.

To conceal his approach into the citadel, Montgomery decided to attack under cover of darkness during a snowstorm. The first such opportunity came on the evening of December 27 and Montgomery alerted the army for action. The storm blew over, however, and a clear night sky illuminated the scene, so the troops stood down. Besides the unfavorable weather, more bad fortune dogged the Americans that night. During all the activity, a Rhode Island sergeant deserted to the British and divulged to Carleton all he knew about Montgomery's intentions. Montgomery learned of this and modified his concept somewhat, though in essence it remained unchanged—launch in limited visibility, feint against the gates of the upper town, and make the main effort through the lower town.

A fierce blizzard assailed Quebec on the evening of December 30 and in the predawn hours of the 31st the Americans began their attack in four columns. Arnold, with 600 men, moved out from the northern edge of Quebec and skirted the river on his left hand side as he headed south toward the lower town. This force represented one prong of the main effort. A mortar battery that he had left behind began lobbing shells into the upper town as a diversion. Two smaller elements to the west demonstrated ineffectively against Quebec's walls, exchanging fire with sentries. Their only accomplishment was to alert Carleton that something was on. Montgomery headed the other attack column of about 300 soldiers. This force also approached from the west, but then descended south to pick its way along the river at the base of the cliffs into the lower town. The plan was for Montgomery and Arnold to converge, and then jointly enter the upper town. In order to succeed, this fairly complex scheme required more coordination than was possible to achieve this night. Units lagged as they trudged through deep snow drifts, dragging heavy assault ladders and other equipment. Biting wind that blew snow horizontally into their faces further impeded the attackers. The files became dangerously spread out as men straggled. Montgomery led his band personally from the front, not only because this fit his leadership style, but also because experience had shown him that this was the only way to get his sometimes-hesitant troops to advance.

Montgomery's men surmounted two barricades the British had emplaced to block the narrow streets of the lower town. The general was exhorting his men to catch up and come on when a flash and roar erupted in the darkness. At almost point blank range, an enemy cannon in a blockhouse loosed a fearsome blast of grapeshot, which cut down Montgomery and the small group of aides accompanying him. Montgomery, struck in the head and body, died instantly. This was too much for the survivors; Montgomery's second in command decided to terminate the attack and withdraw. Meanwhile Arnold's men, with no idea of Montgomery's fate, fought a desperate, losing struggle in the lower town. Arnold fell wounded and Carleton surrounded this detachment. Ultimately, most of them surrendered, though Arnold eluded capture and subsequently took command of the remnants of the American army outside Quebec.

It took several days for the British to realize that they had killed an important American general. When Carleton found out, he insisted on a dignified burial with military honors. Montgomery was interred inside the upper town on January 4, 1776. For the Americans, the defeat at Quebec and Montgomery's death came as twin shocks. There was much lamentation over the fallen hero. Congress resolved to purchase a monument and held a memorial service. Thomas Paine and many lesser propagandists held him up as a martyr to the cause of liberty and independence, although it is unlikely that Montgomery's thinking had progressed as far as the latter. The pressing business of war delayed the procurement of the memorial, but it was eventually installed at St. Paul's Chapel in New York City in 1787, where it remains today. It includes an inscription extolling:

> The patriotism conduct enterprise & perseverance of
> *Major General* RICHARD MONTGOMERY Who after
> a series of successes amidst the most discouraging
> Difficulties *Fell* in the attack on QUEBEC.[13]

Much later, in 1818, due to the persistence of Montgomery's now-aged widow Janet, his remains were recovered from Canada and conveyed with much solemn pomp to New York and entombed beneath the St. Paul's monument. Although the subsequent fading of his fame proves the dictum that all the world's glory is fleeting, Montgomery's selflessness, courage, and devotion to duty remain to inspire all who choose to look.

CHARLES LEE

It would have been infinitely better for Charles Lee's historical reputation had he, like Montgomery, found a patriot's grave early in the war. He would

have been universally mourned by contemporaries and history would today remember him as a staunch advocate of American independence, an astute trainer and organizer, and his adopted country's first soldier-intellectual. This complex, bizarre, and fascinating figure possessed genuine talent, but joined it to a penchant for self-destructive behavior. It has been observed that rather than an historian, it requires a psychiatrist to understand and explain Charles Lee. He was a man of confounding paradoxes—adventurous freebooter and devoted patriot, romantic and realist, too blunt and honest for his own good while simultaneously capable of great dissimulation. Instead of achieving heroic martyrdom—like Montgomery or Joseph Warren or Nathan Hale—he died alone, disgraced and impoverished, in a dingy Philadelphia inn and is largely forgotten today.[14]

At the struggle's outset, however, he, along with Washington, was the brightest star in the patriots' military firmament. Lee initially impressed virtually everyone he encountered in America. When Congress was selecting generals for the new army, Lee actually garnered some support for the commander in chief position. Ultimately, he received the third ranking general's billet, after Washington and—in another instance of sectional balancing—Massachusetts's Artemas Ward. John Adams expressed confidence that Lee would "do great service in our army at the beginning of things, by forming it in order, skill, and discipline."[15] His wife Abigail, normally an astute observer, saw Lee as a "Brave and Experienced General" possessed of "an unconq[uerable] spirit. . ."[16] Washington himself at one time regarded him as "the first officer in military knowledge and experience we have in the whole army. He is zealously attached to the cause, honest and well meaning." Perceptively, however, he also noted that the mercurial Lee was "rather fickle and violent I fear in his temper."[17]

What was it about Lee that so captivated those he met early on? It certainly was not his physical appearance. Descriptions by those who knew him and surviving engravings depict him as a slight, rather ugly man whose most prominent features were an outsized nose and darting, nervous eyes. He was careless in dress and in his personal habits. His manners were no better, although he could be charming, especially with the ladies, when he chose. More often he was coarse, profane, rude and abrupt with a sarcastic, even caustic sense of humor that bit deeply. What did impress about Lee were his keen intelligence, varied and extensive military experience, and vociferous support of American liberty.

He was born into a reasonably well-to-do family in Chester, England. The exact date is uncertain, but he was baptized on January 26 (old calendar), 1731. His father was a British army colonel of the 44th Foot and an uncle on his mother's side was a Member of Parliament. Four of his six siblings died young, his father was frequently away, and his mother apparently never warmed to him. The closest attachment Lee ever formed in his entire life was with his older sister. He received an excellent education from tutors, attendance at King Edward VI Grammar School in Suffolk, and a sojourn at a private academy in Switzerland. He learned both classical and modern European languages, excelled at history and literature, memorized Shakespeare, and imbibed the heady thinking of Rousseau and Voltaire, which may have influenced his subsequent political radicalism.

Lee followed the paternal path into the king's service, receiving an ensign's commission at age 15 in his father's regiment. Military duties were hardly onerous; indeed, the young ensign spent much of the time in school or abroad. His father's death in 1750 changed everything. Lee became executor of an extensive estate and—in accordance with the English custom of the day—purchased a promotion to lieutenant in the family regiment. Four years after this he found himself bound for America as part of General Edward Braddock's ill-starred expedition to conquer the French stronghold of Fort Duquesne (present-day Pittsburgh). Doubtless fortunately for him, after arrival in Virginia, Lee was detached to a sister regiment to handle logistical affairs and missed the bloody debacle on July 9, 1755, on the Monongahela River. French and Indians ambushed Braddock's column, killing the commander and many others. Among the wounded were two friends Lee had made in the course of the campaign, Lieutenant Colonel Thomas Gage and Captain Horatio Gates. The remnants, including Lee, limped to Philadelphia and thence north as the British sought to regroup and reinvigorate their North American campaign.

Lee spent the next 3 years in the Hudson River–Lake Champlain region. He sent rhapsodic descriptions of the scenery to his sister and became intimate with some friendly Indians, who bestowed upon him the name *Ounewaterika*—"Boiling Water." He also took an Indian concubine to help pass the time and fathered at least two children with her. A succession of British commanders and schemes came to naught, and Lee was already indulging the indiscretion of tongue and pen that would eventually cause him so much grief. Of one superior who had been slightly wounded in the head by a cannonball, he snidely exclaimed "I'll resign tomorrow. None but a fool will remain in a service in which generals' heads are bomb-proof."[18] Lee, now a captain, finally tasted combat in leading his company in an assault on the French works at Fort Carillon (renamed Fort Ticonderoga by the British once they eventually took it) on July 8, 1758. The experience was brief enough; a musket ball shattered his ribs and he was evacuated from the field. The British attack failed and once again he excoriated the stupidity of his commander, General James Abercrombie, referring to him as a "damn'd beastly poltroon" and "our booby in chief," and writing to his sister that "there can be ... no success & victory so certain ... but that miscarriage may be brought about by the incapacity of a single person ... Fortune ... had cram'd victory into [Abercrombie's] mouth, but he contrived to spit it out again."[19]

Lee recuperated first in Albany, then on Long Island, though not without incident. Displaying his unerring capacity for displeasing others, he goaded an army surgeon into trying to shoot him in November 1758 in response to an insult. The attempted assassination miscarried and the aggrieved physician was subsequently discharged. Lee returned to active service in July 1759 and participated in the successful British campaigns that forever ended French control of Canada, including the siege of Fort Niagara and the capture of Montreal. He also commanded a daring independent mission through the wilderness in an ultimately futile pursuit of fleeing French troops. With victory won, the ambitious Captain Lee had no desire to remain stranded in America on backwater occupation duty, particularly after an altercation with a Philadelphia constable in April 1760 that led to a stiff fine of 50 pounds. He contrived to get sent home and made his way to London. There he hobnobbed with intellectuals such as Dr. Samuel Johnson and engaged in political chatter with assorted Whigs. Hungry for action, he sought and gained preferment as a major into a newly raised regiment that shipped for the Iberian Peninsula in 1762. Spain had entered the war against England and here was a new arena for fame and glory. Lee earned both soon enough. Under the command of General John Burgoyne, in October 1762 Lee won accolades for leading a successful night assault against an isolated Spanish outpost. Winter brought a halt to further campaigning, so Lee returned to the warmth and stimulation of London's drawing rooms, taverns, and coffee houses as a half-pay lieutenant colonel—the highest rank he achieved in the British army.

Still feeling restless and waiting for his estranged mother to die so he could come into his inheritance, Lee crossed the English Channel and made for the Continent in late 1764. His itinerary included stops in Holland, Prussia—where he met Frederick the Great—and Warsaw. There his erudition and charm helped him inveigle an appointment as an aide-de-camp to the King of Poland. The radical-minded English aristocrat enjoyed the splendor of court life, but was simultaneously appalled by the absolute power wielded by the nobility over their wretched serfs. Learning of the Stamp Act crisis in the distant American colonies, he wrote to his sister in March 1766, "May God prosper the Americans in their resolution, that there may be one Asylum at least on earth for men, who prefer their natural rights to the fantastical prerogative of a foolish perverted head because it wears a Crown."[20] Lee's mother died that same year and—following a visit to Constantinople—by its close he was back in London to settle affairs and enjoy some of his old haunts in the company of like-minded gentlemen. Among the celebrities with whom he consorted was Benjamin Franklin, who invited the well-traveled and outspoken Major Lee, along with Major Gates, to his Craven Street salon. A revolt against his patron, the Polish King, and a commission as a major general in the Polish army brought Lee back to Warsaw in 1769. He commanded no troops in either the reactionary struggle against Polish rebel bands or later when seconded to the Russian army fighting the Turks. Nevertheless, he once again confirmed his dripping disdain for the military abilities of anyone other than himself, writing of his experiences that "I knew before that blockheads in command could render abortive the valour of Troops."[21] He may also have noted while in Poland the relative effectiveness of marauding partisan bands against well-drilled regular formations. By 1771, by way of the Mediterranean, he had returned once again to England.

In addition to being an indomitable traveler and soldier of fortune, Lee also proved to be a formidable polemicist, radical in print as well as thought and private speech. His personal correspondence of this time contains references to George III as a "reptile" and a "despicable and tho stupid at the same time not innoxious dolt."[22] In an anonymous essay published in July 1770 he publicly assailed the king and his courtiers, attacked tyranny and corruption, and sounded the Whig, not to say republican, themes of liberty and virtue. His circle at this time included Burke, a stout friend of the American colonists, and Catherine Macaulay, a historian devoted to liberal principles similar to those espoused by Lee.

Continued repugnance at the English political scene, a desire to seek his fortune, and perhaps his natural wanderlust as well, drove Lee to take passage back to America in August 1773. He arrived at an exciting juncture in American affairs. Political ferment and agitation abounded, and Lee immersed himself in it, rapidly abandoning a projected trip to consummate a real estate deal in west Florida. Over the next year and a half Lee engaged in what we today would call "networking," peripatetically making the rounds in New York, Philadelphia, Boston, and Williamsburg, the capital of Virginia. He met and exchanged ideas with the likes of Thomas Paine, Thomas Jefferson, Patrick Henry, John and Sam Adams, and a galaxy of other leading American figures. He also renewed ties with his old comrade in arms, Gates, now a Virginia landowner. He was Washington's house guest twice at Mount Vernon, and managed to involve himself in a dispute between the Virginia assembly and the royal governor of that colony. Although not a delegate, he was present in Philadelphia when both the first and second Continental Congresses convened in September 1774 and May 1775.

He employed his sharp pen as well. He conducted an extensive correspondence both with luminaries back home in England and his fellow British officers in America, many with whom he had personally served. The most notable of these was General Gage, the beleaguered British commander in chief in Boston. In late 1774 Lee wrote an impassioned letter that, after assuring Gage of his respect and affection, informed him that "I hold in such utter abhorrence the conduct temper and spirit and measures of our present Court, more particularly their present diabolical measures with respect to this Country that I cannot bear to see [you] . . . one of their instruments." Lee went on to invoke "the bright Goddess Liberty" and declared that, having been driven from England and Europe, "here is her last asylum."[23] Additionally, Lee published several articles and one significant pamphlet that appeared first in Philadelphia in November 1774 and was reprinted numerous times throughout the colonies. Entitled *Strictures upon A "Friendly Address to All Reasonable Americans,"* this essay offered a stinging and effective rebuttal to an earlier pamphlet written by a Loyalist supporter of the crown, the Reverend Dr. Myles Cooper. Cooper had strenuously argued to his fellow Americans that it was both wrong and foolish to oppose the king and his ministers. The strongest part of his thesis emphasized the futility of standing up and prevailing against the mother country in an armed showdown—the redcoats, augmented by German mercenaries and many loyal Americans—would crush any ragged forces that dared oppose them. Lee—drawing upon his immense fund of historical knowledge, extensive practical experience of soldiering, and literary skills—compellingly refuted Cooper. The English firebrand pointed out previous examples where a people in arms had bested trained soldiers, and downplayed the importance of drill and parade ground precision in an environment such as

America's. On the eve of the Revolution, Lee made himself one of the leading lights of rebellion based upon his military reputation, assiduous cultivation of leading patriots, and eloquent advocacy of American liberty.

Thus, it is not surprising that this relative newcomer to American shores should have been offered a major general's commission by the Congress in June 1775. Interestingly, before accepting, this ardent supporter of America's cause requested that Congress indemnify him against the financial losses that he stood to incur, not only from loss of his British army commission, but through the expected confiscation of his English property once he turned coat. Lee's detractors since then have singled this out as an illustration of his fundamentally flawed character. In his defense, some have noted that, unlike Washington or other native born Americans, he stood to lose financially regardless of whether the patriots ultimately triumphed. In any case, the Congress readily agreed and Lee submitted his resignation to the British secretary at state for war, grandiloquently noting his continued willingness to fight for king and country in a just cause, meanwhile admonishing his majesty "into measures more Consonant to his Interest and honor, and more conducive to the happiness and glory of his People."[24]

On June 23, 1775, Washington, Lee, and Schuyler departed Philadelphia amid much pomp and circumstance. Escorted by militia units and a troop of light horse, Washington and Lee were Cambridge-bound while Schuyler was destined to take command not far from his own holdings on the vital Canadian frontier. It was a royal progress of sorts, the entourage being met and feted along their route through New Jersey, New York, and Connecticut. Among those greeting the new commander in chief and his lieutenants was Brigadier General Montgomery and other members of New York's Provincial Congress. At a reception given by this body in New York City, Washington made a justly famous statement of his view of the subordination of military to civilian concerns, "When we assumed the soldier, we did not lay aside the citizen; and we shall most sincerely rejoice with you in that happy hour, when the establishment of American liberty on the most firm and solid foundation shall enable us to return to our private stations in the bosom of a free, peaceful, and happy country." Lee's most sympathetic biographer speculates that this felicitous phrasing may owe something to Lee, noting that Washington often solicited drafting assistance from his more eloquent subordinates.[25]

Upon arrival in Cambridge, Washington assigned Lee to command the left or northern wing of the patriot army opposite the Charlestown peninsula and the British on the dearly bought Bunker Hill, with Ward, the previous commander of the "army of observation," taking the right and another venerable New England soldier, Israel Putnam, holding the center. Lee had about 8,000 men at his disposal. His two subordinate brigadier generals were John Sullivan, a New Hampshire lawyer, and Nathanael Greene. At some point Lee acquired a retinue of dogs that followed him wherever he went, whether trooping the line or calling upon Boston's social elite. This fondness for canine companionship was much noted by contemporaries, although none seem to have attributed it to Lee's fundamental loneliness and inability to get on with two-legged creatures for long. A dinner companion from this period annotated this succinct description in his diary, labeling Lee "a perfect original, a good scholar and soldier, and an odd genius; full of fire and passion, and but little good manners; a great sloven, wretchedly profane, and a great admirer of dogs—of which he had two at dinner with him."[26]

Lee busied himself assisting Washington instill discipline and order into the heretofore rather independent-minded patriot host, composed largely of free-thinking New Englanders. More so than some of the Virginians, however, while sensible of their faults and lack of traditional martial virtue, Lee also judged the New Englanders to be fine material, capable of being molded into first class fighting men. Nevertheless, as was his wont, Lee found much of which to complain, notifying his longtime Philadelphia associate and business agent Robert Morris, "We found everything the reverse of what had been represented . . . we were assur'd . . . the army was stocked with Engineers. We found not one." Somehow overlooking the 300-pound presence of Henry Knox, he continued, "We were assur'd that we should find an expert of artillery. They have not a single Gunner."[27] It was true enough, however, that there were few guns, a state of affairs that Knox would personally remedy that coming winter. Lee also maintained his correspondence with his former British army colleagues, trading barbs with his old commander in Portugal, Burgoyne, as well as with Gage.

Lee remained among the leading radical voices in or out of the army. For instance, he implored John Adams to have Congress seize the estates of leading Loyalists or at least tax heavily those "notorious enemies of American liberty."[28] He further recommended that American ports be opened to all European vessels and fulminated against the reluctance of Pennsylvania Quakers to contemplate American independence. He bombarded Congress with suggestions and advice, urging that patriotic New Yorkers be given the go-ahead to arrest the colony's royal governor and essentially hold him hostage against any British reprisal. And, in early December 1775, he sent Benjamin Franklin a full-fledged war plan that called for wholesale confiscation of Loyalist property, reorganization of the army with the creation of a national militia and roving partisan bands—"flying camps"—under Continental Army control, and fortifying or razing key cities, including New York.

Between December 1775 and the end of June 1776 Lee reached his zenith as a hero of American liberty. During this 6-month span he served as Congress's chief trouble shooter, rushed to wherever the need seemed most critical. This whirlwind of activity commenced when patriot leaders in Rhode Island pleaded with Washington for assistance in contending with native Loyalists, as well as with a feared British seaborne landing. The commander in chief dispatched Lee with a small detachment in response to this call for help. Lee immediately made his presence felt; in 5 days over Christmas he inspected and made recommendations for fortifications, and terrorized local Tories by demanding oaths from them not to support the British or hinder the patriots. Those who demurred found themselves tossed into jail. Then, the cause and patriot morale sufficiently shored up, Lee raced back to Cambridge with praise ringing in his ears and plans for a similar mission to New York City maturing in his head.

New York City was as important a strategic spot as existed in the colonies; both Lee and Washington fully expected the British at some point to transfer their forces to the mouth of the Hudson, as they eventually did. New York also harbored considerable Loyalist sentiment. Thus Lee argued both to friends in Congress and to Washington the need to prepare the city's defenses and sort out the obnoxious Loyalists. Lee was persuasive and in January 1776 he set out for New York on a Congressionally authorized mission, picking up Connecticut and New Jersey militia en route. A spell of a chronically recurring ailment—gout— laid Lee low for more than a week and delayed his arrival. Nevertheless, he kept at his extensive correspondence, taking time to tout to Washington the "masterly, irresistible performance" by his fellow English immigrant Thomas Paine in his new pamphlet *Common Sense*. He felt that it would "give the Coup-de-grace to Great Britain" and, as with many others, "I own myself convinced, by the arguments, of the necessity of separation."[29] He also learned of Montgomery's bitter setback at Quebec, which perhaps increased his concerns about the security of New York now that the British could conceivably assail it from Canada as well as the sea. Lee entered New York in early February—the same day that a fleet with a contingent of redcoats under General Clinton appeared in the harbor—and found city leaders apprehensive not only about the British and Tory sympathizers, but about Lee's already great reputation for fire-eating zeal and the possible repercussions his activities might bring.

Lee lost no time in confirming the worst fears both of the city's Loyalists and more timid patriots. Once again he displayed almost superhuman energy in carrying out his duties. On the political front, he imposed a reign of terror upon known and suspected Tories. As in Rhode Island, these individuals were compelled to swear oaths, with those who refused carted off to jail. These strong arm tactics proved a bit much even for the anti-British New York Provincial Congress, which instructed its delegates in Philadelphia to protest Lee's high-handed methods. Eventually the Continental Congress responded with a watered down resolution forbidding military officers in the future from demanding oaths from civilians. Lee, unnamed in this resolution, felt unjustly censured, though hardly chastened, and friends in Congress assured him that they privately applauded his revolutionary spirit. Meanwhile, the town's Committee of Public Safety was petrified at the prospect of a British bombardment in response to Lee's activities. Lee's rejoinder that he doubted the British would do so and that if they did, "the first house set in flames by their Guns shall be the funeral pile of some of their best friends" may not have entirely set their minds at ease.[30]

In the military sphere, Lee did his best to put New York in a defensible position, though as he presciently advised Washington, the place was "so encircled with deep navigable water, that whoever commands the sea must command the town."[31] He developed plans to situate batteries around Manhattan Island to drive off any British fleet, as well as on Long Island, along with provision for infantry units to cover them. Additionally, to the north at Kings Bridge, he proposed a garrison to secure the only withdrawal route from Manhattan to the mainland. All these ideas were logical, though Lee's basic point about hostile sea power rendering New York indefensible still obtained, as events would show. In any event, the old shortages of artillery, engineers, and manpower that had plagued the effort in Boston were in evidence in New York too. For the moment, however, the British held off and Clinton sailed south, where he and Lee would ultimately cross swords.

On February 19, 1776, John Adams penned a fulsome letter to Lee. Congress had just selected him for the supremely important command in Canada. Reflecting Lee's status as the indispensable man of the hour, Adams wrote, "We want you at N. York—we want you at Cambridge—we want you in Virginia—but Canada seems of more Importance. . ."[32] This commendation arrived along with the official notification from Congress's president John Hancock, along with similar praise-filled letters from the likes of Franklin. All lauded Lee for his efforts in New York and predicted glory for him in the north. The bearer of these missives was that other celebrity of the moment, Tom Paine, who volunteered to carry them to New York in order to congratulate the renowned Lee. Yet Lee had barely begun his preparations to move when another communication from Hancock informed him of a change in plans. Instead of Canada, Lee would command a new southern department that included Virginia, the Carolinas, and Georgia.

This abrupt shift owed not to lack of confidence in Lee, but rather to the concerns of southerners in Congress, who greatly feared a British attack in their home region. Their arguments carried the day against the northern delegates, who preferred to have Lee closer at hand, and so the general headed south. He was now the second ranking officer in the Continental establishment, as Ward, whom Lee contemptuously dismissed as a "church-warden," had retired.[33] By the end of March, Lee and his personal staff were ensconced in Williamsburg. As before, he applied his customary and formidable energies. He even injected himself into areas not within his orbit, directing patriots in Maryland to arrest the royal governor of that colony. As had occurred previously in New York, local patriots took umbrage at this sort of preemptory interference; ultimately Congress backed Lee, and the situation resolved itself with the governor removing himself to the safety of England. Lee passed about 6 weeks in the Old Dominion, fortifying likely British targets at Yorktown and Williamsburg, harrying unfortunate Loyalists, and attempting to isolate Virginia's royal governor, who had taken refuge in the coastal town of Norfolk. The indefatigable Lee also found time to impart his wisdom to Congress on naval affairs and the importance of seizing the western outposts at Niagara and Detroit. Most dramatically, he implored them to proclaim American independence. In a letter to Virginia's Richard Henry Lee, he starkly exclaimed, "If you do not declare immediately for positive independence, we are all ruined."[34]

Meanwhile, alarm ran up and down the coasts of the Carolinas as citizens there anticipated a descent by Clinton's floating expedition, now reinforced with ships and troops from England. Again displaying his inherent radicalism, Lee suggested to North Carolinians that they take the families of prominent Loyalists hostage to guard against their giving aid and comfort to the enemy. Lee's operational problem was to divine exactly what Clinton's objective was and move himself to that point.

Complicating his calculus was the mobility advantage the seaborne British had; if he guessed wrong, the British would attack their target before Lee could recover. In early May, based upon sightings of the British fleet off the North Carolina coast, Lee set out for that colony with over 1,000 Virginia troops to repulse them. On the way, he received intelligence that led him to conclude that Clinton was aiming instead at Charleston, South Carolina, so he pressed on to that seaport city.

He found the anxious South Carolinians working to erect forts on two islands at the entrance to Charleston's harbor—Fort Johnson on James Island to the south and Fort Sullivan on the southern tip of Sullivan's Island to the north. They had also mustered nearly 5,000 men, a hundred or so cannon, and ample quantities of powder. Artillery ammunition was in short supply, however, and the defensive works were no where near complete when the British armada of over 50 ships hove into view in early June. Tricky tides and poor weather helped preclude an early British assault and Lee used the time to energize the defenders, who in his eyes failed to exhibit the requisite sense of urgency. By mid-June, most of the British force had landed on Long Island, to the north of Sullivan's Island, and it thus appeared that they would make their attack from that direction. Lee dispatched forces to the end of Sullivan's Island closest to Long Island to check a British maneuver against the fort. He further emplaced a sizeable contingent on the mainland north of Charleston to block any attack directly from Long Island. He also barricaded the city itself. And he ceaselessly hectored the commander of Fort Sullivan, Colonel William Moultrie, to hasten completion of his works and to build a bridge from Sullivan's Island back to the mainland to facilitate a withdrawal from what Lee regarded as little more than a death trap. Once again, Lee's aggressiveness, not to say abrasiveness, grated local sensitivities and only the diplomatic skill of South Carolina's chief executive, John Rutledge, salved the wounds.

The British assault began on June 28, 1776, and good fortune in the form of rough weather once more smiled upon the Americans. British warships moved up the channel to Fort Sullivan's south and began a bombardment to silence its guns. With that accomplished, the British could then safely concentrate on reducing the city proper. Simultaneously, Clinton planned a ground attack on Fort Sullivan at low tide, since one could normally walk across the channel separating Long and Sullivan's Islands during such periods. The wind, however caused three British frigates to run upon a shoal, where they were exposed to American fire. The same gusts also whipped up the bay's water to such a degree as to make a foot march from Long to Sullivan's Island impossible, even at low tide. Lee attempted to go by small boat to the scene of hottest action, but the wind prevented him reaching Moultrie at Fort Sullivan. The fort's soft palmetto logs easily absorbed the British shot and Moultrie's guns gave a good account. Lee eventually made it to the position in late afternoon, exposing himself to enemy fire while encouraging the gallant defenders. One humorous anecdote surrounding this event had Lee mock-rebuke an aide for seeming to shrink under fire. Lee told the young officer that Frederick the Great had once lost over a hundred aides on campaign, to which

Lee's aide dryly replied, "So I understand, sir, but I did not think you could spare so many."[35] By evening the British elected to withdraw with one ship lost, two seriously damaged, and dozens of casualties. American losses were minimal. Here was a glorious patriot victory. Lee had read the battlefield correctly, disposed his forces intelligently, and displayed physical courage. The laurels bestowed upon him were justly deserved.

For another month or so, Lee occupied himself with his southern duties. Clinton and his wounded flotilla remained off Charleston, while his troops occupied various adjacent islands, and Lee contemplated striking an offensive blow against them. By late July, however, Clinton had departed to join the Howes in their New York campaign. Lee also attempted, with indifferent success, to knit southern officials more closely together in cooperative defense schemes. His most ambitious planning centered on a projected attack against the crown's post at Saint Augustine, Florida, whence the British incited the fierce Seminoles into forays against the Georgia colonists. He also learned of the Declaration of Independence and was especially transported, predicting to Virginia's Patrick Henry, "We shall now, most probably, see a mighty empire establish'd of Freemen whose honour, property and military glories are not to be at the disposal of a scepter'd knave. . ."[36] Soon after, however, he needed to lay aside his southern schemes and glorious forecasts for the new nation. The storm had broken in New York and in early August Congress urgently recalled its military champion north to the scene of action and maximum danger.

Lee arrived in Philadelphia on October 7, 1776, spent a few hours with members of Congress, and then continued to join Washington in New York. By then, General Howe had won a shattering victory at Long Island, occupied New York City, and threatened to cut off and defeat Washington's army, then occupying Harlem Heights. John Adams hopefully wrote to his wife that Lee's "Appearance at Head Quarters on the Heights of Ha'arlem, would give a flow of Spirits to our Army, there. Some officer of his Spirit and Experience, seems to be wanted."[37] Lee's estimate of the situation was that the only sound course of action was a withdrawal, either into Connecticut or up the Hudson. This Washington, pressured by Congress, was reluctant to do. Lee gave vent to his frustrations in a letter to Gates, then commanding the remnant of American forces on Lake Champlain, "the Congress seem to stumble every step—I do not mean one or two of the Cattle, but the whole Stable." Significantly, he now began to fault Washington as well, "in my opinion General Washington is as much to blame in not menacing 'em with resignation unless they refrain from unhinging the army by their absurd interference."[38] From this point forward, Lee and Washington would seldom see eye to eye.

By mid-October Lee had command of the army's left wing and under him it helped thwart a British flanking attack that followed a landing at Throg's Neck. Nevertheless, Lee felt the American position was precarious in the extreme and, when Washington summoned a council of war on October 16, argued strenuously for withdrawal. Lee's advocacy carried the day—at least partially. The army did retire to White Plains in time to save it from being bagged by Howe. Subsequently, in early November, Washington with the bulk of the army crossed the Hudson into New Jersey, leaving the rump of the Continentals and some militia with Lee at White Plains. Washington, however, in attempting to follow Congress's intent, refused to abandon the Hudson River forts—one named for him on the Manhattan side and Fort Lee across from it on the New Jersey bank. Fort Washington was especially exposed, as Howe demonstrated by gobbling it up, along with 3,000 prisoners on November 16. Lee went wild with rage and wrote intemperate letters to Washington and various Congressmen venting himself and decrying the war's inept management.

Washington's prestige plummeted with the disastrous New York campaign and continued to sink as he retreated through New Jersey, just ahead of the conquering Howe. Lee, on the other hand, was riding high and there were those, in and out of the army, who thought that perhaps the ex-English officer was better suited for the supreme command. One of these was Washington's military secretary, Colonel Joseph Reed, who penned an almost-incredible letter to Lee. Reed informed Lee "that it is entirely owing to you that this Army & the Liberties of America ... are not totally cut off" and lamented the commander in chief's indecision and slowness to act.[39] He broadly hinted that Lee was the man to give the army the leadership it required and added that this view was widely shared. Lee responded by agreeing with Reed about Washington's "fatal indecision of mind which in war is a much greater disqualification than stupidity or even want of personal courage."[40] Unfortunately for Lee, Washington himself opened this reply. Although he refrained from making a public issue of the manifest disloyalty in this private exchange, this episode doubtless confirmed Washington's concerns about Lee's "fickle" nature.

Washington would soon have further reason for displeasure. Once Howe turned west and south for New Jersey, Washington expected Lee to bring his forces across the Hudson to link up with him. Lee had other ideas, however, and treated several missives from Washington to this effect as suggestions rather than orders, even after he finally crossed the Hudson on December 2. Rather than obey his chief, Lee pondered independent action against Howe's dispersed forces and lines of communication across the New Jersey countryside. Whatever the military merits of Lee's ideas, it was clear that Washington wanted Lee to join the main army, which by now had crossed the Delaware into Pennsylvania. On December 10, Washington commanded Lee "to march and join me with all your whole force with all possible expedition ... Do come on."[41] At Morristown, New Jersey Lee mulled these instructions, and then began moving ponderously toward the Delaware. He also unburdened himself in a letter to Gates, then hastening south with eight regiments to join Washington. Lee sarcastically wrote, "The ingenious maneuver of Fort Washington has unhing'd the goodly fabrick We had been building." Then the condemning phrase, "*entre nous*, a certain great man is most damnably deficient—He has thrown me into a situation where I have my choice of difficulties..."[42] While bemoaning the predicament he believed Washington had fashioned for him, Lee chose to spend the night of December 12 with just his personal staff at an isolated inn at Basking Bridge, New Jersey, about 3 miles from his army's main camp. This was a mistake. A patrol of British dragoons in the neighborhood learned of his presence and a sudden raid on the morning of December 13 resulted in Lee's capture. When the news got out, it created jubilation among the British and plunged the American patriots into even deeper despair than they had already known.

Lee's being taken set in motion a complicated, intrigue-filled 15-month period. Lee undoubtedly feared for his life and with good reason. Howe regarded him as a base traitor, and desired to execute him. Nevertheless, the British commander, sensitive to the political implications, and also concerned about American retaliation, chose to consult London first. Lee meanwhile was moved to New York, where he lived in fairly comfortable circumstances under a sort of house arrest. For months Congress and Washington wrangled among themselves, and with the British, on how to protect and ultimately repatriate Lee. The issues encompassed arcane eighteenth-century conventions such as parole—where in return for release a captive gave his word not to take up arms—prisoner exchanges, and Lee's actual status. In the latter instance, Lee's formal and public resignation from the British army in 1775 likely helped save him. The British ultimately determined that he had ceased to be a king's officer and eventually they accorded him "ordinary" prisoner status, making him eligible for exchange for a British officer of equivalent major general's rank.

While his fate and disposition were being decided, Lee involved himself in a bizarre negotiation with Howe. During the Revolution, the British frequently sought to gain information from senior captives or even turn them against the patriot cause and Lee was no exception. The voluble, opinionated Lee proved very willing to talk with his captors who were, after all, fellow English gentlemen and former comrades-in-arms. Discussions apparently centered on how to achieve Anglo-American reconciliation. Lee's best biographer perceptively notes that, for all his rhetoric, Lee was more of an English radical than an American nationalist. That is, despite his ostensible support for independence, he likely saw this as a bargaining point to achieve greater liberties for Americans within the British Empire. In March 1777 he drafted a truly amazing document and presented it to Howe. Lee observed that the British would likely subdue the Americans, but only after a long and bloody struggle that would drain both sides. He proposed a plan of campaign that would bring a more speedy English victory, to be followed by a generous peace that would benefit all parties—to include the Howe brothers, who would reap the glory that accrued from such an outcome. Lee must have known or guessed that British intentions for 1777 included Burgoyne's move south from Canada and Howe's advance on Philadelphia. In addition to this, Lee recommended seizing key points in Virginia and Maryland to cut the southern states off from the middle ones. According to Lee, this combination of activities would embolden Loyalists and "unhinge and dissolve" American defenses, bringing a rapid end to hostilities.[43]

Howe did not act on this document and even if he had, it seems unlikely that it would have had the decisive effect touted by Lee. What was Lee trying to accomplish? Was he a traitor to the American cause? Adding to the air of mystery, shortly after Lee wrote it—and there is no doubt about its authenticity—this paper sunk completely out of sight, only resurfacing in a collection of General Howe's effects more than 70 years later. Mid-nineteenth-century writers excoriated Lee, already in generally low repute for his conduct at the battle of Monmouth and his resulting court-martial. More recent and sympathetic biographers have suggested that Lee was playing a sophisticated game by attempting to mislead Howe and divert him from supporting Burgoyne's potentially deadly offensive. One of the Revolution's most perceptive historians, John Shy, considered all the possibilities and offered another—that the compulsive and egotistical Lee simply could not resist the opportunity to be at the center of affairs.[44]

Whatever its causes and purposes, his proposal to Howe remained unknown when Lee finally was finally exchanged in April 1778. Washington warmly received him at the American encampment at Valley Forge. Congress, which with Philadelphia in enemy hands had relocated to York, Pennsylvania, also welcomed him. After a brief period of convalescence at his farm in Virginia, he rejoined the army in May and resumed his post as Washington's deputy. Lee by this time had matured his thinking on organization and strategy, which he outlined in a paper entitled "Plan for the Formation of the American Army." He argued that it was foolhardy to think that Americans could best the British in traditional, European-style warfare and advocated what today we would call a guerilla war as the only reasonable patriot course of action. Unfortunately for Lee, he was out of step with his commander and an army that had spent the previous winter perfecting its professionalism under the stern tutelage of Baron von Steuben. And in little more than a month, his career and reputation were in ruins.

While Lee was re-acclimating himself, Clinton had relieved Howe as the overall British commander. In reaction to France's entry into the war, England took up the strategic defensive, and this included ordering Clinton to quit Philadelphia and move to New York. The Americans detected this withdrawal and Washington called a council of war with his generals—his standard decision-making style—on June 17 and asked for opinions. The general consensus, shared by the cautious Lee as well as fire-eaters such as Benedict Arnold, resolved to attempt to harass Clinton while avoiding a major engagement. The Continental Army, some 12,000 strong, began to parallel Clinton's line of march east across New Jersey. Washington summoned another general officer meeting on June 24 at Hopewell, New Jersey. He clearly ached to strike a blow at Clinton. Lee again led those who urged against any precipitate move that could bring on a general action; indeed he averred that if it were in his power, he would build a "golden bridge" to expedite Clinton's retirement.[45] One of Washington's young staff officers, Alexander Hamilton, later described the deliberations as akin to those of a group of midwives. After the council, several officers including Nathanael Greene, the Marquis de Lafayette, and Anthony Wayne, sought out Washington and convinced him at least to increase the pressure on Clinton. Accordingly, Washington pushed forward Daniel Morgan and a regiment of riflemen to link up with New Jersey militia already operating against the British right flank and ordered another brigade to harass their left. He also sent Wayne's division ahead and placed this entire advance guard of almost 5,000 men under Lafayette's command. Learning of this injured Lee's *amour propre*; though he had doubts about any attack on the British, he asserted his right to command so large a detachment as the senior major general. Washington assented and Lee went forward to take command on June 26. By the morning of the 27th, with the main body under Washington still far behind him, Lee and his detachment were in Englishtown, some 6 miles distant from Clinton, who was resting his weary men at Monmouth Courthouse.

Washington now called Lee and his principal subordinates back to his head-quarters and issued instructions for an attack on Clinton's rear. Throughout the day, he supplemented these via messengers. The general tenor remained to harass, skirmish, and annoy the British rearguard. For his part, Lee issued no specific orders. He had little knowledge of the ground over which he would pass or the enemy situation. Rather than conduct a reconnaissance, he decided that it would be better simply to develop the situation as he moved forward. Three imperatives drive successful battlefield commanders: see the terrain, see the enemy, and see friendly forces. Lee was largely blind to the first two and would experience much difficulty with this last during the ensuing battle of Monmouth.

June 28, 1778—2 years exactly since Lee's victory at Charleston—dawned hot and humid. As for the past several days, the midday temperature approached 100 degrees Fahrenheit. The ground over which the battle took place consisted of sandy pine barrens and numerous small streams. Three large ravines, each about a mile apart and running north-south, were the key features along the route the Lee's force followed toward Monmouth. These have become known as the West, Middle, and East ravines in accounts of the battle. The West and Middle ravines intersected the main road Lee took to Monmouth; a bridge and a causeway, respectively; spanned these. The East ravine was about a mile north of courthouse. Clinton had started his baggage train, with the main body, north along the road to Middletown. Aware that he was being followed and also conscious of the harassing activities of the New Jersey militia, he left a 2,000 man rearguard under Cornwallis at the courthouse. Lee, as he felt his way ahead, began to receive conflicting reports—the British were moving away; no, the British were not moving. Lee pressed on and around noon the Americans discovered Cornwallis's men drawn up in good order north and east of the courthouse and the final ravine. Lee now decided to attack and cut off Cornwallis. He pushed Wayne's unit forward in the center and elected to make his main effort by flanking the British right.

Wayne soon engaged in a sharp fight and Clinton, hearing sounds of battle, began to send reinforcements from the main body back to support Cornwallis. This force began to menace the American right and Lee ordered Lafayette to take a brigade and meet this new threat. Simultaneously, Lee ordered two aides to find his left flank commander who was to make the all important attack on the British right and urge him to remain firm. The aides failed to locate him in the difficult terrain and general confusion. It often happens in battle, especially when communication and understanding of the commander's intent are poor, that the retirement of one or several elements can precipitate a more general pullback. This is what now occurred, starting on the American right. The first unit to retrograde was an artillery battery, for the perfectly good reason that it had run low on ammunition and was heading back to its trains to gather more. Then Lafayette, feeling exposed, ordered the three regiments under him back to a new position in the vicinity of the courthouse. Wayne, convinced that the size of the British force did not warrant retreat, remonstrated with the young French nobleman, but to no avail. Since his own right flank support was disappearing, Wayne also reluctantly withdrew. And Lee's left flank commander, discovering all this and fearful of being cut off, also retreated to the west side of the East ravine. In fact, though Lee was exerting no great control over his men, this sequence of withdrawals probably spared the American vanguard from being crushed against the East ravine—overwhelmed by a superior British force while the difficult terrain to Lee's rear impeded Washington from coming to his rescue with the bulk of the army.

Lee quickly realized that the courthouse and surrounding village were unsuited to defense, and looked for better ground. Spying a promising looking series of hills just west of the Middle ravine, Lee ordered his men back across the causeway to take up positions there. Nevertheless, once Lee achieved this eminence himself, he found it unsatisfactory, becoming concerned that a British attack might sweep his men down toward the West ravine and pin them there. Therefore he decided on a third backward movement, toward a hill on the west side of the West ravine—an excellent defensive position as it turned out. Lee deployed four regiments and some artillery to cover this latest leapfrog movement to the rear; this force effectively delayed the advancing British for a time. By now, however, the American retirement had deteriorated into something of a shambles—the terrible heat, a lack of water, and the seeming absence of control took their toll. Men and units began to straggle; some continued past the latest designated defensive line and acted as if in headlong retreat. For American hopes, this was a fortunate time for Washington, who had been coming on since early morning himself, to arrive with the main army. For Lee personally, it was a disastrous occasion for an encounter with the commander in chief.

The two met on horseback just east of the bridge over the West ravine. Lee apparently believed he had done a creditable day's work in preserving his force in the face of superior numbers. He was therefore shocked when Washington angrily upbraided him in the presence of a large group of officers, "I desire to know, sir, what is the reason, whence arises all this confusion?" The stricken Lee could only stammer "Sir, sir . . ."[46] Washington was famous for his self-control, but he also possessed a ferocious temper. On this day, perhaps the combination of fatigue, heat, stress of battle, and Lee's previous hints of disloyalty got the best of him. He continued to harangue Lee, who was decidedly not famous for his self-control. Lee vigorously defended himself, to include blaming some of his subordinates and reiterating his opposition from the beginning to the whole notion of a major battle with the British. Washington broke off and began to take personal charge of the battle. Superb as always in crisis, the Virginian rallied the rearward streaming elements of Lee's command and gave orders for the main force to itself position on the hill Lee had previously chosen on the west side of the ravine. He then asked Lee to take charge of the covering force on the east side of the bridge while he saw to the final defensive line on the hill. Lee accomplished this task in a satisfactory manner, buying time until heavy pressure forced him back across the bridge. He then asked Washington for further orders and was told to take his fought-out elements back to Englishtown and reform them there. An exhausted and likely demoralized Lee complied. Meanwhile Washington had formed a very strong position that successfully resisted a ragged series of British attacks. Nightfall rang a curtain on the battle and in the darkness Clinton pulled away and resumed his trek to New York. The Americans had no desire to pursue. Casualty figures are unreliable, but both sides appear to have lost around 400 men. Heat stroke killed a number in each army. Both sides with some justification claimed victory. Clinton had fought a successful rearguard action and protected his main body. The Americans had indeed harassed the British and stoutly defended themselves behind the West ravine.

Charles Lee was incapable of leaving well—or bad—enough alone. Washington normally displayed greatness of spirit and had Lee let the episode pass, Washington might have done likewise. Lee, however, began speaking bitterly to others of his treatment even as he departed the battlefield. He then wrote three increasingly intemperate letters to Washington demanding the opportunity to clear his name and reputation, which he felt had been impugned. Among the most insolent and incendiary passages Lee wrote was the following, "You cannot afford me greater pleasure than in giving me the opportunity of shewing to America, the sufficiency of her respective servants. I trust, that the temporary power of office, and the tinsel dignity attending it, will not be able, . . . to offiscate the bright rays of truth. . ."[47] Washington obliged Lee with a court-martial, which charged him with disobeying orders in not attacking, misbehavior before the enemy in retreating, and disrespect to the commander in chief.

The court-martial convened between July 4 and August 9, hearing evidence on the move as the army continued to shadow the British. The charges were extraordinarily grave and the first two theoretically carried the death penalty. From an objective viewpoint more than two and a quarter centuries after the event, it seems unlikely that Lee was truly guilty of disobedience or cowardly behavior. Even less credible is the idea that he was guilty of treason, although in the later, nineteenth century, furor over his activities while in British captivity, that charge was leveled too. While his generalship may have been less than inspired that fateful day, he tried to attack and, at worst, lost control of his units. At best, he may have saved them by pulling back. On the other hand, he clearly showed disrespect to Washington. Nevertheless, although Lee may have been blind to it, once the Lee–Washington dispute became a public contest, there was little chance of the court not convicting him on all counts. This it did. Pure justice may have been on Lee's side, but by this time considerable animus toward him existed throughout the army, based in large measure on what was known of his fraternizing behavior while a British prisoner. Further, the court certainly realized that finding for Lee meant, in essence, finding against Washington and could conceivably even lead to the resignation or retirement of this one truly indispensable man. Public interest trumped private justice. As if in recognition, however, of Lee's claims, the court passed the odd, relatively light sentence of suspending him from command for a period of 1 year.

It required Congress to approve the convictions and Lee hastened to Philadelphia to plead his case and fight for vindication. Congress delayed in the collective hope that the whole ugly mess might go away through the expedient of Lee quietly resigning. When it became apparent that Lee would not go gently, Congress took up the matter and in early December 1778 narrowly affirmed the court-martial's verdict. Lee remained combative as ever. He unlimbered his formidable pen in a torrent of private correspondence and published essays that trenchantly laid out his side of the story. Through his efforts at setting the record straight, he managed to get himself challenged to no less than three duels. He was able to deflect two of these—from fellow generals Baron von Steuben and Anthony Wayne, who felt their courage had been questioned by Lee—and fought the third. He conducted this "interview" (to employ the delightful nineteenth-century euphemism) with Henry Laurens, son of a Congressman and one of Washington's aides, who felt compelled to defend his chief against Lee's scribbling. The two met and exchanged pistol shots, with Lee sustaining a slight wound and honor being satisfied all around. Lee also cornered a less gentlemanly adversary—an editor who had offended him—with a horsewhip in a tavern.

No doubt to the relief of Congress and Philadelphia authorities, in April 1779 Lee retreated to the farm he had purchased some years earlier in western Virginia. Here he led a sad existence with his valet, housekeeper, and dogs. He continued writing to defend himself and attack his enemies. Though not exactly destitute, his financial condition was precarious and he traveled throughout Virginia and Maryland, staying with friends and occasionally borrowing money. Among his favorites was a young man and former army officer, James Monroe, the future fifth President of the United States. When Horatio Gates was appointed chief of the southern department that Lee had commanded years earlier, Lee supposedly issued him a famous warning to beware having his northern laurels (earned at Saratoga) turn to southern willows. Of course, this is exactly what happened. After Gate's disgrace in South Carolina, he and Lee were congenial neighbors until a falling out occurred due to Lee's disdain for Mrs. Gates. By late 1782, in failing health, Lee attempted to sell his estate and traveled to Philadelphia to complete the transaction. Death claimed him the evening of October 2, 1782. His last words were supposedly "Stand by me, my brave grenadiers!" Sensing the end, he had completed a will en route that included a bitter, sardonic last paragraph, "I desire most earnestly, that I may not be buried in any church, or church-yard, or within a mile of any Presbyterian or Anabaptist meeting-house; for since I have resided in this country, I have kept so much bad company when living that I do not chuse to continue it when dead."[48] Frustrated to the end, he was buried just outside the entrance to Christ Church in Philadelphia.

HORATIO GATES

Gates's career as a Revolutionary general, if not as colorful, is at least as controversial as Lee's. The great American historian Allan Nevins long ago observed that Gates's place in our national story is generally held to be that of "a weakling, a bungler, and a marplot … the whipping-boy for the generals and statesmen of the Revolution."[49] Nevins himself disagreed with that characterization, largely the product of nineteenth-century pietistic historians who damned anyone who came into conflict with Washington. Modern scholarship has taken a more nuanced view of Gates "as neither genius nor fool but as a modestly gifted military officer with both commendable and damaging traits of character."[50] On the positive side of the ledger, Gates was instrumental in organizing troops and instilling a modicum of discipline in them; his only rival in this sphere was the Prussian Baron von Steuben. Under his command, the patriots halted two British invasions from Canada in 1776 and again in 1777, with the later occasion—the battle of Saratoga—representing the war's turning point. He was humane, cared well for his men, and was a loyal friend and family man. He devoted himself to the cause of American liberty. Counting against him were an awkwardness and bluntness, especially in written correspondence, that annoyed superiors and subordinates alike, and a tendency to be quarrelsome. This deficiency helped drag Gates's name into a dispute over supreme command of the Army in 1778, which seriously blackened his subsequent reputation. In his maturity, he hardly looked the part of a hardened professional soldier. His demeanor—thinning, gray hair, weak chin, large nose with spectacles perched upon it—led troops to call him "granny Gates." Several times he begged off from difficult assignments, claiming sickness from the dysentery that plagued him most of his life. Like many of his peers, he was contentious and displayed overweening personal ambition, which sometimes led him to unfortunate displays of pettiness or self-pity. An army under his command was routed at Camden, South Carolina, in 1780 a humiliation compounded by his rapid and unseemly flight from the battlefield. And in 1783 at Newburgh, New York, he was associated with a handful of officers who preached mutiny against Congressional authority. A simple, uncomplicated man, he left a most complicated legacy.

Very little is known of Gates's early years—even the date and place of his birth are uncertain. Gates himself appeared unsure of his birthday, hinting at differing dates in letters written in the latter part of his life. His best and most recent biographer opts for April 1728; others claim July 1727.[51] His birthplace is traditionally given as Maldon, England, about 40 miles northeast of London, though no birth record exists. Like Lee, Gates grew up in an aristocratic household. Unlike him, however, it was not as a family member, but as the son of the Duke of Leeds's housekeeper. Normally, someone as low born as Gates would have had little chance of gaining an officer's commission in the British army, but association with a wealthy, noble family proved advantageous in several regards. The boy received a fairly decent education; though not as erudite as Lee, years later colleagues wrote to Gates in French and he often spiced his letters with classical allusions. His Christian name also resulted from his connection to a prominent family; he was named for his 10-year-old godfather, a future illustrious statesman, Horace Walpole. And it is likely that the Leeds provided the necessary assistance for him to purchase a junior officer's commission. Why all this good fortune should have been lavished upon young Horatio is unknown. No evidence exists at all for the most obvious speculation—that he was an important person's bastard son.

Gates's career began in earnest in 1749 when he volunteered for overseas duty under Edward Cornwallis, governor of Nova Scotia. Cornwallis was the first of two senior officers who would do much to assist Gates's progress in his early years. Interestingly, three decades later Gates would confront the governor's nephew, Lord Charles Cornwallis, in battle. He passed his time in routine garrison duty and, in 1754, married Elizabeth Phillips, the daughter of a fellow officer. Depicted by some as harridan and memorably described by Charles Lee as a "Medusa" who "governs with a rod of scorpions," she was nonetheless devoted to Gates and they seem to have enjoyed a good marriage.[52] That same year he also purchased a captain's commission and shortly afterward the newlyweds moved to New York City, where Gates took command of an infantry company. It was here, in the society of the city's Whig circle, that Gates gained his first exposure to the radical political ideals that would animate him later on.

Domestic bliss, easy duty, and politics all went on the backburner in the spring of 1755 when Gates and his company received orders to join Braddock's expedition against the French at Fort Duquesne. When this force began its march to disaster in June, Gates rode with them. Like many of his fellow officers, he was wounded in the ambush of July 9. A private named Francis Penfold dragged Gates to safety and, years afterward according to an anecdote, the down and out former soldier applied to Gates for help. Gates's generous reply instructed Penfold to "come and rest your firelock in my chimney corner, and partake with me; while I have, my savior Penfold shall not want; and it is my wish, as well as Mrs. Gates's, to see you spend the evening of your life comfortably."[53] Indeed, throughout his career one of Gates's most notable traits—very unusual in eighteenth-century officers and admirable at all times—was his solicitousness toward enlisted soldiers. Gates soon recovered and spent the next several years shuttling between New York City and duty on the colony's western and northern frontiers. Professional fortune smiled upon him in 1759 when, through the efforts of his mentor Cornwallis, Gates became the military secretary to General John Stanwix, commander of British forces in Pennsylvania. More luck followed when General Robert Monckton, a former comrade and friend from his Nova Scotia days, and now recently a hero from the glorious British victory at Quebec, replaced Stanwix in Philadelphia. The two got on famously—the general was only 2 years older than his subordinate—and when Monckton's meteoric rise continued with his appointment in 1761 as governor of New York, he took Gates with him.

Gates soon was hard at work as the British prepared to mount an expedition, under Monckton's command, from New York City against the French-controlled island of Martinique in the West Indies. Undoubtedly, his experience as Monckton's primary assistant in solving the myriad administrative and logistical problems associated with this effort served as a great school for Gate's similar accomplishments with the Continental Army years later. The invasion force sailed in late 1761 and rapidly conquered the island. Monckton honored Gates's service by choosing him to deliver the glorious news to London. In accordance with the custom of the time, the crown rewarded the herald of victory with a promotion.

Advancement to major represented the high water mark of Gates's British Army career. The war with France was winding down and even well-to-do and well-born officers, such as Charles Lee, found it difficult to gain preferment in a reduced, peacetime army. Gates's circumstances, even with his powerful friends, made his professional road much rockier. He spent most of the 1760s angling for rank and position, even voyaging back to America in an unsuccessful attempt to lobby the British chief there for a choice staff billet. Disappointed at every turn, he descended for a while into a routine of excessive drinking and gambling, only to be rescued by exposure to the ideals of the great Methodist preacher, John Wesley. His was not a complete conversion—he remained notably profane and continued to enjoy his glass—but he emerged relatively intact from his brush with dissolution. His political maturation continued apace through renewed contact with English Whigs and encounters with—and cultivation by—the likes of Benjamin Franklin in London. By the decade's end, Gates's friends referred to him as a "red hot Republican."[54]

Gates finally left the army in 1769. His professional frustrations joined to his growing dissatisfaction with the state of British politics caused him to consider removing himself and his family to America. Several of his old New York Whig friends encouraged him along these lines. In May 1772 he wrote his fellow survivor of the Braddock disaster, Washington, to inquire about the availability of land in Virginia. Later that year, like so many before and since, he fled the Old World's economic and political distress for a fresh start in the New. Within 6 months he had purchased a plantation in Virginia's Shenandoah Valley that he dubbed Traveller's Rest. Unlike the energetic Lee or even Montgomery, Gates was hardly active politically in his new home, preferring the peaceful lot of a moderately wealthy country squire, noting "I lead a Life very different from your Elegant Virginians, as I seldom see Company, Drink little, & never Game."[55] Nevertheless, he closely followed the roiling politics of the day and maintained an active correspondence with leading figures close to the tumult. These included his old colleague Charles Lee, with whom he shared his disdain for the measures taken by General Gage in Boston: "I have read with wonder & astonishment Gages Proclamations, surely this is not the same man you and I knew so well in days of yore." Gates closed this missive with a ringing declaration, "I am what I have allways profess'd myself to be, & ... I am ready to risque my Life to preserve the Liberty of the Western World."[56] On May 2, 1775 Gates visited Washington at Mount Vernon, where they must have discussed the colonies' military situation. Washington departed for Philadelphia and the Second Continental Congress the next day. Two days after that body chose Washington as commander in chief, it commissioned Gates as a brigadier and assigned him as the army's first adjutant general.

Gates arrived in Cambridge a week after Washington and quickly made himself indispensable. Drawing upon the staff skills developed years earlier, he firmly grasped the army's administrative reins and started to impose order on what had been slightly more than an armed, patriotic mob investing Boston. He wrote the American army's first disciplinary regulations and set up rational systems for supply, sanitation and medical service, and recruiting. He also advised Washington on operational issues, displaying the innate caution and patience that—with one fatal exception—would mark most of his battlefield endeavors. He opposed any initiative to attack the British in the seaport city, in line with a philosophy contending that "Our Business is to Defend the Main Chance; to Attack only by Detail; and when a precious advantage offers."[57] He preferred to let attrition— desertion, sickness, and supply shortfalls—wear the British down. He noted the enemy plight with satisfaction: "Bad Salt Pork and Dry Pease is all their Soldiers have had to Eat since the beginning of May."[58] Yet if he was conservative in the military realm, politically he veered sharply in the radical direction, forcefully advocating independence in letters to the likes of Jefferson and the two Adamses. Gates's vociferous advocacy even struck that other English expatriate Charles Lee, no shrinking violet himself, who told a friend, 'Poor Gates ... has frighten'd [the moderates] out of their Wits."[59]

Following the British evacuation of Boston in March 1776, Gates accompanied Washington and the army to New York to prepare for the expected onslaught there. Meanwhile, Congress promoted Gates to major general in May and cast about for where best to employ him. American arms in Canada had experienced nothing but reverses since Montgomery's failed attack on Quebec. Under the nominal command of Schuyler and a succession of subordinate generals, the Americans had been falling back under pressure from the British commander in Canada, Carleton, who had mounted a spring counteroffensive. To stem the tide, Congress named Gates to command the American forces in Canada on June 18. As John Adams wrote him, "We have ordered you to the post of Honour, and made you Dictator in Canada for six months."[60] What Congress had also wrought was an extraordinarily snarled command scheme that would bedevil the northern army over the next year, and create great acrimony and friction for itself and the officers concerned.

Schuyler of course still held his post as commander of the northern department. Congress's intent for Gates could be understood in a couple of ways— narrowly, to command American forces solely within the geographical boundaries of Canada or, more broadly, to exercise field command of the northern army, which when Gates was appointed, was still in Canada. This quickly became an important distinction. By the end of June the patriot forces had been entirely pushed out of the putative "14th colony" and were clinging to the ramshackle fortifications at Crown Point and Fort Ticonderoga on Lake Champlain in upper New York. Schuyler favored the narrow interpretation, which reduced Gates to serving under him. Gates believed that he was entitled to an independent command in the north. Both generals turned to Congress, which for the moment resolved the dispute in Schuyler's favor.

In a more practical sense, Gates wielded great authority anyway, since as was his wont, Schuyler was generally content to remain, for all purposes, an absentee commander on his estate near Albany, 100 miles south of the immediate scene of action. In many ways it was a thankless honor for Gates. When he arrived at Crown Point in July his men were in wretched shape, as had been graphically described to him by Benedict Arnold, who now served under Gates. According to Arnold, the army was "neglected by Congress ... Distressed with the small Pox, want of Generals, & Discipline in our army which may rather be called a great Rabble."[61] As he had at Cambridge, Gates went to work with a will, taking measures to improve welfare and morale through a blend of discipline and compassion. Already well regarded by militia and particularly New Englanders, in contrast to the rather imperious New Yorker Schuyler, Gates's activities on their behalf further endeared him to his men. Letters written by his field grade officers reflect the rapid improvement under Gates's aegis. One reported, "General Gates ... is putting the most disordered Army that ever bore the name into a state of regularity and defence" and another flatly stated "General Gates is reforming the Army and is very successful."[62]

While reinvigorating the army, Gates worked to develop a defensive scheme to halt Carleton's anticipated drive into New York down the Champlain–Hudson waterway. He and Schuyler jointly decided to abandon decrepit Crown Point as indefensible, and to concentrate on strengthening Fort Ticonderoga while building a fresh water fleet to oppose Carleton on Lake Champlain. Many not on the scene, including Washington, challenged the evacuation of Crown Point. Gates answered matter of factly to the commander in chief and engaged in a bit of disarming badinage with General Israel Putnam, who had helped construct the fortress nearly two decades earlier, "Every fond mother dotes on her booby, be his imperfections ever so glaring and his good qualities ever so few. Crown Point was not indeed your immediate offspring, but you had a capital hand in rearing the baby. You cut the logs, which are now rotten ... and tumbled to the dust ... Don't be uneasey."[63] Gates also appointed Arnold, who had prewar seafaring experience trading in the West Indies, to oversee the shipbuilding and outfitting effort. Gates worked tirelessly to support Arnold by procuring necessary materials and skilled personnel. By the end of July, Arnold commanded a flotilla that would ultimately grow to comprise 16 vessels and more than 100 guns, crewed by nearly 900 men. This motley force met Carleton's larger fleet October 11, 1776 at the battle of

Valcour Island. The British destroyed the makeshift American armada, but then paused to reorganize at Crown Point before attacking Gates's now formidable position at Fort Ticonderoga. Thinking better of it, Carleton eschewed a siege so late in the year and elected to withdraw into Canada for the winter.

Gates, with some help from Schuyler and due in great measure to Arnold's fighting spirit, had accomplished much in the north. He had little time to reflect on this, however. In late November Washington, defeated in New York and chased through New Jersey, summoned Gates to bring reinforcements and join him in Pennsylvania. Gates had foreseen this contingency and responded with alacrity. He appointed Colonel Anthony Wayne to command at Fort Ticonderoga and headed south with 1,200 men of the Continental line. En route, at Goshen, New York, the state's Council of Safety, a subordinate body to the legislature, propositioned him to disregard Washington and to join forces with General Lee's command—still on the east side of the Hudson—in order to shield the Hudson Highlands. To his credit, Gates ignored this incitement to disobedience and pressed on to link up with Washington December 22 on the west side of the Delaware River, northeast of Philadelphia. Here Gates's operational caution asserted itself, and he urged the Virginian to abandon any hope of guarding the capital and to continue the westward retreat across the Susquehanna River. Washington had other plans and would soon launch his legendary strokes at Trenton and Princeton. Gates played no part in these engagements, no doubt to the considerable detriment of his reputation. Just why he failed to participate is something of a mystery. Perhaps he simply vehemently disagreed and wanted no part in Washington's scheme. More likely, his absence was due to one of the recurring bouts of ill health that plagued him throughout the war. In any case, he repaired to Baltimore, temporary seat of Congress, to importune his friends in that body to give him the northern command in preference to Schuyler.

While Gates recuperated and lobbied, Washington named him military commandant of Philadelphia, once again the capital after Howe's threat to the city had abated. Shortly after this, Congress sought to reappoint Gates to his former position as the army's adjutant general. He demurred, despite Washington's desire to have him resume. Gates, having tasted command, wanted no part of staff work and continued to hunger for the top post in the crucial northern theater. His New England friends in the national legislature partially succeeded in getting him his wish. They embroiled Schuyler in an angry dispute with Congress that resulted in a curtailment of the New Yorker's authority and the award to Gates of command at Fort Ticonderoga, independent of the northern department. Schuyler was not the man to take a slight lying down; in April 1777 as Gates headed north, Schuyler sped south to Philadelphia to fight for his prerogatives in person. Meanwhile Gates further aggravated Schuyler by refusing to confine himself to Ticonderoga, establishing his headquarters at Albany, and acting as if he had supreme command in the north. While the British threat gathered in Canada, the squabbling between the two generals and their supporters continued. Schuyler and the rest of the New York caucus prevailed in Philadelphia, and once more he was named undisputed chief. Now it was Gates who flew to the city of brotherly love to plead his case. On June 18 he subjected Congress to an embarrassing harangue that one member later described as "a Compound of Vanity, Folly, and Rudeness."[64] Unimpressed, Congress ordered him to "repair to headquarters, and follow the directions of General Washington."[65]

It must have appeared to the disgusted Gates that the great summer drama of 1777 in upper New York would play out while he watched from the wings. Fate's wheel had another turn, however. General Burgoyne had temporarily eclipsed Carleton and now led a large, combined British–German force of nearly 8,000 men from Montreal aimed at Albany. In early July the supposedly impregnable Fort Ticonderoga fell to this juggernaut without a shot being fired. Great consternation in Congress greeted this setback; there was even truly revolutionary talk by John Adams of shooting a few generals, presumably *pour encourager les autres*. While the firing squads remained idle, Congress reopened the question of the northern command, so recently settled. Schuyler did not help his case with the desponding letters he sent back to Philadelphia. His seeming defeatism, combined with New England's—which supplied the bulk of militia in the north—manifest lack of confidence in him and growing disenchantment even among his fellow New Yorkers sealed his fate. Congress overwhelmingly voted Schuyler out and Gates in on August 4, 1777. Two weeks later Gates assumed command of the northern department.

The situation was not as dire as it may have appeared to American pessimists. Even before Gates arrived to take charge, a combination of poor decision making by Burgoyne and good work by Schuyler and his subordinates had improved patriot chances. Following his seizure of Fort Ticonderoga, Burgoyne conducted a vigorous pursuit of the fleeing Americans that brought him to the settlement of Skenesborough by July 7, only 70 miles from Albany. He needed to cross over from the east to the west bank of the Hudson River at some point in order to gain that objective. The easier course would have been to backtrack to Ticonderoga, reembark his force on boats, and advance on Lake George to a point within easy marching distance of a Hudson crossing. Instead, he elected to continue overland on the eastern side of the river along torturous wilderness tracks. Oppressive summer heat, along with the column's massive amount of baggage and other impedimenta made the going agonizingly slow. Worsening Burgoyne's ordeal, Schuyler proved a master of delaying tactics. He employed militia to harass the enemy and obstacle the already treacherous terrain, while requiring locals to carry off or destroy any provender to deny it to Burgoyne's men. It took the British 21 days to stagger 23 miles to Fort Edward; from where they would ultimately cross the Hudson a month and a half later. The glacial pace of this movement and the ensuing halt gave the Americans valuable time to gather forces and prepare stout defensive positions.

Additionally, Burgoyne's operation suffered severe checks on both flanks in August. To his south and west, Lieutenant Colonel Barry St. Leger headed a supporting attack moving east along the Mohawk River Valley toward Albany.

St. Leger's heterogeneous force of about 2,000 redcoats, Hessians, Canadians, Indians, and Loyalists besieged Fort Stanwix, an old colonial wars outpost now held by a regiment of New York Continentals. A patriot relief attempt was ambushed at Oriskany on August 6; what ensued was a bloody though inconclusive hand-to-hand fight. Schuyler then dispatched Arnold with a second rescue effort. The fierce Connecticut native, who normally thrived in combat, instead devised a clever *ruse de guerre* that demoralized St. Leger's Indian allies—about 50 percent of his force—and caused him to lift his siege and retire back up the Mohawk and into Canada without a shot being fired. The Mohawk Valley secure, Arnold hastened back to join the main northern army. Meanwhile, Burgoyne had dispatched a 1,000-man contingent from his own army to the east into the upper Connecticut River Valley in what is present-day Vermont. Their mission was to obtain badly needed supplies for Burgoyne's stalled advance. Some 1,500 patriot militia hastily assembled to oppose them and on August 16, in the battle of Bennington, they crushed the foreign invaders. Burgoyne lost approximately 10 percent of his total strength—200 raiders killed and 700 captured—in return for minimal American losses.

These victories had already begun to lift Yankee spirits when Gates took over from Schuyler, but he still had much work to do in preparing to meet Burgoyne. His mere presence acted as a tonic to those who had detested the autocratic New Yorker. Gates had always displayed a sure hand in dealing with the free-thinking New England militia, praising their virtues and ignoring their defects. Now they rallied in large numbers to his encampment at the mouth of the Mohawk River. As he had done at Cambridge and the previous summer at Crown Point and Ticonderoga, Gates reinstilled discipline in a heretofore down-at-the heels army. He also made brilliant use of what modern-day soldiers call "information warfare" to demoralize his enemy. In July a young American woman named Jane McCrea had been killed by marauding Indians. In Gates's hands she became a "young lady lovely to the sight, of virtuous character and amicable disposition . . . scalped and mangled in a most shocking manner" by forces under Burgoyne's command.[66] The beautiful Jane—in reality a Loyalist sympathizer affianced to one of Burgoyne's officers—became a patriot martyr, whose story aroused Americans and eventually led to Burgoyne's censure even in England.

Gates moved north on September 8. In addition to the militia that continued to stream in, Arnold had returned from his foray to the west with 1,200 men and Washington had reinforced Gates with Colonel Daniel Morgan's elite corps of roughly 400 riflemen. Gates possessed a keen eye for terrain and read the battlefield perfectly. He wished to fight a defensive battle on ground that would negate the European troops' advantages in artillery and close order tactics. Therefore, in conjunction with the talented Polish engineer Thaddeus Kosciusko, he established his main line of fortifications on Bemis Heights, hard on the Hudson's west bank and dominating the main road along which Burgoyne must pass to get to Albany. The terrain in front of this position was a tangle of streams, marshes and thick woods, broken only by a few clearings and trails—perfect for Gates's purpose.

The Americans rapidly dug trenches, and erected earth and log breastworks. Gates initially arrayed his forces, about 7,000 Continentals and militia, in three subelements. Arnold commanded the left wing; his troops included Morgan's men as well as 250 light infantrymen under Major Henry Dearborn. Brigadier General Ebenezer Learned oversaw the center force, and the right wing's senior leaders were Brigadier Generals John Glover and John Paterson. Gates set up his command post about a mile to the rear.

Burgoyne began crossing over a bridge of boats to the west side of the Hudson on September 13 and within 2 days was safely across. He began to feel his way south. His "eyes and ears"—his Indian scouts—had grown disenchanted and deserted him, so the British general had little idea of what he faced. Gates, on the other hand, had superb intelligence. Indeed, he contemplated a strike at Burgoyne's divided force as it crossed the Hudson, but the militia on the east side were neither agile nor strong enough to respond in a timely or effective fashion. Therefore, Gates waited with the advantages of space and time in his favor—the former due to the terrain, the latter since Burgoyne had only 30 days of supplies on hand upon which to subsist until he attained Albany and the opportunity to reprovision.

The opposing armies skirmished on September 18. Arnold had sortied out to meet Burgoyne's advance guard. The results were tactically inconclusive, but the clash had two significant results. First, Burgoyne now had some sense of where the Americans were. Second, the encounter led to the first inklings of a rift between Arnold and Gates, who had previously worked well together. Arnold concluded from the fracas that the patriots should attack the British in force instead of waiting for them to advance. Gates wanted to await them in his strong defensive works. This tactical disagreement would grow increasingly contentious between them.

Burgoyne initiated the first of the twin battles of Saratoga on the cool, clear morning of September 19 by advancing in three columns. The ensuing fight is also known as the battle of Freeman's Farm, after the farmstead clearing that was the center of the day's action. Quickly apprised of the Anglo-German advance, Gates ordered Morgan's riflemen and light infantry forward to compel the enemy to deploy. Shortly after noon, Morgan's men began losing furious volleys on British pickets in the vicinity of Isaac Freeman's cabin. Throughout the day, vicious fighting ranged across the 350-yard-long open area about a mile north of Bemis Heights. Both sides poured additional units into the contest and bodies stacked up as the combatants exchanged fire, charges, and countercharges. Arnold controlled the American forces while Burgoyne was personally on the scene for the British with his center column, which bore the brunt of Yankee fury. Gates had not intended to conduct the main battle outside his fortified positions and only reluctantly furnished reinforcements to Arnold, who raged and pleaded for more combat power to smash the enemy then and there at Freeman's Farm. The intervention of Burgoyne's left wing and the onset of darkness ended the fray. The Americans pulled back into their lines, having inflicted about 600 casualties that Burgoyne could not replace in return for about 300 of their own. British veterans of European combat later testified that they had never seen a more brutal firefight. The Anglo-Germans held the worthless clearing but Gates still blocked the way to Albany. Most fatefully, Burgoyne elected to dig in his force rather than retreat to Ticonderoga and thence to Canada—in essence, pinning himself down in front of Bemis Heights.

The two armies thus confronted each other. Burgoyne's strength waned due to the attrition of sickness, desertion, and continual American harassing fire. Gates's waxed as more militia—individuals and units—arrived to be in on the kill. By the first week of October, Burgoyne fielded about 5,000 effectives while Gates boasted some 11,000–2,700 Continentals, the rest militia. In early October, General Henry Clinton in New York made a foray up the Hudson from New York City that temporarily promised to relieve Burgoyne. But while Clinton seized some patriot outposts in the Hudson highlands and pushed a small detachment upriver to within 50 miles of Albany, he ultimately withdrew. As he did, he composed a fatuous note to Burgoyne, "I sincerely hope this little success of ours may facilitate your operations . . . I heartily wish you success."[67] Too little, too late; the second battle of Saratoga took place the day before Clinton penned his message. The only problem on the American side was the now-bitter split between Gates and Arnold. In addition to disagreeing on how to fight Burgoyne, Arnold's considerable ego was further wounded when Gates failed to mention his gallantry at Freeman's Farm in his after action report. Gates also withdrew Morgan's detachment from Arnold's control and, on September 25, relieved him from command of the left wing. Arnold was reduced to sulking in his tent like a Revolutionary War Achilles outside the walls of Troy.

Burgoyne meanwhile disregarded the counsel of his subordinates, who one last time advised him to retire and salvage his army. Instead he chose to hurl his much-weakened forces at the Americans again. His new plan was similar to his previous scheme of maneuver. On the morning of October 7, three columns sallied forth from their fortifications around Freeman's Farm to conduct a reconnaissance in force, precipitating the second battle of Saratoga, frequently referred to as the battle of Bemis Heights. These units advanced three quarters of a mile, then formed a line of battle about 1,000 yards long. Gates once more sent forces out to break up the enemy approach. Morgan swept around the British right and Gates launched a brigade-sized assault on their left. In a well-synchronized maneuver, both British flank elements were sent back reeling. Only the center, composed of German units, stood firm. It was at this point that Arnold, again like Achilles, roused himself to Homeric action. Without orders and indeed to Gates's anger, Arnold rode to the sound of the guns and joined the fight. He took overall command of the disparate American units on the field and personally led them in furious charges against the Anglo-Germans, who by now had all retired into their fortified lines. The enemy buckled and broke before the inspired Americans. Perhaps patriot victory could have turned into a rout had Arnold not been shot down—not in the heel, but in the same leg that had been previously wounded at Quebec. Without his fiery leadership to direct a pursuit and exploitation, the Americans contented themselves with seizing the enemy's positions. On the night of October 9, Burgoyne pulled his battered force back to Saratoga having lost another 600 men in return for about 150 American casualties.

The contest was up for the British general Gates referred to as the "old gamester." By October 12 Gates had cut off all possible escape routes and Burgoyne was forced to seek terms. The British general insisted upon a "convention" rather than an unconditional surrender or "capitulation" agreement. Gates acceded to this semantic distinction; although later criticized by some in Congress, Gates at the time was uncertain about the threat to his rear posed by Clinton and felt impelled to conclude a settlement. Under the convention's provisions, Burgoyne's army was to be repatriated to England and never fight "again in North America during the present contest."[68] On October 17 the British and Germans formally laid down their arms in a ceremony conducted under an American flag sewn together from old military garments and affixed to a rough-hewn pole. Burgoyne, resplendent in full dress, offered his sword to Gates who, garbed in a properly republican plain blue coat, gallantly refused it. Then, in true eighteenth-century gentlemanly fashion, Gates and his senior officers hosted their recent opponents at a banquet where toasts were drunk to both king and Congress.

Gates had achieved the apogee of his career and, to his great credit, was effusive in praising Arnold's and Morgan's gallantry in his final report to Congress. Even though peace would not be concluded for six more years, Saratoga was the turning point battle of the war. At home, it heartened patriots, particularly in light of the beatings Washington had taken around Philadelphia in the summer of 1777. Abroad, it emboldened France to declare openly for the United States, drastically tipping the strategic scales in the Americans' favor. Trailing clouds of glory, the "Hero of Saratoga" removed himself to Albany. From there he dispatched the majority of his Continentals south to Washington and to Putnam in the Hudson highlands, while his militia returned to hearth and home. His immediate military task was to secure the upper Hudson River valley against Clinton's raiding parties, which wantonly burned and pillaged along the waterway. At one point Gates chided the British general, "Destroying defenceless Houses and Villages cannot in the least contribute to the Conquest of America nor to encrease the Revenue of your King ... This Conduct sufficiently evinces Your despair of ever Conquering this Country."[69] But even as Gates coped with Clinton, activities brewed that would plunge his name into the heart of a civil–military storm that would make the earlier affrays with Schuyler and Arnold look tame.

The so-called Conway Cabal—a purported plot in late 1777 and early 1778 to replace Washington with Gates—almost certainly never existed. The suspicions of Washington and his supporters, later reinforced by some nineteenth-century writers and Washington's hagiographers, are what gave it resonance. Only the cooler deliberations of later scholars have consigned the idea of a malevolent conspiracy against the commander in chief to a figment of fevered imaginations. Indeed, the whole episode is best understood in the context of its particular historical moment and environment. All revolutions are accompanied by seething intrigue, infighting, and, inevitably, conspiracy theories. The American Revolution was no different; a kaleidoscope of factions and interests held their own views about how best to proceed in prosecuting the struggle. The modern concepts of loyal opposition and even constructive criticism were alien to this period. Further, real animosity, misunderstanding, and recriminations divided Congress, temporarily at York, Pennsylvania, and the suffering main army 60 miles away at Valley Forge. Add to these ingredients the touchy, hair-trigger pride of eighteenth-century gentlemen quick to perceive offense—in an era where affairs of honor were not infrequently resolved on the dueling ground—and one has a recipe for a poisonous atmosphere where the notion of a plot could thrive.

While there was no nefarious scheme, as the saying goes even paranoids have enemies. Washington attracted his share of detractors within the officer corps, and among civilians in and out of Congress. One of the former was Brigadier General Thomas Conway, an Irish-born French officer and another of Congress's foreign imports. In late October 1777 he wrote a letter (now lost) to Gates highly critical of Washington's performance. As noted earlier, Charles Lee had previously sent similar missives to Gates. Although such conduct fails to comport with modern ideals of military professionalism, this practice was not that uncommon in eighteenth-century European armies. What touched off all the excitement was the indiscretion or mischievousness of Gates's adjutant, Colonel James Wilkinson. Wilkinson, a highly unscrupulous character (one modern biographical dictionary entry lists him succinctly as "Continental officer, scoundrel") who years later would involve himself in the equally shadowy but more tangible intrigues of Aaron Burr among other tawdry affairs, apparently rifled Gates's private correspondence and then spread news of Conway's opinions to fellow officers and sympathetic civilian ears. Soon enough this came to Washington's attention. The Virginian icily confronted Conway, who averred the sentiments, if not the exact words attributed to him. And Washington exchanged letters with Gates—a correspondence of two men talking past each other.

Relations between the two had been somewhat strained in the past—as recently as when Gates had seen fit to notify Congress, but not Washington about the results at Saratoga. Still, Gates was by and large a loyal subordinate. Indeed in his reply to Conway, Gates had actually defended Washington. Instead of smoothing his commander's ruffled feathers however, Gates exacerbated the situation by failing to condemn Conway and by focusing on the injustice done him in the rifling of his papers by persons still unknown to him. It fell to Washington to inform Gates that his own aide—Wilkinson—was the culprit. In the eyes of Washington and his supporters, Gates was clearly implicated in an affair to undermine the commander in chief. By this time—January 1778—Congress had reassigned Gates to the Presidency of its Board of War in an effort to improve that body's slipshod performance in sustaining the Army in the field. This move supplied further proof to those who believed in a cabal that something was afoot. Unfortunately, while Gates's handling of his administrative tasks was as competent as ever, some of his activities gave credence to the worst interpretation.

The most egregious was his involvement in a Congressional initiative for another "irruption" into Canada, a move Gates had long advocated. In the interests of expediting this newest invasion, conceived as a winter thrust across Lake Champlain while frozen solid, no one bothered to consult Washington about it. To add insult to injury, Congress chose Conway as one of the expedition's leaders. Ultimately, the plan fell apart, largely due to the actions of its designated commander, Lafayette. He first objected to the alleged slighting of his idol, Washington. By the time Congress satisfied the marquis—including replacing his countryman Conway—logistical preparations were too far behind to pull off the operation and it was cancelled in February 1778. Gates faced one more bit of unpleasantness stemming from the Conway business. He had fallen out with Wilkinson when he learned of his former aide's role in the affair. Meanwhile Congress appointed Wilkinson a brevet brigadier general and found the worst possible billet for him—as the Board of War's secretary. The two soon clashed and the bumptious Wilkinson challenged Gates to a duel. Although Gates accepted, a mutual acquaintance intervened. He got the antagonists to stand down for the moment, although the animosity flared up again several months later. On the field of honor, this time in New York, Gates allowed the rascally Wilkinson three unsuccessful shots before their seconds halted the proceedings. Honor was satisfied, although the two men never reconciled.

Congress delivered Gates from these travails in April 1778 by appointing him to command in the Hudson highlands. Congress made clear that in this post he was directly subordinate to Washington. This represented a change from previous practice, where lines of authority involving the northern department, Congress, and Washington were blurred. No doubt it also reflected Congress's desire to mollify Washington after the Conway affair. Gates rode to New York with Colonel Ethan Allen, recently freed from British captivity after being taken at Montreal in September 1775; the Green Mountain Boys' leader and Gates became fast friends. Establishing his headquarters in Fishkill, Gates faced two challenges: keeping the British forces in New York City from breaking out to the west to intervene against Washington's pursuit of Clinton from Philadelphia, and securing New York's northern and western frontiers against raiding Indians. He was effective in accomplishing the first, less so in the second. In fact, he deliberately dragged his feet in carrying out express Congressional directives in the summer of 1778 to mount campaigns against hostile tribes in order to advance his own long-preferred goal of leading the conquest of Canada. Whether his strategic vision was keener in this instance than Congress's—or Washington's, who also wanted a pacification effort—Gates clearly defied his superiors' intent. The year ended with neither an Indian nor a Canadian excursion.

After the battle of Monmouth, Clinton safely withdrew into New York City, and Gates found himself somewhat uneasily colocated with Washington, chafing under the latter's personal supervision at Peekskill. By the fall of 1778 and under these circumstances, Gates developed the conviction that the war's decisive theater would shift to Boston and angled for the command there. New England friends in Congress obtained the post for him in October; once again he was free from Washington's direct control. Gates's wife and son joined him in Boston, which despite his earlier surmise, remained removed from any hint of military conflict. The winter of 1778–1779 was only enlivened with some spiteful correspondence from Gates to Congress over the missed opportunities to invade Canada. In March 1779 Washington asked Gates if he felt up to leading the long-delayed expedition against the Indians in Mohawk country. Gates declined, observing "The man who undertakes the Indian service should enjoy youth and strength; requisites I do not possess." Somewhat sourly he added, "It therefore grieves me, that your Excellency should offer me the only command to which I am entirely unequal."[70] The assignment devolved upon the American commander in Rhode Island, General John Sullivan. With a British garrison in Newport, Rhode Island was somewhat closer to the scene of action than Boston and Gates replaced Sullivan in Providence in April. There he spent most of his time battling smugglers and profiteers, and bemoaning the lack of republican virtue among the Rhode Islanders. After the British evacuated Newport in October, an unhappy, worn out Gates asked for and got Washington's permission to winter with his family at Traveller's Rest.

While recovering at his Virginia estate, Gates keenly followed diplomatic and military developments. He corresponded with many notables, including John Adams and Ben Franklin in Paris. He must have especially enjoyed the latter's sending him a copy of Burgoyne's recently published apologia for his defeat at Saratoga. Gates avidly sought an important command for the upcoming 1780 campaign season; he even journeyed to Philadelphia briefly to explore his options with Congress. His opportunity came when the British seized Charleston, South Carolina on May 12, capturing the 5,500-man garrison, including its commander, Gates's former subordinate at Saratoga, General Benjamin Lincoln. One month later, a worried Congress appointed Gates to replace Lincoln in the southern department, giving him broad authority to requisition supplies and call on state militias. En route to joining what remained of the army in North Carolina, Gates conferred with the governor of that state, Abner Nash, as well as Virginia's chief executive, Thomas Jefferson. He also wrote a letter to the unfortunate Lincoln, dwelling on the challenges ahead: "I feel for you, I feel for myself; who am to Succeed to, what! To the command of an Army, without strength; a Military Chest, without Money; a Department apparently Deficit in Public Spirit; & a Climate, that increases Despondency, ..."[71] On July 25 he joined his bedraggled command, relieving its temporary commander, the Bavarian-born French army veteran and volunteer for America, Johann Kalb.

Based upon his previous record and the dire situation of the troops he inherited, one would have expected the cautious Gates to have deliberately set about rebuilding the men and units under his command. Instead, he immediately set his mixed force—Maryland and Delaware Continentals; North Carolina and Virginia militia—in motion toward a reported British concentration at Camden South Carolina. He compounded this dubious decision by choosing the most direct path, through blasted territory empty of anything except Loyalist sentiment. This even though a slightly longer route recommended by his subordinates offered promise both of provisions and recruits to the cause. The only possible reason for Gates's uncharacteristic precipitancy was his desire to strike a tide-turning blow before Lord Cornwallis, his opposite number in the south, could reinforce his Camden outpost.

As his hungry, tired army straggled south—subsisting mostly on green corn and unripened peaches—Gates pleaded with Nash and Jefferson for support. He also began to formulate his tactical plans. In early August, he ordered the South Carolina partisan leaders Thomas Sumter and Francis Marion to threaten the British line of communication between Camden and their main base at Charleston to the south. Arriving at Rugeley's Mill, several miles north of Camden on August 14, Gates apparently intended to go over to the tactical defensive as he had at Saratoga, taking up fortified positions along a nearby creek and challenging the British to attack him. The next night he sent his men forward to occupy his chosen ground under cover of darkness, a tricky maneuver even with rested veterans and one that taxed his exhausted, mostly inexperienced force even more. Even worse for Gates, though unknown to him, Cornwallis had just arrived at Camden with reinforcements. Aware that Gates was to his front, he too began moving toward his enemy on the evening of August 15. Around midnight the two armies bumped into each other. As the sun rose the next morning they faced off along the north-south road halfway between Rugeley's Mill and Camden in an open field flanked by swamps. Both sides deployed in line of battle. Gates placed the proven Maryland and Delaware regiments under Kalb to his right and the untried North Carolina and Virginia militia to his left, with more Maryland Continentals in reserve. Cornwallis, outnumbered, but possessing better trained, equipped, and rested units chose a scheme the inverse of Gates's. The British general covered his left with irregular, Loyalist units and emplaced veteran redcoat regiments on his right, with the formidable Banastre Tarleton's cavalry to the rear as an exploitation force. In another judgment error, Gates had left the bulk of his cavalry behind in North Carolina, not wanting to wait for it to refit. The small squadron he retained had been scattered by Tarleton in the predawn skirmish. Thus Gates had no counter to a mounted attack in an open field.

The battle commenced on this hot, humid morning with the advance of the British right. Inexplicably, Gates sent the Virginians forward to meet them. Predictably, the hardened regulars sent the raw, terrified militia reeling, casting away their weapons as they fled. Panicked, the North Carolina militia also broke and ran. Tarleton's legion then charged on the now-unprotected left flank of the Maryland and Delaware regiments as the rest of the British force conducted a frontal attack. Although the Continentals put up a stiff fight, the battle was over in less than an hour. Casualty estimates vary, but figures of between 600 and 1,000 Americans killed or wounded are generally given, along with another 1,000 captured. Among the dead was General Kalb. British losses of all types were around 300. With the pursuing Tarleton on their heels like a vengeful banshee, it was every man for himself. Gates and several aides rode all the way to Hillsborough, North Carolina, covering the 200 miles from the battlefield in 3 days. Alexander Hamilton, no friend of Gates, later asked savagely in a letter to a fellow Gates enemy, "Was there ever an instance of a general running away as Gates has done from his whole army?" and, observing the distance covered, mockingly adding "It does admirable credit to the activity of a man at his time of life." Hamilton also staked out the position of those who viewed citizen soldiers as far inferior to regulars, "[Gates's] passion for militia, I fancy will be cured, and he will cease to think of them as the bulwark of American liberty."[72] Camden was a patriot disaster; for the second time in 3 months an American army in the south had been taken off the board and its commander humiliated. Charles Lee had been prophetic when he cautioned the "Conqueror of Burgoyne" about northern laurels and southern willows.

Gates showed remarkable resiliency in planning to parry Cornwallis in the south and reconstitute his army even as Congress moved to relieve him. As he noted in a somewhat self-pitying letter to Washington, "I shall continue my unwearied endeavours to stop the Progress of the enemy, to reinstate our affairs . . . But if being unfortunate is solely a reason sufficient for removing me from Command, I shall most cheerfully submit to the orders of Congress and resign a office few Generals would be anxious to possess."[73] The efforts of the South Carolina partisan forces under Thomas Sumter, Francis Marion, and Andrew Pickens aided him greatly, as they would his eventual successor, Nathanael Greene. And a combined force of Carolina and Virginia militia won a heartening October victory over a Loyalist contingent at King's Mountain on the western North and South Carolina border. He did his best to rebuild the army, while bemoaning the lack of support, "I am tired of writing to Congress, to Governors . . . upon this miserable detail of wants & Deficiencies."[74] He also engaged in a typical civil–military dispute that plagued all Continental generals during the war—arguing with North Carolina's governor and legislature over who controlled militia employment. Gates moved his army into winter quarters near Charlotte in November. Congress had recently resolved to replace him and he turned command over to Greene on December 3, 1780.

Gates trudged back to Traveller's Rest with a heavy heart. Disgraced, in hopes of clearing his name he had demanded the court of inquiry mandated by Congress, only to find no one interested in actually convening it. Worse, his only child—22-year-old Robert, the apple of his eye—had died suddenly of a mysterious illness. Once again in retirement, he followed events closely and stayed in touch with army and well-connected political friends, eager to redeem himself and return to duty. In addition to Charles Lee, his neighbors included a third general who had been discharged—for drunkenness at Germantown—by Congress, Adam Stephen. As the inimitable Lee allegedly said at a convocation of the commiserating officers, "The county of Berkeley is indeed to be congratulated. She can claim as citizens three noted major generals of the Revolutionary War. You, Stephen, distinguished yourself by getting drunk when you should have been sober. You, Gates, were cashiered for advancing when you should have been retreating, while your humble servant covered himself with glory and laurels and was cashiered for retreating when he should have been advancing."[75] A move by Congressional friends to get him appointed secretary at war under the new Articles of Confederation came to naught, but in the summer of 1782—10 months after Yorktown—Congress rescinded its earlier resolution faulting him for Camden and reinstated Gates to serve as directed by Washington. Gates soon set out for the main army, now camped on the Hudson near Newburgh, New York.

Gates reported for duty in October and Washington gave him command of one of the army's wings. All was largely quiet as the patriots and the British in New York City confronted each other uneasily while peace negations proceeded. But if the battlefront was placid, the same could not be said of the American army's internal workings. Throughout the war, officers and men had frequently gone unpaid and developed other compensation-related grievances against Congress, such as demands for postdemobilization pensions and half-pay. Several in and out of Congress saw an opportunity to use the threat of army dissatisfaction as a spur to achieving the political goal of strengthening the woefully weak central government. Their thinking was that in order to escape the army's wrath, Congress would need to empower itself to tax the states—a substantial aggrandizement of power. Whether the somewhat complementary objectives of a few soldiers and politicians added up to a so-called Newburgh Conspiracy remains open to conjecture. Probably, as with the earlier Conway Cabal, there never was anything close to a fully matured plot—the actors were too disparate a cast. Nevertheless Washington, who ultimately proved a strong nationalist in his general acceptance of enhanced central power and who certainly wished to see his men's claims addressed, was rightly alarmed. As he wisely pointed out, in words that have been proven time and again in other historical settings, an army is a "most dangerous instrument to play [politics] with."[76]

In March 1783 two anonymous pamphlets circulated among the officers at Newburgh. Highly inflammatory and seditious, and almost certainly written by at least one of Gates's aides with the general's knowledge and approval, these Newburgh Addresses threatened Congress with dire consequences should it fail to satisfy the army's demands. Washington assembled his grumbling officers on March 15 at a meeting that Gates chaired. The Virginian left them in no doubt as to his feelings, counseling them to trust in Congress to make good on previous promises and not to "lessen the dignity and sully the glory you have hitherto maintained." In a superb piece of political theater, Washington stumbled over his prepared remarks and reached for his eyeglasses, while apologizing, "Gentlemen, you will permit me to put on my spectacles, for I have not only grown gray, but almost blind, in the service of my country."[77] Washington's stern admonitions and emotional string-tugging carried the vast majority of his listeners. After the Washington departed, Gates chaired the remainder of the session, which drafted a respectful communication to Congress reaffirming the army's loyalty, rejecting the notorious addresses, and expressing faith in the legislators' doing them justice.

Although Gates was most likely too much a republican to have been involved in any political conspiracy, he had good reason to sympathize with demands for financial relief. He himself, like many veterans, suffered considerable economic

distress. Compounding his woes, in addition to his own chronic ill heath, by the spring of 1783 his wife hovered near death. In late March he took leave from the army, never to return, and was at Traveller's Rest when Elizabeth died on June 1. Alone and quite destitute, despite his estate and more land voted him by a Virginia legislature grateful for his war service, Gates wallowed in misery. In his loneliness, he wooed Janet Montgomery, whom he met on a visit to New York. The widow of Montgomery, the fallen hero of Quebec, gently rebuffed him. Things began to look up when he successfully courted a wealthy Maryland spinster named Mary Vallance. In addition to being "good, sensible and cheerfull," she was also worth half a million dollars, an enormous sum.[78] They married in 1786 and 4 years later moved to New York City. As Gates liquidated Traveller's Rest, he made provision for his 17 slaves to be eventually freed by their new owner. Although short of immediate emancipation, Gates's action compares favorably with the practices of many slave-owning contemporaries.

Gates passed his last years in comfort. Always generous financially, he loaned large sums of money to friends and associates, most of which were never repaid. He took an interest and became active in the new republic's nascent political party system, becoming a Jeffersonian Democratic Republican. He was even elected to a single term in the New York state legislature in 1800. Conscious that his life was drawing to a close, 6 weeks before he died, he wrote in a letter, "I have lived long enough, since I have Lived to see, a Mighty people animated with the Spirit to be Free & Governed by Transcendant Abilities and Honour; If when I am going, I am allowed to look down & behold the world I leave; I shall rejoice to find the U.S. beyond Example, a Great and Flourishing People."[79] He died on April 10, 1806, and was buried in the yard of Trinity Church in lower Manhattan. Just as his name rapidly fell into oblivion, so too with his mortal remains; no trace of his resting place now exists. Tarnished historically, and unfairly, by the Conway Cabal, and with somewhat more justice by defeat at Camden, and association with the Newburgh Conspiracy, Gates deserves better from posterity. While his all-too-human flaws were real, so was the decisive victory he won at Saratoga and his devotion to his adopted country.

Self-Educated Fighters

Henry Knox and Nathanael Greene

MONTGOMERY, LEE, AND GATES were professional soldiers who spent years on active service for His Majesty before enlisting in America's cause. They learned their trade in tradition-laden regiments on parade ground and battlefield. While none were wealthy, all came to own estates and live as landed gentlemen. Hardly scholars, each nonetheless was capable of turning a fine Latin or French phrase in correspondence or conversation. The contrast between them and Henry Knox and Nathanael Greene could not have been more pronounced.

Knox and Greene were quintessential New England Yankees—shrewd, practical, and ingenious. These self-made men sprang almost miraculously from the ranks of tradesmen to high command. A Boston book dealer in 1775, Knox became the American army's youngest major general in just 6 years. Greene, a Rhode Island ironmaster, advanced from militia private to Continental Army brigadier in a matter of months. Both had rudimentary formal educations, but were autodidacts who learned by reading, observing, and most of all by doing. Critical thinkers, their Revolutionary careers transformed them into vociferous nationalists. Each died shortly after the war and well shy of the Biblically allotted three score and ten. Had they lived longer, it is likely they would have contributed much to the early national period. As it was, these close friends and self-taught military geniuses rendered extraordinary service while becoming Washington's best and most-trusted commanders.

HENRY KNOX

Henry Knox was a giant of a man. In full maturity he exceeded 6 feet in height and approached 300 pounds in weight. Despite his considerable girth, his was an attractive, gregarious personality—active, intelligent, and relentlessly optimistic. His early years were almost Dickensian. He was one of ten children—all boys— born in Boston July 25, 1750, to Scots-Irish parents. His father deserted his wife and her brood in 1759, leaving the family near destitute. To help out, young Henry quit school and went to work in a book shop to augment the family's income. Although his formal education ceased, Henry read voraciously on the job. His favorite subject matter was military art and science. In further pursuit of this interest he joined local militia units and closely observed the drill of the British regulars, who by his teens were occupying his restive native city as the result of imperial troubles.

In addition to being a military buff, Knox was ambitious. In 1771 he opened his own bookstore. The shop's congenial atmosphere soon made it a popular gathering spot for Boston's more clever and sociable set. The acquaintances and friends Knox acquired there included Paul Revere, John Adams, and a young man from Rhode Island who shared his interest in military affairs, Nathanael Greene. An emerging patriot, Knox witnessed the infamous Boston Massacre in March 1770. He unsuccessfully attempted to intervene and prevent bloodshed after a crowd began to taunt a British sentry outside the city's customs house. Ultimately, a squad of redcoats fired on the mob, killing five and handing patriot agitators a major propaganda coup. When he courted his wife-to-be, Knox's views on the imperial–colonial dispute, as well as his modest origins, gained him the stern disapproval of his prospective father-in-law. A staunch Loyalist, Thomas Flucker was England's royal secretary in Massachusetts—the last as it turned out. He wanted no part of Knox for his daughter Lucy. A plump, gay, high-spirited girl—a perfect match for Knox—she defied her father and the two wed in 1774. After the battles of Lexington and Concord in April 1775, the couple slipped out of Boston and entered patriot lines. Lucy never saw her parents again.

Knox immediately volunteered his services to Artemas Ward, who initially commanded the New England "army of observation" gathered outside of Boston. Although holding no military rank, Knox drew upon his military studies, and rendered invaluable service in helping plan and supervise the patriot fortifications surrounding the city. He caught Washington's favorable eye soon after the Virginian arrived in July, beginning a long and admiring relationship between the two men. Indeed, Knox served at Washington's side during every campaign the commander in chief waged. By November Washington recommended to Congress that "Mr. Knox, a gentleman of Worcester" be given command of the army's artillery.[1] Congress responded with a colonelcy for Knox dated November 17, 1775.

The Continental Army lacked virtually everything, including artillery. In addition to making something of a mockery of Knox's position, it also meant that Washington had no real means to drive the British out of Boston. Knox proposed an imaginative solution to both problems. He offered to journey to Fort Ticonderoga, recently taken by the Americans, retrieve whatever usable guns he could find there, and haul them back to Boston. Washington assented and Knox set out, reaching

Ticonderoga on December 5. There, from a park of mostly old, worn-out pieces he selected 59 serviceable tubes and began an epic of ingenuity and endurance. As he reported to Washington, "I have made 42 exceeding strong sleds, and provided 80 yoke of oxen to drag them. . ." Proceeding down the Hudson and then east through the Berkshire Mountains over 300 miles of ice and snow, in January 1776 he made good on his vow to deliver a "noble train of artillery" to Washington.[2] By early March, the British were staring up at the barrels of those guns, trained on them from Dorchester Heights, and were forced to evacuate Boston. Knox enjoyed the signal honor of riding alongside Washington at the head of the liberating army as it entered the city.

The scene of action now shifted south. After detours to Rhode Island and Connecticut to assist in laying out coastal fortifications, Knox joined the army in New York City, accompanied by his wife and their infant daughter. One morning in early July, he and Lucy woke to an awe-inspiring view from their house at the foot of Broadway. As he subsequently wrote, "From the hall window, where we usually breakfasted, we saw the [British] ships coming through the Narrows" between Staten Island and Long Island. "You can scarcely conceive the distress and anxiety . . . The city in an uproar, the alarm guns firing, the troops repairing to their posts. . ."[3] Although this proved a false alarm, Knox hastened his family away. With 120 guns at his disposal, but crews for only about half of them, he worked tirelessly to put the city in a state of defense. He also kept an extensive correspondence. Knox had early on won the confidence of John Adams and now served as a sort of "directed telescope" into the army's workings for the great patriot statesman, providing him with incisive opinions on men and events.

The storm broke on August 27, 1776, when General Howe, who had earlier begun landing troops on Long Island, attacked and drove the defenders back into Manhattan. Knox helped oversee the perilous retrograde move across the East River that saved the patriot army from Howe's clutches. Two weeks later the British executed a right hook amphibious maneuver up the East River that nearly succeeded in trapping the Americans in lower Manhattan. Knox was one of those almost caught or killed. He had attempted to rally fleeing Connecticut militia and was overseeing the preparation of a last ditch defense when a staff officer—Aaron Burr—materialized and showed this desperate band an escape route to the north. Upon entering into Washington's new defensive line on Harlem Heights, Knox received an emotional welcome from his brother officers and the commander in chief himself, who had feared him lost. Knox redoubled his efforts, noting in a letter to his brother, "My constant fatigue and application to my department has been such that I have not had my clothes off o' nights for more than forty days."[4] Howe continued to bang away at the Americans and drove them back to White Plains, before Washington escaped across the Hudson River. Howe followed him through New Jersey during November and December, and held possession of that state as year's end approached. Meanwhile Washington's army clung to life on the Pennsylvania side of the Delaware River, south of Philadelphia.

Knox played a key role in Washington's storied crossing of the Delaware on Christmas night, 1776. Placed in charge of the critical ferrying operation,

Knox displayed extraordinary personal, charismatic leadership similar to his performance on the Ticonderoga expedition—urging, encouraging—in getting men, horses, and guns across the river in the teeth of an icy gale. The consensus of many present that night was "but for the stentorian lungs of Colonel Knox" the crossing could not have succeeded.[5] In his own words, "The floating ice in the river made the labour almost incredible. However, perseverance accomplished what at first seemed impossible."[6] Knox's artillery was a vital component of the attack. His cannoneers manhandled 18 pieces in support of the 2,400-man assault force. This represented an unusually high ratio of guns to troops in an age where the normal proportion was three guns to every 1,000 infantrymen. The larger artillery complement provided both tangible and intangible support to the infantry. The added firepower compensated for the wet weather that rendered muskets largely unusable and the cannon's thunderous roar provided psychological reassurance to the nervous troops. Knox's detachment also included a party equipped with ropes, hammers, and iron rods. Their task was to seize enemy artillery if possible and turn it against them. Failing that, they would disable or "spike" the enemy's guns by driving the rods into the cannons' touchholes and breaking them off flush with tubes.

Once across the river, the shivering, wet Americans marched 9 miles to Trenton where, at daybreak, they attacked the Hessian garrison there. As Knox later described it, "here succeeded a scene of war of which I had often conceived but never saw before. The hurry, fright and confusion of the enemy was [not] unlike that which it will be when the last trump[et] shall sound."[7] Knox contributed greatly to this chaos by emplacing his guns at the head of the town's main streets and blasting the hapless Hessians as they attempted to form themselves. The Americans killed about 20 enemy soldiers and took nearly 900 prisoner, along with six enemy guns, in return for negligible losses themselves, before retiring back into Pennsylvania.

Washington was eager to resume the offensive in New Jersey, but first he needed to confront the imminent year end expiration of many of his soldiers' enlistments. Some responded to patriotic appeals; others extended for 6 weeks in return for a 10-dollar bounty. Ultimately, he mustered 5,000 fighters, which after another frozen Delaware crossing, he had concentrated in Trenton by December 30. General Howe, alarmed at this patriot impertinence, dispatched Cornwallis with 8,000 men, including six battalions of Hessians hot to avenge their comrades. Leaving a brigade at Princeton as a rear guard, Cornwallis bore down upon the Americans to the south, encountering the patriots' covering force, reinforced with some of Knox's guns, north of Trenton on the morning of January 2, 1777. A daylong fight ensued, with the Americans brilliantly delaying the enemy advance by forcing them repeatedly to deploy and contest every ridge and wood line. As darkness set in, the British reached Trenton and discovered Washington's main force dug in just south of town on the high ground overlooking Assunpink Creek. Some 30–40 guns formed the backbone of the American defense, covering the available crossing sites. They gave a good account of themselves, repulsing three enemy attempts to force the creek with severe casualties. An American artillery sergeant wrote, "They came on a third time. We loaded with canister shot and let them come nearer. We fired all together . . . and such destruction it made, you cannot conceive. The bridge looked red as blood. . ."[8] Cornwallis pulled his tired regiments back into town and planned a coordinated assault for the following morning. For several hours after dark an artillery duel angrily lit the night sky.

Confronting superior numbers, their backs to the Delaware, the Americans faced a dire predicament. In all likelihood, if they stood they would be overwhelmed. If they retreated south or tried to recross the river, they risked annihilation. In this circumstance Washington resolved upon a bold maneuver. He would slip around the British left under cover of darkness and strike deep against their rear at Princeton. Leaving campfires burning to deceive the enemy, and wrapping artillery carriage wheels in rags both to muffle noise and provide greater traction on icy roads, the Americans stole away in the predawn hours. En route to Princeton, the Americans collided with the British brigade that had previously been Cornwallis's rearguard, rushing forward to reinforce him. A fierce meeting engagement occurred about a mile and a half outside of the college town. Eventually, the American swept past this British force, but the gunfire to his north alerted Cornwallis that he had been outfoxed and he hastened back to catch his elusive quarry. He was too late, however, to prevent the Americans from routing Princeton's defenders. British casualties totaled about 450 killed, wounded, or captured. Washington, with the very considerable assistance of his artillery chief, Brigadier General Knox—he had been promoted on December 27—had in a week's time won a series of crucial victories. The two battles of Trenton and the fight at Princeton not only inflicted heavy casualties on the enemy, but also, in conjunction with the activities of New Jersey partisans over the following months, drove the British out of the state, reversing much of what Howe had achieved the previous autumn. Most important, they lifted patriot spirits at a crucial juncture of the war.

While the Continental Army went into winter quarters at Morristown, New Jersey, Washington dispatched Knox home to Massachusetts to supervise cannon and gunpowder production. This provided a welcome respite, not least because it offered a chance to reunite with his beloved Lucy. In addition to providing Washington with cogent recommendations on how to improve American armaments, Knox continued to reflect on other ways to upgrade the American army. Throughout the previous months Knox, like Washington, had despaired over the lack of professionalism displayed by patriot troops. An authentic republican, he developed a comprehensive vision of military reform that in some of its particulars was anathema to his fellow strugglers for liberty. He had written earlier, perhaps with the self-righteousness of the self-educated, that "the bulk of the officers of the army are a parcel of ignorant, stupid men . . . We ought to have academies, in which the whole theory of the art of war shall be taught. . ."[9] In a similar vein he flatly declared, "We must have a standing army. The militia get sick, or think themselves so, and run home; and wherever they go they spread a panic."[10] In addition to advocating professional officer training and long-service soldiers, Knox also called for the establishment of foundries and laboratories to forge the sinews of national defense. In time much of this would come to pass, if only years later. The establishment of the military academy at West Point and a system of arsenals, such as the famous small arms works at Springfield, Massachusetts, furnish two illustrations. On the other hand, the issue of professional and citizen-soldiers, and how to balance the two, would remain vexatious.

Besides thinking about the big picture regarding the American military, Knox also focused his restless mind and relentless energy on perfecting the artillery arm that was his special charge. At the behest of John Adams, he had composed a paper entitled "Hints for the Improvement of the Artillery of the United States," which contained the recommendations enumerated above. Additionally, he experimented constantly with ways to make his guns more mobile, such as the introduction of lighter carriages. Later in the war, during a lull in the fighting, he actually established a camp specifically designed to instruct his corps of artillerymen on gunnery and tactics. Although Knox was constantly hampered by the eclectic assemblage of guns at his disposal—old French and Spanish pieces, captured British cannon, as well as native-cast tubes that all required different types of ammunition—he proved himself a master organizer, trainer, and motivator. By the war's end, Knox's gunners were the equal of Europe's finest in terms of tactical and technical proficiency, as well as esprit de corps.

Knox rejoined the army at Morristown to make ready for the campaign of 1777. Before he could take the field, however, he suffered an unpleasant surprise that he took as a personal and professional insult. At Congress's behest, American agents abroad, in addition to searching for financial and logistical support, also solicited professional military expertise and recruited a number of European officers, of various degrees of ability. One such was a Frenchman, Phillipe Charles Tronson de Coudray, a supposed artillery and engineering expert. The commission he received designated him a major general and commander of American artillery and ordnance, in other words, Knox's superior. This was too much for Knox and he composed a curt note to Congress. He asked whether Coudray was to be artillery chief and, if this proved so, "I beg the favour of a permission to retire, and a proper certificate for that purpose be sent me immediately."[11] Greene and John Sullivan, two other Continental generals whose seniority Coudray's elevation affected, sent similar missives. Washington wrote strongly worded letters to Congress praising Knox to the heavens and urging his retention as artillery chief. Congress elided the difficulty by affirming the Frenchman as a major general, but assigning him other duties. Coudray himself permanently resolved the problem by falling off a barge in the Schuylkill River and obligingly drowning in September 1777.

In the spring of 1777 American military leaders anxiously attempted to divine General Howe's intentions. Would he try to join hands with Burgoyne's expected thrust down the Hudson? Return to Boston or aim for a southern objective such as Charleston? Or attempt to seize the patriot capital at Philadelphia? Not until August was Washington sure that Howe had fixed upon Philadelphia. Washington therefore broke camp and paraded his army, 11,000-strong, through the capital on August 24—in part to hearten its citizenry—en route to meeting his adversary, who approached from the southwest. Washington chose to block the way to Philadelphia along Brandywine Creek, about 25 miles west of the city. His defense concentrated on Chad's Ford, which lay astride the main road. Unfortunately, the Americans failed to screen adequately to their right or north where additional fords existed. This proved their undoing. On the morning of September 11, Howe sent Cornwallis with 7,500 men as his main effort around the patriot right while occupying the patriots' attention with a secondary attack at Chad's Ford. The British gained almost complete surprise and by mid-afternoon the Americans were fighting for their lives in two directions. The artillery "did me great honour; they behaved like men contending for every thing that's valuable," wrote Knox.[12] Nevertheless, the Americans lost 11 guns in addition to nearly 1,000 soldiers killed, wounded, or captured. The remainder of the army retreated to the east.

Exhibiting the same dilatoriness he displayed in the New York and New Jersey campaigns, Howe made little effort to pursue and crush the Americans. Philadelphia's fate was sealed, however. Washington was in no position to contest Howe and the British occupied the city 2 weeks later. Meanwhile, approximately 30 miles to the northwest, the Americans licked their wounds and contemplated their next move. It was not long in coming. Aware that a detachment from Howe's army—Cornwallis with about 9,000 redcoats and Hessians—occupied the village of Germantown, 5 miles above Philadelphia, Washington devised an ambitious plan to strike it. It called for 11,000 men in four separate columns to march some 16 miles under cover of darkness on the night of October 3 and conduct a coordinated assault on the unsuspecting British. Small parties of militia screened the extreme left and right flanks. The two central columns—two divisions on the right led by Sullivan, a similar force led by Greene on the patriot left—represented the main effort.

The leftmost flanking column, as well as Greene's, got lost in the dark and the intended simultaneous, four-pronged attack never came off. Nevertheless, the action began well for the Americans. Sullivan's command crashed into the enemy pickets and precipitated a sharp fight. The patriot line subsequently surged forward and, his men reeling, Howe briefly considered a general retreat. Fatefully though, in the wake of the seemingly irresistible American tide, an enterprising British officer and 120 redcoats occupied a large stone mansion and turned it into a near-impregnable bastion. Washington and several of his key aides, including Knox, soon arrived on the scene and debated what to do about this stronghold. Knox, drawing upon his intensive study of military theory, urged that "an occupied castle" not be left in the friendly rear. Here was a classic instance of the truism that the art of war has no traffic with rules; in retrospect, the correct solution would have been to bypass it. Knox, however convinced Washington; testimony to the commander in chief's trust in him. The patriots began throwing reserves and shot at the house, to no avail. This effort stole momentum and resources from the main attack. Soon it stalled and the British began to stiffen.

Then disaster struck. The fog of war that morning was literal; dawn brought a thick haze that the smoke of musketry only amplified. Greene's column had finally arrived on the battlefield and deployed in line of battle. One of his divisions, commanded by Adam Stephen who was later found to have been drunk that day and subsequently relieved, encountered a line of troops to their front. Through the mist they fired—into Anthony Wayne's division, a part of Sullivan's corps. Despite Wayne's frantic efforts, his men began to fall back, unhinging the entire American advance. The British, sensing their advantage, began to counterattack, but gave up their pursuit after about 5 miles. Germantown ended as another patriot defeat, with about 1,000 American losses balanced against 500 enemy casualties. Washington had thrown a scare into Howe, but was undone by his own overly complicated scheme and some bad fortune.

Despite the poor tactical advice he offered at Germantown, Knox retained Washington's confidence. Further, he continued to exhibit considerable strategic acumen. Previously he had noted that despite all Howe's success in marching about the countryside and seizing cities, "no people or country can be permanently conquered where the inhabitants are unanimous in opposition."[13] This remains as perceptive an observation on the nature of insurgency today as it was 225 years ago. In the fall of 1777 and again in the spring of 1778, he wisely advised Washington not to launch contemplated attacks on Philadelphia. His recommendation recognized not only the operational advantages held by Howe, but also the crucial point that the city possessed no intrinsic strategic value, whereas the Continental Army was the real American center of gravity. Accordingly, the army went into winter quarters at Valley Forge.

After a harrowing ordeal—made terrible not so much by the cold, as legend has it, but by American supply difficulties—the patriot army had some reason for optimism as spring arrived. Foremost was the announcement of the French alliance. The army celebrated with a parade and artillery salutes, directed of course by Knox. Several of the officers' ladies also arrived to brighten the scene, among them Martha Washington and the vivacious Lucy, escorted to camp from New Haven by Benedict Arnold. When Clinton, the new British chief, began to evacuate Philadelphia in June 1778 as part of a general British retrenchment, the Americans gave chase.

Washington's subordinates divided whether simply to see Clinton off or to essay a sharp blow at him. Charles Lee was the leading proponent of the former course. Knox's friend Greene and a few others inclined to the latter view. For his part, Knox was prepared to abide by whatever decision Washington took. Writing to his brother after a fateful council of war on June 24, Knox revealed his understanding of the immense burden under which the Virginian labored, as well his admiration for him. Noting the pros and cons of an attack, he concluded "the fate of posterity, and not the illusive brilliance of military glory, governs our Fabian commander, the man to whom, under God, America owes her present prospects of peace and happiness."[14] What resulted was the battle of Monmouth, fought in sweltering heat on June 28.

An American advance guard under Lee attacked the British as they marched north from the small New Jersey village. The British reacted fiercely and the patriots fell back. When Knox came up, he personally helped rally the retreating men. Exposing himself to withering enemy fire, he placed his batteries, which in turn helped supply a decisive check to the British and retrieved the day for the Continentals. One observer wrote, "In the hard-fought contest of Monmouth no officer was more distinguished than General Knox. In the front of the battle, he was seen animating the soldiers and directing the thunder of their cannon."[15] Another frontline participant called the fire of Knox's guns "the finest music I ever heard."[16] Knox himself noted that "my brave lads behaved with their usual intrepidity..." on "a field of carnage and blood."[17] Washington specifically cited Knox and his men in general orders after the battle, declaring "no artillery could have been better served than ours."[18]

Knox saw no more fighting in the 3 years following Monmouth. He continued to train his men, establishing an artillery school at Pluckemin, New Jersey, in the winter of 1779. These years represented in many ways the patriots' gloomiest period. The failure of Congress and the states adequately to sustain the troops led to restiveness among both officers and men. Several mutinies occurred among Continental troops in 1780 and more serious ones in early 1781. While fully supporting the firm suppression of these outbreaks, Knox and many other senior commanders also understood the underlying justice of their men's complaints. At Washington's behest, Knox was one of several officers to petition their native regions to seek relief for the ranks. In a letter to New England leaders, Knox vividly depicted "the aggravated calamities and distresses that have resulted from the total want of pay, for nearly 12 months, the want of clothing in a severe season, and not infrequently the want of provisions."[19] In this instance, Knox succeeded in obtaining some satisfaction from the governments of Connecticut, Massachusetts, New Hampshire, and Rhode Island, which agreed to send money and clothing to their soldiers. Knox would return to this critical issue of soldier support after Yorktown. Among the other duties he performed during this juncture was one distasteful in the extreme. Following Arnold's attempted treason in September 1780, Knox sat on the court-martial that condemned Major John Andre, Arnold's British army liaison who had been captured while the traitor escaped, to hang.

The Yorktown campaign of 1781 was the war's culminating act and Knox played a key role. The prelude had been Greene's brilliant series of operations in the first part of the year that ran the British army in the south ragged and reversed many of their previous conquests. By June, a worn-out force under Cornwallis had reached Williamsburg, Virginia. Clinton, the British commander in chief in New York City, fearful of an attack on him by Washington with a combined Franco-American force, wanted Cornwallis to send reinforcements north. London, however, refused to allow any British troops to leave the Chesapeake. Accordingly, Clinton instructed Cornwallis to establish a base in that vicinity. Cornwallis chose Yorktown, with a satellite outpost directly across the York River at Gloucester. Meanwhile, in mid-August Washington received the exciting news that a powerful French fleet would arrive off the Chesapeake by the end of the month. He marshaled his forces and deceived Clinton into thinking he would attempt to storm New York.

Then he and his French counterpart, General Rochambeau, marched 450 miles south, to link up with the French fleet, as well as an American army already in Virginia under Lafayette, by mid-September.

Yorktown was not a favorable position for Cornwallis. The ground was flat and he was heavily outnumbered—about 20,000 to fewer than 9,000. After the French bested a British fleet off the Chesapeake Capes, he was trapped between the allied land forces and the sea. He also lacked the equipment to prepare works needed to withstand a siege and was short of provisions. His constricted perimeter—1,000 yards long and on average only about 300 yards deep—further hampered defense. Washington invested Yorktown in late September and initiated formal siege operations on the evening of October 6 by digging the first trench, or parallel, about 800–1,200 yards from the British lines. Artillery was the decisive arm here and Knox meticulously prepared his gunners. He designated specific field-grade officers to aim and level pieces, and to record rounds expended and the results. On October 9 Knox's batteries, along with the French, commenced a devastating fire on the British. One allied observer noted, "This artillery was always well served, the general [Knox] incessantly directing it and often pointing the mortars . . . we French were . . . impressed by the extraordinary progress of the American artillery."[20] Lafayette enthused to an American comrade-in-arms, "the progress of your artillery is regarded by everybody as one of the wonders of the Revolution."[21]

It ended quickly. The allies commenced a second parallel 300–500 yards closer to the British on the night of October 11 and secured it by storming two enemy redoubts the evening of the 14th. The cannonade was thunderous. In 12 days of remorseless shelling, over 100 Franco-American guns hurled more than 15,000 rounds at the enemy. Often they used a ricochet technique, deliberately bouncing cannonballs along the ground to sever the limbs of enemy troops. A British sortie to spike the tormenting guns brought them no relief and Cornwallis's desperate attempt on the night of the 16th to ferry his battered command across the river to Gloucester failed. On the morning of October 17 Cornwallis asked for terms; on the 19th his men laid down their arms and marched into captivity.

Victory at Yorktown did not end the war. Two years passed before the conclusion of peace and the final departure of British troops from United States soil. During this uncertain period, Washington and most of the Army returned to the Hudson highlands to watch Clinton and the British garrison that occupied New York City. Knox, who had been made a major general following Yorktown, commanded the American fortress at West Point. A major concern and danger were the rampant discontent in the army over an accumulation of grievances revolving around compensation. To gain justice, as well as to silence the mutinous rumblings of some officers and men, Washington appointed Knox to chair a committee of general officers, which drew up and presented a respectful petition to Congress in December 1782. The national legislature, in truth a weak and ineffective body, made no semblance of acting and Knox privately railed. "Posterity will hardly believe that an army contended incessantly for eight years under a constant pressure of misery to establish the liberties of their country, without knowing ... whether they were ever to receive any reward for their services." Nevertheless, he could never contemplate a military coup: "I consider the reputation of the American army as one of the most immaculate things on earth, and that we should suffer even wrongs and injuries to the utmost verge of toleration rather than sully it to the least degree."[22]

Some others were less forbearing, however, and as a result the "Newburgh Addresses" circulated through the army in March 1783. Washington confronted the issue of army disloyalty head on and soberly reminded his officers of their duty in a session with them on March 15. After the commander in chief had brilliantly defused the crisis and departed, General Gates as senior man present, assumed the chair. Knox then quickly moved several resolutions thanking Washington for his leadership and expressing the army's confidence in Congress's good faith and ultimate redress of its claims. By this time Knox, like many military officers who had suffered under an impotent Congress, was well along the way to becoming an ardent Federalist. These men believed in the absolute necessity of creating a stronger national government. Years before the Constitutional Convention met, Knox insisted to colleagues that a new constitution was essential to replace the weak Articles of Confederation among the 13 states.

It was also during this period that Knox conceived of a postwar organization of Revolutionary officers to perpetuate their wartime comradeship and patriotic ideals. The name chosen was Society of the Cincinnati, for the Roman Cincinnatus, who after fighting for the republic declined all honors and humbly returned to his plow. Although a number of dyed-in-the-wool republicans derided the idea as antidemocratic, aristocratic or worse, Knox succeeded in getting the society launched with Washington as its first president. Meanwhile, as American and British negotiators haggled in Paris, day-to-day command of the Continental Army devolved upon Knox, while Washington remained as commander in chief. Knox's principal chore was to disband the army—a delicate task given the feelings of men still unpaid and the continued British presence in New York. By November 1783 word arrived in America that a treaty had been concluded and Knox negotiated the British departure from New York with his opposite number, General Carleton. On November 25 Knox led his troops into the city in a joyous spectacle. A more intimate and emotional ceremony occurred on December 4 when Washington took leave of his officers at Fraunces Tavern in lower Manhattan. Addressing them, Washington said "With a heart full of love and gratitude, I now take leave of you. I most devoutly wish that your latter days may be as prosperous and happy as your former ones have been glorious and honorable."[23] He then asked them to come forward individually. Knox was the first and the two embraced tearfully.

Knox retired from the army in 1784, but returned to public life in March 1785 when the Confederation government appointed him as Secretary of War. He retained the post after the Constitution was adopted and remained in President Washington's cabinet until the end of 1794. There his political views led him to support the nationalist policies of Alexander Hamilton against the states-centered outlook of Thomas Jefferson. In the teeth of lingering republican resentment against "standing armies," Knox managed to achieve the creation of a small American fleet, construction of coastal fortifications, and an increase in the regular army's size. His tenure also witnessed several campaigns to pacify native American tribes, the most successful being one conducted by Anthony Wayne during Knox's last year in office.

After nearly 20 years of often arduous service, Knox finally settled down with Lucy on some property they had acquired in Maine. They lived comfortably, even extravagantly, in a mansion they built in Thomaston. Their personal fortune fluctuated as Knox assayed a variety of business ventures with differing degrees of success. Outwardly, the couple presented a gracious and winning picture. They entertained frequently, traveled, and were socially popular. Knox also displayed great generosity to those in need. Among those benefiting from his largesse was Nathanael Greene's widow. Privately, the couple experienced considerable sorrow; Lucy bore 12 children of whom only three survived to adulthood. The vibrant Knox died suddenly after a brief illness on October 25, 1806, at the too-young age of 56 and was buried on his estate.

Knox's contributions to American independence were as outsized as the man himself. He created an artillery branch in the Continental Army and deserves recognition as the father of the United States Army artillery. He was Washington's most loyal and reliable companion. His courage and skill contributed measurably to the great victories at Trenton, Princeton, and Yorktown. Perhaps equally as important, his unflagging optimism buoyed the commander in chief during the war's darkest hours. Another Washington—Washington Irving, the literary figure of the early republic—wrote, "Henry Knox was one of those providential characters which spring up in emergencies as if formed by and for the occasion."[24] This seems a just summing up, as does George Washington's pithier assessment, which referred to Yorktown but can stand for Knox's entire career, "the resources of his genius supplied the deficit of means."[25]

NATHANAEL GREENE

This great American strategist and fighter was born into a Quaker family on August 7, 1742, in Warwick, Rhode Island. The prosperous Greenes operated grist and saw mills, as well as ironworks, in southern New England, but neither Nathanael nor his siblings received much formal education. Their father was a hardheaded businessman who insisted that his sons gain the practical experience of learning a trade in lieu of attending school and, in any event, the Society of Friends frowned upon excessive, "frivolous" learning. In keeping with patriarchal design, the future American general took charge of the family's principal foundry at early age. Nevertheless, the youth thirsted for knowledge and spent many a hot work day at the forge immersed in books. Later in life he still regretted his father's stricture, writing, "I lament the want of a liberal education."[26] His love of learning eventually brought him to Henry Knox's Boston book shop, where their shared interest in military subjects initiated a lifelong friendship.

Greene grew into a sturdy, handsome youth of just under 6 feet tall. He was physically active, despite suffering from occasional bouts of asthma and walking with a slight limp, the result of a boyhood accident. He became a substantial and well-regarded citizen, and developed many important business and political connections. A passion for militia units existed in much of colonial America, particularly amid the ferment during the years immediately preceding the Revolution. Much like Knox, Greene helped raise a unit in his hometown. To his great disappointment, however, he was not chosen as an officer—probably due to his disability, which hindered him on the drill field. Thus he served in the Kentish Guards as Private Greene. His martial activities caused him to run afoul of the Quaker hierarchy, which sorrowfully expelled him from their meeting in 1774.

In the tumult immediately following the battles of Lexington and Concord, the Rhode Island Assembly, along with those in the other New England colonies, voted to dispatch militia units to reinforce their Massachusetts brethren. The legislature then promoted Private Greene to brigadier general and chose him to lead the Rhode Island contingent north to Cambridge. This extraordinary advancement reflected his peers' acknowledgment of Greene's natural leadership abilities and character, as well as his family connections and repute as a man of affairs. It also implicitly recognized that cutting a fine figure on the parade ground is a peacetime luxury, not a wartime necessity. In a letter to his still-new bride Kitty on the eve of his departure, Greene expressed sorrow at the imminent separation and bravely averred that "the injury done my Country, and the Chains of Slavery forgeing for posterity, calls me forth to defend our common rights, and repel the bold invaders of the Sons of freedom."[27] The Rhode Islanders arrived in May; shortly thereafter the Congress in Philadelphia confirmed Greene as a Continental brigadier, the youngest of the initial slate of general officers.

Washington, upon taking charge of the army, soon noted Greene's skill and energy, commenting that the Rhode Island men "are under much better government than any around Boston."[28] The Virginian was not an easy man to get close to, but he and Greene quickly warmed to each other. The christening of Greene's first child—George Washington Greene—born shortly after the two met, provides one indication of this. The boy later gained a sister named Martha. In addition to instilling a modicum of discipline, Washington reorganized the army encircling Boston. Greene served as a brigade commander under Charles Lee with the left or northern wing. Mingling with men from other colonies and regions occasionally induced friction and misunderstandings, but for many of the Continental Army's officers it led to a greater national sensibility. This was the case with Greene, who wrote approvingly from Cambridge that Washington had "a great desire to Bannish every Idea of Local Attachments."[29] Greene was well on the way toward becoming a committed nationalist, declaring that "The interests of our colony are in no ways incompatible with the interests of another."[30] Indeed, along with Lee and Gates, he was in the forefront of those soldiers calling for independence.

Following the British evacuation of Boston in March 1776, Greene shifted to New York City with the rest of the army. Congress promoted him to major general in August, in response to Washington's endorsement and pleas for more senior billets with Horatio Gates in upstate New York and Lee down south fortifying Charleston. Washington assigned Greene the vital task of defending Long Island from positions on Brooklyn Heights. Greene worked hard to prepare his troops for an anticipated British blow; unfortunately a raging fever laid him low in mid-August. This proved a crippling loss; not only was Greene a superior general, but his replacements were unfamiliar with the terrain and the defensive plan. Greene was still bed-ridden when the British attacked on August 27, routing the maldeployed Americans, who had ill-advisedly come forward from the imposing heights whence they stood a better chance of stemming the enemy. Washington, aided by a dense fog on the night of August 29, did well to ferry most of his beaten troops back across the East River into Manhattan. Several of Greene's friends, including Knox, thought that the battle might have turned out differently had Greene been on the field, though the latter humbly maintained "I have not the vanity to think the event would have been otherwise ... yet I think I could have given the commanding general a good deal of necessary information. Great events sometimes depend upon very little causes." Nevertheless, in strong language for a Quaker, he also fumed, "Gracious God! To be confined at such a time!"[31]

Greene recovered sufficiently to return to duty in early September. He participated in deliberations at Washington's headquarters over whether and how to defend the city. Greene argued for a total evacuation, noting the British superiority in both troops and the maritime assets to move them up either the East or Hudson rivers to cut off the Americans. In Greene's view the wise course was to withdraw north into Westchester County and establish stout winter quarters. He further advocated putting the city to the torch to deny its comforts to the British, a suggestion that found little favor in American councils. The generals debated and Washington consulted with Congress. Meanwhile Howe struck on September 15, breaching the East River at Kip's Bay near modern-day midtown and brushing aside the defenders. The American troops on Manhattan's southern tip barely escaped entrapment. Ultimately, the patriots temporarily stabilized the situation and reestablished new lines along Harlem Heights, from where they repulsed a halfhearted British assault on the 16th. Here Greene got his first real exposure to combat as he rode forward to rally and encourage the defenders. In addition to Harlem Heights, farther north the Americans held Kingsbridge on the Harlem River, which secured a potential line of retreat upstate. Just above the Heights the patriots manned two Hudson River posts—Fort Washington on the New York side and Fort Constitution, later Fort Lee, directly opposite on the New Jersey bank. Greene made his headquarters at the latter after Washington assigned him the important responsibility for guarding the river against British attempts to sail up it, as well as maintaining the patriot line of communications across New Jersey to Philadelphia.

When Howe attempted another envelopment of the American left or eastern flank on October 18, Washington pulled his army back to White Plains, where he fought a defensive battle a week and a half later. The Americans retired north once again in reasonably good order, but in early November Washington decided to cross into New Jersey with the larger part of the army. He left the rump in Westchester County under Lee, recently returned from his victory at Charleston, along with a smaller detachment to protect the Hudson highlands. Howe shifted his immediate attention to the now dangerously isolated Fort Washington and began to invest it.

Fort Washington fell under Greene's area of responsibility and here he committed his most serious error of the war. Interestingly, although he had previously advocated ceding New York to the British, he believed that the fort could withstand an enemy assault or siege, despite the works being unfinished and the garrison outnumbered by their potential assailants. He compounded this dubious conviction by steadily feeding men and supplies across the river into what proved a trap. When the commander in chief arrived at Greene's Fort Lee command post on November 13, he allowed his subordinate, against his better judgment, to convince him. Three days later the two were personally inspecting the place when an all out British attack began. The fort's commander, a colonel, insisted that the generals depart immediately. Horrified, Washington and Greene watched helplessly from the Jersey side as, minutes after their getaway, the enemy overwhelmed the fort, taking 3,000 prisoners. In the aftermath there were voices calling for Greene's censure or worse, but Washington stuck by him. Something of Greene's deep personal anguish comes through in a letter he wrote to Knox shortly afterward, "I feel mad, vexed, sick, and sorry. Never did I need the consoling voice of a friend more than now. Happy should I be to see you. This is a most terrible event: its consequences are justly to be dreaded. Pray, what is to be said upon the occasion? A line from you will be very acceptable."[32]

Time allowed for neither criticism nor introspection. Events pressed and Washington's bedraggled army abandoned Fort Lee and retreated across New Jersey into Pennsylvania. Although Lee had been tardy in answering Washington's summons, eventually that portion of the army linked up with the main force—absent Lee who had carelessly allowed himself to be captured. Gates arrived with further troops from upstate New York, and some Pennsylvania and New Jersey militia also presented themselves, as Washington strove to hold an army in being and launch a riposte. On Christmas Eve, 1776, at Greene's headquarters Washington and his subordinate commanders worked out the details of his bold decision to raid the Hessian garrison across the Delaware River at Trenton the following evening. The countersign for the operation, personally written out by the Virginian, was "Victory or Death."

Once across the river that stormy night, Greene, accompanied by Washington, led the army's left wing south toward the unwary Hessians while General John Sullivan headed the right wing as it paralleled the river. Thanks in large measure to the brutal elements—wind, snow, sleet—that assailed them, the patriots gained complete surprise. Sullivan's men had circled around to enter the town from the southwest as Greene's force drove in from the north. It was a one-sided contest, Knox's guns visiting great destruction upon the enemy by sweeping the streets with hot grapeshot. In a hasty council amid the Hessian surrender, Greene and Knox urged their chief to continue the attack and pick off other enemy outposts, but Washington declined. Still, the exhausted but jubilant Americans withdrew with hopes renewed after a tremendous ordeal. Greene's account to his wife echoed many others when he wrote that he endured "thirty hours in the Storm without the least refreshment."[33]

Scarcely 3 days later, Washington followed up with another foray across the Delaware, this time in greater strength. The army concentrated again at Trenton, so recently cleared of enemy troops, and prepared to fight a defensive battle against troops led by Cornwallis, who had been forced to cancel a leave home by the Americans' audacity. Recent experience had shown Washington that Trenton itself was indefensible, but there was favorable terrain south of town and here the patriots established their lines. From a base at Princeton to the north, Cornwallis advanced against "the old fox," as he called Washington, on January 2. Washington had emplaced a covering force north of Trenton to harass the enemy and late in the afternoon he sent Greene forward with reinforcements to direct it. The successful delaying action bought valuable time, but by nightfall the Americans faced seemingly imminent destruction on the morrow, with a larger force to their front and no way to cross the Delaware behind them. To escape this trap, Washington conducted a masterful night march around the British left and struck their rear at Princeton. The Americans then skipped away, just beyond the reach of the angry Cornwallis, and eventually established their winter quarters at Morristown. These signal victories reversed the British tide in New Jersey and caused them largely to withdraw from the state. Some patriots gave a providential interpretation to these events, including Greene, who wrote that "the Lord seems to have smote the Enemy with a Panic."[34]

While waiting for spring and the onset of a new campaign season, Washington dispatched his generals on various embassies to their states or to Congress to make the case for the army's needs regarding men, money, and supplies. Greene journeyed to Philadelphia on such a mission in March 1777. Greene was never reluctant to share his views with civilian leaders. Earlier, in the December crisis, he had urged Congress to delegate extraordinary powers to his idol Washington, assuring them that "There never was a man that might be more safely trusted, nor a Time when there was a louder Call."[35] Like his fellow officers, he was extremely sensitive concerning issues of rank and promotion, and flatly informed John Adams that he thought Washington, not Congress, should be responsible for the selection of generals. At the same time, he hardly advocated military supremacy. When General Philip Schuyler was briefly considered for the Presidency of Congress, Greene strongly opposed it, telling Adams "No free people ought to admit a junction of the Civil and Military, and no man of good Principles, with virtuous intentions, would ask it..." Such a combination was "incompatable with the

Safety of a free people."[36] He and Adams profoundly agreed in this instance, but regarding the officer corps' seemingly constant upheaval over promotions and seniority Adams was not so understanding. He poured his frustrations out to his wife, "I am wearied to death with the wrangle between military officers, high and low. They quarrel like cats and dogs. They worry one another like mastiffs, scrambling for rank and pay like apes for nuts."[37]

The Coudray affair was a prime illustration of this. Greene joined Knox and Sullivan in vehement protest to Congress against the Frenchman assuming Knox's position as artillery chief. Congress in turn exploded at the effrontery of this hectoring from the generals. Philadelphia echoed with cries for their dismissal or, at a minimum, censure. Fortunately, cooler heads—Washington's among them— prevailed and the furor died down. After Congress shunted Coudray off to another post, all eyes turned to the movements of Burgoyne's army descending from Canada and the intentions of Howe's mighty host in New York.

The Philadelphia campaign of 1777 began with Howe's and Washington's armies conducting a midsummer series of marches and countermarches in New Jersey. The British evidently wished to find advantageous ground, go over to the tactical defensive, and lure the Americans into battle, but Washington refused the bait. Regarding these maneuvers Greene mused that the army seemed "compeld to wander about the country like the Arabs."[38] The only real fighting took place on June 22 when two of Greene's brigades bloodied a British detachment outside of New Brunswick. Having failed in his gambit, Howe quit New Jersey entirely and embarked his men on ship from New York. About this time Greene revealed some of his strategic perceptiveness in a letter to a brother. Ticonderoga had fallen to Burgoyne in the north and there was much alarm in patriot circles. Greene thought "General Burgoyne's triumphs and little advantages may serve to bait his vanity and lead him on to his total ruin."[39] This indeed proved the case at Saratoga. Meanwhile, the American command played a high-stakes guessing game to anticipate where Howe's blow would fall. Not until the third week of August could they confirm a British landing at the northern tip of Chesapeake Bay, about 60 miles southwest of Philadelphia. The Continental Army moved to interpose itself between the enemy and the capital along Brandywine Creek.

The morning of September 11 found Greene's division, along with Anthony Wayne's, covering the most direct British avenue of approach at Chad's Ford. The day began with an artillery duel as American gunners traded shot and shell with a large Hessian force opposite them. Greene was at Washington's headquarters about a mile behind the front line when word arrived that a sizeable British element had been spotted skirting the American right flank, the assigned responsibility of General John Sullivan's division. Seeing a magnificent opportunity to strike a divided enemy, Washington ordered Greene and Wayne to cross the Brandywine and pass over to the offensive. Before the command could be carried out, however, new reports indicated no British presence on the American flank. Washington countermanded the attack order. Shortly afterward came the shocking information that the British indeed had crossed the upper Brandywine fords in considerable strength. Worse, they had turned the American right flank, manned by Sullivan. Sullivan's division tried to reorient itself and make a stand, but soon crumbled under intense pressure. Late in the afternoon, a portion of Greene's division came to the rescue. His lead brigade, Virginians under General George Weedon, marched to the sound of the guns and covered 4 miles in under an hour, an incredible feat. Although the Americans had been surprised and outmaneuvered, Greene and his men saved the army from total annihilation. Some time later, in an interesting denouement, Greene asked Washington why he had not seen fit to mention this performance in his dispatches to Congress. Washington replied, "You, sir, are considered my favorite officer: Weedon's brigade, like myself, are Virginians; should I applaud them for their achievement under your command, I shall be charged with partiality; jealousy will be excited, and the service injured."[40]

Following Brandywine, Howe occupied Philadelphia while the Continental Army lurked to the northwest. The American generals were eager for another crack at Howe and his dispositions invited attack. An exposed portion of his army garrisoned the village of Germantown outside of Philadelphia and Washington devised a daring, if complex, scheme to take them unawares. On the night of October 3, four separate American columns moved out from their encampment at Metuchen Hill toward Germantown, 16 miles distant. Sullivan and Greene led the two main thrusts in the center, with militia on each flank. Sullivan struck first and drove in the enemy's light infantry pickets, but the attack bogged down as the Americans occupied themselves with a well-defended British bastion they should have bypassed. Further unhinging Washington's plan, Greene's guides had gotten lost in the dark, taking this element of the force some 4 miles out of the way before it could arrive on the field. Elements of Sullivan's and Greene's corps then engaged in a fratricidal exchange, and the fight rapidly degenerated into a swirling, confused melee in the dense morning fog. So thick was the mist that Howe's prized dog crossed over into the American lines, later to be returned to him under a flag of truce. Eventually, the British broke the patriot momentum and emerged masters of the field as the Americans pulled back.

The two armies sparred for a couple of months longer, most notably with the British reducing two American forts on the Delaware just below Philadelphia, before going into winter quarters. Washington's army built its encampment at Valley Forge. As had become the army's custom, several of the ranking officers' wives—including Martha Washington, Lucy Knox, and Kitty Greene—joined their husbands in camp and furnished a bright spot in a winter of discontent and suffering. Greene, as one of Washington's staunchest supporters, became embroiled in the acrimony that swirled around the so-called Conway cabal. He excoriated the somewhat hapless Gates for being a party to the alleged plot to unseat Washington. In writing the President of Congress, he linked the machinations against Washington to his favorite theme of officer promotions. If Congress did not mend its ways, he warned, "Military ardor will languish; a spirit to enterprize will cease; Men of honor will decline the service; art and cabal will succeed, and low intrigue will be the characteristick and genius of the Army."[41]

Thankfully, much of this poisonous atmosphere of court intrigue seemed to dissipate with the spring thaw. The army's supply situation, however, remained desperate. American logistical procedures—these could hardly be dignified with the term "system"—were abysmal. Given the extreme republican aversion to centralized power, coupled with primitive manufacturing and finance sectors, it perhaps hardly could have been otherwise. Needing to do something, Washington turned to his trusted and highly capable subordinate Greene, and asked him to take on the thankless burden of being the army's quartermaster general. There certainly was no glory to be won. As Greene mordantly remarked some time later, "Nobody ever heard of a quartermaster in history."[42] Out of loyalty to Washington and in recognition of the army's dire straits, he reluctantly accepted the position after Congress appointed him in March 1778, replacing Thomas Mifflin, who had essentially abdicated the post some months earlier.

Greene went to work with a will, employing his business acumen, as well as the impressive energy and organizational skills that had always won him notice. He rationalized the previously chaotic workings of his department, creating mechanisms for procurement, transportation, storage, and distribution. The army felt the effects almost immediately and embarked upon the campaign of 1778 in much better shape due in large measure to his efforts. Inevitably, as a consequence of the bruising political warfare among various factions in Congress and the army, his enemies—Mifflin included—whispered accusations of malfeasance and corruption against Greene. In accordance with established procedure, Congress had allowed Greene to earn a 1-percent commission on his departmental expenditures. In addition to claiming that he spent excessively to increase his profits, his foes also accused him of speculation and nepotism. It is true that Greene liked money. Just before taking the job he penned these quintessentially American lines, which could have been written by Jay Gatsby, "Money becomes more and more the American's object. You must get rich, or you will be of no consequence."[43] Likewise he invested his profits in a number of enterprises, including a fleet of privateers, and sent considerable business to family and cronies in Rhode Island. Even in an age less scrupulous than our own in drawing lines between public and private interests, Greene was probably guilty of some irregularities, though none were ever substantiated. No doubt, he did well while also doing good. Still, Washington's opinion should carry the most weight. He offered this heartfelt and grateful verdict upon Greene's labors as quartermaster, "When you were prevailed upon to take the office . . . it was in great disorder and confusion, and, by extraordinary exertions, you so arranged it as to enable the army to take the field the moment it was necessary. . ."[44] Greene certainly was more successful at provisioning the army than either Mifflin or his own eventual successor, Timothy Pickering.

Greene served a little over 2 years as the army's chief logistician while continuing as a valued source of operational advice to Washington. He also took the field and commanded in battle on three occasions during this interlude. The first was at Monmouth in June 1778. Greene had been one of those, as opposed to the eventually disgraced Charles Lee, urging boldness on Washington from the start of the campaign. He frankly told Washington, "I cannot help thinking we magnify our deficiencies beyond realities ... marching until we get near the enemy and then our courage fails. People expect something from us and our strength demands it."[45] When battle was joined, Greene had come forward with Washington. Following the Virginian's stormy interview with Lee, he made Greene responsible for the right wing of the final American defensive line. It was the enfilade fire from Greene's troops that helped break the British advance on that hot and bloody day.

A month later, Washington sent his quartermaster to Rhode Island to participate in the Newport campaign, the war's first combined Franco-American venture. Greene agreed without murmur to serve under his junior Sullivan since the latter was already established as the overall commander. Doubtless, his friendship with Sullivan and eagerness to fight in his native state contributed to Greene's willingness to overlook the precedence of rank. As it turned out, the expedition miscarried badly. The plan called for the Americans to attack one side of the British defensive works while French marines landed and menaced the other. With the Americans in position and the French just ashore, however, a British fleet appeared in view. The French commander, the comte d'Estaing, reembarked his marines and sailed out to challenge the ancient enemy on August 10. This left the patriot force in the very uncomfortable position of confronting an entrenched force that now outnumbered them. A devastating hurricane 2 days later wrecked both fleets, as well any residual American thoughts of assaulting without their Gallic allies.

Already angry, Sullivan and the other American generals became incensed when d'Estaing decided to sail off to Boston for repairs, taking his marines—who could have played little role in any sea fight and none whatsoever in the refitting—with him. The hot-headed Sullivan allowed himself some choice and decidedly undiplomatic words, which threatened the new and dearly sought alliance. Washington turned to Greene to pour oil on the troubled waters, informing him "I depend much upon your temper and influence to conciliate that animosity which ... subsists" between American and French officers.[46] Greene did tolerably well as a peacemaker, but it was too late to salvage the Newport operation. Already weakened by the French withdrawal, mass desertions of militia, who used the French departure as an excuse, further depleted Sullivan's little army. Sensing an advantage, the British sallied out of their works on August 29 and engaged the Americans. Greene skillfully handled his troops in a sharp skirmish that traded about 200 patriot casualties for 300 enemy. Both sides retired; the British held Newport until they voluntarily evacuated in October 1779.

For the next 2 years Washington's army postured in New Jersey and above New York City. While protecting against a renewed British attempt on Philadelphia, a foray into New England, or another try to force the line of the Hudson, Washington unsuccessfully tried to coordinate offensive action with his French allies—an endeavor that would not bear fruit until the fall of 1781. After Newport, Greene returned to his quartermaster post and seemingly endless squabbles with Congress. Only his sense of duty and loyalty to Washington kept him at a job he hated. Due to his efforts, the Army passed the winter of 1778–1779 in relative comfort. One high point of the social season at the Middlebrook, New Jersey, camp was a soiree at which the flirtatious Kitty danced 3 hours nonstop with Washington. A year later, he kept the army from freezing and starving at Morristown during the century's worst recorded winter. Greene's final opportunity to lead men in battle while laboring under his quartermaster duties came in June 1780. Getting wind of attempted mutinies in various American regiments, a strong British detachment of 5,000 men marched into New Jersey to exploit presumably weakened patriot morale, and also as a diversion for a projected attack up the Hudson against West Point. Washington hastened north to the Hudson highlands, leaving Greene with about 2,500 men at Springfield, New Jersey. Greene beat back the enemy after a daylong fight on June 23. Meanwhile the intended British thrust up the Hudson also failed.

Worn out by his critics' sniping, as well as the rigors of the job, Greene submitted his resignation as quartermaster to Congress, effective August 1, 1780. This hardly ended his torment, however. Congress took umbrage at his tone, and his enemies persisted in demanding investigations of his tenure and his dismissal from the army. Washington calmed ruffled feathers in Philadelphia while eloquently defending Greene. Eventually, the affair blew over and Greene set to work transitioning his responsibilities to Pickering. He was at his headquarters at Paramus, New Jersey, on the evening of September 25 when he received a startling communication from Alexander Hamilton of Washington's personal staff. Benedict Arnold, recently installed as the commander at West Point, had been found out in a plot to turn the vital fortress over to the enemy. Washington had been en route to visit when patriot militia fortuitously apprehended Arnold's liaison with the British, Major John Andre, and discovered the treasonous scheme. Greene immediately dispatched troops to reinforce West Point and forwarded Hamilton's note to Congress. Arnold escaped, but Andre was not so fortunate. He had been caught in civilian disguise, and justice was both swift and harsh. Washington appointed a military court with Greene presiding. On September 30 the court sentenced Andre to death as a spy. British appeals for the young officer's life did not avail; the only deal acceptable to the Americans would have been an exchange that brought them Arnold. The young Briton was hanged on October 2. Shortly after this unpleasant affair Greene succeeded to the command of West Point, but he would not remain there long.

While stalemate reigned in the north, in the south the Americans had suffered two crushing defeats within a span of 3 months in 1780. Charleston fell in May, with the loss of 5,000 prisoners. Gates's rout at Camden in August destroyed another patriot army. The British rapidly overran the southland, and established a chain of posts in the South Carolina and Georgia countryside that complemented their control of the coastal cities of Charleston and Savannah. While they had not completely pacified the region—partisan bands sprung up in the mountainous western areas as well as the eastern low country of South Carolina—the British bid fair to extinguish the Revolution below the Potomac. Patriot leaders in North

Carolina and Virginia trembled as Cornwallis, the British commander in the south, poised to invade their states.

In this grim circumstance, Congress, whose previous choices had fared so disastrously, asked Washington in October who should be sent south to retrieve patriot fortunes. Washington did not hesitate to designate Greene. The Rhode Islander set out from West Point almost immediately for his new post, taking along Baron von Steuben as his deputy. En route, Greene stopped in Philadelphia to pay obeisance to Congress, and ask for money and supplies. As he made his way, he appealed as well to the legislatures and governors of the southern states. Occasionally he indulged in the blunt, direct talk that had so irked Congress from time to time. Like many military men Greene took a national and practical view of the Revolution. As such, the frequent invocation of local concerns by civil authorities and their republican reservations against the broad exercise of power greatly exasperated him. For their part, leaders such as Virginia's Governor Thomas Jefferson resented being lectured, as for example, in a dispute over providing cavalry mounts where Greene pointedly asked whether horses were dearer to Virginians than their liberty.

Greene reached the remnants of the army at Charlotte, North Carolina, on December 2, 1780, and formally took command the next day. He treated the disgraced Gates with the utmost sensitivity and consideration, setting aside their previous animosity centered on the Conway cabal. He inherited a truly dismal situation. His "army" existed in name only. The 2,000 odd men on hand were broken physically and in spirit. Many were literally clothed in rags and without weapons. The only activity that seemed to rouse them from their torpor was plundering nearby settlements in search of something to eat. When his newly appointed commissary general protested his lack of skill at accounting, Greene sardonically reassured him—the army had no money anyway. There were a couple of reasons for optimism, however. The partisans in South Carolina were driving Cornwallis to distraction; indeed, one of his reasons for projecting operations farther north was his disgust at the inability of native Loyalists to support the suppression of revolutionary activity. Not that they weren't trying; the backcountry struggle between crown adherents and patriots was extraordinarily savage—a merciless farrago of bushwhacking, murder, and reprisal—whose only contemporary parallel lay in the Indians fighting on the frontier. Patriot militias had won a particularly one-sided victory in early October when they slaughtered or captured over 1,000 Loyalist irregulars at King's Mountain in southwestern North Carolina. Another bright spot was the presence of Daniel Morgan. This estimable warrior had gone home in 1779 after being passed over for promotion. Before departing, Gates had coaxed him out of retirement and gotten Congress to give him the brigadier's rank he coveted. Morgan would play a vital part in the opening phase of Greene's campaign.

The new commander took stock and determined his operational design. He resolved to wage what he termed a "fugitive war."[47] By this Greene intended a contest of hit and run, advance and retreat. He would rely heavily upon superior mobility, conferred not only by lightly equipped partisans and cavalry, but also by a sturdy supply system and solid information about the terrain. He left Steuben in Virginia to coordinate logistics and recruit; dispatched teams to survey the numerous trails, rivers, and fords in his operational area; and established an intelligence system. He built supply magazines and collected not only horses, but also every boat he could find—both to equip himself and deny them to the enemy—and built more, which he placed on wheeled carts to enhance flexibility. The boats would prove indispensable. And he established communications with the leading partisan chieftains—Thomas Sumter, Francis Marion, and Andrew Pickens—lauding them for their previous efforts and impressing on them the need to synchronize their operations with his army.

Greene quickly vacated the depleted countryside around Charlotte and by the end of December established a new main camp at Cheraw, South Carolina. Besides offering access to ample food stocks and other supplies, this site conferred several operational advantages. From Cheraw, Greene could readily support Marion's partisans and threaten the enemy's flanks, as well as their exposed line of communications from Camden back to Charleston. In a highly unorthodox move, Greene also divided his already tiny force, dispatching Morgan and some 600 men to the west to harass the British frontier posts. Greene explained, "I am obliged to put everything to the hazard; and contrary to all military propriety am obliged to make detachments that nothing but absolute necessity could authorize or even justify."[48] Part of Greene's rationale included easing his supply problem; there were fewer mouths to feed at Cheraw and Morgan could easily live off the land. But more importantly, tactical virtue inhered in this logistical necessity. As Greene wrote, splitting his command "compels my adversary to divide his [forces], . . . He cannot leave Morgan behind him to come at me, or his posts [in the west] would be exposed. And he cannot chase Morgan far, or prosecute his views upon Virginia, while I am here with the whole country open before me."[49]

In mid-January, Greene sent Lieutenant Colonel Henry Lee and his cavalry–infantry legion—recently arrived after being sent down by Washington—to support Marion's operations in the eastern part of South Carolina. His predecessor in the southern department, Gates, had disdained cavalry, but Greene would come to rely greatly on the mobility afforded by Lee's mounted troops, as well as their professionalism. Meanwhile, Morgan threatened British garrisons to the west. To quash him, Cornwallis sent Lieutenant Colonel Banastre Tarleton, a notoriously savage cavalry leader known to patriots as "bloody Tarleton" for atrocities committed by his men. Tarleton gave chase until he cornered Morgan at Cowpens on January 17, 1781. Here Morgan turned and inflicted a surprising and one-sided defeat on the British, killing more than 100 and capturing another 800. Tarleton himself barely escaped.

Morgan's astonishing victory changed the entire dynamic of the campaign. Cornwallis now vowed to pursue and punish Morgan, as well as recover the captives taken at Cowpens. To expedite the hunt, Cornwallis burned his baggage to increase his command's mobility. Greene soon perceived Cornwallis's intent and sped to join forces with Morgan. The rifleman wanted to retreat into the mountains, but Greene saw an opportunity to lure his antagonist to ruin. When Morgan disavowed responsibility for such a risky gambit, Greene told him "I shall take the measure upon myself."[50] Greene then led the British on a desperate, arduous chase along the atrocious back roads and across the swollen rivers of western North Carolina. Greene's prior study of the terrain, and his foresight in preparing and positioning boats now served him extraordinarily well. In this "race to the Dan"—the river marking the Virginia–North Carolina border—Greene just managed to outpace the angry British nipping at his heels, crossing into the Old Dominion on February 13. An exhausted Cornwallis gave up the game and retired to rebuild his strength, but Greene was only just beginning. To Jefferson he wrote, "I have been obliged to practice that by finesse which I dared not attempt by force."[51]

Formerly the mouse, he now became the cat. He sent Lee, who had rejoined the main army in early February, back into North Carolina to join with the partisans tormenting the British, then reentered the state in force on February 23, his army augmented by fresh levies from Virginia. After his futile pursuit, Cornwallis also welcomed the prospect of a fight, even though Greene outnumbered him in effectives by something like 4,200 men to 2,000. Cornwallis was certain his disciplined regulars could make up for the numerical disparity. What followed was the first of three major battles that Greene fought in the south. Though tactical draws, at best, for the Americans, they contributed immeasurably to continued British attrition and eventually cost them control of the region. As Greene aptly put it, "We fight, get beat, rise, and fight again."[52] The two armies spent 3 weeks maneuvering and occasionally skirmishing. Remarkably, Greene had already selected the ground upon which he desired to fight while still scurrying to the Dan. Guilford Courthouse sat upon a wooded hill overlooking a narrow valley, about 100 miles northeast of Charlotte. Greene arrayed his men there on March 14 and awaited the British attack.

It came the next day. Cornwallis, approaching from the south along a road that ran through the valley to the courthouse, found the Americans drawn up in three lines. Militia composed the bulk of first two ranks—North Carolinians up front at the edge of a field, with Continentals anchoring each end, and Virginians about 300 yards behind them in the tree line. Greene trooped the militia line before the fight, imploring them to loose just "two rounds my boys, and then you may fall back."[53] At the top of the hill, 550 yards distant from the second line and just below the courthouse, Maryland and Virginia Continentals represented the main line of the defense. After a brief exchange of cannon fire, Cornwallis launched an assault that quickly scattered the first line of militia. Fierce, semi-independent battles broke out, however, between his lead elements and the patriot regulars who stood fast on both flanks.

Cornwallis threw in more troops in the center, who collided with the tenaciously resisting Virginia militia. The opposing sides rapidly became disorganized in the tangled undergrowth of the surrounding woods. The British regiments eventually emerged piecemeal from this fracas and clashed with the Continentals at the top of the hill. Another confused melee ensued that featured small combats, and numerous charges and countercharges. In desperation, Cornwallis brought up two light guns and ordered them to fire grapeshot into the intermingled British and American units. This temporarily separated the combatants and, at this juncture, Greene disengaged and withdrew his troops. He might have been able to regroup and sweep the enemy away, but felt he could not risk his army after having already so grievously wounded his adversary, who lost more than a quarter of his force killed or wounded. Greene left the field to Cornwallis and wrote afterward, "The Enemy got the ground the other Day, But we the victory. They had the splendor, we the advantage."[54]

Following Guilford Court House, Cornwallis's battered army staggered east to Wilmington on the North Carolina coast to regroup. Greene briefly pursued, then decided to make the liberation of the lower south his objective instead. As he pondered his return to South Carolina, he explained his reasoning to Washington, "the Enemy will be obliged to follow us or give up their posts in that State."[55] Greene half expected that Cornwallis would trail him south, where he could continue to lacerate the English lord. With some surprise, therefore, Greene subsequently learned that his opposite number elected to invade Virginia in lieu of a return to the Carolina hornet's nest. Cornwallis of course met catastrophe 7 months later at Yorktown.

Unsure for the moment of Cornwallis's intentions, in early April Greene made for the British garrison at Camden, site of Gates's earlier misfortune. He now confronted the main British force remaining in South Carolina, a mixture of redcoats and Loyalists under the command of a young nobleman, Colonel Francis Rawdon. Upon arriving at Camden, Greene found an enemy garrison of just under 1,000 men barricaded inside strong fortifications. Rather than throw himself upon these works, he attempted to entice Rawdon into attacking by deploying on Hobkirk's Hill, about a mile and a half north of Camden. The aggressive Rawdon accommodated by assaulting the patriots on the morning of April 25. This time Greene had placed his Continentals in front, with militia and cavalry in reserve. As the British moved uphill, Greene ordered a section of six-pounders to blast them with grapeshot, cutting a swath through their ranks. He then launched two regiments downhill to meet the enemy, while attempting a double envelopment by throwing a regiment at each of Rawdon's flanks. To complete the maneuver, he swung his cavalry around to sweep the British rear.

These were all sound tactics, but war is preeminently the realm of chance. The British neatly countered the flanking moves by extending their lines. Greene's cavalry drove too deep and bogged down raiding enemy supply trains. And for inexplicable reasons, one of the two charging regiments of veteran Continentals faltered, which in turn spread alarm and panic to its sister outfit. Then one of the regimental commanders was shot down, and the British exploited the disarray to shove the Americans off the hill. Greene was in the center of it all and even helped his gunners haul off their pieces so they might be saved. The late arriving cavalry, along with one Virginia regiment, fought a determined rearguard action long enough for the Americans to withdraw in reasonably good order. Each side lost approximately 250 men killed, wounded, and missing. Once again the British gained the ground but suffered casualties that they, unlike Greene, could not easily replace.

Besides fighting the fierce battle at Hobkirk's Hill, Greene had simultaneously unleashed the lethal combination of Lee's rapidly moving dragoons and marauding partisans. These forces raised havoc with British supply lines and picked off isolated enemy outposts one by one throughout the backcountry. Greene himself commanded the siege at Ninety Six, a Loyalist stronghold in western South Carolina. A hastily assembled relief expedition out of Charleston headed by Rawdon forced Greene to try a premature assault on June 18, which was bloodily repulsed. Greene gave up the siege 2 days later in order to avoid Rawdon's more powerful force. In this he succeeded and Rawdon elected to evacuate Ninety Six anyway as untenable. By mid-summer 1781, in a brilliant campaign, Greene had effectively broken the British hold on the region. Rawdon, the nominal victor at Hobkirk's Hill, was even forced to abandon the base at Camden. Shortly thereafter he returned to England, his health broken at age 27. The only British holdings remaining in the deep south were in and around Savannah and Charleston, where small garrisons sat, effectively bottled up. Greene colorfully described his method in this way: "There are few generals that has run oftener or more lustily than I have done . . . But I have taken care not to run too far and commonly have run as fast forward as backward, to convince our Enemy that we were like a Crab, that could run either way."[56] Despite his success, he remained in the field with his army for another 18 months, contemplating ways of forcing the British out of their remaining coastal enclaves.

For the hot summer of 1781, Greene moved his army to a plateau known as the High Hills of the Santee, roughly 100 miles north of the swampy, fetid low country surrounding Charleston. This area was somewhat cooler and healthier, and also defensible. Here he rested and awaited developments in Virginia as Washington, Rochambeau, and the French fleet closed upon Cornwallis. Naturally, he was not completely idle. He continued to orchestrate partisan efforts to plague the British and their Loyalist auxiliaries. And he dealt with a number of headaches originating not in the enemy, but rather the friendly camp.

The first two were perennial challenges faced by all American generals in the Revolution: maintaining an army on a shoestring and handling prickly, headstrong subordinates. From his perch above the Santee River, Greene continually reminded Congress that "To conduct a war which is carried on so much at arm's end . . . so remote from supplies of every kind . . . without money . . . is an unenviable task . . . this cannot be expected to continue without more effectual support."[57] Likewise, he had practically to beg hard-pressed and parochial state governors for support, and put up with the militia's short-term availability and maddening practice of going home at the worst possible moments. Regarding his lieutenants, Greene was fortunate in their fighting qualities, but several were difficult. Sumter was a South Carolina grandee who often seemed to be fighting his own private war. He also became sick—like Morgan, who had to leave for home shortly before Guilford Court House—and Greene had to cajole him to remain in the fray. Marion, who generally cooperated much better than Sumter, intensely disliked his fellow partisan and Greene had to manage their relationship carefully. Additionally, Marion had little use for many of the ragged men who joined his band and he yearned for a commission in the Continental line. Greene, of course, needed him to continue his highly effective leadership of irregulars. Finally, there was the mercurial "Light-Horse Harry" Lee, ambitious for glory, and often prone to feeling unappreciated and insufficiently recognized. Greene had to soothe his ego as well.

A problem rather more unique to the southern department concerned a scenario all-too-familiar to twenty-first century American soldiers—internecine struggle and the related challenge of restoring civil government. While patriots and Loyalists clashed in all of the 13 former colonies, conflict in the south was on a far greater scale and took on the aspects of a blood feud. In Greene's description, the appalling struggle was "truly shocking to humanity" and "rages like a fire and devours everything before it."[58] British occupation had destroyed state and local government in South Carolina and Georgia, creating a sort of Hobbesian state of nature. The clear-sighted Greene saw that the only practical way to bring peace and stability to the war-ravaged states lay in reestablishing the rule of law, which could proscribe murderers on both sides while simultaneously taking measures, such as pardons, to bring about reconciliation. Greene devoted much effort to urging these ideas on southern leaders.

In late August, guided by a combination of apprehension and opportunism, Greene sought to engage and destroy what remained of the British army outside Charleston. He feared that Cornwallis might quit Virginia at any moment and return to Charleston to shore up the British position in the Palmetto state. Simultaneously, he detected what appeared to be crumbling British strength and resolve. If he succeeded, Greene thought he might be able to retake Charleston and decisively finish the campaign. Greene's army of about 2,200 men moved stealthily southward until they came upon an enemy force of approximately equal size camped at Eutaw Springs, 30 miles northwest of Charleston. That this approach went undetected indicates how completely Greene's cavalry and partisans had won the intelligence battle over the preceding months.

On the morning of September 8, Greene's advance guard startled a foraging party that Lieutenant Colonel Alexander Stewart, Rawdon's successor, had sent forward to dig up yams for his hungry command. The Americans shot up the unarmed detail, as well as a smaller force that had been sent to watch over it, and took a considerable number of prisoners. Alerted by the firing and the fleeing survivors, Stewart deployed skirmishers to buy time to draw up the rest of his army. Greene came on in two ranks with North and South Carolina militia in the lead, backed up by Continentals from Virginia, Maryland, Delaware, and North Carolina. He placed cavalry on his flanks and kept a squadron of horse in reserve as well. Unlike previous battles, Greene's militia did not cut and run, but rather slugged it out with the British, exchanging several volleys with them. When the militia wavered, Greene sent forward a regiment of Continentals to stiffen them. The battle surged back and forth until Greene ordered his entire second line of Continentals forward with the bayonet. They drove the enemy before them and burst into the British camp.

It seemed Greene, the master strategist, had finally won the tactical victory that had heretofore eluded him. Fortune proved perverse however. Much of the enemy force had taken to its heels, save for the stubborn fighting of two right flank enemy battalions that prevented the Americans from exploiting their gains. One of them had occupied a large, three story brick house; the other a dense thicket. Both refused to be dislodged while keeping up a brisk fire. The scene was reminiscent of Germantown, 4 years earlier, where a similarly defended strongpoint had absorbed and dampened the momentum of an apparently irresistible American attack. Further contributing to disorganization and hampering any chance of decisive results, some of the Americans became engaged in looting the British camp, paying particular attention to its ample supply of rum. Greene, who had been in the thick of the fight and had a horse shot from under him, reluctantly decided to pull back. His men were spent after a long, hot march and stiff fight, and Stewart, a few miles down the road toward Charleston, was rallying his men to renew the battle. In Greene's own words, Eutaw Springs "was by far the most bloody and obstinate" battle of the campaign.[59] The butcher's bill came to nearly 500 Americans and perhaps twice as many British, including 400 taken prisoner.

Before Eutaw Springs, Greene believed he verged on the climactic battle for South Carolina. Indeed, to Henry Lee he dramatically said "we must have victory or ruin."[60] The battle yielded neither and, after Cornwallis's October surrender at Yorktown, the southern department settled into the same kind of tense standoff that obtained in the north. Greene still wished to take Charleston and was disappointed that the French fleet did not make for there following Yorktown. Washington, before returning to New York, did provide some reinforcements, including Anthony Wayne, whom Greene sent to pressure Savannah. Throughout 1782 Greene maintained a loose siege of Charleston. In order to demonstrate and show scorn for lapsed British power, the reconstituted South Carolina legislature convened just a few miles outside the city in January under Greene's protection. Peace negotiations dragged on abroad, but the British has already decided to evacuate their remaining footholds in the new United States. They left Savannah in July and in December sailed away from Charleston forever, taking thousands of Loyalists with them. On the afternoon of December 14, Greene, Wayne, and the governor of South Carolina triumphantly entered the city at the head of a mixed column of soldiers and joyful civilians.

Honors, annoyances, and an ugly contracting scandal characterized Greene's final months in the army. The grateful governments of Georgia, North Carolina, and South Carolina all voted him large tracts of land as a reward for his services. At the same time, Greene occasionally jeopardized this goodwill by quarreling with the states over jurisdiction between himself as a military commander in the field and civil authority. He also indulged his habit of preaching to them the virtues of a national vice local outlook. More seriously, he confronted soldier unrest and threats of mutiny in the face of continued supply shortages and their desire to go home after the fighting had stopped. The genesis of the contracting mess lay in Greene's determination to obtain food and clothing for his men during the winter of 1782–1783. Two of Greene's subordinates were secret partners of the commercial agent with whom he made arrangements to supply his men. Soon they were not-so-secret partners and rumors ignited—doubtless fueled by the controversy surrounding his quartermaster troubles—that Greene had speculated with government funds and worse, that he himself held an interest in the company. Predictably, his friends defended and enemies assailed him. A contemporary investigation revealed no hard evidence of improper behavior and historians have found none since. Nevertheless, it was not only homesickness that made Greene glad to relinquish his command and head for home in August 1783.

His return north was a leisurely and adulatory procession. Southerners especially hailed him for delivering their states. He frequently visited with old comrades along the way before reuniting with Washington at Trenton in early October. One can only imagine the emotions felt by two men who had not seen each other for 3 years, meeting at the site of their desperate Yuletide triumph in perhaps the Revolution's darkest hour. Taking leave of Washington and Congress, Greene finally arrived to a hero's welcome in Newport. Along with Kitty and his brothers he resumed both family life and business career, but poor investments and bad luck, as well as the overall sluggishness of the postwar economy, plunged him into debt. A brace of suits brought by various creditors exacerbated his difficulties. During his time in the south Greene thought he perceived great opportunities, and now he traveled back and forth to the region on business. Eventually, in the fall of 1785, he moved to Georgia and settled at Mulberry Grove, the plantation given to him by the state. One of his neighbors was Anthony Wayne, who had been the recipient of a similar gift. Fate granted him precious little time to enjoy his new home. While inspecting a neighbor's fields in early summer 1786 he evidently fell victim to sunstroke and he died a week later on June 19. He had not yet attained age 45.

The days and weeks following Greene's death witnessed an outpouring of praise and honor. Initially laid to rest at an Episcopal church in Savannah, in 1820 his remains were reentombed beneath a monument to him in the center of that beautiful city. Although his memory has faded, no doubt due in some measure to his untimely demise, the historical record is clear for those who care to examine it. He and Washington were the only two generals at the siege of Boston who served continuously throughout the 8 years of the war. Washington relied heavily upon him for operational advice until Greene went south in 1780. In the event of his own death, incapacity, or capture, the Virginian viewed Greene as his logical successor. Greene's actions as quartermaster probably saved the army at Valley Forge. Most notably, his southern campaign remains unique in American military annals. Fighting from a position of inferiority in materiel and trained soldiers, he combined partisans and regulars, retreat and advance in such a way as to prise the countryside from the enemy's grip and wreck his armies. These accomplishments entitle him to recognition as the preeminent military strategist of the Revolution.

Ambitious Fighters

Benedict Arnold and John Paul Jones

THE OLD CADET CHAPEL overlooks the Hudson River on the grounds of the United States Military Academy at West Point. This beautiful Greek Revival structure, built in 1837, stands watch over a cemetery that began as a Revolutionary War burial ground and today contains dead from all of America's wars. Inside, along the east wall, are black memorial tablets to George Washington and each of his generals. One plaque differs from the others. Near the choir loft hangs a tablet where the name has been effaced, leaving only the words, "Major General, Born 1740."[1] According to Academy legend, generations of nineteenth-century cadets succeeded in scratching out the name of Benedict Arnold, disgraced by treason.

Some 250 miles to the south, at Annapolis, Maryland, the green patina dome of the United States Naval Academy Chapel commands the skyline. Beneath the transept, in a magnificent marble sarcophagus, lie the mortal remains of John Paul Jones. For nearly a century, Midshipmen have been inspired by the words carved on the tomb, "He gave our Navy its earliest traditions of heroism and victory."

In spite of their radically different legacies at the United States' premier service academies, Arnold and Jones shared important similarities. They stand as two of the Revolution's most capable and ferocious fighters. Each was ambitious in the extreme—for recognition, rank, and financial reward. In their hunger for the first of these they resembled Shakespeare's Henry V, who confessed, "If it be a sin to covet honor, I am the most offending soul alive." Their victories on land and water came at crucial moments, and count among the Americans' most vital. Each felt, with some justification, that Congress and their fellow officers overlooked their sacrifices and service. Consequently, they nursed grievances against that body and those who had been preferred over them. Arnold succumbed to his resentment while Jones rose above his. Oddly enough, each died in a foreign capital essentially as men without a country—Arnold in London, Jones in Paris—alone and unhonored. The former remains eternally notorious while time, in the case of the latter, has rescued merit from oblivion.

BENEDICT ARNOLD

Benedict Arnold was a study in extremes and contrasts. Shrewd and calculating in business and war; he was simultaneously impulsive and unwise in politics and his personal relations. He possessed a hot, quick temper, and an excessive belligerence. He gloried in hardship and danger, and loved luxury. He became America's greatest traitor, coming nearer to ruining her bid for independence than any one man. And he was perhaps the patriots' greatest battlefield general, whose actions at critical moments did as much as anyone to preserve that same cause. Indeed, his perfidy shook the Revolutionary generation to its core precisely because he had been such a towering hero prior to his treason. He was a Miltonian figure, resembling the Lucifer of *Paradise Lost* who fell from luminous glory to the darkest pit.

Arnold was born in Norwich, Connecticut, on January 14, 1741. He had five siblings of whom only a sister, named Hannah after their mother, survived to adulthood. His father was also called Benedict; in fact, the future general represented the fifth generation to bear the name. An older brother, who died in 1739 before he achieved the age of one, was christened Benedict as well; necronominy was a common practice in colonial America, reflective of the grimly high rates of infant mortality in those times. The family had come to New England in the seventeenth century and prospered. A distant ancestor, the first Benedict as it happened, had been a colonial governor of Rhode Island.

The family's fortunes fluctuated, though young Benedict spent his early years in relative comfort. That changed as his father began a descent into financial ruin and alcoholism when the boy was only 13. His cash-strapped parents withdrew him from the boarding school he had been attending and ultimately apprenticed him to wealthy relations on his mother's side. These gentlemen, who operated a successful apothecary and general merchandise business, gladly took him on. Arnold demonstrated great aptitude for trade and spent his teenage years learning it thoroughly, with only the briefest interruption to muster for militia duty in 1757, in response to an invasion scare during the French and Indian War. By 1761, both his parents were dead. He had no inheritance to speak of, but his patrons saw great potential in Arnold and they set him up as a merchant in New Haven.

Arnold—by now a good-looking, solidly built young man of about $5\frac{1}{2}$ feet tall with a dark complexion and jet black hair—thrived as a businessman. He dealt in a variety of products, ranging from patent medicines to books to rum and sugar. He found commercial partners with whom he purchased and operated three sailing vessels, which carried his goods to and from Canada and the West Indies. Arnold himself took to the sea and frequently sailed to distant ports as his own shipmaster. Based upon his apothecary trade and ocean voyages, his respectful fellow townsman commonly addressed him as both "Doctor Arnold" and "Captain Arnold." As befitted a very eligible bachelor, and up and coming gentleman, Arnold took Margaret Mansfield, daughter of New Haven's sheriff, as his wife in 1767. She bore him three sons before her untimely death in 1775.

As a leading citizen and merchant, Arnold could not avoid engagement in the imperial crisis that brewed up between Great Britain and her 13 American colonies following the conclusion of the French and Indian War in 1763. The Stamp Act and other British legislation such as the Townshend Duties directly affected his livelihood, as well of those of hundreds of other merchants, including such luminaries as Boston's John Hancock. Like Hancock, Arnold routinely engaged in smuggling to circumvent the laws and also participated in antitax agitation in his community. His radicalism increased when he learned of the Boston Massacre in 1770. He wrote passionately about the "cruel, wanton, and inhuman murders committed" by the redcoats and asked, "Good God, are the Americans all asleep and tamely giving up their liberties ... that they don't take immediate vengeance on such miscreants."[2] He also joined a militia company composed of New Haven's leading citizens—formed to defend their liberties against Parliament's encroachments—in late 1774 and his fellows elected him their captain.

When fighting broke out at Lexington and Concord in April, 1775, Arnold, like many New Englanders, burned to march his company to the sound of the guns and join the patriot hosts assembling in Cambridge. The somewhat more conservative New Haven town meeting, however, displayed reluctance to give Arnold access to the community's store of ball and powder. Arnold, backed by his wildly enthusiastic men, threatened to break down the door to the magazine, vowing that "None but Almighty God shall prevent my marching!"[3] The thoroughly intimidated town fathers surrendered the key.

Somewhere along the road north, Arnold conceived the idea of seizing the ramshackle and lightly defended British fortress on Lake Champlain, Fort Ticonderoga. This "Gibraltar of the Wilderness" had been a vital position during the earlier war for empire between Great Britain and France. It contained a large artillery park, whose pieces the patriots could use to drive the British out of Boston. Shortly after arriving in Cambridge, Arnold presented his thoughts to the Massachusetts Committee of Safety, a subordinate element of the Bay Colony's Provincial Congress that provided political direction for the patriots in the ongoing crisis. This body readily assented to Arnold's proposal and commissioned the Connecticut captain a colonel in the service of Massachusetts.

The notion of a *coup de main* against Ticonderoga had simultaneously occurred to other Americans as well, most notably a collection of Connecticut men of affairs. These worthies approached Ethan Allen, the leader of a freebooting outfit—the Green Mountain Boys—that operated in what is modern-day Vermont, an area that both New York and New Hampshire claimed. Allen agreed to take charge of an expedition to seize the fortress. By May 9, 1775, a combined force of Connecticut and Massachusetts volunteers, and Allen's rollicking Boys, numbering around 250 men, had assembled on Lake Champlain's eastern side, ready to cross by boat and seize the fortress.

Arnold moved to the Champlain region ahead of his Massachusetts command, which was in the process of being recruited by his subordinates, and soon got wind of Allen's expedition. Spurring his horse, he came upon the attack force while it was in the midst of final preparations for a predawn assault on May 10. An indignant Arnold protested his right to command; the truculent Boys retorted that Colonel Arnold had no troops and that they would follow Allen or no one. Arnold possessed but one trump card—his Massachusetts commission. Perhaps fearful that he had no official authorization—his Connecticut backers represented no one but a group of private citizens—Allen eventually agreed to allow Arnold to accompany the enterprise as a "volunteer."

Although a shortage of boats permitted only one third of the rebels to make the crossing, the operation came off with ridiculous ease. The attackers caught the sleepy British completely unawares and Ticonderoga fell bloodlessly in under a quarter of an hour. Allen's exuberant ruffians began to celebrate their triumph, lubricated by 90 gallons of rum belonging to the fort's late commander. Never tightly disciplined to begin with, the intoxicated Boys offered insults and threats to the presumptuous Arnold, and a couple even discharged their muskets in his direction. Arnold displayed great sangfroid, correctly guessing that, their heroic deed accomplished, most of Allen's rabble would melt away back to their homesteads, which is what occurred.

Meanwhile, Arnold's Massachusetts captains began arriving with their recruits in tow. By May 14, commanding the majority of on-hand troops, Arnold found himself in the position of advantage previously held by Allen. The latter ceded primacy to Arnold over not only Ticonderoga, but also the smaller bastion of Crown Point, 10 miles north, which also had fallen into patriot hands. Arnold was not slow in exploiting opportunities to strike further blows. Some patriots had confiscated a lake schooner belonging to a wealthy Loyalist and sailed it down lake to Ticonderoga. Arnold armed it with small cannon and boldly mounted his own private invasion of Canada. On the morning of May 18 Arnold's raiders fell upon the—incredibly enough given recent events—unwary redcoats at St. John's, 25 miles north of the New York border. Arnold took them prisoner, burned some boats, and made off with several others.

These warlike activities on Lake Champlain presented an embarrassing quandary to the Second Continental Congress, which had convened the very day that Ticonderoga fell. The delegates, faced with the outbreak of shooting in Massachusetts only weeks earlier, wavered between defiance and reconciliation. Advocates of the latter course temporarily gained the upper hand in Philadelphia and ordered withdrawal from the captured forts, with the captured cannon and other stores to be safely guarded until the hoped for restoration of harmony between Great Britain and her colonies. Arnold and Allen, still on the scene, both agreed that this was madness. Arnold wrote Congress that evacuation would throw those patriotic Americans living in Ticonderoga's vicinity "into the greatest confusion" and expose them to British and Indian reprisals from Canada. He considered the old fort "the key of this extensive country" and believed that the cost of quitting it would be much heavier "than the expense of repairing and garrisoning it."[4] Going much further, he also advocated using the upper Champlain forts as a launch point for an invasion of Canada aimed at gaining control of Quebec province.

Others—particularly those from the New England colonies most directly menaced by a British descent from Canada—voiced similar views. Congress quickly reversed itself, and dictated the fortification and strengthening of the captured outposts. By late June 1775, Congress also voted to add Canada to the patriot fold as the "fourteenth colony." Although this represented a victory of sorts for Arnold, overall, his initial foray into war, and especially the politics of war, proved frustrating. He had demonstrated commendable tactical acumen, strategic insight, and initiative. Still, he had earned little credit or renown. Allen proved much more skilled in the art of self-promotion, trumpeting his role far and wide, while failing to acknowledge Arnold. Other officers in the Champlain theater denigrated Arnold in reports back to Congress or their home colonies. Arnold confronted one of these and challenged him to a duel. When the man refused to offer satisfaction, Arnold contented himself with applying a swift kick to the man's backside. Worst of all, Massachusetts, whose writ had been Arnold's source of authority at Ticonderoga, demoted him to serve under another officer there. Thoroughly fed up, Arnold "resigned my commission, not being able to hold it longer with honor."[5]

Arnold started home in early July. While passing through Albany he looked in upon the newly installed commander of the patriot's northern department, General Philip Schuyler. Arnold created a favorable impression, which augmented positive—especially in contrast to the confusion and disorder reigning under his successors—accounts of his conduct on Lake Champlain that also reached Schuyler. Word of his wife's death caused Arnold to cut short his Albany sojourn and speed his way to Connecticut. After settling his sons with his sister, and newly buoyed by Schuyler's patronage, he traveled to Massachusetts to settle his expenses with the Provincial Congress and, more significantly, offer his services to the Continental Army's commander in chief, George Washington.

Congress had authorized Schuyler to lead the main invasion force into Canada, but several other patriots contemplated a supporting attack up through the Maine wilderness aimed at Quebec City. Arnold was one of these and he found a receptive listener in Washington. As had been the case with Schuyler, Arnold's qualities of imagination and energy impressed him greatly. The Virginian rapidly secured a Continental colonel's commission for Arnold and designated him to conduct the operation. Arnold began logistical preparations, to include ordering the construction of 200 light bateaux for negotiating the northern waterways. Washington called for volunteers and ultimately some 1,100 men (and two women—soldier's wives) answered. These represented two battalions of musket-carrying infantry, as well as three companies of riflemen under the control of Daniel Morgan.

Interestingly, among those on the expedition were a pair officers who, along with Arnold, later achieved great infamy: Aaron Burr and James Wilkinson. Nevertheless, the latter two behaved creditably on this occasion; Arnold's performance was epically heroic.

The force marshaled at Newburyport, Massachusetts, boarded ship, and set sail September 19, 1775, up the New England coast. They arrived at Gardinerstown, Maine, 3 days later and found their bateaux, along with supplies, waiting. Arnold was eager to commence, not only in hopes of reaching Quebec before the British reinforced it, but also to complete the journey before the arrival of ferocious winter weather. In the event, fortune deserted him on both accounts. The British quickly learned of the expedition from their Indian auxiliaries and by intercepting Arnold's couriers, and the elements ultimately proved atrocious. The 45-day, 350-mile ordeal began in earnest on September 25. Arnold divided his command into four separate columns in order to preclude them becoming entangled at the many portage spots—places where the men would have to carry their boats from one stream to another—along their route.

Morgan's woodsman led the procession up the Kennebec River while Arnold and a small party, including friendly Indian scouts, moved among the separated elements in a dugout canoe. The exhilarated colonel shouted "To Quebec and victory!" each time he passed one of his detachments.[6] The first part of the journey was hardly easy; a mere recitation of the itinerary gives a sense of its challenges: Ticonic Falls, Five Mile Ripples, Skowhegan Falls, Bombazee Rips, and three separate Norridgewock Falls. Additionally, the route required numerous portages where the men shouldered their 400-pound boats through the trackless woods and swamps. Nevertheless, the weather remained benign and the patriots obtained needed supplies from occasional settlements that dotted their route. Ominously, however, the bateaux, constructed of green lumber, were falling apart and water had already ruined a large portion of the provisions.

By October 11, Arnold and the lead elements had left all traces of civilization behind. They traversed the Great Carrying Place, which required an 8-mile portage, interspersed with 4 miles of paddling across three ponds. This brought them to the Dead River and an arduous 30-mile ascent. As Arnold, with some understatement, reported to Washington, it was "a very fatiguing time."[7] The temperature plummeted, heavy late autumn rains began to fall, food shortages materialized, and sickness began to take a heavy toll. An especially severe storm on October 21 caused the Dead River to swell to 200 feet in width, more than three times its norm. This played havoc with the boats and led to the loss of a considerable quantity of the meager remaining food stocks, as well as much ammunition and powder. Arnold called a council of war with all his available officers 2 days later to decide whether to press on or abort the mission.

Inspired by their stout-hearted commander, the officers determined to continue. Essentially, the command now engaged in a race against time and distance. It was imperative to reach the French–Canadian settlements on the Chaudiere River and obtain fresh supplies before starvation set in. In order to accomplish this, Arnold evacuated his weakest men and led a handpicked party of 50 to forge ahead, procure the needed rations, and dispatch them back toward the advancing main body. At about this time, Arnold wrote Washington again, confessing frankly "I have been much deceived in every account of our route, which is longer, and has been attended with a thousand difficulties I never apprehended." He then continued, "but if crowned with success, and conducive to the public good, I shall think it but trifling."[8] This advance guard reached a cluster of French *habitant* houses on October 30 and an overjoyed Arnold purchased the desperately needed supplies, including several bullocks. These reached his trailing troopers who "shed tears of joy, in our happy delivery from the grasping hand of death," on November 2.[9]

Although Arnold was unaware of it until later, one of those "thousand difficulties" had transpired in the rear of his column. On October 25, a group of officers decided that it was madness to continue farther and therefore quit the expedition, taking some 300 men with them. In the short term, this desertion ameliorated Arnold's supply difficulties, but in the longer run, 300 muskets would be sorely missed at Quebec. Washington subsequently charged the most senior of the retreating officers with desertion, but a court-martial acquitted him, in part because all those who could have testified against the deserter were by then at Quebec—in many instances dead, wounded, or captive.

Meanwhile, Arnold's refreshed command, reduced to about 700 effectives, pushed ahead, covering the remaining 70 miles or so by foot to the southern shore of the St. Lawrence River in a week's time. En route, the men gathered further supplies and Arnold exhorted the *habitants*, without much success, to join the cause of American liberty. This stage, although much less taxing than what preceded it, was grueling enough, as the men churned through mud and snow. On November 9, Arnold finally laid eyes on his objective, viewing through swirling flurries the walled citadel of Quebec rising on steep cliffs above the northern bank of the St. Lawrence.

Arnold burned to get across, but the requirement to gather boats and gale force winds delayed him until the night of November 13. Despite drawing fire from enemy patrol boats in the river, Arnold was able to assemble his force on the enemy shore by the next morning. He paraded them in sight of the ramparts, unsuccessfully challenging Quebec's defenders to sally forth and fight. This they wisely refused to do, amply supplied and snug behind their thick fortifications. Arnold sent ultimatums, promising mercy for immediate capitulation, but warning "if I am obliged to carry the town by storm, you may expect every severity practiced upon such occasions."[10] This was a hollow threat; the British had managed to reinforce the city and were impervious to assault. Arnold's march had been a magnificent feat of human endurance and a tribute to his indomitable leadership. For the moment, however, all he could do was withdraw to a point outside Quebec to await the arrival of the other American pincer, coming over from Montreal, which had fallen to the patriots the same day Arnold breached the St. Lawrence.

The two commands linked up on December 2, 1775, about 20 miles southwest of Quebec. Overall command devolved upon Brigadier General Richard

Montgomery, an exceedingly competent former officer in the British Army, who had assumed control of the main invasion force when Schuyler fell ill. Although Montgomery arrived with only 300 men, he also brought ammunition, artillery, and supplies that included warm winter clothing, much wanted by Arnold's threadbare troops. The patriots' combined strength now totaled about 1,000 men, half as many as those defending Quebec. The Americans moved to the Plains of Abraham, to the west of the city on December 5. Montgomery subsequently positioned Arnold's men on his left hand side, to the northwestern suburb of St. Roch.

The two American leaders respected each other and worked well together. They faced a daunting challenge. Not only were they outnumbered, but the enlistments of many of Arnold's New Englanders were due to expire by year's end. Viewing withdrawal as unthinkable, Montgomery and Arnold considered two options: siege or storm. Lack of heavy artillery and Quebec's well-stocked commissary forestalled the first. The Americans thus resolved to assault the bastion under the cover of darkness and foul weather prior to January 1. After a false start on December 27, favorable conditions—a howling blizzard—arose on December 30.

Two desultory diversionary efforts—some sporadic firing and the launch of rockets—to the west of Quebec did little more than alert the British defenders. Well after midnight, Montgomery led one column down to the south of the city and along a treacherous footpath with the icy St. Lawrence to his right and the city walls hard on his left. Meanwhile, Arnold personally spearheaded his element of about 600 men around the northern edge of the fortress with the intention of joining Montgomery at Quebec's lower entrance. The two forces would then attempt to fight their way in and carry the remainder of the town.

This desperate plan was doomed from the outset. Arnold's men, advancing single file along a narrow pathway, encountered a wooden barricade erected along their attack route. While Arnold huddled with his officers in the street below in order to devise a breaching scheme, the British loosed a devastating volley of musket and cannon fire. Arnold fell, conscious but badly wounded in his lower left leg. Captain Daniel Morgan bravely strode up and, after briefly conferring with Arnold, assumed command. He arranged for his colonel to be evacuated while he pressed the attack forward. Arnold demurred, but was too weak from blood loss and shock to resist. The patriot surgeon patched Arnold up in a makeshift aid station about a mile to the rear. Arnold, agonizing in body and spirit, could only listen to the dismal reports that floated back to him, carried by wounded and fleeing troopers. Montgomery's column had been repulsed and the American general killed. Morgan made a gallant try, but he and most of the men with him—over 400—had been captured. About 60 Americans across the entire attack force were killed; the defenders suffered negligible losses, fewer than 20 dead or wounded.

Severely hobbled by his wound, Arnold remained defiant. As he wrote to his sister shortly after the defeat, "I have no thoughts of leaving this proud town, until I first enter it in triumph."[11] He reconstituted the shattered American forces and reestablished a partial cordon around the walled city. Fortunately, the British displayed no inclination to venture out and annihilate the ragged Americans. Arnold implored Washington and Congress for more troops so that he could try again before the enemy reinforced Quebec. The thousands he requested were simply not available, nor could they have been expected to march into Canada in the dead of winter even if they had been. Nevertheless, Arnold did receive a trickle of men. General David Wooster, whom Montgomery had left in charge of Montreal when he moved on Quebec, sent 150 troopers. And Congress dispatched others up the Champlain–St. Lawrence corridor conquered by Montgomery the previous autumn.

Arnold's boldness earned him accolades. Washington thanked him for his "enterprising and persevering spirit" and Congress named him a brigadier general.[12] Arnold welcomed these expressions of confidence, but likened his difficulties, bereft of men and supplies, to those of "the Israelites of old, obliged to make brick without straw."[13] His spirits sank further in early April when Wooster, Arnold's senior, arrived from Montreal to take charge of operations. Wooster, a fellow native of the Nutmeg State, was an unpleasant and incompetent 64-year-old veteran of ancient colonial wars. An antagonized Arnold sought and received permission to withdraw to Montreal, in effect exchanging command billets with Wooster.

The Americans had ostensibly invaded Canada in order to win her inhabitants over to the glorious cause. In Montreal, Arnold found himself playing the role of diplomat as well as soldier. Congress attempted to aid him by sending a delegation headed by Benjamin Franklin northward. The new general impressed the commissioners, but their mission, like the entire Canadian venture, proved fruitless. Although Arnold pledged to do "everything in my power ... to keep possession of this country, which has cost us so much blood and expense," by early May he recognized that the tide had turned against the patriots.[14] Over 8,000 redcoats and Hessians arrived to break the siege at Quebec and soon moved irresistibly up the St. Lawrence, pushing the Americans back. Simultaneously, a combined British and Indian force attacked Montreal from the southwest, a maneuver that the energetic Arnold managed to check.

Arnold had set out for Canada 9 months previously; now in June 1776, he prepared to quit that country. He had not lost heart, despite almost unimaginable hardship and reverses. He saw a need to regroup, informing Congress, "We had much better begin anew, and set out right and methodically."[15] His firm leadership, so crucial over the preceding months, proved just as vital in preventing retreat from turning into route. He organized the patriot withdrawal up the Richelieu River and back into New York, commanding the rear guard, and ensuring in a typically flamboyant *beau geste* that he was the last patriot soldier to leave Canadian soil.

The summer of 1776 was tumultuous for Arnold, replete with political, legal, and personal battles, as well as military operations. Besides declaring independence, Congress conducted inquiries into the failure of the Canadian campaign. Rather than investigate its own shortcomings in providing direction and resources, that body cast about for military scapegoats. Arnold, as one of the ranking officers, came in for his share of censure. The aspersions rankled him no end, given his exertions while Congress remained secure in Philadelphia. This was not the first slight to the touchy Arnold's *amour propre*—it reminded him of his earlier ill treatment by the Massachusetts assembly—nor would it be the last, and in time he would come to question both Congress's gratitude and its commitment to the cause for which he was sacrificing so much.

Arnold also became embroiled in a nasty dispute with some of his fellow officers. While in command at Montreal, he had accused a subordinate of dereliction concerning a number of Canadian merchants whose stocks had been plundered. This individual demanded a court-martial. When seated in August, the tribunal outraged Arnold by seeming to question his character and favoring the accused at his expense. Arnold blasted the court both verbally and in writing. Tempers escalated and Arnold wound up offering to meet its members on the dueling ground, declaring, "as soon as this disagreeable service is at an end . . . I will by no means withhold from any gentleman of the court the satisfaction his nice honor may require."[16] The hearing responded by finding the accused not guilty and, further, demanding Arnold's arrest for his intemperate behavior. Arnold's immediate supervisor, Major General Horatio Gates, responded by dissolving the court. Danger threatened from the north and the army's senior leadership recognized that Arnold's talents were indispensable. As Gates told Congress, "the United States must not be deprived of that excellent officer's service at this important moment."[17]

The British in Canada had assembled an enormous army—13,000 men all told, including redcoats, Hessians, Canadian militia, and Indian auxiliaries. In September, this host ponderously began to move south along the St. Lawrence–Champlain corridor. Combined with the equally massive British force that then threatened—and soon would seize—New York City, this posed the supreme danger of splitting New York and the Middle Colonies away from New England. Besides the upper Champlain forts, still in American hands, if in considerable disrepair, the only way to check the enemy advance was by deploying a fleet on the lake to oppose their waterborne progress. By virtue of his previous maritime experience, the commanders on the scene tasked Arnold to organize and lead the American effort. All summer, while simultaneously warring with his antagonists in Congress and the army, Arnold raced to ready his flotilla.

Arnold—displaying the same superhuman drive that characterized the march to Quebec—completed a masterpiece of improvisation in creating a freshwater fleet virtually from scratch. The Americans had begun with three mid-size vessels—two schooners and a sloop—taken from the British earlier. In spite of shortages of materials and ship-building expertise, Arnold managed to have four galleys and nine gundalows constructed. Both types of vessel were propelled by a combination of oars and sails. The galleys, 72-feet long, were crewed by about 80 men each. The gundalows measured just over 50 feet and carried approximately half as many "sailors"—actually, mostly land lubbers. All of these craft mounted a motley armament ranging from 18 to 2-pounders and swivel guns.

By September 23, 1776, Arnold had taken station with 15 vessels at the northern end of Lake Champlain, anchoring in a narrow channel between Valcour Island and the lake's west bank. Here, for nearly 3 weeks, he awaited the arrival of the British juggernaut. On October 11, it hove into view. Arnold and his men anxiously watched as at least 50 vessels—schooners, gunboats, and barges full of troops—majestically glided uplake toward them. Although seriously overmatched in men and firepower, Arnold rejected his lieutenants' preference for immediate flight. He realized that the swifter British vessels, with a strong northerly wind behind them, would overtake his boats in open water and destroy them in detail. Instead, he opted to remain snug and, as yet, undetected, in the three-quarter-mile wide channel. Should his flotilla be spotted, Arnold counted upon the constricted space hindering the enemy from bringing all guns to bear at one time. What he really hoped for was that the British would hug the lake's east shore and cruise past Valcour Island, allowing Arnold to use the wind to advantage in attacking them from the flank and rear.

It played out exactly as Arnold wished. Around noon, he dispatched his fastest vessels, including his flagship, the galley *Congress*, toward the British to lure them into the channel, where the rest of his flotilla waited in line of battle facing south. The enemy fleet took the bait and, with difficulty, turned into the stiff wind and gave chase. Bad fortune now struck the Americans. The schooner *Royal Savage*, Arnold's most powerful ship, ran aground on the island's southwestern edge due to a combination of bad handling, treacherous winds, and British cannonading. Her crew abandoned her as a vicious, 7-hour slugfest commenced in the channel between the remaining American craft and 15–20 British gunboats. Because the Americans "suffered much for want of seamen and gunners," Arnold himself had "to point most of the guns on the *Congress*, which I believe did good execution."[18] The two sides traded shot at a range of about 100 yards, turning the channel into a cauldron of smoke and thunder. Adding to the din and the danger, the British landed troops on both sides of the channel to take the Americans under a hail of musket fire.

At dusk, the British pulled back, confident that they would finish off the Americans the next day. Arnold had other ideas and, under cover of darkness and fog, the American flotilla silently crept past the British fleet along the lake's west shore. Dawn revealed to the British that their quarry had escaped and they turned about to give chase. The wind had shifted 180 degrees and now blew from the south, so both sides had to row against it. The grim chase lasted all day on October 12, with the Americans only covering 6 miles in an ordeal of backbreaking labor. By daybreak of the 13th, Arnold's vessels were still 30 miles from the friendly post of Crown Point. Once again, however, the wind changed and the British profited to close the gap dramatically between them and their prey.

In the middle of the lake, all the advantages lay with the larger, more powerful British armada and by afternoon it had made short work of the Americans. Arnold had *Congress* rowed to the eastern side of the lake and deliberately grounded it, along his other surviving boats. To prevent them from falling into the enemy's clutches, he burned them with their colors still flying defiantly. That night, he led their crews, about 200 men, on a 10-mile march through woods teeming with hostile Indians to Crown Point. Believing that place indefensible, Arnold collected its garrison, set its buildings alight, and continued south to Ticonderoga, reaching it "extremely fatigued and unwell, having been without sleep or refreshment for near three days."[19]

Arnold lost 11 out of the vessels with which he began the Battle of Valcour Island, along with 80 killed or wounded and another 200 taken prisoner. British losses were slight. They had gained a tactical victory, but it turned out to be an American operational and strategic triumph. The overly cautious British commander, impressed by the stoutness of Arnold's resistance and fearing that it augured more of the same, determined that it was too late in the year to press the offensive and retired into Canada. Given the true state of the Americans' position at Ticonderoga, Arnold's performance likely saved upper New York state, and perhaps the entire Revolution.

His aggressive defense of Lake Champlain initially earned Arnold much praise. Soon enough, however, a handful of vengeful junior officers whom he had crossed with his abrasiveness, as well as some overzealous congressmen, began finding fault with him. Comments bruited around Philadelphia portrayed him as a maniacal glory seeker whose inept handling of his fleet had resulted in its annihilation. For Arnold these slurs presently merited no attention. In December, with the enemy's northern threat abated for the winter, Gates led eight regiments from Ticonderoga to succor Washington's army, which was then retreating through New Jersey. Arnold accompanied the reinforcements and actually arrived at Washington's headquarters on the west bank of the Delaware River a few days ahead of the main body. Here the commander in chief apprised him of his daring plan for a Christmas night stroke against the Hessian outpost across the river at Trenton. And he assigned Arnold a new mission: hasten to Rhode Island to stiffen patriot defenses against a threatened British attack there.

After a brief sojourn in New Haven to reacquaint himself with family and friends he had not seen in over a year, Arnold reported to Providence on January 12, 1777. The British had seized Newport a month earlier, but Arnold quickly discerned that they had no inclination to attempt further offensive action. Indeed, His Majesty's forces throughout North America were content to rest on their arms until spring. Restless, Arnold traveled to Boston, where he spent a month caught up in the society whirl. A certain "heavenly Miss De Blois" attracted his amorous gaze, but his affections went unreturned.[20] A more serious rebuff greeted him when he returned to Providence in March.

Washington had beseeched Congress to expand the Continental Army, to include the creation of more general officer positions. As part of this, Congress appointed five new major generals. Despite being the army's senior brigadier and his unquestioned merit in the eyes of senior patrons such as Washington and Schuyler, Arnold was not on the promotion list. He had fallen victim to politics—the furious horse-trading among congressmen to secure billets for their states. Since Congress felt that Connecticut already had its "fair share" of major generals—two—in proportion to the troops it supplied to the war effort, Arnold failed to gain advancement. Washington tactfully informed his valued subordinate of this result and asked that he not take any rash action until he could make inquiries. Washington, always careful to bow to civil authority, circumspectly pressed Arnold's case, but to no avail. Arnold believed that this mortal slight resulted from calumnies heaped on him by jealous rivals "busy with my fame" and the "whim and caprice" of a feckless Congress. He reacted furiously, "By heavens I will have justice, and I'm a villain if I seek not a brave revenge for injured honor."[21]

In mid-April, with Washington's leave, he departed Rhode Island intent on personally tendering his resignation to Congress in Philadelphia. New Haven lay along his route and once again he stopped to enjoy a brief respite with family. Before he could resume his journey, a substantial seaborne British raiding force landed near Norwalk, about 30 miles to the west, with designs on the American supply depot at Danbury. Frantically awakened by his neighbors in the early morning hours of April 26, Arnold set aside his grievances and rode in a pouring rain toward the commotion. By the time he reached the vicinity of Danbury, the enemy had not only destroyed the patriot stores, but had burned most of the town as well and was now withdrawing to their ships. About 600 Connecticut militia had mustered and Arnold, along with other officers on the scene, determined to exact retribution. Arnold took the bulk of the force and established a blocking position along the enemy's return route near the small village of Ridgefield.

The British column, 2,000-strong and flushed with victory, approached the anxious militia, dug in across the road, late on the afternoon of April 27. When a frontal attack failed to dislodge the Americans, the British flanked them and began delivering enfilade fire. This proved too much for the citizen-soldiers and they began to flee. Arnold attempted to rally them and had his horse killed under him for his pains. An enemy trooper lunged at Arnold, pinned beneath the dead animal. Arnold coolly shot him dead with a pistol, extricated himself, and limped off to safety. Still full of fight, he labored all night to reconstitute his force and by the next morning somehow established another defensive position just north of Norwalk. Sadly, the militia proved unworthy of their general. The redcoats easily brushed them aside, despite Arnold's ferocity, and regained their ships. The militia's timidity furnished Arnold another opportunity to reflect on his fellow countrymen's lack of patriotic virtue. "I wish never to see another of them in action," he wrote shortly afterward.[22]

Although the Danbury raid was a relatively minor action, Arnold's gallant behavior caught Congress's notice and perhaps pricked its collective conscience. And Washington's tactful, behind the scenes advocacy must have helped as well. Certainly fighting generals were scarce enough. In any event, on May 2, Congress suddenly named Arnold a major general, approvingly citing "his vigilance, activity, and bravery in the late affair at Connecticut."[23] Arnold remained determined to confront Congress, however. For one thing, although it promoted him, Congress failed to restore his seniority over the earlier named major generals. And he still had expenses to settle dating back to the Canadian expedition, where he paid out of his own pocket to provision his troops. Finally, a scurrilous pamphlet published by an ex-officer attacked his character. Arnold wanted a board of inquiry to clear his name publicly. Although virtually all the pamphlet's charges were baseless, one was eerily prescient: "Money is this man's god; and to get enough of it, he would sacrifice his country."[24]

Feuding, angry generals took up much of Congress's attention in the early summer of 1777. Henry Knox, Nathanael Greene, and John Sullivan all threatened to resign because Congress contemplated elevating a foreign officer, one Baron de Coudray, over them. Coudray's accidental drowning defused this crisis. Schuyler and Gates were at daggers drawn over who would command the critical northern department in the face of the imminent British offensive from Canada. Schuyler initially won out, but fortune's wheel spun again and by late August Gates had superseded him. As for Arnold, Congress gave him the inquiry he requested and declared the offending pamphlet's allegations groundless. He did not get his expenses, although Congress did vote him a new horse, presumably to replace the one shot from under him during the Connecticut action. And Congress did not backdate his major general's commission. On July 11, 1777, concluding that "Honor is a sacrifice no man ought to make," Arnold submitted his resignation to Congress.[25] That same day, the delegates received a letter from Washington, specifically requesting that Arnold be urgently dispatched to the northern theater, where a crisis loomed.

In early July, a large enemy force under General John Burgoyne seized supposedly impregnable Fort Ticonderoga while hardly firing a shot. Burgoyne now threatened Albany, only 70 miles distant, and indeed the entire Hudson Valley. Arnold immediately agreed to Washington's summons, but to preserve his pride insisted that he would only act "as a private citizen to render my country every service in my power."[26] There was no time for niceties and the issue of Arnold's status remained very much up in the air when he reported to Schuyler at Fort Edward, 45 miles north of Albany on July 22, 1777. Delighted to see the combative and capable Arnold, Schuyler assigned him the mission of delaying Burgoyne's advance while the main part of the army established defensive positions farther south. This Arnold accomplished with his usual élan, trading space for time with the enemy advance guard. This allowed Schuyler breathing room to concentrate the patriot forces just below the village of Stillwater, on the west bank of the Hudson.

By the second week of August, Schuyler had bad news on two fronts. Congress sacked him upon learning of Ticonderoga's fall and ordered him to stand before a board of inquiry. The lame duck New York general now awaited the arrival of his replacement, General Gates. Additionally, he had intelligence of an enemy column approaching from the west down the Mohawk Valley, which threatened his rear. This was a 2,000-man force—half comprised of Indians—led by Lieutenant Colonel Barry St. Leger, whom Burgoyne had launched from Montreal as a supporting effort. All that impeded St. Leger was Fort Stanwix, an old colonial wars post 110 miles from Albany that had recently been occupied by about 750 New York Continentals. St. Leger had this place under siege. Schuyler sent Arnold at the head of 900 men to relieve the fort and check this deadly thrust.

Forced marching brought Arnold to Fort Dayton, still 30 miles short of Fort Stanwix, by August 21. By this juncture Gates had relieved Schuyler. Arnold assured the new northern commander that "Nothing shall be omitted that can be done to raise the siege. You will hear of my being victorious, or no more; and as soon as the safety of this part of the country will permit, I will fly to your assistance."[27] Brave words, regrettably, his subordinate officers now appeared reluctant to advance against a force twice as large as theirs.

Arnold fumed, then received a bizarre proposition. A local man and reputed halfwit named Hon Yost Schuyler had been arrested for Loyalist activities in the valley. He now offered, in return for his freedom, to go to St. Leger's Indians, among whom he had once lived, and exaggerate the size of Arnold's column to induce them to flee. The Iroquois evidently regarded his mental incapacity as a sort of gift from the Great Spirit, which made him a seer. To add to the improbability of all this, Hon Yost apparently was a distant relative of the recently departed patriot general. Having no better options available, Arnold acceded. The gambit worked. Hon Yost convinced the hostile Iroquois of Arnold's immense strength. Given that the Indians were already disenchanted with static siege warfare, this proved enough to persuade them to desert St. Leger en masse. The defection of such a large portion of his command in turn caused St. Leger to abandon his plans and withdraw, much to the incredulity and joy of Stanwix's garrison. True to his promise to Gates, Arnold rushed back to join him at Stillwater.

By this time relations between Arnold and Gates had cooled considerably, most likely due to the former's close ties to Schuyler, Gates's rival for the northern command. Fundamental disagreement how to fight the forthcoming battle with Burgoyne exacerbated the bad feelings. The aggressive Arnold wanted to attack; Gates preferred to await Burgoyne inside strongly fortified positions. These differences would soon erupt into an ugly showdown between the two American generals. On September 12, the 7,000-man strong patriot army began entrenching itself on Bemis Heights, a commanding piece of ground 5 miles north of Stillwater and just west of the Hudson. Arnold and the staff engineer Thaddeus Kosciuszko had traced the position's outline beforehand. Arnold commanded the army's left wing, made up of five Continental regiments—three from New Hampshire, two from New York—plus two smaller, but crack units led by veterans of the Quebec expedition. These outfits were Colonel Daniel Morgan's rifle regiment and a detachment of light infantry under Major Henry Dearborn.

Burgoyne's situation was hardly favorable. In addition to St. Leger's earlier defeat, he had suffered the destruction of a large foraging detachment at Bennington, Vermont in mid-August and the desertion of most of his Indian allies. Prudence dictated that he retreat into Canada, but the British general plunged ahead. On September 17, his force, roughly equal in size to the Americans, but already worn out from their exertions and short of supplies, camped 4 miles north of Bemis Heights. Bereft of his Indian scouts, Burgoyne had only the dimmest picture of the American disposition. To get a better read on the British, Arnold prevailed upon Gates to let him lead a reconnaissance in force on the 18th to ascertain enemy strength and intentions. Gates assented, but emphasized that his fighting subordinate was not to bring on a general engagement. Arnold complied and fought a skirmish that afternoon that resulted in about 20 British killed, wounded, or captured. This action probably provided more intelligence to Burgoyne than it did to the patriots, as it alerted them to the Americans' proximity. It also made up Burgoyne's mind to try the American lines the following day.

The battle of Saratoga, a turning point in the Revolution, actually consisted of two separate engagements 3 weeks apart. In turn, these fights go by several names. The first is most often referred to as Freeman's Farm and occurred on September 19, 1777. Burgoyne advanced on Bemis Heights that morning in three separate columns. Gates was soon aware of this movement and appeared content to let Burgoyne come on. Arnold argued forcefully that it made more sense to go out to meet the attackers while they were still in march formation and ensnarled in the woods, rather than allow them to get into a position where they could deploy and use their superior artillery to blast holes in the patriot positions. At length, Gates consented to the dispatch of Morgan's and Dearborn's units. These elements came into contact with portions of Burgoyne's rightmost and center columns shortly after noon near the small farmstead clearing that gave the engagement its name.

Arnold hurried forward to assess the situation and detected a sizable gap between the two British forces. Realizing that he could exploit this circumstance to separate them further and defeat each in detail, he poured his more troops into the fracas, aiming first at the enemy center. Both sides punished each other throughout the remainder of the day across an open area no more than 350 yards wide, exchanging musket, rifle, and artillery fire. One observer later recorded that "Arnold rushed into the thickest of the fight with his usual recklessness, and at times acted like a madman." Another wrote "nothing could exceed the bravery of Arnold on this day."[28] Neither side could gain the advantage and the late intervention of Burgoyne's left hand column ended any chance Arnold had of smashing the enemy there and then. Darkness and mutual exhaustion ended the contest. Burgoyne's battered troopers, who had lost around 600 men, dug in where they lay around Freeman's farm. Arnold's regiments, having sustained 300 casualties, returned to Bemis Heights to lick their wounds.

The Arnold–Gates dispute, smoldering before Freeman's Farm, ignited after it. Gates's tardiness in providing reinforcements when Arnold had requested them was one reason. His refusal to let Arnold attack on the 20th was another. The transfer of Morgan's and Dearborn's units from Arnold's command after the engagement represented a third. But Gates's failure to mention Arnold's role in his report to Congress following the battle was the main cause for the blow up. This omission enraged the hypersensitive and prideful Arnold. In his view, it constituted only the latest in a series of insults and injuries he had endured in return for his sacrifices for liberty. Arnold confronted Gates in a stormy interview in the latter's command post. Gates refused to back down and taunted Arnold by suggesting—as a result of the resignation he had proffered earlier that summer—that he may no longer have even held a Continental commission.

On September 25, Gates relieved Arnold from command of the army's left wing and assumed it himself. He doubtless hoped that Arnold would depart and perhaps he might have, to seek redress from Congress or Washington, but for a very public show of support from his officers, who begged him to remain in camp. While the opposing armies faced off, Arnold brooded in his quarters and penned a letter to Gates, declaring "I am determined to sacrifice my feelings to the public good and continue in the army at this critical juncture, when my country needs every support."[29]

While the two American generals feuded, Burgoyne's situation grew increasingly precarious. He found himself desperately short of supplies and losing men daily to sickness, desertion, and incessant sniping. The American ranks, in contrast, had swollen, as fresh militia units arrived to be in at the death. Burgoyne's lieutenants counseled retiring into Canada to save what remained of their army, but the British commander decided instead on a last bid for victory. On October 7, the tattered redcoats and their Hessian allies once more issued from their positions around Freeman's Farm in three columns. They moved forward less than a mile to a wheat field, then deployed in line of battle and waited. Gates then attacked both ends of the enemy line with brigade-sized units. These achieved much initial success until they ran up against the center enemy column, largely composed of tough Hessian troops. The mercenaries held their ground, even as Gates fed in additional brigades piecemeal. The Germans then heard the sound of cheering coming from the American ranks. A dark-visaged general on a large brown horse had galloped up and was rallying them.

It was Arnold. He had heard the gunfire and no power on earth could restrain him from entering the battle. He led charge after charge, eventually driving the Anglo-Germans back into their fortifications. As he rode up and down the patriot battle line Arnold spied a similarly gallant British officer, General Simon Fraser, doing the same among the enemy troops. Finding Morgan, Arnold pointed out his opposite number and coolly ordered him shot down by one of the riflemen. Soon Simon lie in the dirt, mortally wounded. As his life ebbed, so did enemy resistance. Arnold personally led an assault against a redoubt; when repulsed, he braved a hail of enemy fire to cross an open area to collect more men for a fresh effort. These he led in a renewed attack; as the position yielded, both Arnold and his horse were shot, Arnold in the same leg wounded at Quebec. For all purposes, the second battle of Saratoga—known as Bemis Heights—ended here. Arnold's incredible heroism had gained the day for the patriots. As he was being carried from the field, an aide who had been dispatched by a furious Gates finally caught up to him to pass on the commander's order to return to camp.

Arnold was recuperating in hospital when he learned of Burgoyne's surrender on October 17. The results of the American triumph were immense. On a strictly military plane, it took an entire British army, along with their arms and equipment, off the board. Psychologically, it provided a badly needed boost to patriot hopes, particularly after the enemy's capture of Philadelphia a month earlier. Most crucially, on a diplomatic level, Saratoga convinced France to declare openly for the Americans. And while many hailed Gates as the "victor of Saratoga," others in Congress and the army realized full well that it had been Arnold who provided the impetus to victory. As part of this recognition, Congress belatedly restored Arnold's seniority among the Continental generals.

There is no way of knowing with certainty, but it appears that during 5 long months of painful convalescence, Arnold lost his last ounces of faith in the virtue of his fellow Americans. No apology or Congressional thanks had accompanied the adjustment of his rank. His leg healed slowly and ended up 2 inches shorter than the other; for the rest of his life he walked with a severe limp. Not only had he ruined his health, he had dispensed his fortune and neglected his family and business interests as well—all for an ungrateful public. Meanwhile others, who had not sacrificed nearly as much, received recognition that was due him. Washington still valued him highly and inquired after his recovery, along with asking when he might return to the army. Arnold replied to the commander in chief with a distant-sounding letter that spoke of "your country" and cause, not one they shared together any longer.[30]

In May 1778, Arnold reported to the army's camp at Valley Forge. With the British evacuation of Philadelphia imminent, Washington offered the still frail general a post as the capital city's military commandant. This was a bad fit. It exposed, on a daily basis, the aggrieved and indignant Arnold not only to the Congress he believed treated him so shabbily, but to the radical local authorities, who looked unfavorably on his dealings with politically suspect citizens thought to hold Loyalist sentiments. Prominent among these was the Shippen family, whose head was a distinguished jurist. Arnold became smitten with the judge's youngest daughter, 18-year-old Peggy, whom he wed in April 1779.

The marriage brought Arnold entrée into Philadelphia's high society. He and Peggy entertained lavishly, and often beyond their means. This in turn pushed Arnold into a number of dubious commercial ventures, which led him to run afoul of vigilant Congressional and state officials, eager to trap him in some impropriety. In due course, several charges were brought against him. Despairingly, he wrote to Washington, "Having made every sacrifice of fortune and blood, and become a cripple in the service of my country, I little expected to meet the ungrateful returns I have received . . . but as Congress has stamped ingratitude as the current coin, I must take it."[31] Arnold demanded a military board of inquiry to clear his name. To his dismay and disgust, in January 1780 the court found him guilty on two charges: giving special clearance to a trading ship of which he was part owner and using public wagons to carry his private goods. As punishment, the court recommended that the commander in chief reprimand Arnold, which Washington did, reluctantly, in April. By this time, Arnold had been in secret communication with the British for nearly a year.

Arnold's principal handler was Major John Andre, who served as intelligence chief to the British commander in America, General Henry Clinton. It is more than likely that Arnold made his initial contacts with Andre through the offices of his new wife, who had met him during the occupation of Philadelphia. The British realized that switching sides by a fighter as renowned as Arnold would constitute an extraordinary coup, yet they wanted more. They asked him to contrive to surrender a large patriot force as part of his defection. This opportunity presented itself in August 1780 when, after refusing Washington's offer of field duty, he became commandant of the vital Hudson River fortress of West Point.

Arnold offered to turn the position over to the British for 10,000 pounds. The plot miscarried only due to fortuity. On September 23, a patriot militia patrol below West Point intercepted Andre in civilian clothes while he was making his way back to British lines following a clandestine meeting with Arnold. Discovering incriminating documents on him, they notified their superiors; naturally enough, word soon reached Arnold. Although not yet suspected, he realized it was only a question of time, since the papers found on Andre included treasonous communications from Arnold to Clinton. Arnold precipitately fled down the Hudson to a British warship on the morning of September 25, astonishing breakfast guests at his headquarters by bolting mid-meal, and scant hours ahead of Washington himself, who was on his way to visit.

The Americans tried and hanged Andre as a spy after the British refused to exchange Arnold for him. The gallantry with which the major accepted his fate made Arnold's behavior appear even more craven. The Americans, with no reason to suspect her, allowed Peggy to reunite with her husband. Although the scheme fell through, the British treated Arnold with considerable generosity. They paid him the sum promised and commissioned him as a brigadier general of Loyalist troops. Later, they granted lifetime pensions not only to him, but to his wife and the five children she eventually bore him. Additionally, the crown awarded him over 13,000 acres of land in Canada.

Fighting for the British, Arnold led minor raids into Virginia and his native Connecticut, but otherwise rendered no important service. Following the American victory at Yorktown, Arnold moved his family to London and lived out his remaining years bouncing between there and other outposts of empire, including New Brunswick, Canada, and the West Indies. Respected by some, despised by others, and largely forgotten by most, Arnold died in London on June 14, 1801. Despite romantic legends that on his death bed he asked to be dressed in his Continental major general's uniform, there is no evidence that Arnold ever felt any remorse for his treason. Others among his fellow officers, even the venerated Washington, at times suffered injustices and injuries from those unable to "admire or reward the virtue they cannot imitate."[32] They frequently lashed back with bitter words and threatened resignations that, in some cases, they actually submitted. None, however, no matter how wronged, ever followed Arnold's example of outright betrayal.

A simple monument, standing on a slight rise of ground on the Saratoga battlefield, captures the tragedy of Benedict Arnold. It reads:

> In memory of the most brilliant soldier in the Continental Army, who was desperately wounded on this spot, the sally port, Burgoyne's Great Western Redoubt, 7th October, 1777, winning for his countrymen the decisive battle of the American Revolution and for himself the rank of Major General.

Like the poignantly empty shield in the chapel at West Point, it also refrains from naming America's darkest traitor.

JOHN PAUL JONES

The future scourge of the Royal Navy was born on Scotland's southwest coast, little more than a mile from the sea, near the town of Kirkbean on July 6, 1747. John Paul was one of five children of a gardener and his housekeeper wife who labored on the estate of a wealthy squire. He learned to express himself forcefully—at times even gracefully—at a nearby Presbyterian school before being apprenticed, at age 13, to a ship owner from the neighboring port town of Whitehaven. Aboard the *Friendship*, a small merchantman, the youngster's sharp mind and aptitude for seamanship attracted the captain's eye. Paul thus advanced rapidly from ordinary seaman to junior officer or mate.

Paul's initial voyages illustrate the commercial dynamic of Great Britain's eighteenth-century colonial economy. The *Friendship* plied a triangular route: hauling provisions to Barbados, then West Indian rum and sugar to Virginia, before returning home laden with tobacco. The owner's subsequent bankruptcy—another aspect of the volatile Atlantic economy—ended Paul's apprenticeship in 1764. The young man thereafter experienced a further dimension of imperial commerce. For 3 years he served as an officer aboard slavers transporting human cargo on the horrific "middle passage" between the African coast and Caribbean slave plantations. After quitting this "abominable trade," as he later called it, in Kingston, Jamaica, Paul found passage home aboard a brig—a two-masted, square-rigged craft—bound for Scotland.³³ At sea, both the captain and first mate died of fever. John Paul, the only experienced navigator aboard, bought the ship safely to port. Back in Scotland, the grateful and impressed owners offered permanent command to the 21-year-old.

As master of his own ship, the *John*, Captain Paul established the traits that became his hallmark. Technically, he was a magnificent seaman, whose ship handling competence won the respect of his crew, whose lives, after all, depended on this. He demanded unusually high standards of cleanliness and precision when under way. While sailors thrived on their daily ration of grog—a potent mixture of rum and water—John Paul was an abstemious skipper, whose preferred shipboard drink was lemon or lime juice liberally spiked with sugar, although he would occasionally sip wine after dinner in his cabin. Maritime discipline during the age of sail was strict and frequently harsh, and Paul ran a tight ship; indeed he was something of a martinet. A slight, wiry figure who stood a shade under $5\frac{1}{2}$ feet tall, he exhibited a classic "little man's complex," giving vent to a flaming temper when crossed or challenged. This characteristic landed him in legal trouble on a couple of occasions and eventually led him to flee Great Britain for America, thereby altering the course of United States naval history.

Paul's first brush with the law resulted from his having a disobedient ship's carpenter flogged aboard the *John* in the fall of 1769. Although an Admiralty court in the West Indies cleared him after the aggrieved sailor sued his master, a shocked Paul found himself under arrest when he returned to Scotland. The carpenter had shipped back to England on another vessel, contracted a fever, and died en route. The deceased's father brought murder charges against Paul, claiming the punishment caused his son's death. Released on bail, Paul eventually cleared himself by obtaining affidavits from the Admiralty court and other witnesses demonstrating no connection between the whipping and the victim's demise.

His maritime career progressed handsomely until his second and more serious encounter with justice, which he later described as "that great misfortune of my life."[34] In late 1772, Paul became captain, as well as part owner, of his largest trading ship yet, the *Betsy*, whose home port was London. While docked at Scarborough, Tobago, in October 1773, members of his crew became restive and demanded an advance on their wages, which were due only after the ship returned home. The sole existing firsthand account of the episode lies embedded in a letter Paul wrote to Benjamin Franklin several years afterward. According to Paul, a crewman, a native of Tobago identified only as "the Ringleader," menaced him, forcing the captain in self-defense to skewer him with his sword. Paul then went ashore and surrendered himself to a magistrate, presumably to stand trial. Shortly afterward, before a court could hear the case and apparently fearing any proceeding's outcome, John Paul fled Tobago, leaving his ship and all his possessions, save 50 pounds, behind. Soon the fugitive adopted the surname Jones and, as he told Franklin, after wandering about the West Indies, elected to "retire Incog.[nito] to the continent of America."[35]

John Paul Jones turned up in late 1774 in Fredericksburg, Virginia—a place where he had previously sojourned on his maiden voyage 13 years earlier. Then he had visited an older brother who had settled there and opened a tailor shop. Any hope Jones may have held of fraternal assistance was dashed by that same brother's death shortly before he arrived. A foreigner, on the lam, under an assumed name, virtually broke, Jones's prospects were not exactly glittering. Fortunately for him, years earlier, he had joined the society of Masons. Now, in Virginia, he encountered members of that association who befriended him and provided entrée into tidewater society. For the better part of a year, in the venerable tradition of unemployed gentlemen, he relied upon the kindness of strangers until great events offered him an opportunity to seek glory and fortune. By the summer of 1775, the

Continental Congress had created not only an army, but also a navy and it needed officers. Jones traveled to Philadelphia and the records reveal that one "John Paul Jones Esq." received a first lieutenant's commission in the Continental Navy on December 7, 1775.

This American navy, destined one day to achieve glory as a fighting force with battle honors stretching from "Old Ironsides" to Midway, began insignificantly enough. Largely at the behest of the New England states, in October 1775 Congress authorized the commissioning of four armed vessels. The Royal Navy at this time consisted of more than 250 bottoms, nearly half of which were ships of the line; before the war ended, the British disposed of nearly 500 ships. Congress also appointed a Naval Committee to supervise the nascent fleet's organization and operations. In short order these men drafted a set of regulations, pursued the purchase of more ships, and recommended raising two battalions of Marines. Throughout the war, this civilian body, in various incarnations, set naval policy and supervised maritime activities.

Besides being overwhelmingly outnumbered and outgunned by its opponent, the Continental Navy faced other serious challenges. Geographically, the accessibility of the North American coast, with its numerous estuaries and navigable rivers made it well-nigh impossible to protect against invasion. Another hindrance lay in the United States' uncoordinated naval efforts. Just as the state militias competed with the Continental Army for recruits, so too did various state navies siphon valuable resources—ships, supplies, and men—from the Continental Navy. A further complication was the practice, both by the states and Congress itself, of granting letters of marque and reprisal. Essentially, these were licenses issued to private individuals—privateers—sanctioning what amounted to legalized piracy. American privateers took about 600 British prizes during the war. Once again, however, this drained assets from the navy—especially since privateers got to keep the ships and cargoes they seized. Finally, and much more so than the Army, itself at times a hot bed of intrigue, the navy's officer corps was plagued by favoritism and nepotism.

Lieutenant Jones would encounter all of this soon enough. His first posting was the *Alfred*, a converted merchantman outfitted with 30 nine- and six-pound guns and crewed by about 220 sailors. Jones served as second-in-command under Captain Dudley Saltonstall, member of one of New England's most ancient and prominent families. He proved an ineffable snob and incompetent to boot. Jones took an immediate dislike to him and his "Rude Unhappy Temper."[36] The *Alfred* also served as the flagship of the new navy's first chief, Commodore Esek Hopkins, another difficult New Englander.

Congress did not tarry in directing action. In January 1776, Hopkins received exceedingly ambitious orders to take the American fleet south and, if conditions proved favorable, engage and destroy any British vessels in Chesapeake Bay, as well as off the Carolinas. This directive provided considerable latitude, however, and Hopkins had no intention of engaging the enemy off the American coast. Rather, he steered his eight-ship squadron for the Bahamas in order to raid the

British settlement of New Providence (modern Nassau). Finding the place denuded of troops, the Americans landed unopposed on March 3 and made off with valuable stores for Washington's army, to include 88 cannon and a considerable amount of ammunition. By early April, the patriot vessels returned to America's northern waters.

Jones saw no combat on this cruise, but on April 6 he took part in the United States Navy's first fleet action. This was a 3-hour nighttime encounter with HMS *Glasgow*, fought off the entrance to Long Island Sound. Hopkins did not handle his battle line particularly well, committing his ships piecemeal against the lone enemy frigate. Jones commanded *Alfred's* lower gun deck during the fight, effectively directing the fire of the nine-pounders. Although outnumbered, outgunned, and badly shot up by Jones's gunners, *Glasgow* managed to escape. The Americans then put in to New London, Connecticut, without further incident, at least afloat. Once ashore, however, conflict flared among the fleet's officers. Junior officers, including Jones, hurled accusations of "Rude ungentle treatment," ineptitude and even cowardice against several captains.[37] The Naval Committee conducted hearings and cleared most of the skippers, except one—the captain of the sloop *Providence*. A court-martial—upon which Jones sat—convicted him on several charges and he was relieved. Hopkins offered the vacant command to the Navy's senior first lieutenant and Jones accepted it, along with the temporary rank of captain, on May 10, 1776.

Over the next 6 months, Jones established himself as the navy's fiercest and best combat leader. His new ship was a 70-foot long, single-masted craft mounting 12 guns. Jones passed the early summer of 1776 refitting the *Providence* in the eponymous Rhode Island port and performing sundry escort duties along the New England coast. While awaiting orders, he importuned Congress for permanent captain's grade, as well as command of one of the new frigates that it had recently authorized. In a letter to a member of the Naval Committee, he dwelled upon the necessary qualifications: "in my opinion a Captain of the Navy ought to be a man of Strong and well connected Sense with a tolerable Education, a Gentleman as well as a Seaman both in Theory and Practice."[38] Like many other sailors from time immemorial, and as he would throughout his career, Jones also indulged his fondness for the company of the fair sex. His letters from this period refer to an "agreeable Widow" and a "little affair of the Heart at Providence."[39]

In early August, he obtained the desired permanent rank as well as instructions from Congress. These enjoined him to make for the Caribbean and "to Seize, take, Burn or destroy" enemy vessels.[40] Jones cleared the Delaware Capes on August 21 with a crew of 73 men, sufficient not only to man the *Providence*, but to furnish crews for any prizes taken. Before he reentered Narragansett Bay on October 8, Jones had captured seven British commercial ships. This exploit advanced both his martial reputation and his financial status, for in the age of sail, captains and their crews—both British and American, and indeed of all navies—commonly received a share of the spoils. Jones had preyed upon helpless vessels, but also experienced a couple of brushes with much more powerful British warships. *Providence*'s nimbleness and Jones's adept ship handling, however kept him out of the enemy's clutches. Of one particularly close call, Jones described "Our 'Hairbreadth Scape' and the saucy manner of making it."[41]

Jones embarked on his second independent foray less than 3 weeks later. Commanding his old ship, the *Alfred*, with the *Providence* sailing under his control as well, his mission was to raid British shipping off Nova Scotia. The cruise began auspiciously. The two ship flotilla took three prizes in rapid succession, including a transport carrying to the British army at Quebec a load of winter clothing— some of which eventually found its way to Washington's grateful troops freezing in New Jersey. Shortly afterward, however, an "epidemicall discontent" set in among the officers and men of both vessels.[42] Despite Jones's imprecations to the contrary, the *Providence* turned back after her officers decided that she was leaking too badly to continue northward in the increasingly foul weather. Aboard *Alfred*, his own crew grumbled as he forged ahead. Jones took four more prizes and outfoxed a British frigate off Cape Cod before putting in at Boston Harbor on December 14.

With two highly successful excursions under his belt, Jones had every reason to believe that Congress would recognize his merit. He was therefore deeply cha- grined when he learned in January 1777 that he stood 18th in order of seniority on the list of naval captains drawn up by the Naval Committee. Even more humbling, he was relieved from *Alfred* and reassigned to command the smaller *Providence*. Jones reacted furiously in a fusillade of letters he dispatched to Congress from Boston, where he had been wintering. In these missives, Jones sourly attacked the competence of many of the men placed ahead of him—and with some jus- tification. The truth of the matter, however, was that Jones, as a recently arrived foreigner and a relative unknown in America, could not hope to be preferred over well-established natives. Congress assigned captains partly as a form of patronage and partly to maintain sectional balance. Additionally, it had authorized the build- ing of 13 new frigates and named their commanders based upon their residence near where the construction took place—logical grounds, since the captains were expected to supervise the work and recruit crews locally.

Somewhat perversely, Jones's failure to get command of one of the new frigates in the end worked to the advantage of his reputation—and to that of his adopted country. Most of these vessels never got to sea, as the Royal Navy effectively bottled them up in their home ports throughout the war. Instead, after Jones traveled to Philadelphia in March to plead his case, Congress rewarded him with a newly launched sloop of war carrying 20 guns. Jones accepted with alacrity and hastened to Portsmouth, New Hampshire, to assume command of the *Ranger*.

Jones first laid eyes on the three-masted vessel in mid-July. Plenty of work remained to get her shipshape, to include gathering a crew of about 150, laying in stores and provisions, arming her, and procuring sails and cordage. Jones's vision for *Ranger*, as he informed his officers, was to make her "the best Cruizer in America . . . able to Fight her Guns under a most excellent cover."[43] Portsmouth was a prosperous seaport and when not casting a critical eye on activities down at the dockyard, Jones hobnobbed with the elite of the town's society. He also found time to correspond with a wide variety of people, to include the African-American poet and former slave Phillis Wheatley. And he continued venting to Congress about his treatment, bitterly describing several captains listed senior to him as "altogether illiterate and Utterly ignorant of Marine affairs."[44]

Ranger set sail in November, bound for France where American emissaries were ardently wooing Louis XVI's ministers in order to gain support for the patriot cause. Congress hoped that the French would provide a frigate for Jones to captain. Jones entered the Brittany port of Nantes on the Loire River in early December. After looking to the care of his ship and crew, he made his way to Paris and reported to the American commissioners there. Preeminent among them was Benjamin Franklin, to whom Jones took an immediate shine. While diplomacy proceeded, in true seadog fashion, the gallant Scot immersed himself in a romantic affair with the wife of a prominent French official. This proved no major hindrance to Franco-American dealings; news of the great American victory at Saratoga soon prompted the French to declare openly their heretofore secret support of the rebellious Americans. Nevertheless, negotiations regarding a vessel for Jones dragged out and, in frustration, Jones returned to *Ranger* in late January 1778.

He carried orders from the commissioners to fit out *Ranger* and to "proceed with her in the manner you shall judge best for distressing the Enemies of the United States."[45] Armed with this carte blanche, Jones hatched a truly daring scheme to repay British depredations along America's shores by sailing into the Royal Navy's home waters and raiding the British coast. Specifically, he intended to enter an English port, burn shipping there, and seize a prominent hostage to exchange for Yankee seamen captured and held by the British. Jones's men were nonplussed by their captain's bold vision. Not only did this seem exceedingly dangerous, they had signed on at least partly for the promise of prize money—to seize ships and cargo, not destroy them. Additionally, Jones noted an "Epidemical malady Of Homesickness" among his New England salts. With this unlikely crew of heroes, and after several false starts due to uncooperative winds and tides, *Ranger* got under way on April 10. What ensued was a month of farce, danger, and glory.

Ranger entered the Irish Sea from the south—between Ireland and Wales—4 days later. There Jones captured a Dublin-bound merchant ship, manned it with a prize crew, and dispatched it back to the French port of Brest. Sluicing north, *Ranger* eluded a suspicious cutter and sank a Scottish coastal schooner. Jones now resolved to attack the English harbor of Whitehaven, on Britain's west coast not far from his birthplace, whence he had first gone to sea as a boy.

April 22 began with evil portents. *Ranger*'s crew verged on near mutiny and Jones had to clap a pistol to the ringleader's head in order to quell an uprising on his quarterdeck. When Jones then revealed his plan, a number of his officers and men refused to participate. The grimly determined captain gathered two boatloads of what he thought were loyal sailors and marines, and at midnight set off for

Whitehaven, leaving a trustworthy officer in command of his ship. Exhausting hours of rowing against a strong tide brought them to the harbor side as the sun rose on the morning of the 23rd. The landing party went undetected by a sleeping town, but one of Jones's men proved treasonous. As soon as he got ashore, the turncoat—an Irishman who had signed on at Portsmouth only for a return ticket to the British Isles—broke away and dashed door to door to rouse the somnolent residents. Jones managed to spike most of the harbor defense guns and fire several boats with premade incendiary devices before hundreds of milling, agitated townspeople arrived on the scene. They proceeded to try and douse the flames. A sudden rain squall aided this effort and covered Jones's hasty withdrawal as well. The raiders, minus the traitor, safely regained the *Ranger* by six o'clock. An eventful 48 hours still lay ahead.

Undaunted by the relatively unspectacular, even inglorious, results at White-haven, Jones decided that very same morning to conduct another raid, this time in Scotland. *Ranger* steered north, across Solway Firth, which separates England and Scotland by 20 miles along Britain's west coast. Jones's target was the Earl of Selkirk's mansion on St. Mary's Isle, in the neighborhood of his birthplace at Kirkbean. His intention was to seize the Earl, a very minor Scots peer, and barter his freedom for the release of imprisoned American sailors. In broad sunlight, *Ranger* brazenly entered the bay and for the second time that day Jones led a landing party while his ship lay at anchor. No resistance materialized, but to Jones dismay, he learned that the Earl was away on business.

Jones prepared to trudge back to his boat and row out to *Ranger*, when two of his lieutenants—citing the profitless nature of their cruise thus far—insisted on being allowed to sack the Earl's home. Sensing their ugly mood, Jones consented to the officers and a handful of sailors breaching the house's threshold and making off with the family silver. He admonished them, however, not to take or damage any other property, or harm anyone they encountered. Jones waited outside while the looters went about their work. Lady Selkirk was home and spiritedly confronted them before ultimately yielding her plate. To their credit, the intruders disturbed nothing else and made off with the booty. Jones and his band returned to the *Ranger* without further incident.

This episode had an interesting denouement. Word rapidly spread along the north bank of the Firth of Solway—Jones's native district—that the villainous "pirate" was none other than the Kirkbean gardener's son, John Paul. In early May, once Jones had made it safely back to France, he penned a long and extremely gallant letter to Lady Selkirk. Like a number of the social-climbing founding fighters, Jones possessed a Gatsby-like desire to be a fine gentleman. With numerous chivalric touches that included rhymed couplets of his own composition, and mention of his forsaking "the softer Affections of the Heart" and his "prospects of Domestic Happiness" in order to "Struggle for the rights of Men," Jones assured the good lady of his honorable intentions.[46] He also pledged to purchase the purloined silver from his crew and return it to her, which he actually did, after the war.

Before he could sit down and write to the fair lady, however, Jones and crew faced one more test. By the morning of April 24, Jones's activities had alarmed Britain's west coast and the Admiralty, which urgently dispatched warships to track down the impertinent American raiders. One of the Royal Navy vessels on the lookout was HMS *Drake*, also a sloop of war roughly the same size and armament—20 six-pound guns—as *Ranger*. The two encountered each other off Carrickfergus, on Ireland's northwest coast. *Drake* was inside Belfast Lough, a narrow channel, when its lookout spotted a suspicious hull standing at the waterway's entrance. *Drake*'s captain dispatched a small boat to investigate and Jones responded by taking it captive, hoisting the stars and stripes, and challenging *Drake* to combat.

As excited onlookers crowded the shore, the two equally matched adversaries maneuvered for position. They came to grips shortly before sunset. Jones later reported that "The action was warm, close and obstinate."[47] After an exchange of cannon fire and musketry from the mast tops, lasting about an hour, *Drake*'s surviving officer cried out for quarter. Jones suffered 3 dead and 5 wounded. *Drake*'s losses were 4 dead—including her captain and first lieutenant—and 19 wounded. Jones, ever gallant and observant of the proprieties, buried his opposite number at sea with full honors. After installing a prize crew aboard the captured ship, and making the repairs necessitated by the deadly American gunnery, Jones made for the French coast. Outrunning British pursuit, *Ranger* and its prize entered Brest On May 8.

Jones's exploits on this 28-day cruise had laid the foundation of his legend; Benjamin Disraeli, the famed nineteenth-century British prime minister and also a man of letters, would later write that "the nurses of Scotland hushed their crying charges by the whisper of his name."[48] Nevertheless, for the next 10 months Jones found himself and his career in the doldrums. He spent this period in France bickering with subordinates and superiors, and desperately seeking a ship and command worthy of his ambition and talent. Many of *Ranger*'s officers and men cordially hated him. This resulted not so much from Jones being a tyrannical or even unusually harsh captain. Rather, Jones's vision of martial glory was totally at odds with the more commercial interests of the New England merchant seamen who made up *Ranger*'s company. And his insistence on rigorous naval discipline contrasted with their experience of relatively free and easy shipboard democracy. In a letter about this time he condemned "Gain ... [as] the ruling principle of Officers in an Infant Navy" and "the Mistaken and baneful Idea of Licentiousness and Free Agency under the specious name of 'Liberty.'"[49] His men's 1-year enlistments were set to expire and so, in late August 1778, *Ranger* returned to America under the command of her first officer, whose insubordination had been one of Jones's biggest headaches. No doubt Jones was happy to be rid of them; but now he had another problem—no ship.

"I wish to have no Connection with any Ship that does not sail fast, for I intend to go in harm's way."[50] Jones wrote these stirring words in the midst of his search in the summer and fall of 1778 for a vessel suitable to his needs. He relentlessly lobbied Congress, the French naval ministry, the American commissioners in Paris, and anyone else he thought might remotely be of help. He even wrote directly to Louis XVI. At various times his hopes soared, only to be dashed by this or that change of plans. Notably, he never for an instant thought of following the example of many other captains and going into business for himself as a privateer, much less of resigning or turning coat. At one point, however, Jones grew so frustrated that he contemplated challenging the French Navy Minister to a duel, only to be talked out of it by wise old Ben Franklin.

Unhappy working through official channels, Jones even conducted his own personal search for a ship. In late December 1778 he finally found one that he thought might do. At the port of Lorient, on the southern coast of the Brittany peninsula, he discovered an old, tub-like but sturdy, French Indiaman named *Le Duc de Duras*. He then persuaded the French government—after all, its American allies were penniless—to purchase her for the Continental Navy. In gratitude for Franklin's assistance, Jones renamed the *Duras* in honor of the American *philosophe*'s *Poor Richard's Almanack*. In French, "Poor Richard" became *Bonhomme Richard*. She would not sail fast, but she would carry Jones into harm's way and to immortality.

Jones passed the spring of 1779 converting the merchantman to a warship. He fitted her with 40 guns and recruited a polyglot crew of Yankee blue jackets, French sailors and marines, Royal Navy deserters, and assorted Irish, Norwegian, Portuguese, Scottish, Swedish, Swiss mariners that added up to a total of about 380 officers and men. Four other, smaller vessels, similarly manned, were assigned to Jones's command as well, in effect making him a commodore at the head of his own squadron. These ships were all skippered by French officers to whom the Congress had awarded commissions in the American navy. One of them, Captain Pierre Landais of the frigate *Alliance*, would give Jones as much trouble as any of his previous difficult subordinates ever had.

The Franco-American allies entertained various schemes to employ Jones's task force. The most daring envisioned a joint naval–land expedition—the latter commanded by the young Marquis de Lafayette—to conduct a massive raid on Liverpool. Ultimately, they discarded this idea as too impractical. Finally, after a shakedown cruise in June, spent escorting French merchant ships along the coast, the *Bonhomme Richard* squadron was ready for offensive operations in British waters. The heterogeneous—although each vessel flew an American flag—five-ship element departed Lorient on August 14, 1779. Two French privateers rendezvoused with them shortly thereafter. Jones set a course that would carry in a clockwise direction around the British Isles. His mission was to prey on enemy shipping and generally raise havoc along the enemy's coast.

Making its way deliberately around Ireland's southwest tip, the squadron took several small prizes the first week out. Nevertheless, Jones rapidly found himself taking arms against a sea of troubles. The privateers soon deserted him, which could not have surprised him. A gale blew up off Ireland's west coast on August 25. The frigate *Pallas* sustained a damaged rudder and became separated. The small cutter *Cerf* likewise suffered storm damage and her skipper elected to return to Lorient. Captain Landais, who appears to have been a lunatic, proved ostentatious in his disregard for many of Jones's signals and instructions. He openly disparaged his superior and even raved wildly about killing him once the two men regained dry land. When the storm struck, Landais took advantage of it to go his own way as well. Jones and *Bonhomme Richard*, accompanied now only by the corvette *Vengeance*, pressed on, reaching Scotland's northern edge by month's end.

By then, *Pallas* had caught up and rejoined the flagship, as had *Alliance* under the unchastened Landais. The task force continued to seize British coastal vessels as it traversed Scotland's northern shores and entered the North Sea. Jones now returned to a notion that had long fixed itself in his mind, and had animated his descents on Whitehaven and the Earl of Selkirk's home the previous year. "I was anxious to teach the enemy humanity by some exemplary stroke of retaliation, to relieve the remainder of the Americans from captivity in England."[51] While a handful of American sailors had been exchanged by their British captors the previous spring and Continental soldiers were routinely exchanged, as a rule his majesty's government regarded Yankee seamen as pirates rather than legitimate combatants. Jones hoped to sail up the Firth of Forth on Scotland's east coast to the lightly defended port city of Leith and essentially take the town hostage, threatening to burn it unless the British paid a ransom and released more captive Americans.

On September 16, *Bonhomme Richard*, along with *Vengeance* and *Pallas*— Landais had sortied off on his own again more than a week earlier—entered the Firth flying British colors. Additionally, Jones and his officers sported uniform coats closely resembling those worn in the Royal Navy. Initially, the ruse worked. A harbor cutter approached and, mistaking Jones's flagship for a British man of war, warned of the approach of the "pirate Paul Jones." In perfect Robin Hood fashion, Jones gave the small craft a barrel of gunpowder to defend itself against this "pirate" and then requested that a pilot come on board his ship to guide it into Leith harbor. The cutter's commander complied. Once the hapless pilot stood on *Bonhomme Richard's* quarterdeck, Jones coaxed him into declaring that the villainous Jones deserved hanging before dramatically revealing his true identity. The man pleaded for mercy and a laughing Jones assured him that he was a prisoner, but safe.

Jones almost certainly would have assailed the town but for the advent of divine intervention—or at least a stroke of appalling weather—on behalf of the helpless Scots. As Jones recorded after, "a Very severe gale of Wind came on, and being directly Contrary obliged me to bear away after having in Vain Endeavoured for sometime to Withstand its violence."[52] Blown back to the mouth of the firth and suffering storm damage, Jones reluctantly concluded that he had lost any hope of surprise and that he must sail away. The American squadron bore southward. En route, Jones entertained the idea of pouncing on Newcastle-upon-Tyne, the English coal-shipping port on the Scottish–English border. He argued in vain to *Vengeance*'s and *Pallas*'s captains that burning the port's colliers, or coal ships, would bring home the war to England's people and partially avenge British depredations on America's coasts. These worthies were more interested in prize money than in dangerous, unprofitable raids and declined to participate. Eighteenth-century military professionalism was a far different thing than it is today and Jones had no recourse but to give up this operation as well.

For several days, Jones's ships chased, and occasionally seized, small craft off the Yorkshire coast. On the morning of September 23, 1789 *Alliance*, after a 2-week hiatus, rejoined the squadron, giving Jones four ships in all. And that afternoon, the tiny task force spied a huge merchant convoy of over 40 sail off Flamborough Head, bearing north. Escorting them were the 20 gun sloop of war HMS *Countess of Scarborough* and the frigate HMS *Serapis*, rated at 44 guns and commanded by Captain Richard Pearson, a Royal Navy veteran of 30 years.

Both Jones and his opponent were eager to fight. *Serapis* signaled her flock to hug the Yorkshire shore's protective cover and, accompanied by the diminutive *Scarborough*, moved to meet the American predators. About an hour before sunset, *Bonhomme Richard*'s drummers beat to quarters—the shipboard command for manning battle stations. Jones signaled his nominally subordinate captains to "form line of battle"—a directive, like so many others on this cruise, they ignored, although *Pallas* would eventually come to grips with and best *Scarborough* in a secondary combat.

Serapis seriously outclassed *Bonhomme Richard*. She was newer, faster, more maneuverable, and better armed. Jones, a ferocious fighter and superb tactician, realized he could not win in a prolonged exchange of broadsides. The Americans' only hope lay in killing *Serapis*'s crew with grapeshot and musketry, and ultimately grappling close with hooks and ropes to board her. To effect the first part of this design, Jones sent sailors and marines scurrying to the mast tops, armed to the teeth with hand grenades, handheld mortars, and muskets. Commanding them were young midshipmen, some barely 17 years old. For boarding, he designated parties armed with cutlasses, pikes, and pistols and covered them as best he could on *Bonhomme Richard's* exposed main deck.

The two flagships closed to within hailing distance. Jones had been flying British colors and Pearson wished to be certain of his foe before opening fire. Jones failed to identify himself to Pearson's satisfaction and, as the British captain repeated his challenge, he ran up the Continental Navy ensign. This was the signal for both vessels to thunder broadsides at the other near simultaneously. The crackling of musketry and the screams of the maimed soon added to the din. Near catastrophe struck *Bonhomme Richard* as she attempted a second broadside. At least one of her ancient, French-cast eighteen-pounders burst, leaving a horrific abattoir in the gun room, as well as a gaping whole in her starboard hull. Jones ordered the remaining unreliable guns—his heaviest—abandoned. The desperate night engagement "Continued with Unremitting fury," luridly lit by a harvest moon with the chalky cliffs of Flamborough Head as backdrop.[53]

The more agile and lethal *Serapis* raked *Bonhomme Richard* and "made a dreadful havoc of our crew. Men were falling in all parts of the ship by the scores," recalled one of Jones's midshipmen long afterward.[54] Aided by a favorable breeze, Jones was able to execute the one maneuver that could prevent his certain destruction and offer a chance at victory. After several tries, he succeeded in ramming *Serapis* and grappling alongside her, bow to stern. "Well done, my brave lads, we have got her now," exulted Jones. In almost the same breath he giddily reprimanded his sailing master, who was loosing horrible oaths as only a sailor can. "Mr. Stacy, it's no time to be swearing now—you may the next moment be in eternity; but let us do our duty."[55]

The two ships, now locked like boxers in a clinch, swirled together at the mercy of wind and tide. Fires raged aboard each vessel and their decks, awash with blood, were strewn with splinters and body parts. Pearson's men tried with axes to sever the ropes and hooks binding them to *Bonhomme Richard,* but to no avail as fusillades from the American fighting tops shot them down. At this juncture, *Alliance*, which had heretofore stood off under the unbalanced Landais, circled the two combatants and discharged three broadsides indiscriminately. *Bonhomme Richard* suffered the worst of it; several of her men were killed or wounded and their agonized cries echoed over the water as Landais leisurely glided away again.

The only guns Jones could bring to bear on *Serapis* were three nine-pounders on his quarterdeck, one of which he served with his own hands in a sort of ecstasy of fury. Both vessels were terribly damaged, joined in a death embrace; *Bonhomme Richard* was little more than a floating hulk. She became dangerously flooded below decks, where more than a hundred English prisoners, taken from prizes seized earlier on the cruise, were confined. Hearing their piteous wails, one of Jones's officers released them and enjoined them to man the pumps, which most did with alacrity. Jones was indomitable, almost superhuman, this night. One of his men begged him to surrender and he exclaimed "No, I will sink, I will never strike!" A petty officer made to haul down *Bonhomme Richard*'s tattered ensign and a livid Jones clubbed him with a pistol. And of course, according to legend, at some point during the struggle, Pearson demanded if Jones had struck his colors, eliciting the immortal words, "I have not yet begun to fight!"[56]

The battle had raged over 3 hours and while conditions aboard *Bonhomme Richard* were hellish, they were nearly as awful on *Serapis*. Pearson was a brave captain, who had gone so far as personally nailing his ensign to its staff before the engagement to indicate that he would never give in. Two events now drove him beyond his limit. One of Jones's sailors crawled out on a yardarm that hung over *Serapis*'s main deck and dropped a hand grenade through an open hatch, setting off numerous secondary explosions when it detonated among loose lying powder charges on the gun deck. And Jones's nine-pounders succeeded in felling *Serapis*'s mainmast. Pearson ripped his flag down and cried for quarter. Jones acknowledged his call and dispatched a boarding party under his first lieutenant to take possession of *Serapis*. Shortly thereafter, Pearson crossed over to *Bonhomme Richard* and offered his sword to Jones. One can only imagine the pride swelling in the gardener's son as he gallantly returned the blade to his late adversary and invited him down to his wrecked cabin for a glass of wine.

Thus concluded the most famous ship-to-ship engagement in naval history. About half of each ship's company—150 men on both vessels—had been casualties, although Jones survived unscathed despite almost constant exposure to enemy fire. For 36 hours after the battle, *Bonhomme Richard's* crew worked heroically to save the crippled ship, but to no avail. Jones reluctantly gave the order to abandon and the old war horse sank beneath the waves on the morning of September 25. Jones transferred his flag to *Serapis* and with the rest of his small fleet sailed to the port of Amsterdam in compliance with his earlier instructions from the French naval ministry. A British flotilla gave futile chase; once Jones anchored, the Royal Navy warships lurked on the edge of Dutch waters to bottle him up and await his emergence.

Jones remained in Amsterdam until the end of the year. His presence created difficulties for the Dutch government, since, unlike France, the Netherlands was officially neutral in the Anglo-American contest. In practice, of course, the Dutch had heavily supported the rebels through contraband trade. While diplomats from four countries, including the infant United States, wrangled over Jones's legal status, he busied himself repairing his ships, settling prize money, and arranging the status of the 500 English prisoners he had taken. He also basked in the adulation of the Dutch public, which admired him for having twisted the British lion's tail. Meanwhile, the unspeakable Landais made his way to France to intrigue against Jones with the American commissioners, the French government, and anyone else who would listen. Jones reestablished his flagship on *Alliance* and on December 27, 1779, aided by foul weather that blew the British blockaders temporarily off station, sailed away. After a desultory cruise to the south, he made Lorient on February 19, 1780.

For the next 10 months, spent in France, Jones experienced both the best and worst of times. Acclaimed in Amsterdam, he was lionized by *le tout Paris*. Audiences with the king, attendance at the smartest salons, and numerous love affairs occupied much of his time. At one notable court dinner, someone mentioned that Captain Pearson, late of HMS *Serapis*, had been knighted by George III for his gallantry in the losing contest with *Bonhomme Richard*. "Let me fight him again," the feisty Jones retorted, "and I'll make him a lord!"[57] When not playing the celebrity, Jones unsuccessfully angled for fleet command and floated daring strategic options that interested no one but himself. Meanwhile, Landais, with the connivance of an impatient American commissioner named Arthur Lee, usurped command of *Alliance* and sailed it for America in July 1780. Edifyingly, the Frenchman wound up being relieved and court-martialed, and ultimately ended his days in deserved obscurity and disgrace.

Having had his ship snatched from under his nose, Jones cast about for another. Franklin and the French eventually found him one, the frigate *Ariel*. Loaded with much needed supplies for Washington's army, she began the Atlantic passage in October, only to meet an epic tempest. Jones's extraordinary seamanship saved *Ariel* from going to the bottom, but he was forced to limp back into Lorient and did not get under way again until December. Finally, in February 1781, he arrived at Philadelphia, back in the United States after an absence of over 3 years. He probably did not realize it at the time, but he had already reached the peak of his glory, though he would ardently pursue it through the final decade of his life.

From Congress he sought an admiral's rank—unsuccessfully; the U.S. Navy would not have its first flag officer until the Civil War. Congress, however, did award him command of the 74-gun frigate *America*, then building in Portsmouth. Jones hastened to New Hampshire in August to supervise the work, stopping off in New York to meet with Washington, who was then preparing for his decisive march to Yorktown. That climactic battle, in October, hinged greatly on seapower, but it was the French Navy, without any American assistance, that did so much to assure victory. Jones missed out on the triumph while alternatively being feted by Portsmouth's upper classes and fretting over the glacial pace of *America*'s construction. As the war wound down with Jones on the sidelines, another cruel blow from Congress awaited. In September 1782, short of funds and discerning no need for a navy with the end of hostilities imminent, Congress voted to give the still unfinished *America* to France as a gift.

As with all the other indignities visited upon him, Jones complained, but remained the loyal sailor. Ever the professional, he got himself attached to a French naval expedition against British holdings in the West Indies. The fleet, with a large contingent of marines embarked, sailed from Boston in late 1782. Jones thought he might profit by observing how such a large force was handled. In the event, there was nothing for Jones to learn; the operation miscarried and was aborted in April 1783.

This misadventure represented Jones last spell of active service on behalf of the United States. He spent his remaining years drifting abroad, unsuccessfully seeking command in the French Navy before Catherine the Great of Russia offered him the coveted admiral's flag and an opportunity in her fleet, then warring against Ottoman Turkey. Jones performed more than capably in what was essentially a mercenary role, but proved woefully out of his depth in the Byzantine court politics of St. Petersburg. Having made use of him, his enemies among Catherine's retinue trumped up a sex scandal involving a 12-year-old girl, which caused him to quit Russia in disgrace in 1790. He wound up in Paris, where, his health broken due to years before the mast, he lived out a solitary existence. France, in the early stages of her own revolution, was a far different place from what it had been when he was last there under the ancien regime, but most Frenchmen admired him for his services in the name of liberty.

When Jones died on July 18, 1792, alone in a tiny apartment, having just reached the age of 45, it was the French National Assembly that organized a dignified funeral for him after the apathetic and penurious American embassy could not be bothered. It took more than a century for him to receive a much grander one. In 1905, President Theodore Roosevelt, desiring a symbol for a rising America's powerful new navy, had Jones's remains exhumed and carried across the Atlantic. A cruiser, escorted by a flotilla of battleships, brought home America's first and greatest naval hero to a fitting resting place at Annapolis.

Partisan Fighters

Andrew Pickens, Thomas Sumter, and Francis Marion

THE AMERICAN south proved the decisive theater of the war. More than any other, this arena also assumed the aspect of a civil war in which Americans savagely fought each other. Nowhere in the south were the results more important or the struggle more vicious than in South Carolina. Over 200 skirmishes and battles took place throughout the state. From the Revolution's earliest days, patriot militia and irregulars bitterly fought the British and their Loyalist and Indian auxiliaries. After the twin disasters of Charleston and Camden in 1780, the leadership of three very different South Carolina partisan fighters prevented the British from completely dominating the state and eventually contributed significantly to expelling them from the entire south.

ANDREW PICKENS

Tall, lean, and severe looking, Andrew Pickens resembled an Old Testament prophet—minus the flowing beard—in the sternness of his rectitude and the righteousness of his aroused anger. He was a devout and taciturn Presbyterian elder who, according to lore, held his words "between his fingers and examined them" before speaking.[1] When he did speak—or act—men heeded him for he was a natural leader and warrior. At the same time, this dour figure was also a man of uncommon compassion, rigid honor, and fairness. He came from a clan of Scots-Irish pioneers who migrated steadily southward during the middle of the eighteenth century. Pickens, born in Bucks County, Pennsylvania, on September 19, 1739, trekked with his family from Virginia to North Carolina, before finally settling in South Carolina's Waxhaws district in the northern portion of the colony.

Out on the frontier, he grew up in a culture that equally prized the Bible and the long rifle.

Pickens followed in his father's footsteps and became a respected local magistrate and militia officer. In 1760, the quiet young man embarked upon the first of his several campaigns against the neighboring Cherokees and began constructing a formidable reputation as an Indian fighter. On this expedition he also developed empathy for the Indians' predicament which, while hardly romantic or sentimental, was rare enough in any frontier settler—especially one whose mother-in-law and brother would be killed by hostiles. Serving under overall British command and watching Cherokee villages burn, he additionally discovered his lifelong antipathy to what he regarded as a British penchant for cruelty. Returned to peacetime pursuits, he lived as a prosperous farmer and trader. In 1765 he married and built a homestead on Long Cane Creek, some 20 miles west of Ninety Six, a trading settlement whose unusual name derived from its purported distance from an important Cherokee town.

The South Carolina backcountry was relatively isolated from coastal society or the lowcountry centered on the capital, Charleston. Indeed, as in several other colonies, the tension over taxation and representation between frontier westerners and seaboard easterners replicated to some degree the similar dispute aggravating the 13 colonies and Great Britain. In addition to the conflict between leaders in Charleston and London, and ill feeling dividing settlers and coastal elites, there was also considerable bitterness among factions in the interior itself, where the coming struggle against England exacerbated existing political rivalries and personal feuds. Further roiling this backcountry witch's brew was a general climate of violence, fueled by lawlessness and reinforced by no-quarters frontier combat with the Indians. Pickens, already strongly Whig and anti-British, inclined to the patriot side, though many of his neighbors were strong Loyalists or Tories. Word of Lexington and Concord led South Carolina patriots and Loyalists to arms by mid-1775. While leaders in Charleston engaged in relatively decorous debate over the implications of rebellion, open warfare broke out in the backcountry.

In early November 1775, Captain Pickens and his followers joined a larger patriot militia force that engaged in a 2-day fight with Loyalists at Savage's plantation, near Ninety Six, the first land battle of the Revolution in South Carolina. The colony's lieutenant governor managed to broker a temporary truce, but fighting flared again a month later. Pickens led his company deep into Cherokee country as part of a massive expedition against Loyalists who had taken refuge there. Later memorialized by participants as the "snow campaign" for the unusually harsh weather they endured, the operation turned into a great patriot success. Descending upon an unsuspecting camp—a tactic Pickens would repeatedly employ with great success—on a wintry dawn, the patriots seized 130 of the crown's supporters. In a grim portent of atrocities to come on both sides, only the leaders' exertions prevented their aroused men from massacring the helpless prisoners.

During the first months of 1776, as Washington and the British maneuvered against each other between Boston and New York, Pickens gathered a regiment of fighters pledged to him. The Cherokees, partly stirred up by British agents and seeing an opportunity in the white man's struggle, went on the warpath. Pickens gathered his family and neighbors in a blockhouse he had built, made provision for its defense, and took the field. A brutal, no-quarters campaign conducted jointly by North and South Carolina militia killed over 2,000 Indians, destroyed 32 villages, and broke Cherokee power. Pickens experienced many close calls, including a celebrated fight on August 12, 1776, in the upper part of what is today Pickens County, South Carolina. Nearly 200 braves ambushed a 25-man reconnaissance party led by Pickens. Forming a tight circle and coolly directed by him, the outnumbered detachment fought the Indians with accurate musketry. Having lost almost half their number killed or wounded, the Indians retired just before militia reinforcements could arrive. The pious Pickens, known to drop to his knees and pray within sight of the enemy, rebuked his brother Joseph, one of the late arrivals, for the violent oaths he uttered upon viewing the bloody scene. Afterwards, the Cherokees respectfully dubbed Pickens *Skyagunsta*, the "Wizard Owl" or "Great Warrior."

Subduing the Indians temporarily brought peace to the backcountry and Pickens returned to his farm and family. His next spell of active service occurred several hundred miles distant from his home. In the spring of 1778, the patriots resolved to invade Florida and Pickens's regiment received orders from state authorities to join the expeditionary force marshaling in Georgia. The operation was a debacle from the start. Traversing swampy ground in oppressive summer heat, assailed by insects, and inadequately supplied, the advancing army wilted and began to disintegrate from sickness and desertion. The bedraggled invaders eventually reached the St. Mary's River on the Georgia–Florida border and managed to reduce a weak British outpost. The American leaders thereupon declared victory and withdrew to the north. Scarcely had Pickens regained home before the heretofore dormant British, with their Loyalist and Indian allies, went over to the offensive in Georgia in late 1778. Two sizeable British columns—one advancing from the British base at St. Augustine, Florida, the other landed by sea just below Savannah—crushed patriot resistance. Simultaneously, Creek and Chickamauga tribesman began raiding outlying settlements. By early 1779, the British had captured Savannah and Augusta, and seemingly conquered the state.

During this gloomy interval, Pickens's regiment served along the South Carolina–Georgia border. In early 1779 he learned of a planned British incursion into Georgia's interior designed to eliminate any remaining patriot resistance. Pickens—now a militia colonel—notified his superiors and plunged into Georgia, taking command of about 350 men drawn from the militia of both states. Pickens shadowed and skirmished with the British during the first part of February before receiving intelligence that a contingent of 700 Loyalists was approaching his rear en route to joining the royal garrison at Augusta. Displaying commendable agility, Pickens reoriented his command to intercept this latest threat. On the morning of February 14 his scouts stalked the enemy to their camp on Kettle Creek, 50 miles west of Augusta. Pickens split his force into three detachments, sending two around the Loyalist flanks while he himself led the assault in the center. Pickens's column surprised the enemy pickets and began to attack down a ravine and into the hostile bivouac. The Loyalist commander, Colonel James Boyd, was a brave and competent fighter himself, as well as an old acquaintance whom Pickens respected. Boyd rallied his men, who gained the upper hand in the duel, when Boyd sustained a mortal wound. The Loyalists panicked and tried to escape across the creek—right into a murderous crossfire from the patriot flanking elements. Some 70 enemy died and another 70 were taken prisoner; five of these were subsequently hanged for treason, a telling indication of the stakes and passions on both sides. The rest—reduced to a disorganized mob—fled into the wilderness. The cost to the patriots was 9 dead and 23 wounded. Coming upon the dying Boyd, Pickens gravely told him, "I am pained to see you in such suffering and in such a cause."[2] He then accepted a brooch from Boyd, along with a request to deliver it to his wife, and ordered two men to stay at the fallen Loyalist's side and comfort him until he expired.

Pickens always regarded the battle of Kettle Creek as "the severest check and chastisement the Tories ever received in South Carolina or Georgia."[3] A few days later, he struck another blow—this time some 65 miles southwest of Augusta at an encampment of Creek Indians reported to be on their way to join the British. He scattered the Indians and took several prisoner, including one chief. These victories induced the British to withdraw from Augusta, and temporarily reduced Loyalist and Indian depredations in that state.

The British next set their sights on Charleston and marched from Savannah with 4,000 men. Arriving outside South Carolina's capital on May 12, the British demanded its capitulation. The Charlestonians refused in hopes that the overall American commander in the south, General Benjamin Lincoln, would come to their rescue. Lincoln, who had been unsuccessfully attempting to eject the British from Georgia, redeployed his Continental and militia troops—including Pickens's regiment—to confront this menace. Outnumbered, the British commander prudently withdrew to Savannah, taking with him several hundred African-American slaves, to the great consternation of their owners. Lincoln decided to attack the enemy rear guard—about 900 redcoats, Hessians, and Loyalists—at Stono Ferry, south of the city. The American advance commenced late on the evening of June 19 with Continentals on the left and militia led by Pickens on the right. Darkness and rugged terrain made for slow going, and the patriots did not encounter the enemy's pickets until after sunrise on the 20th. The British resisted stoutly and after several hours of close quarters combat that included Pickens having his horse killed beneath him, Lincoln ordered a retreat, having lost 300 men while inflicting only minimal casualties on the enemy.

Following this fiasco, one of several over which Lincoln presided in the south, word spread of another Indian uprising in the backcountry. Pickens requested and received permission to return home with his men. There they remained until fall 1779, when they mobilized to join the combined Franco-American siege of

Savannah. Lincoln and a French amphibious force under the Comte D'Estaing moved steadily on the British outer works, and began to bombard the city from both land and sea on October 4. Although the British defenses had hardly been reduced or breached, d'Estaing—concerned about his ships' safety in the face of storm season or the arrival of a British fleet—insisted on a full scale assault for the morning of October 9. An overly complicated allied scheme of maneuver featured five separate columns moving in the dark. The brigade to which Pickens was assigned sustained heavy losses and was easily beaten off. The same held true for the other attacking elements and the allies called off the operation. D'Estaing, himself badly wounded, sailed away to the West Indies and Lincoln pulled the bulk of the Americans back to the vicinity of Charleston. Pickens and his men remained in south Georgia for several more months, where they waged a smoldering, low-intensity conflict against assorted Loyalists and Indians.

Pickens's regiment returned home to South Carolina's Ninety Six district in early 1780. Terrible news soon reached them: General Lincoln had surrendered Charleston to the British on May 12 after a lengthy siege. In a dreadful coda, 2 weeks later a combined force of Loyalists and regulars, commanded by Lieutenant Colonel Banastre Tarleton, rode down a fleeing patriot force at Waxhaws. Allegedly ignoring a white surrender flag, Tarleton's troopers massacred more than 100 helpless men and captured another 200. This action made Tarleton's name—along with "Bloody Ban" and similar monikers—a byword among patriots and gave birth to the notorious phrase "Tarleton's quarter," which meant no mercy to captives. Concurrently, British forces and their allies flooded the state, establishing garrisons at Ninety Six, Camden, and a host of smaller locales. They reoccupied Augusta, Georgia as well.

These reverses momentarily stunned South Carolinians into submission. The state's revolutionary governor, John Rutledge, fled and many prominent men made their peace with the occupiers and pledged not to resist further. When Pickens polled his followers, almost to a man they expressed a desire to give up the struggle. Thus even the fierce Pickens, seeing no prospect in continuing to fight and with a family to protect, gave his parole and went home. The colonel spent the summer in the bosom of his family, working his holdings with them and his slaves. As the weeks and months passed, reports occasionally arrived of renewed British affronts or Loyalist outrages. Some of his neighbors took up arms again and looked to Pickens to lead them, but to Pickens an oath was a solemn thing and he upheld his word. The British commander in the south, Lord Cornwallis, issued orders to visit severe reprisals upon those who refused positively to support the crown. This in turn increased the cycle of violence. Pickens remained true to his bond until late 1780, when marauding Loyalists descended upon and burned his plantation while he was away on business. Adding insult to injury, they heaped abuse upon his wife and children. Presenting himself to a local British official, Pickens stiffly informed him, "I have honorably and conscientiously adhered to the rules laid down in the protection I took but now I consider myself completely absolved from its obligation by the plunder and wanton waste which has been committed on my farm and the insults and indignities that have been offered to my family."[4] He had rejoined the fight with a vengeance.

Having withdrawn his parole, Pickens fully realized that in British eyes he was an outlaw and subject to hang if captured. He again bade his family farewell and took to the woods, where he recruited and sent messages to the new American commander in the south, Nathanael Greene, offering his support. Greene instructed Pickens to join his partisans with General Daniel Morgan's command, which Greene had recently detached to operate in western South Carolina. By the end of December Pickens and 350 mounted followers reported into Morgan's camp on the Pacolet River near Grindall's Shoals. Other militiamen flowed in as well from the rest of the Carolinas and Georgia.

Cornwallis watched the division of Greene's army and imitated it. He dispatched Tarleton with 1,100 men, included his dreaded, green-coated legion, to hunt down and destroy Morgan, who by now mustered a similar-sized force of Continentals and militia. For the first half of January 1781 Tarleton dogged Morgan up the west side of the Broad River. Pickens's scouts helped keep Morgan apprised of Tarleton's progress and thanks in part to Pickens's reporting, Morgan realized that his remorseless opponent was closing on him. He decided to stand and fight, rather than be caught on the march as had happened to the hapless patriots at Waxhaws. After consulting officers familiar with the area, Morgan chose a spot some 5 miles from the Broad River in northwestern South Carolina to make his stand.

The Americans assembled throughout the day on January 16 at the northern, upper end of a gently sloping meadow known as the Cowpens. Morgan expected Tarleton to slam into him on the morrow from the south, making his approach along the road that bisected the open field. Morgan planned to receive him by arraying his men in three ranks. The first would be a skirmish line of handpicked riflemen whose task was to pick off enemy officers and cause the British to deploy. The second rank consisted of the bulk of the militia—nearly 300 men—under Pickens's steady command. Veteran Continentals comprised the third and main line. A squadron of about 125 dragoons, poised to exploit success, made up the American reserve. The night before the battle Morgan and Pickens made the rounds of their men, outlining the plan to the anxious soldiers huddled around their campfires and attempting to allay their nervousness. Pickens explained to his militiamen that they were to stand fast once the first rank of riflemen withdrew and not to fire "until the enemy is within thirty paces; then aim low and fire in relays, picking off the officers first; every third man fire, while the others hold their fire in reserve."[5] Once they had discharged their weapons, they would then make an orderly withdrawal to the left rear of the American position, behind the Continentals.

Somewhat astoundingly, and in defiance of the maxim that no plan survives contact with the enemy, Morgan's design worked almost exactly as he drew it up. On the morning of the 17th, Tarleton's men, already exhausted from a 5-mile, predawn approach march, began their attack up the meadow. The front rank rifle-men took their toll and then it was the turn of Pickens's ragged but determined fighters. They traded volleys with the enemy and demonstrated a firmness wholly at odds with previous—and many subsequent—militia performances. Some Con-tinental officers later averred that it was here that the battle was won. Pickens's men bloodied the oncoming enemy and in particular shot down many officers and sergeants. Then, in the face of glittering steel bayonets that had cowed other patriot militia from Manhattan to Camden, Pickens's men smartly leapfrogged to their alternate position. While Pickens reorganized his jubilant troops, the enemy regiments and Continentals locked up in a death struggle. Tarleton committed his infantry reserve—the crack 71st Highlander Regiment—against the American right to decide the issue. Morgan countered by sending his cavalry thundering against the British right while Pickens led his swarming irregulars against the enemy left—creating in effect that classic battlefield maneuver often sought but rarely attained by commanders, a double envelopment. Pickens later recalled that the enemy began to throw down their arms en masse, "That part of the 71st, which was there, surrendered to me, and I believe every officer of that regiment delivered his sword to my hand."[6]

Tarleton's attempts to rally his troops failed and soon he joined the remnants of his command fleeing the Americans' pursuit. His loss of over 900 men killed or captured dealt a crippling, if not fatal, blow to Cornwallis's plans for a southern offensive. Though Morgan rightfully deserves the greatest credit for the victory, there was plenty of glory to share. In the battle's aftermath, Governor Rutledge commissioned Pickens as a brigadier general in South Carolina's militia and the Continental Congress thanked him in a resolution that included the eventual award of a commemorative sword.

Following Cowpens, the contending armies tramped into North Carolina. An enraged Cornwallis set after Morgan while Pickens, tasked to deliver over 600 enemy prisoners to safe custody north of the Yadkin River, followed a separate route. After discharging his responsibilities, Pickens hastened to Salisbury, North Carolina, which General Greene had designated as the rallying point for the scattered elements of his army. Greene's intended to make for the Dan River and cross into Virginia, wearing down Cornwallis's pursuing force and setting himself up to recross into North Carolina and strike a counterblow. He assigned Pickens, now in command of a mixed detachment of Carolina and Georgia militia, the critical mission of getting behind Cornwallis to harass his supply lines and foraging parties. Additionally, Pickens would provide intelligence and attempt to attract as many new fighters to the patriot standard as he could. With this assistance, Greene won this "race to the Dan" by mid-February and began to refurbish his troops for the planned offensive.

To begin this next phase of the campaign, on February 18 Greene dispatched the dashing patriot cavalry officer, "Light-Horse Harry" Lee and his legion—a combined cavalry–infantry force organized similar to Tarleton's outfit—back into North Carolina to link up with Pickens. Several days later, Greene himself, with a small cavalry escort, crossed the Dan to brief the two men personally at their austere camp. Their task was to raise havoc in the enemy's rear and, more particularly, discourage Loyalist sympathizers from rallying to Cornwallis. The commanding general then slept on the ground, under a blanket borrowed from Pickens. Early the next morning he shared a meager breakfast of cornbread and salt meat with the South Carolinian. The two then separated, Greene back to gather the main army and Pickens, with Lee's considerable assistance, to embark on this latest mission. In the course of this, and in a struggle replete with atrocities both real and alleged, Pickens was involved in one of the most infamous episodes.

Pickens had learned that none other than Tarleton himself, leading a reconstituted force, was operating in the country between the Deep and Haw Rivers, generally regarded as a hotbed of Loyalist sentiment. Pickens and Lee decided to attempt to corner him. While unsuccessful in this endeavor, on the morning of February 25, Pickens and Lee learned of a column of 300 North Carolina Loyalists who were marching to join Tarleton at Hillsborough. In an elaborate ruse, Lee and his Legion, whose green jackets resembled those worn by Tarleton's men, pretended to be the British force. With Pickens and the militia hidden in the nearby woods, the *faux* "Tarleton"—that is, Lee—requested the Loyalist leader, a local doctor and self-styled colonel named Pyle, to draw his troops up alongside the road so that "Tarleton's Legion" might get by. As the Legion passed, a melee broke out—perhaps begun by a keen-eyed Tory who spotted Pickens's ill-concealed militia in the tree line. Lee's men, aided by the militia, quickly fell upon the stunned, helpless Loyalists and made short work of them with blade and musket at point blank range. Nearly 100 Loyalists died; the others were virtually all wounded and dispersed. That all were not killed owes something to Pickens and Lee, who made efforts to restrain the slaughter. There were no patriot casualties. To them the result was a great victory and condign revenge for Tarleton's action at Waxhaws. To the British and their supporters it became the "Pyle Massacre." Regardless, the gory affair represented another savage chapter in the southern struggle. It also considerably dampened Loyalist ardor in the region.

In the March days leading to the clash between Greene and Cornwallis at Guilford Courthouse, Pickens continued to slash away at British detachments and supply trains. Nevertheless, his South Carolinians and Georgians had grown weary of their hardships. For over 3 months, they had waged a brutal struggle under the most appalling physical conditions of danger and privation. Additionally—a recurring reality with all militia—the safety of their homes and families concerned them; after all, local protection was what militia forces were really all about. Pickens requested from Greene the release of himself and his men, citing not only their exhaustion, but also the continued threat of British reprisal and Indian uprising. Bowing to Pickens's persuasiveness, Greene assented on March 8, ordering him to place himself under the command of Thomas Sumter, the ranking partisan general in South Carolina, once he arrived.

As Pickens made his way home, Greene and Cornwallis fought the battle of Guilford Courthouse. Afterwards, the British general marched to Wilmington to refit his troops, then made his momentous decision to abandon the Carolina hornets nest and invade Virginia. Greene countered by heading the opposite way into South Carolina. Although the British still had some 8,000 troops remaining in that state and Georgia, they were scattered in packets across a wide area. Greene hoped to pick them off one by one through the combined efforts of his army and the aroused partisans. As part of this design, by April Pickens, in cooperation with Georgia militia, was operating between the two westernmost British posts, Augusta and Ninety Six. Shortly before Pickens's arrival, Georgia partisans had captured a notorious Loyalist named James Dunlap—the man responsible for burning Pickens's farm. Pickens eschewed personal vengeance and agreed with his Georgia counterpart to send the man away for trial. Another partisan, however, mad with rage, overpowered Dunlap's guards and killed him in cold blood. Pickens duly reported the murder to the senior British officer in the area, expressing his "horror and detestation," but also adding that the retaliation stemmed in part from "the many barbarous massacres committed by those calling themselves officers on our people after their capture."[7]

Throughout the spring of 1781 a succession of British outposts fell to the patriots—either captured by them or evacuated by the British as untenable. By the end of May, the only remaining British backcountry strongholds were Augusta and Ninety Six. Greene sent Henry Lee, fresh from successful operations with Francis Marion, to join Pickens near Augusta. While the high-strung Lee and Sumter, along with the moody Marion, had driven Greene to the verge of despair with their quarrels, no similar problems arose between "Light-Horse Harry" and Pickens—a tribute to the latter's tact and calm, dignified demeanor. Reunited in action, the two devised a plan to reduce the enemy works. Augusta's defenses consisted of two forts—Fort Cornwallis in the town itself and Fort Grierson, after the British officer who commanded there, just outside it. They agreed to attack the exterior position first and seized it on May 23 after a sharp fight. In a grimly familiar ritual, Pickens later had to inform Greene about another "very disagreeable and Melancholly affair"—patriot militiamen shot and killed the captured Colonel Grierson and several other captives.[8]

Fort Cornwallis, held by 250 Loyalist militiamen and 300 Creek Indians, resisted longer. The patriots began digging approach trenches to get close enough for an assault. They also erected a tower—a proven technique from previous sieges against the British posts—and emplaced sharpshooters and even a cannon. Pickens personally led a force that countered a Loyalist sortie in a desperate hand-to-hand fracas the night of June 1. Pounded into submission, the enemy surrendered 4 days later. Taking account of the locals' high feelings and having learned from the fate meted out to previous captives, Pickens took extra precautions in safeguarding the ranking Loyalists who fell into his hands. And, as he had done in the case of Dunlap's assassin, he offered a reward for the apprehension of Grierson's killer. After securing his prisoners, distributing captured supplies, and establishing a patriot garrison at Augusta, Pickens made for his home district of Ninety Six to join the siege of the lone hold out British backcountry post.

General Greene himself, with slightly over 1,000 Continentals and militia, had been supervising the investment of Ninety Six since May 22. The village had been transformed into an imposing Loyalist stronghold, manned by 550 men, supported by their womenfolk and a number of slaves. In addition to the walls surrounding the town itself, the fortifications consisted of an obstacled ditch, and redoubts to the east and west. The defenders skillfully parried Greene's approaches by frequent sorties and countersaps. By the time Pickens arrived on the scene in early June, none of the gambits—a tower from which to fire into the fort, even flaming arrows—that availed the patriots in previous sieges had succeeded. Snipers took a toll on both sides. A Loyalist marksman killed Pickens's brother Joseph, who was a militia captain. Then Greene hit upon a winning stratagem—cutting off the garrison's water supply, which came from a spring guarded by the western redoubt. Given time, this might have worked, but the British launched a powerful rescue expedition from Charleston. Greene ordered Sumter and Marion to check this force, but neither accomplished the task. Years afterward Pickens criticized his fellow partisan chiefs: "They had a number of men in the Low Country and knew every defile on the way—and I believe not the least attempt was made by them"[9] The impending enemy relief compelled Greene to try a last-ditch assault, which failed to carry the enemy position.

Greene reluctantly lifted the siege on June 20, forcing Pickens once again to leave his wife and children behind in a district still teeming with Loyalist sympathies and resentment. Pickens's men screened the main army's withdrawal and maintained a watch on enemy movements, including their eventual evacuation of Ninety Six in early July. While Pickens and the other partisans continued their activities, Greene refitted his main force on the high ground above the north bank of the Santee River. By late August, Greene felt strong enough to return to the offensive. He also feared that Cornwallis might return from Virginia and thus he sought to crush the remaining enemy forces in South Carolina before that could occur. Greene issued the call and the far-flung partisan bands rendezvoused with the rest of the army on the Santee. This host then marched southeast toward Charleston. Though largely blinded by the partisans' efforts, the British obliged by moving northwest out of the capital to challenge the patriots. Greene's vanguard collided with the unsuspecting British on the morning of September 8, 1781, at Eutaw Springs.

South and North Carolina militia advanced side by side as the patriots' first attacking wave. Pickens commanded on the left, Marion on the right and a French nobleman, the Marquis de Malmedy, led the North Carolinians in the center. The British veterans rapidly organized themselves and offered stern resistance. While the flanking elements under Pickens and Marion pressed ahead, the North Carolina militia faltered. Then the South Carolinians began to stall as well. Seeing this, Greene fed in his Continental regiments, who comprised his second echelon. The battle, already furious, became a smoky, earsplitting cauldron of shot and shell. The Americans gained the advantage with a bayonet charge and might have routed their foes but for the unrelenting fire of two enemy battalions—one barricaded in a solid brick house, the other in a dense thicket off to the American left. Somewhere in the donnybrook, Pickens was shot out of his saddle. His men carried him from the field, certain he was mortally wounded. By an incredible stroke of fortune, however, the ball had struck his sword belt and been deflected, pounding the buckle deep into his breast bone. After three hours of violent combat in brutal heat, the American assault ran out of steam and Greene ordered a retreat. The last major battle of the Carolina campaign, and the bloodiest, ended with both sides pulling back to lick their wounds and await further developments.

Cornwallis surrendered at Yorktown on October 19, 1781, but British troops remained in Charleston another 14 months. During this period of stalemate, Pickens recuperated and contended with Loyalists and Indians. Pickens was magnanimous, despite his implacable wrath in battle and the personal losses he had endured, toward those former crown supporters who wished to be reintegrated into society in the aftermath of British defeat in America. He strongly supported Governor Rutledge's and General Greene's efforts to pardon and safeguard them in their return to their homes. For his part, Pickens issued strict orders against reprisal and plunder to his followers. Nevertheless, roving Loyalist bands—little more than bandits—continued to plague the backcountry. Some of these freebooters also managed to stir up the Cherokees again. In a particularly horrific episode, one of Pickens's brothers fell into the Indians' clutches and was roasted alive. In retaliation, Pickens led militia from several states in multiple campaigns to eradicate the outlaws and pacify the Indians. The culmination, after much blood and fire, was a treaty Pickens negotiated with a dozen Cherokee chiefs in October 1782. This marked the end of Pickens's active military career, but hardly his public role.

Pickens served his neighbors, state, and the new republic in many capacities. In the second half of his long, productive life he acted as an elder of his church, justice of the peace, member of the South Carolina legislature, and United States Congressman. Governors and presidents appointed him to numerous state and federal commissions, where his most important work lay in marking boundaries and concluding Indian treaties. He became wealthy through his ownership of several large plantations. He remained a man of considerable influence; the Pickens name ranks with Rutledge, Pinckney, and Calhoun among the great families of antebellum South Carolina. Indeed, Pickens mentored the young John C. Calhoun and the future statesman married into the Pickens clan. A Pickens son and grandson became state governors. Like some Biblical patriarch, he died peacefully in his 78th year, surrounded by family and while gazing across his fields toward the mountains. The simple marker above his resting place near Pendleton, South Carolina notes that he was "a Christian, a Patriot and Soldier."[10]

THOMAS SUMTER

Thomas Sumter, the highest ranking of the South Carolina partisans, was not the most capable or successful among them, but certainly the most charismatic and contentious. "The Gamecock" earned his nickname from the cock's feather with which he adorned his uniform hat, but the soubriquet neatly fit his feisty, combative personality as well. He was more adept at execution than planning and his fearlessness led him to ill-judged tactical decisions on occasion. Henry Lee described him as so "Enchanted with the splendor of victory, he would wade in torrents of blood to attain it."[11] Sumter's independence and stubbornness made him at times an uncooperative subordinate, but the same traits impelled him to resist British power during his state's darkest hours. He was born in the Blue Ridge foothills of frontier Virginia on July 14, 1734. His Welsh-English immigrant parents eked out a living farming and operating a gristmill. Sumter received little schooling and helped augment the family income by hiring out as plow boy for a neighboring farmer. He grew into a tough, sinewy man of medium height who displayed a decided wild streak. His favored pursuits included gambling, cockfighting, and horse racing.

His taste for excitement led to his enlistment in a militia regiment at the start of the French and Indian War. He took part in the British-led expedition into western Pennsylvania that captured the French stronghold of Duquesne in November 1758. Sumter, like many rambunctious young men before and since, thrived under the military's unique blend of action and routine, freedom and discipline. He rose to the rank of sergeant and in 1760–1761 distinguished himself in the same series of punitive expeditions against the Cherokees in which Andrew Pickens and Francis Marion also fought. Following the eventual peace settlement with the Indians, Sumter volunteered for the hazardous chore of delivering the treaty to the Over the Hill tribes in the Great Smoky Mountains region of what is modern-day Tennessee. While among the Indians he endeared himself to their chiefs and escorted three of them back to Virginia's capital. When the tribal leaders subsequently voyaged to London, Sumter accompanied them. His sojourn at the apex of imperial civilization was as eventful as his earlier stay among the savages. All London feted the Indians and their minder. After several months basking in celebrity, including an audience with George III, Sumter and his charges returned to America.

Sumter landed in Charleston and lingered in South Carolina, making new acquaintances among the lowcountry gentry and visiting in the backcountry with his old Indian friends. Among the latter, he got involved in a scrape with a French agent provocateur, seized him after a hand-to-hand brawl, and dispatched him off to British captivity. This escapade won him more plaudits. When the young hero finally returned to his Virginia settlement in late 1763, however, he got a less congenial reception than those afforded by tribal chiefs, his majesty's court, or Charleston aristocrats. The local magistrate clapped him in prison for defaulting on an old debt. No cell could contain him for long; he broke jail and headed south. He turned up in South Carolina and rather brazenly petitioned the crown for compensation for his late services escorting the Indian chiefs. Fortune favors the bold; he received 700 pounds and with this stake he opened a trading post in Eutaw Springs, along the boundary between frontier and the more settled low country.

He prospered, especially after marrying a rich widow 11 years his senior in 1767 and settling in at her plantation above the Santee River. As befit a man of his newly enhanced stature, he took an interest in politics and held minor local offices. Sumter also became an ardent Whig and exponent of colonial liberties in the mounting revolutionary turmoil of the early and mid-1770s. Consequently, his neighbors elected him to a new body formed to confront the royal governor, the South Carolina Provincial Congress. Convening in Charleston in early 1775, this assembly corresponded with the Continental Congress meeting in Philadelphia and compiled a list of grievances revolving around imperial misdeeds while avowing its continued loyalty to the king. Radicalization swiftly set in however, spurred chiefly by news of Lexington and Concord. By June, the Provincial Congress, concerned about possible Loyalist contamination of the militia, raised three new regiments to defend patriot liberties. A dismayed Sumter, not wealthy or well connected enough, failed to receive a commission, so he formed his own independent company. His men in turn elected him their captain. When fighting broke out between Loyalists and Whigs around Ninety Six in November, the Provincial Congress ordered a reinforcing detachment to aid the patriots. Captain Sumter distinguished himself as the commander's adjutant on the expedition. This backcountry foray culminated with the December "snow campaign," which netted over 100 Loyalists who had taken refuge in Cherokee country.

Over the next 3 years Sumter attained the rank of colonel and participated in four major campaigns, none of which brought him much personal satisfaction or martial renown. In early 1776, amid mounting excitement over renewed Indian threats and fear of a British assault on Charleston, the Provincial Congress authorized the raising of more regiments and commissioned Sumter to command one of them as a lieutenant colonel. Sumter recruited that spring among the riflemen of the backcountry and by early summer was encamped on the outskirts of Charleston. On June 1 the British threat to the city materialized in the form of a fleet carrying the British General Henry Clinton and a landing force. General Charles Lee was on hand to direct the patriot defense, which centered on Fort Sullivan, located on the island of the same name guarding the entrance to Charleston harbor. Lee posted Sumter's men on the mainland just above the city to repel any British attack there. From this vantage point Sumter watched Fort Sullivan's defenders beat off Clinton's attack on June 28.

As the British sailed off, action in South Carolina shifted to the frontier and the threat posed by the resurgent Cherokees. Sumter marched his troops west to participate in a vicious campaign of scorched earth throughout the second half of 1776. This drove the Indians to make peace. While several battles occurred, Sumter did no fighting. Rather, he and his men grimly put villages and fields to the torch. Following this arduous, if inglorious, period of field service Sumter brought his regiment to a comfortable bivouac conveniently located just 5 miles from his plantation, which also served as his headquarters. In a further blow to Sumter's already bruised ego, the local magistrate fined him for having failed to fulfill his duties as a grand juror during his absence. Meanwhile, Sumter's command, along with the other South Carolina state regiments, had been inducted into the Continental line at the Philadelphia Congress's request. Sumter's men were now regulars, at least in name.

A British probe—little more than a foraging expedition—into Georgia from St. Augustine, Florida in February 1777 aroused the southern patriots once again. Lee's replacement in the southern department, General Robert Howe, mobilized his South Carolina regiments and ordered them to Savannah. By the time they arrived, Georgia militia had turned away the intruders short of that city. Sumter aggressively pursued them nearly 100 miles through the pines and swamps. Howe hoped to mount a counteroffensive into British East Florida, but Georgia's cutthroat internal politics forced him to discard that notion almost immediately. A power struggle between two magnificently named and bitter rivals—Lachlan McIntosh, Georgia's senior Continental officer, and Button Gwinnett, the state's chief executive and a signer of the Declaration of Independence—scuttled the project and culminated with McIntosh killing Gwinnett in a duel. In such circumstances, it was impossible to prosecute an invasion, and Sumter's footsore and dispirited men were back in Charleston by May.

The Continental Congress subsequently investigated the Georgia–Florida disaster and called Sumter to Philadelphia to give evidence before an inquiry. Congress ended up reassigning McIntosh to the Pennsylvania frontier—in part to spirit him away from murder charges sought by Gwinnett's friends. Sumter made good use of his time in the corridors of power; by summer's end he had secured a new commission as a full colonel in the Continental line. He returned to South Carolina in August. The rest of 1777 passed uneventfully for Sumter and his men, who wintered comfortably in Charleston. In the spring of 1778 Howe began preparing another effort to eliminate the British base in Florida. Sumter's regiment dutifully tramped southward through Georgia once again, but misfortune plagued the expedition from the start. Poor logistical planning, the nightmarish terrain and summer climate, and the usual disputes among state and military officials, caused the invading patriots to grind to a halt near the Florida border. Sumter himself, like many of his men, had succumbed to malaria and returned to his plantation above the Santee before then. For 3 years, he had marched all over the Carolina backcountry and Georgia low country without firing a shot in anger while others won laurels. In ill health, he was disgusted as well. In September, he resigned his commission.

Sumter stayed out of the fray for 20 months. His retirement coincided with the onset of military stalemate in the north and the British shifting their main effort to the south. Sumter developed his extensive land holdings and got elected to the state assembly. He refused all entreaties to take up arms however, even after the British threatened Charleston at the beginning of 1780. He watched throughout the spring as numerous refugees, slipping through the tightening British ring around the city, fled past his home en route to North Carolina. One of these was Governor Rutledge, who left a bag of state funds with Sumter for safekeeping. Once the British took Charleston, in early May, they began to overrun the rest of the state. Columns fanned out in all directions. The most energetic, led by Banastre Tarleton, slashed its way up the Santee. Sumter had been a well-known Continental officer and on May 28 Tarleton's men burned his home as his wife and small son watched. Sumter, anticipating this, had departed scant hours earlier, now intent upon mounting resistance against the British.

Other South Carolinians had similar ideas and they coalesced in the vicinity of Salisbury, North Carolina on the Catawba River. South Carolina's patriot government was in disarray, so these men organized themselves without any official sanction. Applying the freewheeling method of the frontier, they elected Sumter as their leader. The Gamecock had no overarching strategy or plan of campaign other than to terrorize Loyalists and raid enemy posts. He did, however, write to the temporary head of Continental forces in North Carolina—the Baron de Kalb, who awaited the imminent arrival of Horatio Gates to assume the southern command—and offer him what intelligence he could. By mid-July, Sumter had gathered approximately 500 fighters—their numbers fluctuated daily—and reentered South Carolina. Over the next 30 days he sparred with Tarleton and the Loyalists along the Catawba–Wateree River valley above and just below the British base at Camden.

Sumter's partisans made plans in the same democratic spirit with which they chose officers. A council of colonels devised a scheme and then put it to the men. In accordance with these procedures, all agreed to an operation against an outlying Tory station at Rocky Mount, an eminence overlooking the Catawba about 40 miles north of Camden. Approximately 150 Loyalists manned the site. Launching diversions against other British posts in the immediate area, Sumter attacked on August 1. Alert enemy pickets foiled an attempt to take the place by stealth and a daylong firefight ensued. The Loyalists holed up in a fortified house and could not be forced out. Late in the day, Sumter tried to set fire to the building, but a sudden downpour stymied this plan. Low on ammunition, he withdrew, having inflicted and suffered about a dozen casualties.

Five days later, Sumter struck again, this time against a substantially stronger enemy position east of Rocky Mount. Several enemy regiments, totaling 1,400 redcoats and Loyalists, including elements of Tarleton's Legion, occupied a series of fortified camps along Hanging Rock Creek. Sumter crossed to the east side of the Catawba with about 600 South and North Carolina militia on the morning of August 6. He had divided his force into thirds with the intention that each portion assault a different camp. As it turned out, the thick woods and channeling effects of terrain caused all three units to crash into the northernmost bivouac. The stunned Loyalists were driven back and the patriots proceeded to roll up the parallel encampments. The Legion infantry put up a stiffer fight and some British regulars managed a flanking maneuver that enabled them to pour a devastating fire into the patriot advance. The battle became a confused melee and here Sumter was in his element. Astride his horse, he shouted directions and encouragement above the din, even after being grazed by a musket ball in the thigh. Eventually the redcoats formed a square and the militia became too disorganized to press further. Realizing that his attack had culminated, Sumter yelled "Boys, it is not good to pursue a victory too far!"[12] The Americans withdrew while the British gave three cheers for King George. The patriots answered with three cheers of their own before they retired. Well they might; Hanging Rock was a clear cut patriot win. In return for about 70 men lost, Sumter's raiders killed, wounded, or captured over 200 of the enemy.

"Both British and Tories are panic struck," is how Sumter described the effect of Hanging Rock.[13] Perhaps this overstated the case, but by now the British were alarmed, not only due to Sumter's aggressiveness, but also because of the approach of an American army led by the latest southern commander, Horatio Gates. Cornwallis began concentrating forces at Camden to deal with both these threats while Gates attempted to coordinate his advance with Sumter and another partisan leader farther south and east, Francis Marion. In order to isolate the enemy at Camden, Gates instructed Sumter to move down the Catawba and Wateree Rivers to secure the crossings above Camden. He later gave Marion a similar mission proceeding up the Santee River. Sumter's fortunes rode high. News of his success swelled his ranks with new recruits and Gates even reinforced him with 400 Continentals and some artillery. By August 15 Sumter's forays down the Wateree had reached south of Camden and netted him over 100 prisoners and much booty—more than 40 supply wagons, a herd of cattle, and a flock of sheep. Here, however, the patriot idyll ended.

On August 16 Cornwallis routed Gates at the battle of Camden. The terrible Tarleton flayed the remnants of Gates's army before Cornwallis summoned him back and loosed him on Sumter. The Gamecock had been creeping north along the west side of the Wateree when he received news of Gates's defeat. He attempted to increase his pace, but his captured goods slowed him. Tarleton now shadowed Sumter up the east side of the waterway. On the evening of August 17, the Briton spied the patriot campfires on the opposite bank about a mile distant and forbade his men to light any of their own in order not to give away his position. Early next morning Tarleton's men crossed at Rocky Mount and continued to stalk Sumter. By noon they caught up with their prey. The exhausted patriots had only managed to stagger a few miles farther before establishing another campsite at Fishing Creek, beside the Catawba. Oblivious to their peril, they stacked arms and proceeded to cook rations or bathe in the river. Many were drunk on captured rum. Sumter was literally caught napping, under the shade of a wagon. Tarleton's men descended like banshees, killing at least 150 and taking twice as many prisoner, while freeing their comrades and recovering the looted materiel. The survivors of this onslaught scattered for their lives, including a bootless and half-dressed Sumter, who barely got away on an unsaddled horse.

One of the more remarkable aspects of the war in the south was the patriots' ability to reconstitute forces following catastrophic defeat. So it was with

Sumter's followers. Over the next week or so, those who had escaped from Fishing Creek, augmented by newcomers, assembled on the Gamecock in the relative safety of North Carolina. By the end of August, Cornwallis complained that "the indefatigable Sumter is again in the field and is beating up for recruits with the greatest assiduity."[14] Shortly thereafter, as Cornwallis himself drove into North Carolina to expand his southern conquests, Sumter with nearly 1,000 adherents slipped back across the border into the Palmetto State. In addition to Sumter's renewed presence in the region between the Broad and Catawba Rivers, Marion bedeviled the British in the lowcountry above Charleston. Most ominously for Cornwallis, on October 7 a combined force of Carolinian and Virginian "over mountain men" cornered and destroyed a 1,000-man Loyalist army at King's Mountain along the border between the two Carolinas. These developments all led Cornwallis to give up his North Carolina invasion; by the end of October he was back in South Carolina and determined to extinguish the partisan threat there.

Sumter meanwhile had weathered a command controversy. In early September, one James Williams, another of the numerous elected or self-appointed irregular "colonels" waging war in the south, materialized at Sumter's camp, proclaimed himself a brigadier general, and asserted his right to command. Even without a bad personal history that already existed between the two men, this was not calculated to sit well with the proud Gamecock—or his troops—who refused to submit to Williams's authority. In fact, the exiled Governor Rutledge had, somewhat ill-advisedly, just commissioned Williams as a brigadier. After their typical fashion, the troops deliberated and decided to send a delegation to Rutledge to make their case. Williams rode off in a huff, Sumter temporarily suspended his command, and the delegates proceeded to North Carolina. The emissaries were more persuasive than they could have hoped. On October 6, the governor commissioned Sumter as a brigadier general, gave him command of all the militia in the state, and instructed him to cooperate fully with any Continental forces. As it developed, others would challenge the former imperative and Sumter frequently flouted the latter. For the moment, however, he busied himself complying with his other charges to raise troops and harass the enemy. Williams helped resolve any immediate difficulties by injecting himself into the fight at King's Mountain and becoming one of the very few patriots killed in that one-sided battle.

Throughout the late fall of 1780 the British doggedly sought to bring the partisans to heel. In one of the many paradoxes of this type of warfare, their ardor to stamp out insurgents created more, most notably in the case of Andrew Pickens, who came out of retirement after Loyalists fired his home. Sumter fought two engagements in November. The first was in defense of his bivouac at Fish Dam Ford, on the Broad River 30 miles northwest of Winnsboro, where Cornwallis had concentrated the bulk of his army. Acting on good intelligence, a mounted force of 200 redcoats swooped down on Sumter's camp in the dark, early morning hours of November 9. The British had gone so far as to detail a special 5 man squad with the express mission of capturing or killing Sumter in his tent. Similar to Fishing Creek, Sumter once again was rousted from slumber and scrambled off barefoot and partially clad to take refuge along the riverbank. Unlike Fishing Creek, the patriots were on their guard. In a surreal nighttime battle luridly illuminated by campfires, they repulsed the enemy with heavy losses. Among those captured was the British commander. At daybreak Sumter interviewed the wounded officer and discovered on his person a sheet of paper listing houses he had previously pillaged and burned, and men he had hanged. Realizing that his partisans would impose the roughest sort of justice should they learn of this, Sumter magnanimously destroyed the paper, thus sparing the man who had plotted his assassination.

Hoping to be done with Sumter once and for all, Cornwallis again unleashed Tarleton, who had been fruitlessly chasing Marion through the low-country swamps. The cruel British dragoon turned his attention to Sumter, and for a week relentlessly hunted him across innumerable streams and rivers in the north-central portion of the state. For his part, Sumter sought a place to make a stand. He selected his ground at Blackstock's plantation, high above the Tyger River, 60 miles northwest of Winnsboro. It was a strong natural position and Sumter situated his men in the wooded hills that covered both sides of the road leading up to the main house, as well as the surrounding fields. The impatient Tarleton, anxious lest Sumter give him the slip, had left behind his artillery and slow-marching infantry to pursue with dragoons and what infantry he could mount. He approached Blackstock's late on the afternoon of November 20 with about 270 men.

Being outnumbered by nearly two to one failed to deter Tarleton. He advanced up both sides of the road with his now-dismounted infantry on his right, while he personally led the heavy cavalry to the left. Sumter, at least as impetuous as his adversary, refused to wait on an assault and precipitated the fight by ordering troops on his left forward to meet the enemy infantry. His men complied and got off a ragged volley at too great a range to do any damage. The disciplined redcoats then charged with fixed bayonets, sending the militia reeling. The British infantry proved too fierce for their own good, however, for their surge carried them within range of riflemen in and around the house. A hail of lead broke the British charge and thinned their ranks. Simultaneously, Sumter ordered the units on his right to flank Tarleton's dragoons. A powerful salvo emptied 20 British saddles. Tarleton then led his remaining troopers away from this threat and across the road to the aid of his embattled infantry. A withering patriot crossfire filled the lane with dead and dying horses and men. All Tarleton could do was call retreat. Riding to the scene of action to savor his triumph, Sumter caught a fusillade from the retiring but still lethal British infantry. Struck multiple times in the right chest and shoulder, he grimaced and simply asked an aide to return his sword to its scabbard. Not wishing to demoralize his men, Sumter hung on for as long as he could until, weak from loss of blood, he relinquished command to a subordinate. He then cantered over to the main house and was led inside where he collapsed. The Americans claimed to have inflicted nearly 200 casualties while Tarleton only admitted 51. Regardless of which figure is accurate, Blackstock's was Sumter's finest hour as a battlefield tactician. In return for a handful of American losses—including the wounded general—Tarleton had been badly beaten.

While Sumter slowly recovered from his painful and debilitating wounds, great changes were underway. In early December Nathanael Greene took command of Continental forces in the south. One of his first moves was to journey from North Carolina with Governor Rutledge to visit the ailing Sumter. Greene commended Sumter for his previous resistance activities and discussed strategic options. Rutledge confirmed Sumter's command of all state forces, including the numerous partisan bands that had sprung up. While all proceeded well in this session, within weeks Greene badly ruffled the Gamecock's feathers. In a letter to Sumter elaborating on his strategic vision, Greene had deprecated irregular efforts, "The salvation of this Country don't depend upon little strokes . . . Partizan strokes . . . are like the garnish of a table . . . but they afford no substantial national security."[15] Worse, Greene detached General Daniel Morgan to operate in the Carolina backcountry and authorized him to command any militia there. While Greene had not intentionally meant to snub the still hobbled Sumter, the feisty partisan leader viewed this as a clear violation of his command prerogatives. Greene, Morgan, and Rutledge all attempted to mollify him with some slight success. The contretemps was a harbinger of frustrations to come on both sides. Neither Greene nor Sumter would ever clash openly; indeed each remained excruciatingly polite to the other. But more and more, Greene would view Sumter as unreliable. For his part, Sumter simply ignored Greene whenever it suited him.

Sumter remained sidelined while Morgan—with some of Sumter's men—won his great victory at Cowpens. In mid February, while Greene led Cornwallis in a ruinous chase across North Carolina, Sumter felt sufficiently rejuvenated to take the field in South Carolina. He had designs on a series of British outposts along a 50-mile stretch of the Congaree–Santee waterway running through the center of the state. Sumter ordered Marion to cooperate in this scheme, but the Swamp Fox's recalcitrance mirrored Sumter's own stance toward Greene. Marion thought the plan was unrealistic; consequently he wanted no part in it. Over time, Sumter would discover Marion to be every bit as difficult and independent as Greene found Sumter. Nevertheless, Sumter set out for Fort Granby, located on the site of present-day Columbia, with 300 men. The Loyalist garrison there easily repelled his attack on February 19. Undismayed, instead of retreating, the Gamecock drove 35 miles farther south and assaulted another post at Belleville. Once again, he lacked the strength either to carry the place or mount a siege. Additionally, the British command in the lowcountry was now alerted and several detachments had orders to ride him down. Sumter temporarily fooled them by continuing his raid to the south instead of retreating north as expected. On February 28 he struck Fort Watson, a well-defended strongpoint just above Eutaw Springs. Once again he failed, this time with significant casualties. Sumter now decided to pull back. Pausing at his Santee plantation to pick up his wife and son, he retired all the way to Waxhaws, but not before taking more losses in a clash with Loyalist militia on March 6.

Still outwardly confident, despite this recent string of setbacks, Sumter began fretting about the quality of his troops. Though he himself often bridled under discipline, he concluded that poorly trained and equipped militia, who only turned out for short periods and often refused to serve far from their homes, were inadequate for the great task of liberating South Carolina. He conceived of the creation of State Troops, a mounted force that would be more akin to regulars in that they would be enlisted for 10 months. To raise men, he proposed to pay recruits primarily in slaves confiscated from Loyalists, in addition to a fixed share of all other goods taken from the enemy. As the senior officer in the state establishment, and in the absence of any civil authority, he felt within his rights to establish this program, which became known as "Sumter's Law." Some troops were raised in this fashion, though never in the numbers that Sumter had hoped. "Sumter's Law" horrified Marion who, as a resident of the low country where the slave-owning planter-class dominated, opposed the idea of confiscating this sort of property. He even wrote Sumter a long letter maintaining that the Gamecock had no authority to issue such a subversive proclamation. Sumter's action merely confirmed Marion's view of him as a dangerous freebooter. Greene acted more circumspectly, telling Sumter that, as a rule, he opposed plundering and hoped that certificates would be issued for any confiscated property.

By this time—in early April—Greene had seen Cornwallis off to Virginia and determined to return to South Carolina. This invigorated Sumter, who burned several Loyalist settlements along the Broad River and noted with satisfaction that "upon the whole they have been pretty well scurged."[16] Meanwhile, Greene moved toward Camden, looking for a showdown with the main enemy army. Sumter protected the right flank of this advance and forwarded supplies to his nominal chief, but refused his repeated requests to combine forces. Sumter went long stretches without answering Greene's frequent missives and when he did respond, he generally evaded Greene's increasingly pointed questions. Although the Gamecock claimed that he had "been under Great perplexity" due to recruiting problems, he clearly had no wish to subordinate himself or South Carolina volunteers to Greene.[17] Accordingly, Greene fought the battle of Hobkirk's Hill on April 25 without any aid from Sumter, who was only 30 miles away. With a combination of anger and resignation Greene complained that while Sumter and Marion were "brave good Officers . . . the people that are with them just come and go as they please."[18] Greene bowed to the inevitable and assented to Sumter's conduct of his own increasingly private war, hoping to salvage some virtue from this necessity.

Greene turned to picking off the numerous isolated British posts throughout the region, counting upon the more reliable Marion and Pickens to assist him. The former worked the lowcountry to the east, while the latter operated in his backcountry haunts in the west. This left Sumter in early May to once again try to seize Fort Granby in the central part of the state. He established blocking positions around the fort to cut it off and waited for it to drop into his lap. While attending this outcome, Sumter led a sizeable portion of his command south to the Loyalist settlement of Orangeburg. A few rounds discharged from a field piece were enough to cow 85 of the king's supporters into surrendering on May 11. Even as Sumter enjoyed this triumph, Greene sent Henry Lee and his Legion to Fort Granby. "Light-Horse Harry" took charge of the siege, overruling Sumter's subordinates on the scene. Sumter's men frantically informed him of this usurpation and the aggrieved Gamecock wrote Greene on May 14 to inform him that he required no assistance from the Continentals. "I have been at great pains to reduce that post, I have it in my power to do it, and I think it good for the public to do it without regulars."[19] Too late—Fort Granby surrendered to Lee a day later. Sumter appeared on the scene on May 16, to find both Lee and glory gone. Outraged, Sumter sent in his resignation to Greene.

Greene displayed considerable wisdom and tact in handling the prickly Sumter. Conscious of Sumter's shortcomings, he also realized that he was a fighter and one of the few men who could inspire large numbers of his fellow South Carolinians. In a letter full of praise for Sumter's service, he gently refused to accept the Gamecock's resignation or forward it to South Carolina's still-exiled governor. Instead he reinforced Sumter's authority, bidding him to "continue your command of this place [Fort Granby], & form and encourage the militia in all parts of the state."[20] Headed west to command the siege of Ninety Six, Greene further directed Sumter to destroy the recently captured enemy posts in the east and confirmed his right to direct Marion. This placated Sumter, though in practice Marion remained largely unresponsive to the Gamecock.

Ninety Six proved a tough nut to crack and Greene's operation there proceeded deliberately. In early June, reinforcements from England arrived in Charleston and with these the British embarked on a relief expedition toward Ninety Six. Getting wind of this, Greene tasked Sumter to intercept and delay them. Sumter assented to these orders, but displayed little energy in carrying them out. Marion's failure to cooperate with Sumter provides one mitigating factor. Sumter thought that the British column would proceed via Granby in its 200 mile march; in fact it followed a different route. When he made contact, he committed the tactical error of throwing small detachments at the powerful enemy force, which easily fended them off. Finally, Sumter's unhealed wounds and the scorching Carolina heat no doubt also contributed to his lethargy. For whatever reasons, he failed to deflect the British rescue mission, and a dejected Greene had to retreat from Ninety Six.

Even as he withdrew, Greene hoped to concentrate his forces and find favorable circumstances under which to give battle to the enemy. For nearly a month he unsuccessfully labored to assemble his disparate units and maneuver the British onto favorable terrain. In mid-July he abandoned the effort and decided to rest his worn out Continentals in the High Hills of the Santee. He left the struggle's prosecution in Sumter's hands and augmented his state troops with the horsemen of Lee's Legion. Sumter quickly passed to the offensive and launched a foray on Monck's Corner, a key crossroads only 30 miles from Charleston. He employed cavalry to isolate his objective from reinforcement and to raise havoc in the surrounding countryside. On July 17, Lee's dragoons captured the rearguard of a retiring British regiment. The enemy main force then went into a defense

18 miles southeast of Monck's Corner near Quinby Bridge, just off the Cooper River. Marion and Lee both agreed that the position was too strong to storm without artillery support. They so informed Sumter when he came up with the main body of infantry late in the afternoon. The Gamecock's blood was up however and he vociferously disagreed. Without sending back for artillery or taking time to perform a detailed reconnaissance, he hurled his troops at the enemy fortifications. The result was a shambles. The patriots did all that flesh and blood could do, but to no avail. More than 50 patriots—most of them Marion's men—were shot down without making a dent in the British defense. Under cover of darkness and broken in spirit, the Americans hobbled away.

The next morning, Lee and Marion took the extraordinary step of withdrawing themselves and their troops from Sumter's command. Marion swore that he would never allow his men to fight under Sumter again. Disconsolate, the Gamecock rode north, ultimately into North Carolina, to brood over his misfortune. Before embarking, he furloughed his remaining troops until the fall, further antagonizing Greene and the other South Carolina generals still in the field. Governor Rutledge, returning to South Carolina in early August, dealt him another blow by issuing an edict against plunder—in effect, repealing "Sumter's Law" and indicting his method of raising troops. After Cornwallis's October surrender at Yorktown, Sumter reappeared at Greene's headquarters, causing a measure of embarrassment. Greene defused it as best he could by detailing this now unwelcome senior general to monitor Loyalist activity in the vicinity of Orangeburg. For a few desultory months he performed this duty, though he realized that his reputation did not shine with either Rutledge or Greene, especially when contrasted with that of the partisan hero of the hour, Marion. Sumter's neighbors thought better of him, however, and elected him to the reconstituted state assembly. In early January 1782 he sent a terse note to Greene that asked permission to "Quit this Place" as "the Assembly is soon to sit."[21] A month later, he formally resigned his brigadier's commission.

Fifty eventful years remained ahead of the Gamecock, who lived to nearly 100 and was the last Revolutionary general to die when he slipped his earthly bonds on June 1, 1832. He served multiple terms in the state legislature and was elected to the United States Congress—including its very first session—as both a representative and a senator. His politics were unabashedly democratic. He sided with the unsuccessful anti-Federalist opposition to the new national Constitution in 1788. Later, he became a fervent Jeffersonian Democrat-Republican, supporting states' rights and sharply limited government power. He made a fortune speculating in land, and lost it through poor investments and bad luck. He defended himself against legal suits for his confiscatory actions during the war and ultimately both Carolinas passed laws indemnifying him. Likewise, when his financial position crumbled, the South Carolina assembly intervened to stem his state creditors. He aged, but did not really mellow, remaining the combative Gamecock until the end. As the Revolutionary generation passed from the stage, he became more and more venerated as an icon of a heroic age. He was not a great strategist or even a tactician. He lost more battles than he won, and his victories were hardly crucial or decisive. Yet he symbolized defiance and resistance at a juncture when these were sorely needed, and animated others to emulate him. That he was a sincere patriot, there can be no doubt. His simple, graceful acceptance of a gold medal for his wartime service provides his best epitaph: "If I have contributed to the relief of this lately oppressed State, the approbation of my Country is full and ample reward . . . I wished for no other."[22]

FRANCIS MARION

Francis Marion is commonly regarded as the greatest irregular fighter America has ever produced. His legendary reputation derives largely from the romantic fictions spun by his earliest biographers, among them Parson Weems, who also gave us George Washington and the cherry tree. This fanciful treatment portrayed Marion as some sort of American Robin Hood or William Tell. Unfortunately, the mythology encrusting the "Swamp Fox"—a nickname originating in the frustrations of the fox hunting British officer class, which displayed a particular fondness for vulpine metaphors (also invoked to describe Washington)—makes it difficult to separate fact from fiction, and recover Marion's true story. As such, these pietistic fables obscure his very real accomplishments, especially his resistance against the British in South Carolina during slightly more than a single year of intense action in 1780–1781.

He was born sometime in late 1732 to a family of French Protestant descent that had settled on South Carolina's Cooper River. While he was still a small boy, his parents established a modest home near the port settlement of Georgetown. Marion received little education and was a scrawny lad afflicted with deformed knees and ankles. Still, his constitution was robust enough for him to go to sea at age 15. Seafaring life proved disagreeable, however—no doubt in some measure due to a shipwreck he barely survived—and by 1750, following his father's death, he was looking after his mother and the family plantation. As a property-owning young man, he had a stake in society and served in the local militia. Like so many combatants on both sides of the Revolution, he gained his first battle experience on the frontier fighting Indians. Along with a number of other future South Carolina notables, he participated in the exterminatory campaign against the Cherokees in 1761. Lieutenant Marion attracted much favorable notice for his efficiency and gallantry. He especially distinguished himself that June in action near present-day Franklin, North Carolina by leading a 30-man detachment that broke up a Cherokee ambush despite sustaining over two-thirds casualties.

By 1773 Marion had amassed the means to purchase his own plantation on the Santee River just below Eutaw Springs. He was a moderate Whig, though not politically active or vocal. Nevertheless, his war record and standing in the community naturally led to his election to South Carolina's first Provincial Congress in early 1775. When that body decided in June to create regiments outside the colonial militia structure to defend the peoples' liberty, it named Marion a captain in William Moultrie's 2^d Regiment. For the next year Marion recruited and trained his company, which was billeted in and around Charleston. South Carolina's capital was an obvious enemy target, especially after a British task force sailed south from Boston in January 1776. As that fleet glided down the coast, Marion—now a major—and his men labored to construct fortifications on Sullivan Island, which guarded the entrance to Charleston's harbor. These works were still only partially complete when the British armada hove into view in early June. The overall American commander on the scene, the just-arrived Charles Lee, considered the fort a potential slaughter pen and wished to evacuate, but the South Carolinians were adamant about holding it. In the event, their judgment proved astute. Fighting bravely behind breastworks made of palmetto logs, Colonel Moultrie and his regiment repulsed the British attempt to force the harbor on June 28. Marion commanded the left side of the fort and controlled half its complement of 26 guns. According to tradition, Moultrie awarded Marion the honor of personally firing the battle's last shot at the retiring British vessels.

In the fall of 1776 the South Carolina regiments entered the Continental establishment and Marion received a regular commission as a lieutenant colonel. In September 1778 he ascended from executive officer to command of the 2^d South Carolina. For more than 3 years following the defense of Charleston, Marion performed garrison duty in that city. Here he displayed a penchant for strict, by-the-book discipline, a trait not normally associated with the kind of bush-whacking warrior he would ultimately become. Waspish and dyspeptic looking, he was reputed regularly to drink a mixture of vinegar and water. He pelted his men with a series of general orders on topics ranging from church attendance to alcohol consumption to grooming. For instance, "Any soldier who comes on parade with beards, or hair uncombed, shall be dry-shaved immediately, and have his hair dressed on the parade."[23] Perhaps this is just what was needed during an extended spell of relatively easy service in a city full of temptation. Apparently, his men did not regard him as a martinet or hold his sternness against him. One of them later wrote, "Marion wished his officers to be gentlemen ... whenever he saw one of them acting below that character, he would generously attempt his reformation."[24]

The call to action finally arrived in September 1779. Marion's regiment moved south to join in the Franco-American attempt to wrest Savannah from the British. This operation culminated in a failed assault upon the city's outer works on October 9. None of the five allied columns succeeded; the one that came closest to breaching the enemy lines included the 2^d South Carolina, which actually managed to plant its colors on a hostile redoubt before being driven back with heavy losses. Marion's second in command described the grim aftermath of "digging large pits, sufficient to retain about a hundred corpses ... taking off their clothes, with heavy hearts, we threw them into the pits ... and covered them with earth."[25] The French sailed off to their bases in the West Indies while the bulk of the American army pulled back to Charleston. The South Carolina regiments were brigaded together and Marion commanded them for 3 months at Sheldon, an advanced post 45 miles below the capital. From here he attempted to discern enemy capabilities and intentions in Savannah.

It was soon apparent that the enemy would use Savannah as a base from which to conquer South Carolina. Consequently, the senior American general in the south, Benjamin Lincoln, called Marion back into Charleston in early 1780. This time there would be no glorious patriot defense. A somewhat embarrassing episode, however, spared Marion the ignominy of surrendering with the rest of the garrison when the city capitulated in May. With the noose tightening, many of the officers gathered for a dinner party that soon degenerated into a drinking bout. The host, following custom, had locked all doors as the bacchanal commenced. Marion, whose asceticism was exceeded only by his stubbornness, had no wish to imbibe. He found a second floor window and jumped to the street below, making good his escape but breaking an ankle in the process. Thus Lincoln included the invalided Marion along with the other sick and injured when he evacuated them from the besieged city in April. Marion took refuge among family and friends along the Santee. When the capital fell and ruthless enemy columns began scouring the countryside for patriots, he and a handful of followers rode north to join an American army rumored to be en route to the Carolinas.

Eventually Marion made contact with the army being led into South Carolina by General Horatio Gates, hero of Saratoga and newly assigned commander of the southern department. Marion's scruffy band did not make the best impression. Gates's adjutant noted that they were "distinguished by small leather caps, and the wretchedness of their attire; their number did not exceed twenty men and boys, some white, some black, and all mounted, but most of them miserably equipped."[26] The patriot army marched toward Camden in early August with Marion riding along as a supernumerary and chafing for action. Gates had been favorably impressed by Sumter's partisan activities above Camden and ordered him to continue in support of his advance. Meanwhile, patriot militia had mustered in the region between the Pee Dee and Santee Rivers, and only wanted a leader. Marion offered to fill this role and Gates readily agreed, instructing him to destroy every boat he could find on the lower Santee to prevent a British escape from the beating Gates planned to administer at Camden. By mid-August, Marion had taken charge of his new command and was busily organizing it when devastating news reached him. On August 16 Cornwallis routed Gates at Camden. Two days later Tarleton destroyed Sumter's unwary partisans at Fishing Creek. Keeping these tidings to himself, Marion sent a detachment to harass the enemy around Georgetown and led the rest of his men up the Santee to begin a series of actions that by the end of 1780 would torment the British, cow the Loyalists, and establish his legend.

Information soon arrived concerning a large number of friendly soldiers, recently taken at Camden, who were being held at Sumter's abandoned plantation above the Santee. Marion hatched a daring scheme to rescue them. He startled the enemy guards at dawn on August 20, killing or capturing 25 and liberating

150 Continentals of the Maryland line. To Marion's great disgust—and indicative of the nadir of patriot fortunes—virtually none of the freed men wished to return to the fight and some even expressed a preference to continue into captivity at Charleston. Aware that British fury would soon be turned full on him, Marion hurried due east and set up camp on the Pee Dee. He had not long to wait. A force of 250 Loyalists began to move down the Little Pee Dee River to the northeast, intent on crushing the impertinent Marion. Outnumbered five to one, Marion refused to flee or passively await his enemy. Instead, he rushed to meet them, bloodying their advance guard, then ambushing the main body at Blue Savannah on the Little Pee Dee on September 4. In his own words and displaying an impish sense of humor he reported to Gates, "I directly attacked them to flight" and sent them reeling "into an impassable swamp to all but Torys."[27] Marion then withdrew farther east into the gloomy Great White Marsh in North Carolina.

Unlike the often rash Sumter, Marion was a meticulous campaigner who took particular pains never to be surprised. He always posted sentinels and patrolled aggressively to retain the initiative. He rose before sunrise and frequently moved his camp in order to avoid detection. While gathering new recruits in his North Carolina lair, Marion learned that 50-some Loyalists had assembled in his home district on Black Mingo Creek, north of Georgetown. Eager to strike another blow, Marion led a similar-sized detachment on a forced march that, just after midnight on September 29, brought them to the edge of the enemy camp. The Loyalists, led by Colonel John Ball, were alert and drew up to meet the patriots as they advanced. A vicious 15-minute skirmish ended with one third of the Loyalists dead, wounded, or captured and the rest dispersed. Marion suffered two killed and eight wounded. A number of horses counted among the spoils of victory, including one that had belonged to the opposing commander. Marion claimed this for himself, puckishly renamed it "Ball," and rode it the rest of war. Marion continued his demoralization of South Carolina Loyalists a month later. His superb intelligence network informed him of a concentration of over 200 newly organized Tory militia near Tearcoat Swamp on the upper Black River. With 150 men Marion fell upon them in the early morning of October 26 and took them completely unaware. As he later reported, "This surprise was so compleat, that I had not one man killed; our loss was only two horses killed."[28] In return, he inflicted more than 40 casualties and captured more badly needed horses and weapons. Several overawed Tories actually chose to switch sides and join Marion. Marion exulted "the Toreys are so Affrighted with my Little Excursions that many is moving off to Georgia with their Effects others are rund into Swamps."[29]

By now, Cornwallis had more than enough of Marion's marauders. In early November he sent Tarleton down the Santee, where Marion had lately been operating, to rid him of this meddlesome brigand. The adversaries, well matched in terms of cunning and energy, began a deadly game of cat and mouse. Tarleton quickly located Marion and set an ambush for him, baiting it by sending out small, seemingly vulnerable patrols. The South Carolinian chose discretion as the better part of valor and escaped eastward instead. Discovering this, Tarleton gave chase "and made a rapid march of 26 miles through Swamps, Woods, & Fastness toward Black River without a Halt."[30] This only proved an exhausting exercise in frustration. Then, perhaps to Tarleton's relief, with Sumter raising havoc to the northwest, Cornwallis urgently recalled him. The Englishmen allegedly exclaimed to his legionnaires "Come, my boys! Let us go back, and we will find the Gamecock . . . as for this damned old fox, the devil himself could not catch him!"[31]

The "damned old fox"—soon to become the Swamp Fox to his admirers—continued to scourge the enemy in the region lying between the Santee and Pee Dee. Although Loyalist reinforcements stymied his November 15 raid on Georgetown, he mounted another major operation a month later. Two hundred English recruits, recently debarked in Charleston, were dispatched in early December to join their regiment inland. Marion gathered what was for him a massive party of 700 mounted men and rushed to cut them off. Riding north along the crude road paralleling the Santee, he caught up to the new soldiers, and the veteran redcoat battalion shepherding them, on December 12 adjacent to a bog known as Halfway Swamp. The two forces exchanged fire and the British established a hasty defense while simultaneously sending out a desperate call for reinforcements. Then, under a flag of truce, the British commander dared the partisans to come out and fight like men. Marion responded with a medieval challenge; each side would choose 20 champions to meet in mortal combat in the open field. The enemy accepted and the two handpicked teams faced off. When the Americans closed to within musket range, however, their opponents rapidly shouldered arms and scurried back to safety. The partisans gave three lusty cheers and retired to their lines to receive their comrades' accolades. Later that evening, leaving their campfires burning and abandoning their baggage, the redcoats skirted Marion's position and silently slipped away. The Swamp Fox had been outfoxed.

Nevertheless, the episode at Halfway Swamp offers a good illustration of the kind of moral ascendancy Marion gained over his foes. Although he inflicted only negligible casualties on the redcoats or Loyalists in many engagements, his adversaries came to dread him. Conforming to the classic insurgent design, while the British and their allies controlled population centers, and moved through the countryside with relative security by day, the night seemingly belonged to the shadowy partisans. Achieving tangible results by intercepting supplies, killing and wounding enemy soldiers, and forcing the British to devote considerable resources to protecting their supply lines and chasing him, Marion's greatest success was psychological. Because of his reputation, many putative Loyalists chose to stay home rather than bear arms for the crown. In some cases, they even elected to join him. Constant themes in communications among British commanders were the threat posed by this elusive partisan and what to do about him. They worried out of all proportion to his actual physical strength. Of course, in addition to vexing the enemy, Marion's boldness inspired his friends.

Interestingly enough, while he preyed upon his opponents' minds, the mercurial Marion himself repeatedly suffered spells of despair. His concerns centered on materiel and external support, as well as the commitment of his own countrymen.

Regarding the former, Marion, like all patriot commanders—irregular or Continental—lacked ammunition, clothing, and virtually every other necessity for waging war. For instance, as he wrote to Gates, "I am Greatly in want of a Surgeon, one of my wounded Bled to Death for want of one, so many is oblige to retreat for want of Medicine, for I have not any whatever." He felt isolated, even forgotten. In the same letter to Gates he plaintively noted, "Many of my people has left me & gone over to the Enemy, for they think we have no Army coming in & have been Deceived, as we hear nothing from you in a great while ..."[32] Marion's anxieties about his men mirrored those of many other American leaders about militia troops. Much less disciplined and not as well trained as regulars, militia answered the call when they felt an imminent threat to their homes, but would rapidly disperse when the immediate danger passed in order to look after their farms and families. Marion never forgot that he was a Continental officer and, unlike Pickens and Sumter, could not reconcile himself entirely to his partisans' coming and going as they pleased. Again, he unburdened himself to Gates, "The People here is not to be depended on for I seldom have the same set a fortnight."[33] One of war's maxims maintains that the view on the other side of the hill is at least as bleak as it is on one's own. Indeed, British commanders frequently despaired over the dependability of Loyalist militia. This same martial truism adds that the side that hangs on just a little bit longer will prevail. Despite periodic doubts, Marion hung on.

Gates, a lame duck commander after his defeat at Camden, had major problems of his own and he paid little attention to Marion. In contrast, when Nathanael Greene assumed the southern command in early December, he immediately reached out to Marion and the other partisans. To the Swamp Fox he wrote, "I have not the honor of your acquaintance but I am no stranger to your character and merit. Your services in the lower part of South Carolina, in awing the tories and preventing the enemy from extending their limits, have been very important."[34] Greene acknowledged Marion's supply difficulties and offered to help to the best of his ability, although in practice, Greene's main army ended up relying more upon the partisans for logistical sustenance. In another gratifying development, the exiled Governor Rutledge also recognized Marion's accomplishments and commissioned him a brigadier general in South Carolina's militia, with command of all detachments in the eastern part of the state. More concretely, in January 1781, Greene temporarily dispatched Lieutenant Colonel Henry Lee and 250 infantry and cavalrymen of his legion to reinforce Marion. Besides the considerable combat power they represented, these Continental veterans provided a stiffening effect to the embattled partisans and a visible reminder that they were not alone.

Together, Marion and Lee designed an elaborate operation against Georgetown, a glittering prize that repeatedly attracted the Swamp Fox's interest. On the evening of January 22–23, they sent their combined infantry 90 miles down the Pee Dee River in small boats to an island hiding spot on just off the town's waterfront. Then, with their mounted troops, the two patriot leaders approached Georgetown's landward defenses. On the night of the 24th the infantry force landed, entered the town, and in a brilliant stroke seized the enemy commandant and his key subordinates in their beds. The cavalry with Marion and Lee brushed aside the British pickets to link up with the waterborne raiders. Now, however a painful and even slightly embarrassing reality intruded. Although leaderless, the British garrison remained snugly inside the formidable walls of their barracks and refused to come out. The patriots had no means to force them and were unprepared to conduct a siege. Marion and Lee would accomplish much together the following spring; perhaps they even drew some important lessons about preparation here. For the moment, however, they were thwarted. Reluctantly, the Americans paroled their doubtless bewildered captives and vanished back into the swamps as the sun began to rise.

While Marion and Lee had been preparing their stroke, Morgan trounced Tarleton at Cowpens. This set in motion Cornwallis's vengeful pursuit of Greene's army across North Carolina. As he began his retrograde, the American commander recalled Lee, once more leaving the South Carolina partisans on their own. The senior patriot fighter remaining in the state—Thomas Sumter—did not hesitate to take the initiative. He commenced an ambitious, if ill-conceived, offensive against enemy posts along the Congaree and lower Santee Rivers. Marion ignored several calls from Sumter urging him to join forces. He was not sanguine about the Gamecock's scheme; he believed that without Continental support the residual enemy forces in the region were too strong to contest openly. Events showed this diagnosis to be correct. Sumter unsuccessfully hurled himself against several British strong points during the latter part of February before being chased back to the northern recesses of the state with considerable losses.

While Cornwallis and Greene fenced in North Carolina, and with Sumter checked, Lord Rawdon, the senior British field commander in South Carolina, focused on Marion with the intent of eliminating him once and for all. Employing an anvil and hammer technique—still a favored counterinsurgency ploy—Rawdon sent one powerful column eastward to block Marion from retreating to his marshy hideaways and ordered another 500-man force of Loyalists and redcoats to drive south and smash the Swamp Fox. Lieutenant Colonel John Watson led this second element down the Santee road on March 5.

Marion chose fight over flight. In a 3-week running battle beginning March 6, he tormented Watson at every turn with a virtuoso display of agility—attacking, defending or withdrawing as the situation dictated and always keeping his opponent off balance. Marion drew first blood at a narrow causeway that crossed Wiboo Swamp not far from Eutaw Springs. Patriot cavalry clashed with enemy dragoons in a daylong whirl of charge and countercharge that ended only when Watson painstakingly unlimbered his artillery and managed to bring up his infantry. Marion withdrew to a nearby plantation and both sides regrouped. The British resumed their march the next morning as Marion tantalizingly lingered just beyond range. After crawling forward a bit and as if tired of the *pas de deux*, the British column suddenly veered from the Santee and pointed northeast along a wilderness road for the Black River, a dozen or so miles away. Rightly viewing this as a threat to his pro-Whig sanctuary, Marion decided to cut the enemy off. He rushed a detachment of mounted riflemen to cover the Lower Bridge, a span over the Black below Kingstree that the enemy must cross. The patriots won this race, destroyed the bridge, and waited on the east bank. When their adversaries appeared, the American sharpshooters took a heavy toll. Unable to dislodge them with artillery, Watson bivouacked his troops at a homestead on the west shore. Marion's men now swarmed around their one-time pursuers, constantly sniping and making life generally miserable for them.

The two commanders had earlier entered a brisk, angry correspondence in the course of which Watson had haughtily lectured Marion on the rules of civilized warfare. Now, with his wounded piling up, Watson contritely asked Marion to allow his casualties to pass safely to Charleston. Marion humanely assented while continuing to harass Watson's beleaguered troops. On March 28 Watson broke out from the trap and made for the safety of the British base at Georgetown. Marion's men chased them the entire distance like vengeful furies. One of his officers later recalled of their quarry, "Never did I see a body of infantry ply their legs so briskly! The rogues were constantly in a dog trot. . ."[35] With brute, desperate force the British fought through a patriot roadblock on the Sampit River, 9 miles from their destination. Arriving in Georgetown, they gratefully collapsed. A chagrinned Watson later wrote of the Swamp Fox and his band, "They will not sleep and fight like gentlemen but like savages are eternally firing and whooping around us by night, and by day waylaying and popping at us from behind every tree!"[36]

The almost equally exhausted patriots, resting on the Sampit, had precious little time to enjoy their triumph. Marion now got the bad news that while he had been punishing Watson, the other enemy force had stumbled onto his main base camp between the Pee Dee River and Lynches Creek. His skeletal rear detachment had to flee, leaving behind their sick and wounded, as well as enemy prisoners they had been holding. The British burned everything that the patriots were unable to carry way. Stung, Marion immediately set out after the despoilers, who nevertheless made their getaway. He gamely established a new base farther north on the Pee Dee. As he reorganized, Marion received a further annoyance in the form of a preemptory letter from Sumter. Ignoring Marion's brilliant handling of Watson—which contrasted starkly with Sumter's earlier bumbling along the Santee—the Gamecock quibbled with Marion's dispositions and even reprimanded him for his troops' alleged plundering. This last struck a sensitive nerve with Marion, who deplored banditry and even advocated summary execution for these activities. Worse yet, Sumter also broached his State Troops scheme, which called for paying long term recruits in confiscated property. To the strait-laced Marion, this represented the vilest sort of anarchic class warfare and he wanted nothing to do with it. For the moment he held his tongue and took solace in the welcome news that Greene was headed back to South Carolina and once more sending Lee's Legion to join him.

Marion and Lee reunited April 14 on the Black River and set their sights on Fort Watson. This British post, named for Marion's erstwhile opponent, overlooked the Santee about 60 miles above Charleston. The patriots rapidly invested the place, but its stout walls offered impervious protection to the 120-man enemy garrison. Marion cut them off from their water supply, but the British countered by digging a well. The situation seemed highly unpromising for the besiegers, who lacked artillery and faced a possible British relief expedition at any moment. Then one of Marion's officers, Hezekiah Maham, ingeniously suggested the construction of a tower from which to pour rifle fire into the bastion. The structure, 5 days in building and erected on the night of April 22, surpassed all expectations. A constant hail of lead commencing the morning of the 23rd prevented the defenders from manning their positions and they surrendered later that day. The "Maham tower" became a standard tool of the southern army in subsequent sieges.

Victory at Fort Watson was the first in a series of American successes that spring that ultimately led to the elimination of British control in South Carolina. After spending a couple of weeks sparring with a Loyalist force in the lowcountry, Marion and Lee next moved 10 miles upstream to where the Congaree and Wateree Rivers merged to form the Santee. Here the enemy maintained an important link in the chain of posts linking Charleston to the interior. They called it Fort Motte, after the wealthy widow's hilltop mansion that formed the center of the base. Consigning Mrs. Rebecca Motte to an outlying cabin, 140 British and Hessian soldiers placed a stockade and other obstacles around the main house to create an impressive strong point. The patriots initiated their siege May 8. Here a tower would not avail, and once again Marion and Lee feared the imminent arrival of an enemy rescue force. This time Lee got the sudden inspiration—to burn down Mrs. Motte's grand home with flaming arrows. The American commanders gently broke the news to the lady and, according to lore, she responded in a manner to make any Roman proud. She brought forth an ornate bow and accompanying shafts that had long ago been a curiosity bestowed upon her as a house gift. Presenting them to Lee she observed that they should do the trick. They did. By noon on the 12th the mansion's roof was ablaze. Patriot artillery discouraged those defenders who tried to douse the flames, forcing the garrison to surrender. Happily for the patriotic lady, both sides then arrested the fire and salvaged something of the house. In a chivalrous denouement, the American and British officers then dined together as her guests before the losers were paroled to Charleston.

While busy picking off enemy forts, Marion also continued feuding with Sumter over lines of militia authority and the Gamecock's confiscation policy. Lee empathized with Marion and even asked Greene to show support to the depressed Swamp Fox, noting "His services demand great acknowledgements, and I fear he thinks himself neglected."[37] Greene, however, refused to enter the dispute and confided his private feelings to Washington, sighing that the bickering brigadiers "deserve great credit for their exertions and perseverance but their endeavors rather seem to keep the contest alive, than lay any foundation for the recovery of these states."[38] Additionally, Greene had his own testy exchange with Marion. On several occasions Greene had asked Marion to forward horses taken from the enemy to provide his Continentals with fresh mounts. Marion had ignored these appeals, but a letter from Greene implying that "the object of the people [Marion's men] is plunder altogether" harmful to the patriot cause sparked his ire.[39] With some asperity, Marion acknowledged his superior's repeated requests for animals and stated that he wished "it had been within my power to furnish them, but it is not and never has been." He pointed out that his unpaid, underequipped soldiers used the horses in the field, not for private gain. He sarcastically offered to dismount his men, but observed that they would all promptly desert. Then he dropped his bombshell, "This would not give me any uneasyness as I have somtime Determin to relinquish my command in the malitia."[40] He concluded by expressing a wish to travel to Philadelphia to seek a Continental command.

Greene realized he had pushed the distracted brigadier too far. He wrote a conciliatory letter granting that Marion was in the best position to judge the disposition of horseflesh and imploring him to stick to his vital militia post. The fall of Fort Motte put everyone in better spirits and Greene arrived at the site the day it surrendered to meet Marion for the first time. The two got on famously and Marion put aside his ideas about resignation. They parted with Greene headed west to besiege Ninety Six and Marion plunging down the Santee, his eye fastened once again on Georgetown. In the event, his long anticipated triumph was anticlimactic. Shaken by the earlier capture of so many other posts, the small garrison there quit the town and embarked on several Royal Navy vessels. Marion rode unimpeded into Georgetown on May 28, destroyed the British works, and awaited developments.

While Greene invested Ninety Six, in early June Lord Rawdon mustered a powerful force to relieve it. Greene admonished Sumter and Marion to stave him off, but for a variety of reasons—including an inability to cooperate, their men's fatigue, and a misreading of Rawdon's intentions—neither partisan general succeeded. Greene's desperate effort to storm Ninety Six before Rawdon arrived failed on June 18 and he had to retreat. The frustrated American commander later allowed himself to fulminate to Lee about the partisans' reliability, "It is next to impossible to draw the Militia of the Country from the different parts of the State to which they belong. Marion is below. Pickens I can get no account of, and Sumter wants to make a tour to Monks Corner, and all I can say to either is insufficient to induce them to join us."[41] Then, as he did so often, Greene made the best of what he had and by the second week of July had actually managed to assemble most of the patriot forces in South Carolina, including Sumter's and Marion's, under his immediate control. He offered battle to Rawdon outside Orangeburg, but the British commander declined. Greene then withdrew his Continentals to the hills above the Santee and left Sumter to keep the enemy off balance below.

Sumter was anxious to conduct his "tour to Monck's Corner" and smite a British post there, manned by a redcoat regiment and assorted Loyalist units. On the evening of July 12 the Gamecock sent Marion's and Lee's mounted elements thundering south to envelop the enemy, while he followed with the infantry along the west side of the Santee. The British commander refused to be trapped and retreated south, eventually occupying a plantation near Quinby Bridge, close by the Cooper River. Both Marion and Lee considered the position too formidable to tackle and so informed Sumter when he caught up to them late on the 17th. Sumter overruled them and ordered an attack. Marion's men bore the brunt of the ill-conceived and poorly supported assault, sustaining some 50 casualties. The debacle marked an inglorious end to the Gamecock's combat career. Marion and Lee withdrew their men from his command the next morning, with the former taking his badly mauled partisans to refit in a camp along the Santee.

Little less than a month later Greene called upon Marion to exert himself to aid a threatened fellow partisan. Colonel William Harden had raised a force in the vicinity of the lower Edisto River west of Charleston. A large Loyalist band now endangered them and had been reinforced by a squadron of British dragoons. Marion selected 200 men and moved undetected, covering 100 miles in a series of night marches that brought him to Harden's side on August 13. He discovered that the enemy cavalry was nearby and set a trap for them along the causeway leading to Parker's Ferry on the Edisto. Marion emplaced riflemen in concealed positions around his chosen ambush site and sent out detachments to gull the enemy into giving chase to the kill zone. The plan worked to perfection. The British horsemen ran headlong into a devastating crossfire. Their attempts to rally and assault the hidden infantry only added to the pile of corpses around the causeway. Marion's men expended all their powder and ammunition before the enemy escaped. The Swamp Fox had evened the score for Quinby Bridge; he estimated that he had killed 100 enemy dragoons while his own losses were nil.

Early September found Marion once more on the lower Santee as Greene moved down that waterway toward a British concentration at Eutaw Springs. Greene sought to surprise them and sent word to Marion to move upriver and join him. The Swamp Fox stole past the enemy unnoticed and linked up with the rest of the American army on September 5 above Eutaw Springs. The patriots advanced on the morning of September 8, with Marion commanding the combined militia forces of North and South Carolina, including the estimable Pickens and his brigade. After the American vanguard skirmished with an enemy foraging party, Greene deployed the militia in the front rank with Pickens to the left, the North Carolinians in the center, and Marion at the head of his brigade on the right. The irregulars slugged it out with the redcoats drawn up to meet them, giving as good as they got before making way for Greene's second echelon of Continentals. Marion later proudly and succinctly stated, "My Brigade behaved well."[42] The battle seesawed back and forth; both sides fought fiercely and courageously on this bloody day, which at its end saw Greene withdraw from the field. Later that night Greene launched Marion and Lee in a last attempt to hector the British, who had also retired. They and their exhausted troops responded gamely, but were unable to forestall the enemy from linking up with reinforcements.

Eutaw Springs was the war's last major battle in South Carolina, although more than a year passed before the British evacuated their one remaining stronghold in Charleston. Marion performed myriad duties during this tense and tedious interval. The most basic were keeping his troops together and staying vigilant against renewed enemy activities. Another was helping administer martial law until the state government could be reconstituted. This mainly entailed keeping the peace between Whigs and former Loyalists, and—increasingly—aiding the reintegration of those one time crown supporters who desired it. If this was a thankless task, so was that of reshaping the militia in accordance with the changed realities on the ground. The inevitable shuffling of commanders and units spurred jealousies among his officers and created more headaches for the Swamp Fox. While contending with the penned-in British, his own restive soldiers and unhappy officers, and angry civilians, he was elected to the newly organized General Assembly. His fellow members included a galaxy of the state's other revolutionary heroes, including Sumter and Pickens. The body convened in January 1782 at Jacksonborough on the Edisto, not far from the site of the Swamp Fox's triumph at Parker's Ferry.

Marion left his brigade on the Cooper River above Charleston to take his seat. He soon grew weary of the grind—"I am tired of Legislating," he wrote—and monitored the squabbling among his irritable subordinates with increased dismay.[43] A sudden British sortie from Charleston on February 23 shook the brigade badly and Marion raced back from the assembly to rally his roughly handled outfit and resume command. As winter melted into spring, and Greene's attention focused on Charleston, a last gasp Tory uprising broke out in the eastern part of the state, as well as in adjacent areas of North Carolina. The two state governors agreed to dispatch Marion to quell it. Marching up the familiar route between the Pee Dee and Little Pee Dee Rivers, Marion cornered the most notorious of the Loyalist leaders and, after a brief skirmish, compelled them into a parley. These negotiations ultimately resulted in more than 500 Tories laying down their weapons and pledging allegiance to South Carolina and the United States. One last fight remained for the Swamp Fox. On August 29, a party of 100 enemy dragoons sallied forth from Charleston to raid American positions east of the Cooper. Learning of this, Marion employed a dodge that had previously served him well. He sent a few riders to gain the enemy's attention and lead them on a chase into a well-prepared ambush at Fair Lawn, which sent them reeling with 20 casualties.

Shortly after the British evacuated Charleston in December 1782, Marion mustered out his men and made his way home. Like many others who had taken to the hills and swamps to fight, he found his plantation in ruins—his house burned, his slaves and other property stolen, and his livestock killed or driven off. With the same single mindedness he brought to war making, he rebuilt his estate. His great renown aided him in gaining credit and marriage to a wealthy cousin in 1786 bolstered his fortune. His fellow citizens showered him with honors and reelected him to the assembly. He served on various committees, participated in the convention that wrote South Carolina's constitution in 1790, and commanded a militia brigade until 1794. Marion died peacefully at his simple home overlooking the Santee on February 27, 1795 and was laid to rest in the family cemetery nearby.

Like Pickens and Sumter, Marion demonstrated tremendous courage and resourcefulness in the face of heavy odds and terrific hardship. Unlike them, he was an authentic military genius—and a highly improbable one. Physically unimposing, barely educated, and given to extreme mood swings, he fit few preconceived images of martial glory. Yet along the rivers and in the trackless marshes of South Carolina, his stamina, imagination, and ability to inspire others led to great accomplishments that left the legend of the Swamp Fox deeply graven in the historical memory of his countrymen.

Frontier Fighters

Ethan Allen, George Rogers Clark, and Daniel Morgan

THE AMERICAN FRONTIER was already a century and a half old by the Revolution's eve. Following the French and Indian War, the boundary between steadily advancing white settlement and the hinterland beyond roughly paralleled a great natural barrier—the western Piedmont and the Appalachian Highland—that extended in a mountainous arc from northern New England to central Georgia. Along this frontier, some particularly venturesome colonists struggled to carve out an existence. Among the many challenges they faced were Indian tribes who already lived on much of land they coveted. Additionally, following the victory over France, the British crown, overwhelmed by the swelling tide of westward migration, imposed restrictions upon further expansion with the Proclamation of 1763. This mandated a temporary halt to new settlement to allow London time to design rational frontier defense, trade, and settlement policies. As such, it also represented another sore spot, along with representation and taxation, between Great Britain and her American subjects.

The American historian Frederick Jackson Turner famously postulated that the frontier experience created an American culture and character that emphasized, among other traits, rough and ready practicality, individualism, and democracy. While generations of scholars have critiqued Turner's thesis as overly simplistic, it remains nevertheless compelling. Certainly the careers of three Revolutionary-era frontiersmen explored below illustrate its explanatory power. Ethan Allen grew up on New England's northern frontier, won a famous victory over the British, and helped create a new state. George Rogers Clark, born in the Virginia backcountry, helped secure American control of a vast region that would ultimately add half a dozen states to the Union. And though he gained fame as a Continental regular on battlefields "back east," Daniel Morgan—farmer, teamster, rifleman, unexcelled combat leader—was the quintessential frontiersman.

ETHAN ALLEN

"Do I contradict myself?" asked that most American of poets, Walt Whitman. "Very well then I contradict myself, (I am large, I contain multitudes)."[1] He might been describing Ethan Allen, a brawny, independent-minded New England roughneck who was variously a farmer, land speculator, soldier, author, blusterer and philosopher, politician, patriot, and perhaps even a traitor. "The Damnedest Yankee"—the title of one popular Allen biography—was many things to many people in his colorful, even mythical life, but he is best recalled as a key figure during the American Revolution's earliest days.

Allen's forebears had come from England to America a century before his birth and the Allen clan was well established in New England when Ethan entered the world on January 21, 1738 (new calendar) at Litchfield on the western Connecticut frontier. He was the eldest of eight siblings, all of whom—remarkably for that era—lived into adulthood. The Allens prospered as farmers whose aspirations toward gentility included sending their oldest boy off to a neighboring town to study with a tutor in hopes that he might gain admission to Yale College. Unfortunately, the death of his father shortly afterward ended Ethan's formal schooling, though throughout his life he would fancy himself a scholar of sorts, even going so far as to close his letters as "The Philosopher."

At 17 he became the head of his family. In addition to working the farm and adding to its holdings, he became a partner in an iron works. He also experienced a brief taste of military campaigning when, as a militia private, he mustered for 2 weeks in the summer of 1757 as part of his community's response to a French incursion from Canada into neighboring New York. Allen saw no action, but on this short campaign he glimpsed for the first time the wild country of what is now southern Vermont. Perhaps this fired his youthful imagination and compelled his multiple excursions into this wilderness in the following years. Or maybe it was the spectacularly unhappy marriage he made with one Mary Brownson in 1762 that fueled his wanderlust. From all accounts, Mrs. Allen was the antithesis of her exuberant husband—dour, pinched, and inclined to scold—and Allen's activities provided her with numerous occasions. The records of several Connecticut courts reveal instances of Allen being hauled to the bar for breaches of the peace and blaspheming. These minor scrapes also likely impelled him to light out for the territory.

Leaving his wife and children settled on a Massachusetts farm, in 1767 Allen started making frequent visits to hunt or spend time with friends in an area bisected by the Green Mountains, and lying between the Connecticut River and the Hudson-Champlain waterway. Several colonies claimed it, but by the late 1760s the two major disputants were the provinces of New York and New Hampshire. Complicating the wrangle, the latter colony's governor had seen fit to sell parcels in the region to land-hungry settlers, hence the area's name, the New Hampshire Grants. Both parties in the squabble had turned to London for a resolution, but the king's ministers moved deliberately. Accordingly, impatient New York officials sought to assert their authority over those thousands who had already established themselves on the Grants, either by taxing them as New Yorkers or evicting them if their holdings conflicted with other titles to the land issued by New York.

Predictably, there was much indignation and furor on the settlers' part and Allen soon immersed himself in the controversy. He participated in court hearings, and wrote pamphlets and newspaper articles in favor of the settlers' position. When the law and the pen failed, Allen and his friends resorted to force. Meeting in Bennington in that sturdy cradle of American liberty—a tavern—in 1770 they created a regiment, of which Allen was elected Colonel-Commandant. When New York's governor learned of this, he allegedly remarked that he would drive this rag-tag mob back into the Green Mountains. The militiamen promptly and proudly adopted the name Green Mountain Boys.

Allen was the perfect choice to head this rough and ready band of about 200 men. No known likeness, or even a reliable physical description of him, exists. Nevertheless, based upon the tall tales that grew up around Allen that include him strangling a bear or knocking out an ox with one punch, we can surmise that he was an exceedingly powerful physical specimen who exuded a natural charisma. Allen and his Boys launched a resistance campaign against the New York authorities that included propaganda, as well as threats, beatings, and whippings. These they inflicted not only upon government officials, but upon wavering settlers as well. Notably, however, they never killed anyone, a fact that contrasts sharply with contemporaneous backcountry vendettas in the American south. While prosecuting this strategy of intimidation, Allen also began purchasing substantial chunks of land in the western Grants, thus adding a financial stake to his love for both freedom and mayhem. By October 1771 New York's governor had issued a warrant for Allen's arrest and placed a reward of 20 pounds on his head. A flippantly defiant Allen responded that "By virtue of a late Law in the Province they are Not Allowed to hang any man before they have ketched him."[2]

The backwoods intellectual even produced a 200-page pamphlet in early 1775 partially titled *A Brief Narrative of the Proceedings of the Government of New York Relative to Their Obtaining the Jurisdiction of that Large District to the Westward of the Connecticut River*, ... By this time, his thoughts were also turning to the Grants' independence from both New York and New Hampshire. Still, Allen might have remained nothing more than a Yankee Robin Hood, a forest outlaw who championed the rights of the oppressed against unjust authority, but for external developments.

Concerned with their own struggle, Allen and his Boys had not given much attention to the trouble brewing between Great Britain and her colonies. Yet when fighting broke out at Lexington and Concord in April 1775, Allen showed no hesitation in declaring himself for the patriot cause. Why he should lead his men in this direction, particularly when a majority of settlers in the Grants probably favored the mother country, is an interesting question. In a memoir, he wrote that:

> Ever since I ... acquainted myself with the general history of mankind, I have felt a sincere passion for liberty ... so that the first systematical and bloody attempt, at Lexington, to enslave America, thoroughly electrified my mind, and firmly determined me to take part with my country.[3]

A less charitable interpretation of Allen's motive is that he suspected, sooner or later, the crown would rule in favor of New York's claims in the Grants dispute and that breaking away from the mother country would be in his best personal interests.

Whatever his reasons, Allen fixed upon seizing the "Gibraltar of the Wilderness," Fort Ticonderoga, at the western edge of the Grants. This massive British post, situated at the head of Lake Champlain on its New York shore, guarded the critical north–south waterway between Canada and New York. An object of fierce fighting in the French and Indian War, by 1775, it had fallen into disrepair. Even after the outbreak of hostilities in Massachusetts, its garrison numbered only 50 men, plus their families. In early May, a group of prominent Connecticut patriots approached Allen with offers of money and support in taking the fort.

Events progressed rapidly. By May 7, some 60 Connecticut and Massachusetts volunteers and 130 or so Green Mountain Boys rallied in the Grants settlement of Castleton. The leaders huddled in a tavern and elected Allen commander of the expedition. They hatched a plan to attack the fort at dawn on May 10, crossing by boat from a cove on Champlain's eastern side only 2 miles distant from the objective. The motley force marched to Shoreham, in the vicinity of the embarkation site, while simultaneously detaching parties to round up all the available watercraft. As final preparations proceeded, scant hours before the scheduled assault, Colonel Benedict Arnold, resplendent in a new uniform, accompanied only by his manservant, and brandishing a commission granted by Massachusetts's Committee of Safety, abruptly descended upon the scene and proclaimed himself in command.

Allen may have been intimidated by the diminutive Arnold. Or he may have expected to have his authority upheld. In any case, he put the command question to the troops' vote and they vowed that they would follow Allen or no one. Tense negotiations between the two would-be leaders ensued—after all, Arnold had an official commission and no troops, while Allen had the men but no credentials— and they hammered out an accord whereby they would jointly lead the enterprise. Meanwhile, a more practical problem threatened the operation. Only two boats had been procured; therefore only one third of the attack force—83 men—were able to cross to Ticonderoga prior to first light on May 10. Landed on the far shore, this intrepid band moved to the silent fort.

Without difficulty they clambered through an unguarded hole in the outer works and shortly encountered a solitary sentry manning the inner gate. The guard gamely aimed his musket at Allen, but the weapon failed to discharge. In a rush, the attackers overran him and tumbled into the main courtyard. Allen's men trained their pieces on the troop barracks and, at his command, issued three lusty huzzas to waken the sleeping redcoats. The only other apparently alert sentinel suddenly materialized and courageously, if ill-advisedly, charged with fixed bayonet. Allen knocked him temporarily senseless with a blow to the head, then ordered the woozy man to take him to the commandant's quarters.

Allen later wrote that, upon encountering a trouserless British officer come to learn the cause of all the commotion, he thundered at him to surrender "In the name of the Great Jehovah and the Continental Congress." While, as one historian has pointed out, Allen possessed a commission from neither, this certainly showed a fine sense of church and state separation. Others who were on the scene later recollected that Allen's equally colorful, if less elevated, demand was more along the lines of, "Come out of there you damned old rat!" Regardless, the British commander prudently conceded to Allen and Arnold. Incredibly, a bastion regarded as impregnable had fallen in mere minutes without loss of life on either side.[4]

Allen followed up his signal conquest by pushing a detachment a dozen miles to the north to topple the adjacent British post at Crown Point, whose nine defenders quickly capitulated. In addition to a strategic fortress and nearly 60 prisoners, who were promptly dispatched to Connecticut, Allen had secured valuable stores. These included nearly 200 cannon, about half of which remained serviceable, much gunpowder, and also 90 gallons of rum from the British commandant's personal stock. This Allen distributed to refresh his men after their exertions. He later recorded that "We tossed about the flowing bowl and wished success to Congress, and the liberty and freedom of America."[5] As he and his men celebrated—and Arnold recoiled in horror at their indiscipline—Allen informed the world of his success. From the Continental Congress just convening in Philadelphia he requested immediate reinforcement, explaining that "We are in want of almost Every Necessity (Courage Excepted)."[6]

While the Americans consolidated their triumph, the relative command fortunes of Allen and Arnold reversed. Many of the Green Mountain Boys, the excitement over and spring planting to be done, struck off for home. And a company of Massachusetts men, who had previously volunteered to be part of Arnold's foray, finally arrived at Ticonderoga. Arnold now disposed the preponderance of troops. Taking charge, he assembled his men upon a commandeered schooner and sailed 100 miles down lake and successfully raided the British post at St. Johns, withdrawing back to Ticonderoga with considerable booty. This retirement was well advised, since a British relief force from nearby Montreal was sure to reestablish control at St. Johns. Nevertheless, Allen, with his remaining followers, resolved to seize and occupy the place despite Arnold's warnings.

Having secured four bateaux, Allen and 100 of his Boys plied up lake to debark ultimately just south of St. Johns on the west bank of the Sorel River. Here they learned that a redcoat force twice their size from Montreal was advancing upon them. They crossed to the east shore and, exhausted, made camp while neglecting to post any watch. The next morning, British grapeshot and musketry awakened them. Adopting a *sauve qui peut* attitude, the Americans scrambled to their boats and barely escaped to make a humiliating return to Ticonderoga on the evening of May 21.

Allen's woes mounted. His men continued to melt away and Arnold ascended to command of Allen's prize fortress. Worse, after the initial euphoria provoked by Allen's coup de main, Congress began to wonder what to do with Ticonderoga. Defending patriot rights at Lexington and Concord was one thing, but a brazen offensive action such as Allen's quite another. After all, at least officially, Congress still hoped to reconcile with the mother country. The delegates in Philadelphia began speaking of demilitarizing the fort and placing his majesty's property under safe keeping until the political difficulties worked themselves out. To Allen and Arnold both this was madness in the face of what they feared was an inevitable British riposte. Their joint missives to Congress finally brought that body around.

But not only did Allen wish to defend Ticonderoga, he viewed it as a natural base for an American invasion of Canada. Free of any command responsibilities, in the early summer he began to proselytize among Canadians and Indians, as well as his own countrymen, for such an undertaking. Eventually, he made his way to Philadelphia, where on June 23 he laid his views before Congress. Apparently he was persuasive, for shortly thereafter, Congress authorized the newly appointed northern department commander, General Philip Schuyler, to enter Canada if he found it feasible and the Canadians seemed favorably disposed. Congress also recommended to New York that it raise a Green Mountain Regiment on the Continental establishment, to be recruited in the Grants and paid for by that colony. Allen hastened to New York City, technically still a wanted outlaw in those precincts, and convinced the revolutionary leadership there to accept the Congressional suggestion. Accordingly, in late July a convention in the Grants elected the men who would lead the new regiment. Two of Allen's brothers were selected as company grade officers. Another individual, Allen's longtime subordinate Seth Warner, was chosen as colonel. The electors completely passed over Ethan Allen.

This outcome shocked Allen and in retrospect still seems puzzling. He had championed the Grants settlers for over 5 years and was a natural leader. Possible reasons for this bitter rejection include Allen's bombastic demeanor and overbearing ego, the feeling among some of the more conservative Grants settlers that he was something of a boor and an embarrassment, and the recent fiasco at St. Johns. Whatever the causes and whatever his faults, the ebullient Allen was never one to sulk or wallow in self-pity. He swallowed his pride and offered his services to Schuyler as a civilian scout. Late August found him operating with a small detachment in advance of General Richard Montgomery's attempt on St. Johns. When Montgomery began a siege there in mid-September, he instructed Allen to head north, and recruit allies among the Indians and Canadians. This Allen did with great success and by September 20, he informed Montgomery that he had 250 men under arms.

Buoyed by this, and burning to recapture the glory dimmed by his checks from the British at St. Johns and from his own countrymen in officering the Green Mountain Regiment, Allen decided to seize Montreal. This was a dubious scheme, to say the least. Even though the British had denuded it of troops and guns to defend St. Johns, Montreal was still one of North America's largest cities with a population approaching 9,000 inhabitants. Further, it made no operational sense to attack; once St. Johns fell to Montgomery—which was a foregone conclusion— Montreal would become untenable, as indeed, events proved. Allen, however, could not resist. He coordinated with a fellow scout leading a similar recruiting mission to launch a coordinated attack on the night of September 24–25. Allen's men, now numbering about 100 after he sent the rest to Montgomery, would attack up the St. Lawrence River from the north. The other contingent, roughly twice the size of Allen's, would simultaneously move down river from the south. At dawn, the plan called for the two forces to swoop upon the stunned garrison and present it with a *fait accompli* a la Ticonderoga.

Under cover of darkness, Allen ferried his men across the St. Lawrence to the outskirts of the city. A shortage of boats necessitated multiple lifts. Sunrise found the intrepid 100 outside the city walls. No trace of the other assault element manifested itself. Why this sister force never arrived is unknown; high winds that made Allen's river crossing perilous may explain it. For several uncomfortable hours Allen's puny, highly exposed force and the denizens of Montreal, safe behind their city walls, faced off. Gradually realizing that the odds decisively favored him, Canada's Royal Governor, General Guy Carleton, sallied forth with several hundred redcoats, Canadians, and Indians to deal with the impertinent Americans. Allen later recorded with notable understatement and honesty, "I perceived it would be a day of trouble, if not of rebuke."[7] I thought to have enrolled my name in the roll of illustrious American heroes, but was nipped in the bud."[8] Due to the boat shortfall, Allen rejected retreat; he refused to abandon any portion of his command. He put up a good fight; a 2-hour gun battle ensued with less than exemplary marksmanship on both sides. Two redcoats were the only men killed. "[S]o much ammunition was expended, and so little execution done by it," Allen testified.[9] Nevertheless, the outnumbered Americans eventually threw down their arms. More than $2\frac{1}{2}$ years of captivity stretched out before Allen.

Once they recognized the conqueror of Ticonderoga, the British clapped Allen in irons and in short order transported him to England in the foul hold of a warship. By late December 1775, he and several other prisoners were lodged in Pendennis Castle, outside Falmouth, England. There was much talk of hanging, until it dawned on his majesty's ministers that such actions would invite American reprisals upon captured British officers. Deciding to treat him as a prisoner of war—even though Allen held no military rank—the British shipped him back to Canada, and ultimately to New York City. Allen remained on parole in Manhattan, under tolerably good conditions, from October 1776 until August 1777. Around that time, Allen impressed a British officer, who declared that he had never met anyone "whose mode of expression was more vehement and oratorical. His style was a singular compound of local barbarisms, scriptural phrases and oriental wildness; and although ... sometimes ungrammatical, it was highly animated and forcible."[10] Unsurprisingly, Allen's penchant for flouting authority led his captors to jail him for various parole violations. Nabbed in an off-limits tavern, he remained in lockup until exchanged in May 1778.

Instead of returning home, Allen made his way to Valley Forge to offer his services to General Washington. Perhaps mindful of Allen's inglorious exploits at St. Johns and Montreal, the Virginian deftly turned him aside, although he did tepidly endorse Allen's bid for a Continental commission. Congress in fact made Allen a brevet colonel, but found no billet for him. Allen would remain in an inactive status for the remaining 5 years of the war. Basking in his returning hero role, Allen now headed home to the Grants, enjoying Horatio Gates's company on part of the journey. He managed to spend 2 whole days with his wife and children, who were installed with one of his relatives, before proceeding to Bennington, where transports of joy awaited. Once again, he and his friends "moved the flowing bowl, and rural felicity, sweetened with friendship, glowed in each countenance."[11]

Many changes had occurred in his absence. Most notably, several of his powerful cronies in the Grants had proclaimed that contested area as the independent Republic of Vermont. Not only did this outrage New York even more, it created a swirling mess of issues centered on sovereignty and territorial integrity that involved several New England states as well. Allen happily plunged into the fray. Although he never won civilian elective office, he became the de facto leader of what was essentially a junta that ruled Vermont for the next decade. He made several trips to Philadelphia to lobby Congress to support Vermont's claims. Appointed major general commanding Vermont's militia in 1779, he suppressed several minor rebellions in Vermont's eastern counties fomented by settlers opposed to their rulers' dictatorial regime. He also published a rip-snorting best seller recounting his adventures. Partially titled *A Narrative of Colonel Ethan Allen's Captivity . . .*, portions of it were even true. More interestingly, its purple prose faithfully transmits the author's uninhibited, swashbuckling nature.

Besides keeping unruly farmers in order, the Vermont militia's other task was to guard her borders. A New York bid to reassert its authority by force represented one potential threat and, of course, the British remained in Canada. The latter recognized an opportunity to exploit the inter-American strife and sometime in July 1780, British agents in Vermont approached Allen. The surviving details are sketchy, but over the next 2 years Allen entered into a secret correspondence with the British commander in Canada. Discussion included the possibility of Vermont gaining sovereignty under the crown in return for supporting his majesty against the rebellious colonies. Allen's critics argue that the Continental colonel and militia general contemplated treason—if not against the United States, then against Vermont, which also was at war with Britain. His defenders maintain that he merely played a deep game to galvanize Congress into recognizing Vermont's independence and accepting it into the Confederation. Whatever the truth, negotiations dragged out until overcome by events in the form of British defeat at Yorktown and the subsequent peace settlement.

The war's end marked the start of Allen's decline in power. As Vermont's population grew—it became the 14th state in 1791—it required a more mature politics than that represented by Allen and his Boys. The old firebrand eased out of public life. His first wife died in 1783 and he took a new bride half his age less than a year later. This union evidently proved much happier. Allen eventually settled in the town of Burlington and though he had acquired 12,000 acres by his death, like most of his fellow citizens in that currency-strapped era, he remained cash poor. He successfully dodged his many creditors and finished a deistic tract he had begun 20 years earlier, *Reason the Only Oracle of Man*. This gained him new notoriety and damnation from many pulpits. A lifetime of rough and tumble caught up with him at the early age of 51; he died on February 12, 1789.

George Washington supplied a succinct—and perhaps the fairest—assessment of Allen: "There is an original something in him that commands admiration."[12] What that ineffable something might have been is best expressed by the historian Turner, celebrating the American character produced by the frontier experience. No more suitable epitaph for the legendary frontier rebel could exist than Turner's lyrical invocation of

> ... coarseness and strength, combined with acuteness and acquisitiveness; that practical inventive turn of mind, quick to find expedients; that masterful grasp of material things, lacking in the artistic but powerful to effect great ends; that restless, nervous energy; that dominant individualism, working for good and for evil; and withal, that buoyancy and exuberance which comes with freedom ... [13]

GEORGE ROGERS CLARK

Most Revolutionary War histories give short shrift to that conflict's western theater. This eastern bias, similar incidentally to that obtaining in most Civil War accounts, stems from three reasons. First, the fundamental question of American independence resolved itself in the east. Next, many more—and much bigger—battles occurred there. Finally, virtually all the war's early chroniclers were easterners. Nevertheless, despite the relatively small number of soldiers involved and the reduced scale of the engagements, the Revolutionary contest for the Old Northwest was fully as desperate as that in Pennsylvania or Virginia, and the stakes similarly high. For at issue was nothing less than the control and destiny of half a continent—the trans-Allegheny region northwest of the Ohio River stretching west to the Mississippi and north to the Great Lakes. No single man was more critical to winning this vast domain and establishing the preconditions for the United States' subsequent postwar expansion than George Rogers Clark.

Clark was born in Albemarle County, Virginia—not far from Thomas Jefferson's birthplace—on November 19, 1752. His Scots ancestors had come to the tidewater in the early 1700s, progressed steadily inland, and prospered as planters. Aspiring to gentility, Clark's parents boarded him with a tutor when he was 11. The lad, whose fellow students included the future president James Madison, proved indifferent to mastering Greek and Latin, and more inclined to the open air. After 8 months his formal education ceased and he returned home. He was hardly a dull youth, however. As he grew into strapping manhood—most contemporary descriptions depict him as tall and well-built with flaming red hair and sparkling black eyes—he took up surveying. This happy choice allowed him to employ his sharp mind while indulging his love for nature and the outdoors.

In 1772 Clark left home with his surveying instruments and a geometry book, and made his way to the frontier post at Fort Pitt (modern Pittsburgh). From there, he journeyed by flatboat down the Ohio River and, in the company of some other equally adventurous souls, explored as far south as the mouth of the Kanawha River into what is today West Virginia. Over the next several years, Clark repeated his voyages down the Ohio and into the immense region claimed by Virginia, as well as several other colonies. He became particularly enchanted with Kentucky, surveying for others and staking his own claims. In 1774, Clark participated as a militia captain in a campaign against the Shawnee nation, which had resisted white encroachments on their lands. The savagery on both sides justified the tribes' name for Kentucky—the "Dark and Bloody Ground."

Concerned as they were with taming a wilderness, the Kentucky frontiersmen had not allowed themselves to be overly caught up in the Revolutionary fever that swept Virginia and the other colonies in 1775. Nevertheless, the lingering threat of Indian attack caused "a Respectable Body of Prime Riflemen" to meet at the tiny Harrodsburg settlement and pledge support to the patriot cause. They also sent Clark as their delegate to lobby Virginia's revolutionary government for political recognition and gunpowder with which to defend themselves. Clark's embassy succeeded on both scores; the Old Dominion granted the embattled settlers 500 pounds of powder and, in December 1776, adopted their settlements into Virginia as Kentucky County. This last prompted Kentucky's earliest historians to label Clark the "Father of the Commonwealth."

These actions could not have been better timed as far as the Kentuckians were concerned. In the spring of 1777, the British began encouraging the Indians to attack the Americans' western frontier settlements, a policy similar to one they had carried out for some time in northern New York, and would later employ in Georgia and the Carolinas. The British headquarters for this campaign was Detroit and its architect was Lieutenant Governor Henry Hamilton, whose grim nickname was "the Hair Buyer." Whether he actually offered rewards for settlers' scalps is unknown, but the rampaging tribesmen from north of the Ohio took a number of them and spread terror throughout Kentucky.

Clark, who now held a major's commission in Virginia's armed forces, was the ranking patriot officer in Kentucky. He gamely attempted to defend the far-flung settlements, but soon concluded that the best defense would be a good offense. Only by carrying the war to the enemy—in this case, driving the British from their posts north of the Ohio and ultimately toppling their base at Detroit—could he end the Indian raids the British fomented. As a campaign plan began to take form in his head, he sent spies into the Illinois country and interrogated travelers to gather information. The intelligence picture he compiled revealed a handful of lightly garrisoned stockades adjoining key river towns, which were occupied principally by settlers of French origin who had no great love for the British. In the late summer of 1777 he sent a letter to Virginia Governor Patrick Henry proposing an expedition to seize the important outpost of Kaskaskia, just off the Mississippi some 50 miles south of the Spanish trading center of St. Louis. Under American control, "it would distress the garrison at Detroit for provisions" and "fling the possession of the two great rivers [Ohio and Mississippi] into our hands" while cowing the Indians.[14]

He followed up this missive with a trip back to Williamsburg to sell his ideas to Virginia's leadership. He consulted with and convinced prominent men of affairs such as Thomas Jefferson, Richard Henry Lee, and George Mason. Governor Henry entertained doubts, but eventually acceded. By early January 1778, Clark had authority to recruit 350 men for 3 months service, 1,200 pounds to expend, and a promotion to lieutenant colonel. He also had two sets of instructions from the governor. Publicly, he was enjoined to seize Kaskaskia. A second, secret set of orders, later supplemented, permitted Clark to operate with considerable latitude in the Illinois country. Henry told him to advance beyond Kaskaskia as "the Interest of your Country directs" and to "proceed to the Enemy's Settlements above or across [i.e., Vincennes and Detroit], as you may find it proper."[15] It is worth remarking that the "Country" referred to was Virginia, not the United States. Indeed, the rivalry between Pennsylvania and Virginia over the territory contemplated for conquest by Clark was one of the reasons for the secrecy.

Clark, competing with Continental Army, as well as other Virginia recruiters, experienced difficulty in gathering men. He only had 150 when he set out down the Ohio in early May to a previously designated rendezvous at the Falls of the Ohio (modern Louisville). Here his lieutenants met him with additional troops. The force established a base camp and began training. Most of the men responded enthusiastically when Clark informed them of the true scope of their mission, although a few deserted. On June 26, 1778 Clark, with between 175 and 200 men, shot the Ohio rapids during a solar eclipse and launched the campaign. Reaching the mouth of the Tennessee River, they grounded their flatboats. Rather than risk detection by continuing along the river route, Clark chose to make a 120-mile cross-country march to Kaskaskia. Outfitted in the frontiersman's garb of long, knee-length hunting shirts, cinched about their waists with broad belts, leggings, moccasins, and floppy felt hats, the expedition padded silently through the forests. In addition to their rifles, each man was festooned with a tomahawk, hunting knife, and powder horn, and carried whatever provender he could manage. By July 4 they had closed to within a mile of their objective.

Kaskaskia, containing an unsuspecting population of nearly 1,000 French-speaking *habitants*, was the largest settlement in the Illinois country. It consisted of the town proper and a nearby fort. As darkness fell, Clark divided his troops into two parties, which crossed the Kaskaskia River in some easily commandeered boats. Clark led one detachment to the fort and took it without firing a shot by surprising the commandant in his bed and inducing him to surrender. The rest of Clark's men surrounded the now-defenseless town. By sunrise, the frontiersmen, looking even wilder than normal after their trek down river and through the woods, patrolled the dusty streets. The terrified citizens expected the worst, but Clark assured them that he had not come to burn and plunder, but to secure the area to stop the Indian raids into Kentucky. The Americans' good behavior, plus Clark's informing them that France had recently declared itself for the American cause, provided reason enough for virtually all the townspeople to swear allegiance to the state of Virginia. A number even volunteered to join Clark's tatterdemalion army.

Clark maintained the initiative. He dispatched troops north to the smaller settlements of Prairie du Rocher and Cahokia, whose denizens quickly fell in line. He quickly established contact with friendly Spaniards in St. Louis, which lay on the west bank of the Mississippi across from Cahokia. Clark also had the important post at Vincennes, nearly 200 miles to the east on the Wabash River, scouted and he guessed correctly that its francophone settlers would be happy—or at least willing—to forsake British masters for loyalty to Virginia. By the end of August, Clark's second in command had assumed control and asserted patriot authority there. Amazing as these bloodless accomplishments were, perhaps even more stunning was the diplomatic offensive Clark undertook to compel the Indian nations in the region to cease their attacks on Kentucky. Throughout the fall, Clark met with their chiefs at Cahokia. Through an astute combination of bluffs, threats, and promises, Clark negotiated treaties with at least ten tribes, convincing them that British dominion had ended and that the Americans were the new white power. Meanwhile, in Detroit, "the Hair Buyer" readied his counterstroke.

Hamilton assembled a motley 250-man force of British regulars, French–Canadian volunteers, and Indians. Starting in early October, he led them on a grueling 10-week expedition—initially along the river network above and below Lake Erie, followed by an arduous cross-country portage to the Wabash, then south to Vincennes. By the time he reached the post in mid-December, Hamilton's ranks had swollen to over 500 as various Indian bands joined him. The French settlers at Vincennes—supposedly converted to the American cause—felt no in-clination to resist such an impressive host and refused to fight. The handful of Americans on the scene had no choice but to surrender. Hamilton, belying his hor-rific moniker, treated his American prisoners humanely and quickly reestablished British authority in the vicinity. The French took their latest in a series of loyalty oaths while Hamilton refurbished Vincennes's defenses, renaming the stockade

Fort Sackville. Rather than push west to the Mississippi in order to crush Clark, Hamilton chose to winter at Vincennes, with the intention of finishing him off in the spring of 1779.

All of this occurred without Clark's knowledge. Operating at the end of an extremely tenuous line of communications, not only back to Virginia and Kentucky, but even with his own scattered forces in the interior of the Illinois country, news reached him slowly. He only learned of Vincennes's fall at the end of January 1779, when a Spanish trader, recently come from there, informed him. Isolated and also with his rifle strength depleted through the expiration of his Virginians' enlistments, Clark nevertheless decided to strike Hamilton at Vincennes rather than retreat to Kentucky or await the blow at Kaskaskia. As he told Governor Henry in a hastily scribbled letter just before he set out, "I am Resolved to . . . Risque the whole on a Single Battle . . . I Shall March across by Land my self with the Rest of My Boys . . . the Case is Desperate but Sir we must Either Quit the Cuntrey or attact Mr. Hamilton."[16]

Clark outfitted a large riverboat—the *Willing*—to carry supplies up the Ohio, then the Wabash, and to approach Vincennes from the south. Then with nearly 200 men, equally divided between his remaining Virginians and a company of French volunteers, on February 6 he plunged into the Illinois wilderness headed east. Despite miserable weather that included torrential downpours, the expedition covered more than 150 miles over the first 6 days of their trek, an impressive rate of march under any circumstances. Clark then encountered the first in a series of water obstacles created by the combination of unremitting rain and melting snow. The Little Wabash River, normally a trickle running parallel to its larger sister to the east, had overflowed to create a floodplain 5 miles wide and 3 or more feet deep. Undaunted, the men lashed together rafts to ferry supplies and those too weak or ill to wade.

Two further rivers remained—the Embarrass and the Wabash—before the bedraggled attackers could attain Vincennes on the Wabash's east bank. One of Clark's colleagues captured the desperate situation in a series of remarkable journal entries: "starving Many of the Men much cast down . . . No provisions of any Sort . . . hard fortune . . . some almost in despair . . . lord help us."[17] Here Clark displayed magnificent leadership. Masking his own deep concerns—nothing had been heard from the riverboat bearing rations and other necessities—he drew more from his men than they thought they could give. Encouraging, cajoling, occasionally even joking, he "gave them great spirits."[18] Slogging through icy, chest-deep water, he led them to a dry knoll whence, on the afternoon of February 23, they finally glimpsed Vincennes, not 2 miles off. A duck-hunting Frenchman from the town wandered into Clark's camp. Interrogation revealed that Hamilton had no inkling that his enemies were so near. Clark released the captive with a message for the townspeople warning them that the Americans intended to attack the fort that night and soliciting their assistance.

The locals, deceived as to the small size of Clark's force, switched sides yet again. As darkness fell, Clark's men occupied the town. While the citizenry fed his grateful troops, Clark reconnoitered the fort and had his riflemen begin sniping at its defenders. On the morning of the 24th Clark demanded that Hamilton surrender, warning him that "if I am obliged to storm, you may depend upon such Treatment justly due to a Murderer" and further threatening that if the Englishman destroyed any stores or papers "by heavens ... there shall be no Mercy shewn you."[19] In his terse, defiant response Hamilton begged "leave to acquaint Col. Clark that he and his Garrison are not disposed to be awed into any action Unworthy of British subjects."[20] In spite of his bold words, Hamilton faced a hopeless predicament. Most of his French militia had slunk off and his only reliable fighters were 35 or so redcoats. The two sides exchanged fire until midday when Hamilton proposed a parley.

Clark agreed, but just before the two commanders met, the American indulged in a bloody bit of psychological warfare. His men had ambushed an Indian war party making its way back from raiding Kentucky. Four of the captured braves were brought into view of the fort's defenders and, before their horrified eyes, tomahawked to death and their bodies cast into the Wabash. During their interview, Clark not-so-subtly informed his counterpart that his men remained eager to revenge themselves on those responsible for pillaging their homes in Kentucky and that prolonged enemy resistance might drive them over the edge. Hamilton negotiated terms that satisfied his sense of honor and the garrison handed over the fort the following morning. No further bloodshed occurred. Hamilton and his regulars were eventually transported to Williamsburg, where "the Hair Buyer" spent several uncomfortable months in chains before being paroled to New York City.

Clark's riverboat belatedly arrived in Vincennes 3 days after the British surrender. In addition to welcome reinforcements and supplies, it also brought the first news that Clark had heard from Virginia in nearly a year. Clark learned that he had won a vote of thanks from the state legislature and a promotion to colonel. He also discovered that Virginia had incorporated the territory he subdued as Illinois County and would soon send officials out, lifting the burden of civil government from Clark's shoulders. The new colonel weighed continuing up the Wabash to strike at the grand prize of Detroit, which he knew would be weakened and demoralized by Hamilton's defeat. He even sent a taunting dispatch to the ranking officer there. Informed that the British were feverishly shoring up their defenses, he wrote, "I am glad to hear it, as it saves the Ammericans some expences in building" once he captured the place.[21] Despite the bravado, this was as close as Clark would ever come to winning this prize. Although tempted to press on against the largely helpless British post, he ultimately chose to await the promised arrival of fresh troops from Virginia and Kentucky. In the event, they never appeared and planned expeditions against Detroit in 1779, 1780, and 1781 never came off.

These disappointments—and many others—lay in the future, however as Clark concluded more treaties with the Indian nations around Vincennes, established a strong garrison there, and withdrew with the bulk of his force back to Kaskaskia at the end of March 1779. When reinforcements failed to reach him in the expected strength, and also plagued by supply problems that forced him to take on large personal debts he never escaped, Clark returned to Kentucky in August to drum up support. He had been gone for 14 months and found much changed. His great campaign north of the Ohio had indeed reduced the Indian danger to the Kentucky settlements. As a result, the population had expanded and prospered. To Clark, it also seemed that his countrymen had grown more selfish; to his disgust, he was unable to garner tangible support either for the Detroit enterprise or a contemplated thrust aimed at British posts on the lower Mississippi. Virginia's new governor, Thomas Jefferson, enthused over Clark's proposals but disposed precious few resources to allocate to him.

In the spring of 1780, Clark had to abandon temporarily his offensive schemes as the British initiated an ambitious series of coordinated attacks intended to reclaim the Illinois country as well as menace Kentucky. Over the next several months, in a breathtaking display of agility, he countered the enemy in an immense geographic area encompassing tens of thousands of square miles. In late May he rushed to Cahokia on the Mississippi, barely arriving ahead of a British column approaching from the north. Coordinating his efforts with Spanish forces in St. Louis, he drove off this attack, and for good measure chased the British and their Indian allies back into what is now Michigan. He then shifted his forces more than 300 miles in an effort to thwart a mixed British–Canadian–Indian blow at Kentucky. Placing the bulk of his men on boats to return via the Mississippi–Ohio River route, Clark sped cross-country to Louisville, but arrived too late to prevent an orgy of burning and hostage-taking. Bent upon retaliation, he gathered a 1,000-man force—much the largest ever assembled in Kentucky up to that time—and set off in pursuit. In early August the angered Americans torched a Shawnee village at Chillicothe on the Little Miami River (in what is today Ohio) and won a one-sided engagement some 10 miles farther north at Piqua. It was the bloodiest battle Clark ever fought; he lost 14 killed and as many wounded in return for inflicting nearly 100 casualties on the Indians. Clark wished to press on, but the victory sated his militiamen, who were also running short of supplies and wanted to return home for the fall harvest.

Still persuaded that the key to bringing lasting tranquility to Kentucky lay in seizing Detroit—an undertaking in "which my very soul was wrapt"—Clark traveled to Virginia in the fall of 1780 to solicit Jefferson's backing for the attempt the following year.[22] The governor in turn importuned the Continental Congress and General Washington for supplies and troops. While Washington had never met Clark personally, he had gained a highly favorable impression of him second-hand. Further, he agreed "that the reduction of the post of Detroit would be the only certain means of giving peace and security to the whole western frontier."[23] Jefferson promised Clark that he would have 2,000 men and an artillery train. And although he failed to obtain a Continental colonelcy for Clark, he made up for it by appointing him a brigadier general in Virginia's state troops.

Subsequent developments quashed Clark's projected campaign. In early 1781, Virginia experienced the war first hand when the turncoat Benedict Arnold led a massive raid up the James River. Clark, still on the scene to coordinate the Detroit expedition, immediately volunteered to help face this threat. Seconded to General Steuben, Clark experienced his only brush with eastern "conventional" warfare when 240 volunteers under his command ambushed some redcoats at Hood's Ferry on January 3. Jefferson then recalled Clark so he could remove himself to Fort Pitt, the intended jumping off point for the Detroit operation. With Virginia itself now a major arena of conflict—Cornwallis entered the state in May and the Americans poured in reinforcements as well—the Old Dominion could not furnish the men and supplies Clark had hoped for and expected. Further hindering his plans, the enemy renewed their attacks all along the Ohio River that spring. To the west, severe pressure forced the American evacuation of Kaskaskia and an outpost Clark had established at the confluence of the Mississippi and Ohio, Fort Jefferson. Indian raids resumed against Kentucky as well. All this reduced Virginia–Kentucky resources and enthusiasm for distant offensive operations. By early August Clark accepted the reality of the situation; Detroit was off again. He wrote Jefferson that he had "Relinquished my Expectations Relative to the plans heretofore laid" and expressed "that the Disapointment is doubly mortifying to me."[24]

Clark left Fort Pitt and moved to Louisville to look after the defense of Kentucky. He found himself in that most unenviable of situations—his brigadier's rank made him nominally responsible, but the fractiousness of his fellow Kentuckians meant that he exercised no real authority. Possessed of greater strategic vision than other men, Clark tried unsuccessfully to interest them in a foray against the Indian tribes along the Wabash, but the settlers' preference was for defense. In October he penned a disconsolate letter, describing himself as being "enclosed with few troops, in a trifling fort."[25] Later that same month came the glad tidings of Washington's victory at Yorktown, but while the war wound down over the next year in the east, the Kentucky frontier erupted in more savage fighting, as the Indian nations to the north of the Ohio sought to eradicate the white settlements across the river before the complete withdrawal of British aid. In 1782 Kentucky lay almost defenseless due to the combination of her parent Virginia's own war-weariness and the fecklessness of her citizens. Rampaging Indians destroyed numerous settlements and massacred the badly handled militia sent out to challenge them. Indeed, it seemed that Kentucky's only shield was Clark's fearsome reputation among the tribes, who steered clear of the "Chief of the Big Knives."

As conditions worsened, Clark became a convenient scapegoat among Kentuckians, including the famed woodsman Daniel Boone, as well as for political enemies back in Virginia. A whispering campaign began a rumor that would dog him the rest of his life—that he was a drunkard. Certainly, like many frontiersmen, Clark enjoyed a tipple now and again, and Kentucky was already justly famed for its whiskey, but there is no evidence that he was in any way impaired during this critical period. Indeed, the settlers finally rose from their torpor and clamored for Clark to lead a punitive expedition against the marauding Indians. In November 1782 Clark entered the Shawnee country along the Miami River and exacted revenge by razing villages and fields. This exploit, as well as winter's onset and the diminution of British support, abated the Indian raids for a considerable interval.

This ended Clark's wartime service. The following year he resigned his commission and, not yet 30, began an unhappy postwar career. In many respects, his after years were as sad and tragic as those of that other youthful Virginia paladin, Henry Lee. He never married and lived for several years with his parents, who had purchased an estate outside Louisville. The financial obligations he had assumed during the war on behalf of Virginia left him destitute. The vouchers he submitted were ignored or lost; nearly 2,000 of them resurfaced in Richmond only in 1913! An Indian uprising in 1786 compelled Virginia to call him to active service north of the Ohio, but the raw militia under his command mutinied and the campaign ended abortively. Once again his enemies bruited charges of intoxication against him; among the gossip spreaders was the unspeakable blackguard James Wilkinson, who had his own schemes for taking power in western politics.

Unfortunately, the drinking accusations became reality. Depressed by poverty and forgotten by his fellow citizens, Clark turned increasingly to the bottle for solace. Thomas Jefferson always retained great admiration for Clark and in 1783 suggested to him an expedition "for exploring the country from the Missisipi to California" and asked "how would you like to lead such a party?"[26] Nothing came of this, although 20 years later Clark's youngest brother William gained immortality while accompanying Meriwether Lewis to the Pacific at President Jefferson's behest. The once-vigorous Clark, who exhibited extraordinary endurance in traversing hundreds of miles of forbidding wilderness as a young man, declined rapidly. He suffered a stroke in 1809 and an accident caused the amputation of his right leg shortly after. He lived with various relatives and his increasing bitterness. The largely forgotten hero died on February 13, 1818 at his sister's home east of Louisville and was buried there.

A monument to Clark erected in Illinois a century after his death hails him as "The Son of Virginia," "The Sword of Kentucky," and "The Conqueror of the Illinois." His brilliant campaigns north of the Ohio—conducted on a shoestring and unsurpassed in terms of audacity—preserved Kentucky's infant settlements from destruction by the Indian nations and the British. His conquests extended Virginia's—and ultimately the United States'—western domains tremendously. Before embarking on the crowning episode of his career, the recapture of Vincennes, Clark wrote a long letter to Patrick Henry. He dwelled on the many obstacles ahead and even appeared to argue with himself as to whether to make the attempt. He concluded, however, by declaring that "Great things have been affected by a few Men well Conducted."[27] Not even a heroic statue excels this noble sentiment as a memorial to this indomitable frontiersman.

DANIEL MORGAN

Daniel Morgan fought directly under George Washington, Benedict Arnold, Horatio Gates, and Nathanael Greene, as well as alongside Richard Montgomery,

Andrew Pickens, and Anthony Wayne. His Revolutionary War service spanned from Canada to South Carolina, encompassing the New England, middle, and southern theaters. The "old wagoner" as he styled himself, was in many respects an exemplar of the rugged frontiersman. Raw and unlettered, he loved to josh, gamble, drink, and roughhouse. Beneath the boisterous exterior, however, lay a stern sense of right and wrong, as well as unwavering loyalty to friends, cause, and country.

His origins are shrouded in mystery. He was most likely born in 1735 or 1736. New Jersey, Pennsylvania, and Virginia have all been suggested as possible birthplaces. He is said to have come from Welsh immigrant stock; Daniel Boone may have been a cousin or an uncle. He first appears on the historical stage in the winter of 1752–1753 in Frederick County, on Virginia's western frontier, as a strapping youth who had recently quarreled with his father and left home— wherever that may have been. He found work at various odd jobs—at a sawmill and as a farmhand and wagon driver. The latter occupation proved the most lucrative and also afforded the restless young man the opportunity to travel the backcountry as well as to Virginia's tidewater.

At the outset of the French and Indian War in 1755, Morgan signed on as a civilian teamster supporting the British General Edward Braddock's disastrous expedition to Fort Duquesne. While on campaign, Morgan apparently struck a British officer during an argument, which earned him a disciplinary flogging. Much later, he gleefully claimed that his punishers miscounted and that he received only 499 of the prescribed 500 lashes. The beating did nothing to tame his spirited nature, but it cemented a lifetime hatred for the British and resolved him never to have misbehaving troops under his command whipped for their infractions. Morgan was well to the rear with the trains when Braddock sustained his fatal defeat on July 9; afterward he witnessed firsthand the human wreckage and helped haul the wounded as part of the doleful retreat.

Shortly afterward, back home in Frederick County, Morgan joined a ranger company formed to secure the Virginia frontier in the face of the expected Indian onslaught. In April 1756 hostiles ambushed him and a comrade on patrol. Musket fire killed his fellow ranger. Morgan, on horseback, barely outdistanced his pursuers, but suffered a gunshot wound that entered his neck and ripped through his jaw, knocking out several teeth. He swiftly recovered from the painful, nonlife threatening injury, but bore the scars the rest of his life. His militia stint complete, he returned to driving and a roustabout life. Tall—at least 6 feet—and athletic, he excelled at horse and foot racing, as well as boozing and brawling. He found himself hauled before local magistrates on several occasions to answer for various misdemeanors. As is often the case, however, the love of a good woman curtailed a young man's wild and wicked ways. In 1763 Morgan took Abigail Curry as a common-law wife—a not uncommon frontier practice. In the ensuing decade, a mere two assault and battery complaints were sworn against him. He settled down to farming, acquired at least ten slaves, reared two daughters, and even had a minister legally tie the knot between him and Abigail in 1773.

As Morgan climbed in respectability, his neighbors conferred a number of responsibilities upon him—county road maintenance supervisor, jury duty, deputy sheriff and—in 1771—militia captain. In June 1774, Morgan led a company on an Indian-fighting expedition into the Ohio country—the same campaign in which George Rogers Clark also served. Morgan later described this summer of village burning and occasional skirmishes as "very active and hard."[28] That same year, many Virginians joined the continental chorus against Britain's attempted coercion against her unruly subjects in Boston. Morgan got caught up in the fervor and vowed to come to the Bostonians' aid if fighting broke out. When hostilities opened a year later at Lexington and Concord, he proved as good as his word.

On June 14, 1775, the Continental Congress created the beginnings of an American army by voting to raise ten companies of riflemen—six from Pennsylvania and two each from Maryland and Virginia. In the skilled hands of frontiersmen such as Morgan, the "Kentucky rifle" was a fearsome weapon. Although it had a slower rate of fire than the standard smooth-bore musket—no more than two shots a minute versus four or five—and wasn't fitted for a bayonet, the rifle was accurate and lethal at ranges out to 250 yards. Muskets, on the other hand—designed for volley fire, not individually aimed shots—were generally ineffective beyond 50 yards. Virginia's leaders solicited one of the prescribed companies from Frederick County and the patriots there unanimously elected Morgan as the unit's captain. Morgan carefully recruited 96 men, conducting shooting competitions to determine the best marksmen. Dressed in long hunting shirts, leggins, and moccasins and armed with tomahawks and scalping knives in addition to their rifles, Morgan's men departed for Massachusetts on July 15. Six hundred miles and 3 weeks later the exotic-looking backwoodsmen arrived to considerable acclaim in Cambridge.

They made themselves useful by sniping at the unhappy redcoats trapped in besieged Boston, but chafed at camp discipline and the relative lack of action. Then in September, General Washington designated Morgan's men, along with two Pennsylvania companies, to join Benedict Arnold's expedition to Quebec. Arnold's fabled march—celebrated in both fact and fiction—through 350 miles of Maine wilderness was ordered up by the commander in chief as a supporting effort to the Congressionally directed attack into Canada led by Richard Montgomery.[29] The 1,100-strong force, which included at least two riflemen's wives, sailed from Newburyport, Massachusetts, on September 19 and debarked at Gardiner, Maine. From there they began an ascent of the Kennebec River in bateaux. Arnold placed Morgan in command of the advance party, composed of his and the other rifle companies. Struggling through rapids and water falls, Morgan arrived at the Great Carrying Place, where his men had the task of clearing a portage route to the Dead River, some dozen miles distant. Under horrendous conditions—continuously cold, wet, short of food, plagued by dysentery—Morgan's men labored as the trailing elements caught up to them.

The ordeal continued as the patriots rowed the 30 miles up the Dead River. An especially powerful storm struck them on October 21, on top of the heavy rains that had already pelted them for days. Some of Arnold's officers elected to turn back, taking 300 similarly faint-hearted and sick men with them. The remaining 700 endured a Calvary of wading through icy swamps, carrying 400-pound boats on raw, aching shoulders, and subsisting on a diet that included roasted dog, moccasin leather, and shaving soap. After negotiating the Chaudiere River, the emaciated survivors reentered civilization at the French–Canadian village of St. Mary's in early November. At least 50 Americans had perished over the course of the journey. After a brief rest, the Americans marched along the east bank of the St. Lawrence River to a point just opposite Quebec. After enduring yet another epic storm, the invaders silently began crossing in canoes the night of November 13. An enemy patrol boat detected them in the predawn gloom and an exchange of gunfire followed. Arnold convened a hasty council of war on the hostile shore and sought opinions. Morgan favored mounting an immediate assault on the fortress, but the majority feared that the loss of surprise and the absence of nearly one third of their force—yet to cross—made the undertaking dubious. Arnold uncharacteristically chose caution. He finished ferrying his troops and established a camp outside the city to await Montgomery.

The two commands rendezvoused below Quebec on December 2. Montgomery had brought about 300 men with him, so he now took charge of a besieging army of 1,000 soldiers. Morgan's riflemen took station to the city's north and made life as miserable as possible for enemy sentries with their well-aimed shooting. Meanwhile, the Americans planned to storm Quebec under cover of the first snowstorm to strike. That opportunity arrived on the night of December 30. Two small parties demonstrated to the west of the walled town to attract the defenders' attention, while Montgomery led a column from the south and Arnold brought his troops—including Morgan's company—around from the north. The plan called for Montgomery and Arnold's forces to combine in the center of the lower town and then fight their way into the citadel above them. The attack stood little chance from the outset. The feints proved ineffectual. Montgomery was killed at the head of his element before it even entered the city and his frightened subordinates retreated. All this was unknown to Arnold and Morgan, however, as they picked their way south along an icy footpath into the teeth of a blizzard.

Receiving sporadic fire from the city ramparts, this one remaining American column encountered a barrier at the lower town's entrance. From there a barrage of musketry and cannon fire thundered at them, and Arnold fell with a leg wound. Morgan, close by his side, took command and led a furious assault. Placing a scaling ladder against the enemy works, Morgan mounted, only to be blown back by another discharge of gunfire. Miraculously unharmed, though his clothing was shredded and his face smarted from powder burns, he leapt back up and surmounted the 10-foot wall. Inspired, his riflemen tumbled after him and captured the position, taking 50 prisoners in the process. Three hundred yards ahead lay another barricade, this one unmanned. Morgan wished to press ahead to the upper town, but two military truisms now obtained, to the patriots' disadvantage. The first insists that the succession of command always be designated before an operation. This was not the case here; no one really knew who was in charge once Arnold became *hors de combat*. The second holds that councils of war invariably breed timidity and indecision. Arnold's officers huddled in the dark streets of the lower town arguing with each other over whether to advance, retreat, or await Montgomery, who, of course, would never arrive.

This gave the British time to organize their defenses. With dawn breaking, the other officers gave in to Morgan's insistence on continuing the attack and asked him to lead it. He personally killed a British lieutenant as part of a ferocious hand-to-hand struggle that broke out at the entrance to the upper town. Gradually, however, the enemy, who greatly outnumbered the Americans, gained the advantage. They also slipped parties around to the patriot rear, cutting off any line of retreat. Americans began to throw down their weapons and call for quarter. Morgan raged and shed tears of frustration. His frantic subordinates pleaded with their cornered captain to surrender as he defied the redcoats to try and take his sword. Just as it appeared he would be shot down, Morgan spied a French priest in the crowd of watching, anxious civilians and handed the astonished clergyman the blade, crying "Not a scoundrel of those cowards shall take it out of my hands."[30]

Morgan spent the next 8 months confined at Quebec. He and his fellow prisoners most certainly rested warmer and better fed than their surviving compatriots outside the city walls, who maintained a shivering, forlorn siege under Arnold. Despite relatively lenient treatment, the captives yearned for their freedom. In September 1776, the British transferred them to New York City and paroled them until they could be exchanged for an equivalent set of British prisoners. Morgan went home to Virginia to await the formalities—which took place in January 1777—that allowed him to return to action. Held in high esteem—Washington praised "his intrepid behavior in the Assault on Quebec" and "the inflexible attachment he professed to our Cause during his imprisonment"—Morgan received a Continental colonelcy and command of the newly created 11th Virginia Regiment.[31] Beginning early in the year, Morgan recruited throughout western Virginia, exasperating some state officials with his insistence upon taking only the best marksmen. Prescribed strengths for Continental regiments ranged from between 600 and 1,000 men (though in the field, effective strengths were much lower), but Morgan had just 180 soldiers by April when he joined Washington's army in New Jersey.

Washington possessed a penchant for what we today would call "special forces" and shortly after Morgan's arrival he placed him in command of a "corps of rangers"—over 400 specially selected riflemen drawn from the regiments of three states. The commander in chief committed this force to harass the British during the opening moves of 1777's Philadelphia campaign. Washington, who knew a thing or two about frontier warfare, went so far as to instruct Morgan to have his men fight "in the right Indian Style" and "Attack accompanied with screaming and yelling as the Indians do, it would have very good consequences."[32] In mid-June, Morgan's rangers and Wayne's brigade, under Greene's direction, dueled with enemy detachments in the vicinity of New Brunswick, New Jersey, before the British General Howe withdrew his forces into New York City. While the Americans pondered Howe's next move, they anxiously looked north to another British army's drive from Canada into upper New York. Washington first dispatched Wayne to the northern theater and in August, with Howe's intentions still unclear, ordered Morgan and his rangers north as well. Washington wrote Morgan, "I know of no Corps so likely to check . . . [the enemy's] progress in proportion to their number, as the one you Command."[33]

Horatio Gates had recently taken charge in the north and heartily welcomed Morgan when he arrived on August 30. By then, Gates's opposite number, General John Burgoyne, had already suffered two costly setbacks. Patriots under Arnold bested a British supporting attack to the west along the Mohawk Valley and New England militia had crushed a sizeable detachment foraging to the east at the battle of Bennington. Gates established his main defensive position on Bemis Heights, a commanding plateau just west of the Hudson that dominated Burgoyne's intended route to Albany, New York. As the British advanced, Morgan's men bedeviled their scouts with their Indian tactics, effectively blinding the enemy general, who had moved his army to within 3 miles of American lines. On the morning of September 19, Burgoyne began feeling his way south, inaugurating the first of the two separate engagements generally referred to as the battle of Saratoga.

The enemy came on in three columns, dangerously divided from each other by the rugged terrain in front of Bemis Heights. Although he intended to remain in his strong position with the bulk of his force, Gates ordered Morgan's unit, reinforced with a light infantry battalion, forward to break up his opponents' advance. Arnold, commanding the American left wing, had instructions to support as necessary. The riflemen moved forward through the woods in skirmish order—two widely dispersed ranks with their commander posted immediately behind the second line to control his men. Sometime after noon on the cool, clear fall day, the Americans collided with Burgoyne's center column at a spot known as Freeman's Farm. Both sides were equally surprised at the encounter and Morgan's lead element scattered like a covey of flushed quail, causing Morgan to despair temporarily that he had lost the battle. A couple of shrill blasts, however, on the turkey call he always carried rallied his men to him and they were soon hammering away at the British.

This meeting engagement turned into an afternoon-long slugfest as Burgoyne and Arnold fed in more troops to the fight that swirled around the farm. Gates's unwillingness to commit more than a portion of his force to battle—which enraged Arnold and led to his estrangement from Gates—and the timely intervention of the enemy's left flank detachment late in the day caused the Americans to withdraw into their lines. Patriot losses totaled about 300 killed, wounded, and missing. Enemy casualties were double that, with much of the destruction accomplished by Morgan's riflemen, who themselves only suffered four killed and eight wounded. Gates attested to the value of this relatively small unit in a letter to Washington shortly after Freeman's Farm, calling it "the corps the army of General Burgoyne are most afraid of."[34]

Morgan's marksmen gave the enemy good reason to dread them over the nightmarish days and nights that followed. Sniping, probing, raiding, they allowed the redcoats and their Hessian allies little respite in their hastily constructed fieldworks. Meanwhile a desperate Burgoyne resolved upon another effort to draw the Americans into pitched battle or at least uncover the extent of their defenses on Bemis Heights. Similar to his earlier gambit, on the morning of October 7, he plunged into the dense woods with three columns. These presently emerged and formed a line of battle three quarters of a mile south of Freeman's Farm along a fold of high ground overlooking a wheat field. In reaction, Gates supposedly called upon Morgan to "begin the game."[35]

On his own initiative, Morgan took his men around the British right flank. Simultaneously, another American brigade of 800 men crept around to the enemy left. Sometime between two and three o'clock this latter force overwhelmed a battalion of British grenadiers. Shortly after this, Morgan struck the enemy right. Soon both British flanks began to buckle; only the enemy center, composed of German units, held fast. Another American brigade struck these Germans and was driven back. At this juncture, Arnold, who had been relieved by Gates in the aftermath of Freeman's Farm, thrust himself—quite without orders—into the fray. The Germans gave ground and joined their English allies in defending a series of redoubts against American pressure. Arnold seemed to be everywhere, dashing from flank to flank to direct and encourage. Making his way to the patriot left, he pointed out a conspicuous, mounted British officer—General Simon Fraser—and coolly told Morgan to have him killed. Morgan spoke quickly to one of his riflemen, who shot Fraser dead. Arnold too was eventually hit—wounded in the same leg as at Quebec. The downing of the fiery American general and dusk combined to end the combat, as well as Burgoyne's hopes. The British commander hung on for another week in vain expectation of a rescue expedition from New York City, then surrendered to Gates on October 17.

"[T]oo much praise cannot be given to the Corps commanded by Col. Morgan," read Gates's official report to Congress on the turning point battle of Saratoga.[36] The northern commander then released Morgan and his fighters back to Washington and the main army, which they rejoined in November for what little remained of the campaign of 1777. Morgan participated in raids across the Delaware into New Jersey, as well as a vigorous action on December 7 north of Philadelphia at Whitemarsh, where he had a horse killed under him while directing a successful defense against a British advance. Following this encounter, Washington installed his army at Valley Forge for the winter. When controversy over the so-called "Conway cabal" against Washington erupted, Morgan was among the most vociferous and outspoken of the commander in chief's champions. Disgusted at the petty intriguing, Morgan applied for and received a furlough home for the rest of the grim winter of 1777–1778, returning in spring eager for more action and responsibility.

The campaign of 1778 started out promisingly for Morgan. Washington reinforced his rifle regiment up to a strength of about 600 and employed it to harass the enemy right flank after the British began to evacuate Philadelphia in June. The morning of June 28 found Morgan positioned about 3 miles to the east of the enemy's encampment at Monmouth Court House, New Jersey. Charles Lee commanded the American advance guard, which included Morgan's unit, and had orders to attack the British as they continued north on their withdrawal. Nonetheless, Lee provided no orders to Morgan; in vain, the rifleman sent a subaltern to find Lee and obtain guidance. In the confusion of the initial American attack and subsequent retirement, this proved impossible. As a result, the rifle corps spent that hot day largely impotent while the bloody battle of Monmouth Court House raged to the west.

Following that engagement—the war's last major clash in the north—Morgan found himself as part of the American contingent arrayed north of British-occupied New York City. Washington disbanded the rifle corps at the end of 1778 and Morgan took command of the 7th Regiment of the Virginia line. When his immediate superior went on an extended leave of absence, Morgan became acting brigade commander, a brigadier general's billet. Colonel Morgan performed competently in this position into the late spring of 1779, when the previous incumbent returned to duty. At about this same time, Washington created a new *corps d'elite* of light infantry—1,200 hand-picked fighters from throughout the army. Morgan, an excellent candidate, sought the unit's top post, which rated a brigadier general, but so did Pennsylvania's Anthony Wayne, another superb combat leader. Further, Wayne was already a brigadier and Morgan's home state of Virginia at that time already exceeded its allocation of Continental general officer billets. And Washington always bent over backwards to avoid even the appearance of favoring fellow Virginians. He thus chose Wayne. A bitterly disappointed Morgan rather sourly observed that he had begun his combat career while Wayne was "still enjoying the sweets of domestic life" and submitted his resignation.[37]

Congress tabled Morgan's request, but allowed him to return home to enjoy some of those domestic sweets until suitable employment could be found for him. Morgan's conduct in this instance hardly comports with the modern military value of selfless service. Perhaps the best that can be said for him is that a number of other Revolutionary heroes—Henry Knox, Anthony Wayne, and Nathanael Greene among them—displayed similar sensitivity and threatened resignation over real and imagined slights. Additionally, the northern and southern battlefronts had remained relatively quiet in the year since Monmouth Court House. Finally, Morgan, who had always enjoyed robust health and performed prodigious feats of strength and endurance, was breaking down physically from what he called his "ciatick"—probably some type of rheumatism— which made it painful for him even to sit a horse.[38]

Morgan followed events from his western Virginia farm and corresponded with his old comrades. He visited on several occasions with Horatio Gates, who also spent the spring of 1780 at his Virginia homestead awaiting a call to action. That summons came following the disaster at Charleston in May, when General Benjamin Lincoln, the ranking American commander in the south, surrendered that city and 5,000 troops to the British. As Gates assumed the reins in the southern department, one of his first acts was to ask Congress to appoint Morgan as a general and assign him to duty in the south. Congress deliberated in every sense of that term; waiting until mid-October to promote him. Meanwhile, the old warhorse reported to Gates that he had "mended amazingly" and began making his way to join him.[39]

En route Morgan learned of Gates's own catastrophe at Camden and found only the remnants of a badly beaten and demoralized army when he rode into Hillsboro, North Carolina in late September. Gates did his best to salvage a bad situation while awaiting his inevitable relief. He placed Morgan in charge of a small, mixed force of Continental infantry and cavalry, and sent him to work alongside various North Carolina militia units to oppose Cornwallis's incursion into that state. Morgan—not yet aware of his elevation to general's rank—chafed at having to subordinate himself to any number of Carolina militia generals and did not accomplish much throughout that dismal fall. In a telling comment on the dire supply situation confronting the patriots—as well as his own professional consciousness despite his frontier origins—Morgan bemoaned his inability to fete his subordinates, "An officer looks very blank when he hain't it in his power to ask his officers to eat with him at times."[40]

The destruction in early October of a large Loyalist force at King's Mountain, along the western border between the Carolinas, ended Cornwallis's foray into the Tarheel state and temporarily eased pressure on the patriot army. Nevertheless, a sympathetic and sober Morgan wrote to Gates, whose departure was imminent, "I am informed you are to be recalled, for which I am sorry and glad both, for I don't think it will be in the power of any Genl. Officer who commands in this country [the south] to add to his reputation."[41] With even his army's most aggressive fighter feeling so demoralized, Nathanael Greene arrived in Charlotte on December 2 and assumed responsibility for the patriots' southern fortunes.

Greene, of course, knew Morgan from the northern campaigns, and quickly augmented his corps with more infantry and cavalry. He then sent him into northwest South Carolina with broad power to act "either offensively or defensively as your own prudence and discretion may direct." More specific orders charged him "to give protection to that part of the country and spirit up the people [and] to annoy the enemy in that quarter."[42] By Christmas, Morgan's force had encamped at Grindall's Shoals on the north bank of the Pacolet River. Among the militia that flocked to him was a detachment led by Andrew Pickens. The terse "fighting Presbyterian" and the garrulous "old wagoner" made quite a contrast, but both were natural leaders and deadly fighters. Morgan's strength increased, although he found South Carolina's senior partisan leader, General Thomas Sumter, resentful of what he perceived to be Morgan's usurpation of the state's militia. Both he and Greene attempted to reassure the Gamecock, but Sumter remained uncooperative.

Toward the end of December, upon discovering that Georgia Loyalists "were insulting and Plundering the good people in that Neighborhood" to the east of his camp, Morgan sent some 300 mounted men to punish them.[43] Led by Lieutenant Colonel William Washington, a portly Virginian distantly related to the commander in chief, this force caught the interlopers near a place called Hammond's Store, and killed or wounded 150 while taking another 40 prisoner. In the same missive in which he described the engagement's results to Greene, Morgan asked for a shipment of pack saddles so he could do away with heavy supply wagons. In a still pertinent observation about infantry he noted, "It is incompatible with the Nature of Light Troops to be encumbered with Baggage."[44]

Morgan also devised a scheme for a raid into Georgia, but Greene demurred. With Morgan already 120 miles distant, he was highly reluctant to have him move even farther away from the main army. Greene also had indications that Cornwallis would attempt to destroy Morgan's isolated command. On January 13, in a letter that did not reach him until after the fact, Greene advised Morgan that "Col. Tarlton is said to be on his way to pay you a visit. I doubt not but he will have a decent reception and a proper dismission."[45] And indeed, on January 14, 1781, Morgan's own scouts informed him that the notorious British dragoon, Banastre Tarleton—another exceptional killer—at the head of over 1,000 men, was stalking him.

Morgan withdrew from the Pacolet in a northeasterly direction and bivouacked on Thicketty Creek, a tributary of the Broad River. His men enjoyed little respite; as they cooked their breakfasts on the morning of the 16th, word arrived that Tarleton had stormed across the Pacolet, headed their way. Hastily the Americans struck camp and resumed their retirement to the Broad. At some point along the way Morgan elected to stop running and make a stand. He chose a site known as the Cowpens from the local herdsmen's practice of wintering their beasts there. As a well-known area landmark, it served ideally for the purpose of rallying scattered militia units in the surrounding countryside; however, as a defensive position little seemed to recommend it. Morgan's back would be to the Broad River, 5 miles distant. And the tree-speckled meadow offered no flank protection—woods or swamps—from envelopment by Tarleton's fierce dragoons. Exactly why Morgan chose the Cowpens to give battle remains a mystery. Afterwards, he claimed that the virtue of his exposed position was that it allowed no place for his militia to flee; they would have to stand and fight. Other writers, starting with Henry Lee, speculated that Morgan's temper and sheer orneriness prompted his decision; he much preferred fight to flight.

Whatever the reason, Morgan made his plans with care. He would dispose his men in three ranks in a pasture that sloped upward from the south and the approaching Tarleton. The initial line, 150 Georgia and North Carolina militia-men armed with rifles, had the task of firing two well-aimed rounds each, then moving 150 yards uphill to the second echelon. These, about 300 Carolina militia commanded by Pickens, had a similar mission—fire to disrupt the enemy's attack formation, focusing on officers and sergeants, then fall back. The third and main line, consisting primarily of 450 Delaware and Maryland Continentals, would array itself just below the crest of the hill, covering a front about 400 yards wide. Morgan would conceal his reserve—including 80 cavalrymen under Lieutenant Colonel Washington—on the reverse slope.

The night of January 16–17 presents an eve of Agincourt aspect. An outnumbered, ragged army anxiously awaited the dawn and, possibly, destruction. Its leader, like Shakespeare's Henry V, circulated from campfire to campfire quietly talking to groups of men—joking, instructing, and most of all, inspiriting. According to some accounts, to inflame them, he even revealed the ancient scars from the flogging he had received under the British a quarter century earlier. Writing in old age about this touch of Morgan in the night, one witnessing officer wrote, "I was more perfectly convinced of General Morgan's qualifications to command militia, than I had ever before been." He added that "I don't believe he slept a wink that night."[46]

Most of his men, however, did get a night's rest and were also fed. This was more than could be said for Tarleton's pursuing force. The British commander rousted his men at 2:00 a.m. Shortly before 7:00 a.m.—and daybreak—after an exhausting approach march of nearly 5 miles, they arrived at the southern edge of the Cowpens. Tarleton saw the front rank of American skirmishers and launched two troops of dragoons—about 50 horsemen—to disperse them. Instead, patriot rifles barked and at least 15 enemy fell. As the riflemen raced back to join Pickens, reloading on the move and periodically turning to fire, Tarleton formed his infantry for an assault. Above their martial music—drums, fifes, and pipes all blaring— Morgan said they "Raised a prodigious yell, and came Running at us as if they intended to eat us up."[47]

The Carolina militia held their fire until the redcoats closed to a range of 100 yards. Most of the killed and wounded suffered by the British occurred here. Despite heavy losses, the disciplined British kept advancing. As planned, Pickens's men retired uphill to a spot behind the left rear of the final American line. An attempt by British cavalry to ride down the retreating militia encountered first the withering fire of the patriot infantry near the crest, then a counter charge from the American reserve under Washington. Prudently, the battered enemy horse withdrew. Meanwhile a thoroughly aroused Morgan shouted to the militiamen to "Form, form my brave fellows . . . Old Morgan was never beaten."[48]

Now the Continentals faced the oncoming redcoats. For nearly 30 minutes the two sides traded volleys. Tarleton committed his infantry reserve, a crack highland regiment, to turn the American right flank. The patriot infantry attempted the intricate maneuver of "refusing" their right—that is, bending back 90 degrees to meet this threat. But, as is frequently the case in battle, the rearward movement of one part of a line precipitates the retrograde of everyone else. The Continentals' immediate commander and Morgan, who rode up, decided to make the best of an awkward situation and pulled the line farther uphill to a position designated by Morgan. Washington informed Morgan that if the American infantry would loose one more salvo, he would charge. The Continentals blasted the still-advancing enemy from no more than 15 yards distance, then charged downhill with fixed bayonets. Washington's cavalry thundered into the enemy right. And Morgan sent Pickens's reformed militia, which had made a complete circuit of the battlefield, at Tarleton's left. The resulting double envelopment overwhelmed the enemy soldiers, who threw down their weapons en masse and cried for quarter. Washington led a pursuit that bagged more prisoners, although Tarleton himself managed to gallop away.

Surveying what he had wrought, an overjoyed Morgan impulsively picked up a 9-year-old drummer boy and kissed him. Several days after Cowpens, he wrote that he had given Tarleton "a devil of a whipping, a more compleat victory was never obtained."[49] The one-sided battle cost the British more than 100 men killed and over 200 wounded, plus an additional 600 who joined their disabled comrades as prisoners. The patriots also captured numerous guns, horses, and wagons, along with at least 60 African-Americans who had been with the British army. Morgan kept two of these—"Nat" and "Toby"—as his personal slaves for the rest of his life. American losses amounted to only 12 killed and 60 wounded. Besides being an almost perfect tactical gem, Cowpens had important operational and psychological results. The destruction of much of Tarleton's Legion handicapped Cornwallis for the remainder of the southern campaign. The humiliation visited upon British arms by Morgan also impelled Cornwallis to launch a vigorous effort to run him down, inaugurating a series of events that ended with the British surrender at Yorktown 9 months later. And news of the glorious victory served as a tonic to patriots everywhere, especially in the embattled south.

As Cowpens's exhilaration faded, however, and before its deeper consequences became evident, Morgan realized that he must escape Cornwallis's imminent fury. Refusing to tarry at Cowpens, he sped his captives north under guard and marched the remainder of his troops into North Carolina, covering 100 miles and crossing two major rivers in just 5 days. It was well that Morgan chose this course; Cornwallis learned of the battle within 24 hours and angrily vowed to hunt Morgan down. It took nearly a week for news of Cowpens to reach Greene. The American commander in the south pointed the bulk of his army toward North Carolina, then rode off with a small escort to coordinate with Morgan. They met on the last day of January at Morgan's camp at Sherrald's Ford on the Catawba River. A hasty council of war determined not to oppose Cornwallis on the Catawba, but rather to reunite the patriot army's two wings farther north. Early the next morning, Morgan's command started out and, after an arduous journey, joined their compatriots near Guilford Court House.

By this time, a month's intense campaigning had taken its toll on the ailing Morgan. His rheumatism flared and an attack of hemorrhoids added incalculably to his agonies. He wrote a desponding letter to Governor Thomas Jefferson cataloging his aches and pains, and also bemoaning the general lack of support for the cause. After pointing out that the American troops were "almost Naked" compared to the well-supplied enemy, he asked, "Great god what is the reason we cant Have more men in the field ... How distressing ... to see the country over Run and destroyed for want of assistance."[50] Morgan also entertained doubts about Greene's plan to lead Cornwallis on a dangerous chase north into Virginia; Morgan's counseled retreat west to the sheltering mountains. Having reached the end of his physical—and perhaps emotional—tether, Morgan requested and received Greene's permission to go on leave to recover his health. Morgan started for Virginia on February 10, the same day that Greene's army began its famous race to the Dan River against Cornwallis's pursuing host.

For all intents and purposes, Morgan's active service career ended there. He worked his holdings, which included two small farms he christened "Saratoga" and "Soldier's Rest," and followed the war as best he could through newspaper accounts and news he gleaned from travelers. When the British under Cornwallis threatened Virginia in the late spring, he responded to his state's call, rounded up some volunteers in Frederick County, and headed east. He arrived too late to take part in any fighting; Lafayette and Wayne had already seen off Cornwallis down the Peninsula. Morgan returned home in August and thus missed the Yorktown campaign as well. Like so many Revolutionary officers, he spent the early postwar years dunning Congress and his state for back pay, expenses, and other emoluments he had been promised. Included among the latter were a special Cowpens medal and a horse, which he ruefully noted upon receipt, manifested "almost every bad quality."[51] And though he hardly wrote as lucidly as "pope, Voltiere or Shakespear," he maintained a lively correspondence with fellow veterans.[52]

Although strapped for cash, like many in the new republic, Morgan prospered not only as a farmer, but also as the owner of a gristmill and a distillery. He and Abigail married off their two daughters. Morgan also sired an illegitimate son sometime during the 1780s; he never acknowledged him publicly and whether his wife knew or not, she stuck by her husband and nursed him through his periodic ailments. The son—one Willoughby Morgan—distinguished himself as a company commander in the War of 1812 and became a career army officer who attained the rank of lieutenant colonel before his death in 1832. Although not a deep political thinker, Daniel Morgan matured into a strong nationalist and thus gravitated to the Federalist party. As a major general of Virginia militia, he led a contingent that helped suppress 1794's Whiskey Rebellion in western Pennsylvania. In 1797, his fellow freeholders elected him to the House of Representatives, where he served an undistinguished term. He lived out his remaining years at his younger daughter's home in Winchester, where he died on July 6, 1802.

As a warrior and inspirational leader, Daniel Morgan had few peers among Continental generals. Wayne and Arnold join him on a short list. Nathanael Greene wrote, "Great generals are scarce—there are few Morgans to be found."[53] Morgan was no strategist, trainer, or administrator—unlike, say, Greene, Knox, or Gates— but he understood tactics, that is, how to combine units and their weapons with terrain. And he knew soldiers profoundly, especially untutored amateurs. Though, like most Continental officers, he despaired of militia, he possessed an ability to communicate with them that stemmed from his simple, rustic background. Independent, strong-willed, and tough, the unpolished Morgan's rise to greatness epitomized the frontier spirit and the possibilities inherent to all who share it.

Born Fighters

Henry Lee and Anthony Wayne

COMRADES AND MUTUAL ADMIRERS, Henry Lee and Anthony Wayne were two of the most professionally able American fighters of the Revolution. Charles Lee—no relation—remarked of "Light-Horse Harry" Lee that he seemed "to have come out of his mother's womb a soldier."[1] "Light-Horse Harry" himself wrote of "Mad" Anthony Wayne that he "had a constitutional attachment to the decision of the sword."[2] Both certainly exhibited an unmistakable aptitude for leadership and war. Yet despite their undoubted boldness and colorful nicknames, rashness was not a trait that described either man. Although they shared the powerful ambition to win martial glory through daring deeds, each married this desire to exceptional competence buttressed by meticulous attention to detail. They were audacious but not foolhardy.

HENRY LEE

Charles Lee's description was typically hyperbolic, but it is nonetheless true that as a flamboyant boy-soldier, Henry Lee appeared every inch the *beau sabreur*. Dashing and gallant as he looked, however, Lee was a much more complicated figure. He earned fame as an orator and wrote a celebrated history of the Revolutionary War. He reached the pinnacle of glory by age 25, but failure, disgrace, and depression that are the stuff of great tragedy marked his subsequent life. Descended from Virginia's illustrious line of Lees, he was born at the family estate of Leesylvania, overlooking the Potomac near the town of Dumfries, on January 29, 1756. As the scion of a clan prominent in the colony's affairs for over a century, young Henry was bred to command. He excelled at horsemanship from an early age and a series of tutors ensured that he gained a solid grounding in the classics, as well as in fencing and handling firearms. Well-to-do southern aristocrats typically sent their sons north to be educated; accordingly, at 14 Henry matriculated to the College of New Jersey in Princeton, where his fellow students included James Madison and Aaron Burr. There he became "Harry" to his intimates and read Greek, Latin, philosophy, and history. Upon completing this curriculum, Lee planned to pursue a legal career that—again following the day's custom—would have taken him to London for further studies and an apprenticeship when hostilities broke out between the American colonies and the mother country.

Harry's older cousin Richard Henry Lee ranked as one of the principal movers for independence in the Continental Congress and most others among the extensive Lee "cousinry" also supported this course, so perhaps inevitably Harry adopted it too. Family connections quickly gained him a commission in a cavalry regiment commanded by one of his innumerable relatives in high places. In the summer of 1776 Captain Lee, by now grown into a blue-eyed and fair-skinned young man of slight build and medium height, began recruiting and training his own troop of light dragoons. Initially the regiment remained in Virginia on guard against a British seaborne incursion or an Indian uprising along the western frontier. By early 1777, however, the unit had joined Washington's army in New Jersey.

Lee's troop acted in an independent capacity—foraging, scouting, and gathering intelligence. Here Lee enrolled in the harsh school of war, or what he more grandiloquently called "the study of Mars."[3] Though daring, he was not reckless and he developed his trademark battlefield habit of prudent risk taking. He was a strict disciplinarian, but a miser with his men's lives and solicitous of their welfare. They responded accordingly. While other units melted away through desertion or refusal to reenlist, almost to a man Lee's troopers elected to stay with him when their original terms expired. Their fancy uniforms—purchased in part by their commander—were soon in tatters, but their appearance was that of a hardened, veteran corps d'elite. Along with his performance and impeccable manners, his family's close connections with Washington made Lee one of the commander in chief's favorite junior officers. While spared much direct combat, he participated in the 1777 Pennsylvania campaign. At Brandywine he served for the first time under Nathanael Greene, with whom in the south he would later win his greatest fame. After Philadelphia fell to the British in late September, Lee scourged enemy supply lines in two directions by assailing their eastward connections to New York City and southern communications with the Chesapeake. During one of these forays, he and Washington's senior aide, Lieutenant Colonel Alexander Hamilton, experienced a near brush with death when a British patrol stumbled upon them. Both barely escaped; as Lee later wrote, "Thus did fortune smile upon these two young soldiers, already united in friendship, which ceased only with life."[4] And at Germantown Lee's troop had the honor of accompanying Washington as his personal bodyguard.

The army went into its winter quarters at Valley Forge at the end of 1777. Lee understatedly commented on this ordeal that "the hardy character of the troops did not degenerate by feminine indulgences."[5] Meanwhile, he continued to torment the British, gathering much-needed supplies for the hungry patriots in the process. Lee's activities so plagued the British that they spied out Lee's bivouac, about 6 miles southeast of the main encampment at Valley Forge, and on the night of January 19, 1778, secretly launched a large mounted expedition intended to kill or capture the troublesome dragoon. The next morning's fight at Scott's Farm made Lee famous throughout the army and turned him into something of a national hero as well. Surprised and heavily outnumbered, Lee and a few of his men barricaded themselves in the main house. He then resorted to the type of clever ruse that characterized his combat career. After repelling several assaults, Lee encouraged his men by loudly shouting that supporting infantry were on the way to rescue them. This spooked his assailants, already chagrinned at their inability to break into the strongpoint, and they fled the scene. Washington praised Lee in an order of the day and newspapers throughout the country soon picked up—and embellished—the story.

Besides renown, more tangible results accrued from this gallant episode. Washington, who had long kept his eye on Lee, offered him the post of personal aide de camp. This prestigious billet not only promised intimacy with the great man himself, but also included a double promotion to lieutenant colonel. Nevertheless, Lee's great ambition ran in a direction different from access to patronage and rank. In a delicately worded declination, Lee told Washington that he was "wedded to my sword" and that his object was the military reputation that could only be won in the field and not on the staff.[6] Washington, far from being put off at Lee's refusal, persuaded Congress to award him a major's commission. Further, Congress augmented Lee's troop with additional cavalry units and established it as an independent partisan force that operated at Washington's personal direction. In endorsing this action, the commander in chief praised Lee's "exemplary zeal, prudence and bravery" and declared "Capt. Lee's genius particularly adapts him to a command of this nature."[7]

Lee's hard-riding new outfit rapidly added to his already formidable reputation with its comprehensive intelligence collection, successful skirmishing, and slashing raids. It was during this period that he acquired the nickname "Light-Horse Harry." To his personal mortification, Lee was on detached service and missed the battle of Monmouth Court House in June 1778. Afterward he wrote his friend, Brigadier General Anthony Wayne, that "the name Monmouth reproached me to the very soul."[8] Little more than a year later, Lee's cavalry furnished an invaluable service to Wayne by its thorough reconnaissance of the British outpost at Stony Point on the Hudson just below West Point. His detailed information about the works and British dispositions were instrumental to Wayne's success in taking the place by storm in the predawn hours of July 16, 1779, with his light infantry corps.

Lee's own *coup de main* and his most famous exploit in the northern theater occurred the next month. By this time, the war there had settled into a stalemate with the main British force of 10,000 or so occupying New York City and outlying points, and Washington's army arrayed in an arc above it, anchored on West Point and the surrounding Hudson highlands. Washington, while guarding the line of the Hudson and hoping ultimately to drive the British out of Manhattan, eagerly sought low-cost ways to strike the enemy. Wayne's assault on Stony Point was one such limited operation. Washington's desires and Lee's ambition to emulate Wayne's success combined to set the stage for another surprise blow against an isolated British outpost.

Lee had minutely surveiled Paulus Hook, New Jersey—site of present-day Jersey City—a narrow, sandy spit of land projecting into the Hudson directly opposite Manhattan, about a mile and a half away. Approximately 200 redcoats, Hessians, and Loyalists manned the site, which was well protected by natural obstacles that included a salt marsh and a creek. Additionally, the British had constructed a tidal moat, a wall, and several redoubts. Lee recommended this place as a raid target. Although at first concerned that an attack there might be too dangerous, Washington eventually acceded to Lee's proposal and reinforced him with several companies of Virginia and Maryland infantry.

Lee's plan had to account for complex time–distance factors as well as light and tide data. On the morning of August 18, 1779, he assembled 400 men, including dismounted elements of his partisan cavalry, at Paramus, New Jersey, some 22 miles north of the objective. He intended to march this force so as to reach Paulus Hook under cover of darkness, assault before high tide—which would make the surrounding waterways well-nigh unfordable for both his assault and withdrawal—and make his getaway before first light at 4:00 a.m. Boats would be waiting 2 miles to the west of the objective at Bergen to ferry the retiring raiders across the Hackensack River, helping shield them from pursuers on the return march north. Unsurprisingly to anyone who has practiced or studied the art of war, friction imposed itself as the operation unspooled. A wrong turn in the dark caused the column to get lost en route, costing valuable hours while exhausting and frustrating the troops. Further, just as the patriots were occupying their assault position 500 yards from the objective, Lee discovered that a company of his Virginia infantry had somehow straggled and gotten separated from the force. It was now well after high tide and dangerously close to dawn. Lee sent a subaltern forward to see if the creek and moat were at all passable. When answered in the affirmative, Lee gave the word to advance.

The men slogged forward with unprimed muskets to avoid alarming the garrison by the premature discharge of a weapon. In the event, wading through the moat's chest-deep water fouled everyone's powder, so that the bayonet became by necessity the tool of choice for the work at hand. The Americans gained complete surprise and were upon the enemy before they could mount much of a defense. Dozens of stunned redcoats surrendered; Lee ultimately made off with 158 prisoners. He had intended to burn the barracks and other buildings, but discarded this plan when he learned that soldiers' families and other camp followers occupied them. Approaching dawn, signs of enemy activity across the river in Manhattan, and unyielding resistance from a platoon of Hessians in one of the redoubts compelled Lee to give the withdrawal signal after less than half an hour on the objective. All went smoothly until Lee reached the Hackensack River and the fortunes of battle played their final trick. The expected boats were no where in sight; since the operation was so far behind schedule, the officer responsible for the craft assumed that it had been cancelled. Lee's men thus had to retrace their long, original route north with all the attendant dangers of enemy pursuit. Indeed, at mid-morning they skirmished with a redcoat patrol, but fortunately had reunited with the previously lost Virginians, whose dry powder enabled them to drive off the enemy. Tired, but justly elated, Lee's raiders reentered friendly lines having suffered only a handful of casualties in return for pulling off a brilliant feat of arms.

Lee's immediate included hearty congratulations from Washington, Greene, and Knox among others—and a court-martial. Lee's success attracted envy as well as admiration within the army and his privileged position as a favorite of the commanding general, as well as his perceived arrogance, earned him further enmity from some quarters. Shortly after Paulus Hook, Wayne had warned him, "be well guarded my friend . . . there are not a few, who would not feel much pain on a small Disaster happening to either you or me." This underlying resentment impelled a handful of officers to demand a court-martial to determine whether Lee had exceeded his authority at Paulus Hook by improperly superseding others on the expedition who were senior to him by date of rank. Other charges included that he had behaved inappropriately by not burning the barracks and by retreating too precipitately. Washington had no choice but to sanction the proceeding. Lee was, by turns, bemused and outraged as the mill of military justice ground on. Eventually, a board presided over by none other than General Wayne found him innocent on all counts, specifically noting that while several other officers involved were senior to Lee, Washington had personally entrusted him with the overall command. Congress, which had figuratively held its breath until the verdict was in, then bestowed a special gold medal upon Lee, one of just eight it awarded to Continental Army officers during the war and the only one given to an officer below the rank of general.

Through another long year Lee continued to act as Washington's eyes and ears in the no man's land between New York and the Hudson highlands. In addition to traditional cavalry patrolling, Lee also operated an espionage network for the commander in chief, running agents in and out of British lines. The most spectacular covert operation occurred immediately after Benedict Arnold's treason in September 1780. Resembling something out an eighteenth-century spy thriller, at Washington's order Lee sent a handpicked volunteer—a noncommissioned officer pretending to be a deserter—over to the British with the mission of getting close enough to the recently defected Arnold to kidnap and bring him back to the American side. Although the plan miscarried due to bad luck—the sergeant, however, eventually made it safely back to American lines, albeit empty handed— it illustrates the sort of derring-do that Lee loved and excelled at.

In November 1780 Lee received a promotion to lieutenant colonel and three infantry companies reinforced his cavalry. This mixed unit became known as Lee's Legion. Its commander personally designed their fancy uniforms of dark green tunics and white breeches, topped by plumed helmets. Meanwhile, Nathanael Greene had been chosen by Washington to recover patriot fortunes in the southern department and he desperately required high-quality Continental troops to assist him. Washington could not spare many men, but he did send him Lee's mobile and hard-hitting new command. Lee reported to Greene at Cheraw, South Carolina on January 13, 1781, with 280 troopers and was almost immediately dispatched farther south to bolster Francis Marion's partisans. After some misadventures in locating the peripatetic Swamp Fox's lair, Lee tracked him down and the two raided the British garrison at Georgetown. Lee later recalled that the operation "although conceived with ingenuity, and executed with precision, was too refined and complicated for success."[9] Nevertheless, it served as a dress rehearsal for future triumphant collaborations between the two leaders. As Marion appreciatively wrote to Greene, "Col. Lee's Interprizing Genius promises much."[10] For the instant, however, Daniel Morgan's stunning triumph over the British at Cowpens had stirred Lord Cornwallis, the royal commander in the south, to vow the American army's destruction and Lee was ordered back to join Greene.

Lee caught up to him at Guilford Court House, North Carolina, on February 7. Cornwallis was only 25 miles away and Greene considered making a stand, but his subordinates, including Lee, dissuaded him. Instead, Greene decided to make for the Dan River and cross into Virginia to refit his tattered army. He gave command of the all-important rearguard to Colonel Otho Williams, whose assignment was to delay Cornwallis long enough to permit the American main body to escape. The key element in Williams's 700-man task force was Lee's Legion. Williams and Lee accomplished their mission initially by luring the British toward fords on the upper Dan when, in fact, Greene intended to cross by ferry farther downstream. Initially duped, Cornwallis discovered this stratagem on February 13, changed course, and was soon nipping at the rearguard's heels. That morning Lee engaged one of Tarleton's detachments in a vicious scrimmage that left 18 enemy dragoons dead. This clash also revealed the rage of which Lee was capable. His 14-year-old bugler—"a beardless, unarmed youth, who had vainly implored quarter"—had been ridden down and hacked to death by the British contrary to all humane practice.[11] Lee prepared to hang a captured captain on the spot in retaliation and would have but for Williams's intervention.

February 13 was a long, hard day for both armies. Late that afternoon, Lee and his men, thinking they had safely distanced themselves from the enemy, finally stopped for breakfast. "Criminal improvidence!" remarked Lee in his memoirs. "A soldier is always in danger, when his conviction of security leads him to dispense with the most vigilant precautions."[12] The remorseless Tarleton unexpectedly interrupted the meal and the chase resumed. Moving at a killing pace over muddy, rutted trails in freezing weather, the British covered the final 40 miles in the last 24 hours of their pursuit. But the Americans traversed this same distance in 16 hours, thus winning the "race to the Dan." Greene and the main body passed the river late on the 13th. The rearguard crossed the next evening. Fittingly, Lee himself took the last boat over.

As Cornwallis fell back toward Hillsborough, North Carolina, in an effort to attract Loyalists to the crown's standard, Greene decided to assume the offensive. As a prelude, on February 18 he sent Lee's Legion, reinforced with two companies of Maryland Continental infantry, back into North Carolina to join forces with Andrew Pickens's militia. Their instructions were to harass enemy foraging parties and discourage the general Loyalist uprising that Cornwallis hoped to inspire. A week later fortune handed them a prime opportunity to achieve this. Getting wind that 300 Loyalists under the command of Colonel John Pyle were headed to join Tarleton at Hillsborough, Lee hatched a typically ingenious scheme. He and his legion—whose uniforms closely resembled those of Tarleton's men— impersonated the British dragoon and his outfit. Meeting up at a ford on the Haw River, Pyle and his Loyalist recruits were completely taken in by the deception. Lee was in the process of shaking hands with Pyle and about to offer him the alternatives of surrendering, disbanding, or joining the patriot side when firing broke out between Pickens's militia and the tail of Pyle's column. Lee's Legion, aided by the militia, violently turned upon the startled Loyalists, killing nearly 100, scattering the rest, and effectively ending any chance of royalist sympathizers in the area rallying to Cornwallis.

Greene reentered North Carolina with the army's main force on February 23. For the next 3 weeks he and Cornwallis maneuvered for advantage while seeking to bring each other to battle. Greene had reconstituted Colonel Williams's light corps—which had served so brilliantly covering the retrograde to Virginia—to act now as the American advance guard. Once more Lee led the van of this force and engaged in almost continual activity, including victorious skirmishes against Tarleton on March 2 and again on March 6. By March 14, Greene had established himself at the position from which he desired to fight, Guilford Court House. Cornwallis, a dozen miles to the southwest, decided to accommodate him. Early that morning he began his approach toward the Americans at Guilford with Tarleton, as usual, spearheading the British advance.

Lee commanded Greene's screening force. His pickets detected the enemy's lead elements around 7:00 a.m., 7 miles in front of the main American line. Lee selected an ideal piece of ground—a narrow lane bounded by high fences on both sides—and ambushed Tarleton's dragoons, sending them into pell-mell retreat. Lee in turn pursued until he encountered Tarleton's accompanying infantry. In the ensuing melee, Lee was temporarily unhorsed and his opposite number slightly wounded. Having succeeded in providing warning to Greene and delaying the enemy—inflicting about 30 casualties in return for minimal losses—Lee pulled back and took up his position on the extreme left of the American first defensive line, one of three Greene had established on the wooded slope leading up to the court house.

Shortly after noon, preceded by a brief cannonade, the British attacked. The North Carolina militia, who comprised the bulk of the American first rank, discharged a ragged volley, then fled in the face of the oncoming redcoats. Lee, who invariably found militia wanting—though in this case Greene had authorized them to withdraw after engaging—recorded that "these unhappy men, . . . throwing away arms, knapsacks, and even canteens, . . . rushed like a torrent headlong through the woods."[13] Lee's Legion and some Virginia riflemen held their position on the American left and poured a deadly enfilade fire into the enemy's scarlet ranks. Another group of Continentals did the same from the American right. The British dealt with these flank threats by diverting their first echelon regiments against them. The Americans on the right gave ground grudgingly and retired to link up with the patriot second line. Lee's force and the Virginians, however, found themselves hard-pressed by the combined assault of a British Guards battalion and a Hessian regiment. A vicious, separate battle involving these forces developed to the south and east of the court house. By the time Lee was able to break contact and move uphill to the main position, Greene had already ordered a general retreat after a day of carnage.

Historians have echoed Lee's eloquent verdict on the battle, "The name of victory was the sole enjoyment of the conqueror, substance belonging to the vanquished."[14] Although Cornwallis might claim a tactical success, operationally he was compelled to withdraw to Wilmington, on the North Carolina coast. Subsequently, he abandoned the Carolinas and made his fateful move into Virginia and, ultimately, Yorktown. Meanwhile, acting at least in part on Lee's advice, Greene chose not to pursue Cornwallis, but rather to drive south and liberate South Carolina and Georgia. While Greene advanced with the bulk of the army on the British position at Camden, he once again detached Lee to operate with Marion against the scattered enemy outposts in the surrounding area. Reflecting back on the army's mood as it prepared to embark on this phase of the campaign, Lee wrote that despite fatigue and privation "we were content; we were more than content—we were happy" with "The improved condition of the South, effected by our efforts" and "anticipations of the future."[15]

Lee and the Swamp Fox linked up in early April, and made Fort Watson, on the Santee River 60 miles northwest of Charleston, their first objective. The post consisted of a small stockade built upon an ancient Indian burial mound and surrounded by various man-made obstacles. The enemy inside the walls refused entreaties to surrender and countered an attempt to cut off their water supply by sinking a well. "Baffled in their expectation, and destitute both of artillery and intrenching tools, Marion and Lee despaired of success."[16] At this juncture, a South Carolina militiaman named Maham proposed the expedient of building a tower from which riflemen could pick off the defenders with impunity. The two American leaders readily assented and under Maham's direction, the structure was ready by dawn of April 23. By midday, helpless under a withering fire, the enemy capitulated.

Dispatching their prisoners back toward Greene, who was approaching Camden, Lee and Marion next focused their attention on a 500-man Loyalist force that had recently occupied itself vainly combing the marshes in the lower part of the state seeking the Swamp Fox. To aid Greene, the two Americans sought to keep this element from joining the main British army. They succeeded, although these activities caused them to miss the battle of Hobkirk's Hill, just outside of Camden, on April 25. There the British claimed another bloody tactical triumph over Greene, although, similar to Guilford Court House, the only recourse for the victors following the battle was retreat. For their part, Lee and Marion resumed the war of posts by initiating a siege of Fort Motte, a strategic point at the junction of the Congaree and Wateree Rivers. A sense of urgency soon impelled the patriots, for rumors had the retreating British army headed straight for the fort. Lee and Marion had to take the place quickly or withdraw. The widow Motte's stately mansion was the key to the enemy position and Lee's fertile brain hit upon the idea of burning them out by setting the house ablaze with fire arrows. Lee gravely explained the necessity for this action to Mrs. Motte, who had been evicted from her home by the enemy. The patriotic lady gratified and surprised him not only by cheerfully assenting, but by pressing him to employ a bow and quiver of arrows she produced from her household belongings. One of Marion's men served as the designated archer and by the afternoon of May 12 Lee's inspiration produced a British surrender.

Greene appeared on the scene later that day and gave new orders. He would proceed west to command the siege of the British upcountry stronghold at Ninety Six. Marion would slice southeast to capture Georgetown. And he directed Lee to take Fort Granby, in the center of the state near the site of modern-day Columbia. General Thomas Sumter's partisans were in the immediate vicinity, although the Gamecock himself was 30 miles farther south besieging another enemy garrison at Orangeburg. Lee arrived at Fort Granby on May 14 and wasted little time. Although the defending Loyalists had temporarily defied Sumter, they showed little inclination to fight Lee, who showed he meant business early the next day by shelling the fort with a 6-pound field gun and deploying the fierce infantry of his legion. The enemy commander offered to surrender on the condition that he and his men might retain the considerable plunder they had taken from the surrounding country and receive safe passage to Charleston, where as prisoners of war they could await exchange. Still concerned that the main British army retiring from Camden might intervene, Lee granted those terms. He subsequently received some criticism for this leniency and Sumter was furious that a prize he felt was rightfully his had been taken by another.

There was little time for recriminations, however. On the evening of the same day upon which Fort Granby had surrendered, Greene ordered Lee west to join Pickens in assailing the British stronghold at Augusta, Georgia. To maintain a rapid pace, Lee's Legion employed techniques they often used—infantry mounted double behind dragoons, as well as infantrymen and cavalrymen alternating on horseback and foot. As he approached Augusta, Lee learned about a large quantity of enemy supplies stored at Fort Galphin, one of his majesty's Indian trading posts, 12 miles south of Augusta. Taking his fittest troops and leaving the others to rest, Lee rode for this tempting target on the sultry morning of May 21. Displaying his genius for the clever *ruse de guerre*, he had some Georgia and South Carolina militia demonstrate outside the fort, which had the desired effect of stirring its occupants to quit the stockade to give futile chase. Lee's Legion then rushed into the unguarded fort from the opposite direction and claimed the spoils—food, weapons and ammunition, clothing and medicine—all badly wanting on the American side. Lee then retired, having lost but one man—to heatstroke—and resumed his march to Augusta.

The patriots confronted two major British positions there. The larger one was Fort Cornwallis, within the town itself. A satellite post, Fort Grierson, covered it about half a mile to the west. Reaching patriot lines on May 23, Lee enjoyed a brief reunion with Pickens, whom he had not seen since their joint operations in North Carolina 2 months earlier. They developed a plan to storm Fort Grierson and deployed their men to attack it from three sides. During the fight, Lee repelled an attempted British sortie from Fort Cornwallis that sought to come to their comrades' aid. Overwhelmed, 80 or so of the hard-pressed defenders tried a breakout to Fort Cornwallis, but were swiftly cut down. Half were killed, the rest wounded and captured. Tensions ran high between American patriots and Loyalists; it was only with great difficulty that Lee and Pickens restrained the Georgia militia from slaughtering all their captives. As it was, several were murdered, including the enemy commandant, Colonel Grierson. Of the repeated atrocities in this internecine struggle in the south, an appalled Lee observed that "It often sunk into barbarity."[17]

Lee and Pickens now turned their considerable energies upon Fort Cornwallis, ably defended by a resourceful opponent, Colonel Thomas Brown, and a combined force of approximately 600 Loyalists and Creek Indians. The Americans dug approach trenches and fought off repeated sallies by the enemy, intent on stopping their work. At Lee's suggestion, the patriots also put up a "Maham Tower," which promised to bring matters to a speedy resolution as had been the case at Fort Watson. Brown furiously countered—first with artillery fire, then with desperate bayonet assaults. When none of this availed, he resorted to subterfuge, sending a pretend "deserter" over to the Americans with orders to burn the tower. He also tried to lure the attackers into a mined house. These gambits failed too; in the case of the fake deserter, Lee was initially taken in, but then his own trickster's instincts took hold and he ordered the man kept under close arrest. On June 5, after contentious negotiations, Brown surrendered the fort. Lee personally took charge of his prisoners to prevent a repeat of the earlier atrocities and hurried off to Ninety Six to join Greene.

Ninety Six was the sole remaining British-held post in South Carolina's interior. It was a formidable objective—a village surrounded by a palisade with a strong bastion at one end known as the Star Redoubt. This redoubt connected via a covered trench to a small stockade—Fort Holmes—at the opposite end. In addition, the usual ditches and an abatis augmented the works. Some 550 Loyalists—many of them long-serving veterans nearly as skilled as regulars—manned the defenses. Greene opened the siege on May 22 by committing several tactical errors. The most significant was focusing his approach on the daunting Star Redoubt instead of the far weaker Fort Holmes, which also guarded the enemy's water supply. In fact, in his memoirs Lee bluntly stated that the failure immediately to cut off the garrison's access to water "lost us Ninety-Six."[18] Lee arrived on the morning of June 8, perceived the problem, and convinced Greene to let him commence sapping against the vital point. On the 11th Greene learned from Sumter that a British relief expedition under Lord Rawdon was en route from Charleston. He detached all his cavalry, including Lee's dragoons, to the Gamecock with the intent of thwarting this effort.

In the event, the British rescue party sidestepped Sumter and with their arrival imminent, Greene faced three options: turn and face Rawdon, lift the siege and retreat, or attempt to storm Ninety Six before Rawdon arrived. Greene felt he had insufficient force for the first and profound distaste for the second. So at noon on June 18, he launched a two-pronged attack. On the American right, Lee's Legion infantry, reinforced with Delaware Continentals, quickly seized Fort Holmes. On the left, a vicious fight took place at the Star Redoubt between its doughty defenders, and a combined force of Maryland and Virginia Continentals. The patriots contested the position gamely, but ultimately were beaten back. Lee's foothold at Fort Holmes meant nothing now. That evening he withdrew his men as Greene ordered a general retreat. During the month-long siege, the patriots lost nearly 200 men killed or wounded; enemy casualties numbered about half that many. The British evacuated the post shortly after the relief column arrived. Greene and Rawdon then spent the ensuing weeks circling each other like wary beasts, but no major engagement resulted and Greene retired to the High Hills of the Santee to rest his army in mid-July.

There was little repose for Lee and his legion, however. While establishing his new base, Greene acceded to Sumter's desire to strike a British outpost at Moncks Corner, about 30 miles above Charleston, and placed Lee's Legion at his disposal. Under the pressure of the patriot advance, the redcoat regiment in the vicinity chose to withdraw. On the afternoon of July 17 Lee mauled the enemy rear guard while his van skirmished with the British main force, which ensconced itself in a formidable position at a plantation near Quinby Bridge, only a dozen miles outside Charleston. Marion, also part of Sumter's force, came up shortly afterward and he agreed with Lee that it would not pay to assault an enemy so well established. Sumter believed otherwise and ordered up an attack that the British easily defeated. The beaten patriots rode off into the night, their numerous dead lying across the pommels of their saddles, to be deposited in a common grave at dawn. The legion had been spared this carnage, but Lee broke away from Sumter in disgust at his squandering of lives in a forlorn effort and returned to the hills above the Santee to join the rest of the army.

By early September, Greene felt strong enough to resume the offensive and began a march down the Santee toward the principal British army in South Carolina, which now concentrated around Eutaw Springs. Moving by easy stages, and drawing various militia and partisan units to his hard core of Continentals, Greene's force swelled to approximately 2,200 men, who on the morning of September 8 remained undetected by a like number of the enemy, encamped just 7 miles away. Lee's Legion comprised a portion of the patriot advance guard that surprised a

British foraging party around 8:00 a.m. and precipitated the day's battle. The Americans deployed from two columns in line of march to two ranks, with militia in front and Continentals backstopping them. Lee positioned his mixed cavalry and infantry on the American right flank. The Carolina militia, particularly those under Marion and Pickens fought admirably, but eventually faltered. Lee held firm on the right against the advance of a British regiment and Greene fed in his Continentals to restore the American line. Momentum swung to the Americans; Lee's infantry along with the advancing patriot regulars drove in the British left. Fighting was hand-to-hand; Lee recorded that "such was the obstinacy with which the contest was maintained, that a number of soldiers fell transfixed by each other's bayonet."[19] The British right, however, refused to yield, and their commander took advantage of their staunchness to begin reorganizing the rest of his command.

Lee, who had been forward with his infantry, thought he saw an opportunity to win the day by unleashing his cavalry to complete the destruction of the still reeling British left. But when he called for his dragoons, he discovered to his astonishment and dismay that they had already been committed against—and defeated by—the British right. Whether Greene or some other officer made this decision is unknown, but Lee believed that "To this unfortunate . . . order, may be ascribed the turn in this day's battle."[20] Instead, the British counterattacked and broke the American assault. Greene, seeing that his forces could do no more, gave the order to pull back. The British, happy to see them off, retired to Charleston. Greene sent Lee and Marion to give chase the next day, but those two astute leaders soon thought it wise to pull back to rejoin Greene and the main army for a return to the Santee hills.

Eutaw Springs was the last major battle Greene fought in the deep south and for all intents and purposes marked the close of Lee's combat career as well. In October, Greene sent him to carry dispatches to Washington on the Virginia peninsula. There he witnessed Cornwallis's epochal surrender at Yorktown, of which he gave a vivid account in his memoirs. He returned to South Carolina in November and participated in a pair of abortive operations against the British outside of Charleston in December. For some time he had been out of sorts, probably from a combination of physical, mental, and emotional fatigue engendered by nearly 5 years of almost unbroken and arduous campaigning. Additionally, his ambition and ego always attracted jealousy and he gave himself over to feelings that his contributions were not fully appreciated—despite this and similar encomiums from Greene, "I am more indebted to this officer than to any other for the advantages gained over the enemy in the operations of [the] last Campaign."[21] Too, he recognized that opportunities to win further battlefield glory were unlikely. For all these reasons, as well as a desire to marry a cousin, Matilda Lee, whom he had long courted, he left the army in February 1782.

Lee settled down to what he charmingly described in the final sentence of his memoirs as "the innocent and pleasing occupations of peace."[22] He served in Congress and as Virginia's governor, where he established a reputation for stirring oratory. It was Lee who eulogized Washington with the immortal line "First in war—first in peace—and first in the hearts of his countrymen."[23] Like a number of regular revolutionary officers—Hamilton and John Marshall come to mind— who attributed the army's persistent suffering to an ineffectual Congress, Lee supported the new Constitution and a relatively powerful national government. When outraged citizens in western Pennsylvania violently protested a federal excise tax in 1794, President Washington appointed Lee to command the forces that helped bloodlessly quell the so-called Whiskey Rebellion. Lee's pronounced Federalist leanings, however, including his advocacy of a strong professional military, put him increasingly out of step with political trends in the 1790s— both in the nation at large and especially in Virginia, bastion of Jeffersonian Republicanism.

Misfortune piled up for Lee. Matilda died and the overwhelmingly Republican state assembly turned him out from the governorship before his appointed term expired. Even remarriage failed to assuage the deep depression that eventually consumed him. Paradoxically, the man who displayed such great prudence in war was reckless in peacetime financial speculation and by the early years of the nineteenth century constantly had to dodge his creditors. In 1809 he was sentenced to a year in debtor's prison. While there, to pass the time and also perhaps in self-justification, he wrote his history of the revolution, one of the finest memoirs ever written by an American soldier and an indispensable source on the war in the south. In its pages he repeatedly struck the themes of the superiority of professional soldiers over militia and the necessity for a robust central government presiding over a tight-knit union of states. This last was unusual for anyone in the early republic, particularly a Virginian. In a peculiar irony, a son from his second marriage—Robert E. Lee, born in 1807—would come closer than any other single man to destroying that union more than half a century later at the head of his own revolutionary army.

Henry Lee ardently believed in what we might term ordered liberty; a strict disciplinarian while in uniform, he feared and despised the unchecked passions of the democratic masses. As if to confirm his worst suspicions, in 1812 an angry mob in Baltimore beat him nearly to death while city officials averted their gaze. His offense was expressing strong and unpopular opinions against war with Great Britain, an undertaking for which he adamantly—and as it turned out, correctly— believed the new nation was woefully unprepared. Broken in health and spirit, he left his wife and children in Virginia, and repaired to the West Indies in a vain effort to recover, as well as remain beyond the reach of all those to whom he owed money. This lonely outcast remained abroad for 5 years. Sensing death's approach, in early 1818 Lee took ship back to the United States hoping to reach his native Virginia. He only made it as far as the Georgia home of Nathanael Greene's daughter. Emaciated and sick, he dramatically announced, "I am come purposely to die in the house and in the arms of the daughter of my old friend and compatriot."[24] He was dead in 2 weeks and buried in the Greene family plot. A century later he was reinterred alongside his more famous son at Virginia's Washington and Lee College.

Henry Lee's story is one of great ambition and enthusiasms, triumph and controversy, and ultimate disappointment and despair. He possessed a genius for war rivaled by few, if any, of his contemporaries. In addition to all the advantages afforded by his aristocratic background, nature lavished immense intellectual gifts upon him—a quick, penetrating intelligence; a soaring imagination; and a keen eye for detail. All these stood him in good stead across those glorious years of the Revolution, but afterwards everything turned anticlimactic and his restless ambition could find no peacetime compass. Shamefully treated in his last, sad years and driven by internal demons, his life turned out badly. Yet "Light-Horse Harry" Lee deserves to be remembered by posterity first and foremost as a patriot, as well as one of the most brilliant soldiers ever produced by his country.

ANTHONY WAYNE

Anthony Wayne possessed many unlovely characteristics. He was vain in the extreme, arrogant, boastful, impatient, and commonly regarded as the most profane officer in an army that contained many who cursed with epic fluency. He was a poor husband and father, and made a hash of his postwar finances, although he avoided—barely—joining Henry Lee in debtors' prison. He was a strict disciplinarian, even a martinet. Wayne acquired the nickname "Mad Anthony" not for his fire-eating style in battle—though dashing he was—but from a displeased private who castigated him for refusing to extricate the soldier from legal difficulties with Pennsylvania's civil authorities. Because it seemed to fit so well, the soubriquet stuck. Yet he was also an extremely charismatic and capable combat leader, ranking with Morgan and Arnold as one of the Continental Army's finest during the War of Independence. Like Lee, soldiering was the only thing he was ever really good at. Due to his overwhelming ambition for martial glory and intense desire to be regarded as a hero, Wayne's two most perceptive modern interpreters have labeled him a "military romanticist."[25]

Again like Lee, he was born on an estate bearing his family's name—Waynesborough—in Chester County, Pennsylvania, on New Year's Day, 1745. The Waynes were well-to-do and respected; the father had served on the colony's western frontier as a militia officer during the French and Indian War, and participated actively in church affairs and local politics. Anthony, an only son, got the beginnings of a good education by studying with a schoolmaster uncle. His academic promise and the family's wealth took the 16-year-old boy to the Philadelphia Academy, only some 20 miles distant from home, but a world away in terms of cosmopolitan splendor compared to Chester County. His formal schooling ended after 2 years, and he emerged as an articulate, attractive, dark-eyed young man of medium height, "his whole countenance fine and animated."[26]

He took up surveying in his home district and quickly made himself a good reputation. Among his acquaintances he counted Philadelphia's, indeed America's, leading citizen, Benjamin Franklin, who in 1764 invited Wayne to join in a commercial venture involving land purchases in Nova Scotia. Wayne acted as the syndicate's agent on the scene for several months and performed acceptably, although the undertaking ultimately failed to pan out. Returning home in the middle of these affairs, he wooed and won the daughter of a prosperous Philadelphia businessman, wedding Mary Penrose in March 1765. Wayne settled down to a comfortable life as a farmer who operated a tannery and surveyed on the side.

As one of his community's leading citizens, Wayne found himself caught up in the revolutionary agitation of the early 1770s. He held firm Whig and republican principles, and in 1774 his neighbors chose him to represent them at a provincial convention called to devise measures in support of Massachusetts, then groaning under British oppression. He took an active role in opposing the crown's measures and so-impressed his fellow citizens that they elected him to back-to-back terms in the Pennsylvania Assembly. While immersed in politics, he also began a study of military tactics and, after fighting broke out in April 1775, started drilling with a collection of local volunteers. In January 1776 the Continental Congress commissioned him a colonel, commanding a battalion of the Pennsylvania line. Wayne resigned political office in order to ready his unit for service and also in conformity with the principle of civil–military separation. In April he arrived in New York City to join Washington and the rest of the army in defense of that city against an expected British attack.

Scarcely had Wayne and his men gotten settled when they were further dispatched, along with other units under the overall command of General John Sullivan, to reinforce flagging American fortunes in Canada. Since Montgomery's and Arnold's defeat at Quebec at the end of 1775, a depleted patriot force had maintained a tenuous position around that walled bastion; now the Americans were retiring up the St. Lawrence River toward Fort Ticonderoga pursued by a vengeful British force. By June 1 Sullivan's command linked up with their bedraggled compatriots at Sorel, on the St. Lawrence's south bank, some 75 miles deep inside Canada. Sullivan was as aggressive as any American general, though unluckier than most. When he learned that a British detachment, rumored to be only several hundred strong, had reached Trois Rivieres, 40 miles downriver to the northeast, he decided to attack.

On the night of June 8, 1,500 Continentals, including Wayne's battalion, boarded bateaux and moved to a point 9 miles below Trois Rivieres, on the river's north bank. Leaving their boats under guard, the rest of the party slogged through marshes, hip deep in mud, toward their objective. Dawn added to this hellish ordeal; British ships anchored in the river detected and opened fire on the attackers. Wayne's unit was the first to break free to dry, open ground only to encounter a redcoat formation. He smartly maneuvered his men to bring a hail of musketry onto the enemy and had the satisfaction of watching the British flee. The other American units dragged themselves out of the mire and together they advanced to encounter not the small enemy force expected, but a well-entrenched one equipped with artillery and numbering several thousand. Gallantly, if unwisely, the patriots assaulted and were cut to pieces. They fell back, reeling under pressure from their front as well as the continuous shelling from the vessels on their right. Retreat turned into disorderly rout as individuals and small groups raced to save themselves. Wayne, despite a "Slight touch in my Right leg" from an enemy musket ball, took charge of several hundred stragglers and led them to where they had left their boats, only to discover that the boat guard had taken them off to avoid enemy capture.[27] Resolutely, Wayne led the despairing men on a 3-day march southward to eventual safety. Trois Rivieres was an American disaster—400 patriot casualties for fewer than ten enemy—but Wayne had admirably passed his baptism of fire. Thus, his claim to "have saved the Army in Canada" was perhaps a pardonable bit of exaggeration.[28]

That army was hardly out of danger, however. The British pressed up the St. Lawrence and the Americans—including Arnold, who withdrew from Montreal— fell back to the southern end of Lake Champlain. Horatio Gates arrived to take command of the "army in Canada," a somewhat problematic charge since the remnants of that particular host were all in New York now. Nevertheless, Gates went to work with a will to rebuild and inspirit patriot forces. Wayne and his men found themselves fortifying Fort Ticonderoga throughout the fall and summer for the anticipated British assault. In the event, it never came. A battle between rival flotillas on Lake Champlain in October resulted in a British tactical victory, but checked their enthusiasm for venturing farther south and they retired into Canada for the winter.

With all quiet on the northern front, attention focused on the plight of Washington's army, retreating through New Jersey after its series of defeats in New York. In November Washington summoned Gates south with eight regiments to join him. Wayne, who had impressed everyone with his performance from Trois Rivieres onward, was left in command at Ticonderoga. The experience tried him in the extreme; he likened the post to "Ancient Golgotha a place of Skulls" as his meagerly nourished and ill-clothed men perished from sickness and exposure in upstate New York's harsh winter.[29] Ticonderoga proved a Calvary for Wayne not only in terms of physical hardship, but also for the vexing challenges posed by the increasingly surly men under his command. The enlistments of many of them expired at the end of 1776 and they desperately wanted to go home. Wayne had orders to keep them there until militia from the various states arrived to relieve them. When the promised units were tardy, some in the ranks grew mutinous. On one occasion, Wayne had to threaten a rebellious soldier with a pistol; on another he struck a private and, when the man's company commander protested, threw that officer in jail. By spring 1777 the long-overdue militia finally arrived, but their lax ways appalled Wayne. While a firm disciplinarian from the start, as a staunch republican Wayne had previously espoused the virtues of volunteer citizen soldiers. His experience at Ticonderoga of commanding both short-term Continentals and then militia soured him forever on his previous ideal and, like many senior Continental officers he became a vociferous advocate of a regular army.

Good news finally relieved his gloom. On February 21, 1777, Congress appointed him a brigadier general. And in April, Washington personally ordered him south to the main army's winter quarters at Morristown, New Jersey, to take command of a brigade. Shortly after his arrival, Wayne advanced to the leadership of one of the five divisions—two brigades—in Washington's newly reorganized army. Wayne immediately began instilling his brand of discipline—rigorous drill, spit and polish—noting to a friend that "I would rather risk my life, my reputation and the fate of America on 5000 men neatly uniformed than on a third more, equally armed and disciplined, covered with rags and Crawling with Verman."[30]

While Wayne shaped up his command, the campaign of 1777 unfolded. The British general Howe, after much feinting, abandoned his few remaining posts in New Jersey, though not before the pugnacious Wayne had skirmished with them in late May and June. Eventually Howe embarked his army aboard ship in New York and for over month left the American generals pondering his destination. For a brief spell that summer Wayne went on detached service back to his home in Chester County to help organize the militia to defend nearby Philadelphia. There he had a chilly reunion with his wife, from whom he had grown increasingly distant over the past year and a half, and indulged his fondness for the company of other, younger women. By early August he rejoined the main army north of Philadelphia, which still puzzled over the seaborne Howe's intentions. The situation soon clarified; Howe sailed into Chesapeake Bay, clearly with the aim of approaching Philadelphia from the southwest. The patriots rushed south and by early September arrayed themselves along Brandywine Creek, 25 miles west of the capital, to await the British advance. Wayne's division, with most of the American artillery, held the left of the patriot defensive line at Chad's Ford, the most direct crossing site along the road to the city. Nathanael Greene's division manned the center, while Sullivan's division held the extreme right covering the creek's upper fords. A small force on the west side of the Brandywine covered the front of Wayne's position in order to provide early warning to the main line of resistance.

On the hot, hazy morning of September 11 the enemy advance drove the patriot covering force back across Chad's Ford and Wayne prepared to meet the expected assault. Instead, a relatively harmless artillery duel broke out as a large force commanded by the Hessian General Knyphausen assembled on the west bank, but did not attempt to advance. Meanwhile Washington, in his command post not far to the rear, was buffeted by confusing reports of enemy activity to his right. At one point, believing Howe had fatally divided his army, Washington ordered Wayne and Greene to come out of their positions and attack Knyphausen, then revoked the order when he got word that the enemy "activity" to his right was in fact Howe's main effort and that it had succeeded in turning his flank to threaten the American rear. Washington pulled Greene's division from the line and rushed it north to stem the enemy tide that threatened to overwhelm the patriots. This left Wayne to face the brunt of Knyphausen's supporting, but still robust, attack, which he finally launched mid-afternoon. Wayne's men yielded ground grudgingly in a tough 3-hour fight that prevented the German general from linking up with the other enemy pincer. Only when he received word that the rest of the American army had extricated itself and was retiring in good order did Wayne break off the engagement and retreat eastward.

Although on the American side Brandywine was in many ways a poorly conducted battle, Wayne emerged with his already formidable fighting reputation considerably enhanced. A week and a half later, however, he suffered the most humiliating setback of his career. While Washington withdrew to the north of Philadelphia, Wayne's division remained south of the Schuylkill River to harass Howe's army. Wayne was operating in familiar country close to his boyhood home. He established a base near Paoli Tavern and prepared a surprise blow at Howe's exposed right flank. Although badly outnumbered, Wayne thought he enjoyed the advantages of secrecy and surprise. Unknown to him, Howe had superior intelligence and on the night of September 21, launched a surprise, preemptive strike of his own. General Charles Grey's raiding force of three regiments crashed into Wayne's bivouac shortly after midnight. To ensure maximum stealth, the British general had ordered his men to remove the flints from their muskets, thus preventing them from discharging and earning him the grim nickname of "no-flint Grey." Relying solely upon cold steel, the British bayoneted some 150–200 sleepy Continentals, about 10 percent of Wayne's command.

Wayne did well to rally his troops and prevent the outcome from being much worse; he expertly reorganized the survivors some distance from the ill-fated campsite and even brought off the four guns and baggage attached to his unit. Wayne, not surprisingly, burned to retaliate, but Washington instead ordered him to rejoin the main army. Over the following days, what Wayne had regarded as a stinging, but still minor, defeat ballooned into a full-blown *cause celebre*. Due to the bloody carnage wreaked by enemy bayonets, and no doubt to serve propaganda purposes, Americans began calling the engagement the "Paoli massacre." Patriots emphasized alleged British atrocities, even though all available evidence—including their taking a large number of prisoners—indicates that the British behaved properly. This version of the action at Paoli also caused Wayne to be condemned for "allowing" the "massacre." Outraged, Wayne demanded that Washington authorize a formal inquiry to clear his name. A board of senior officers duly found Wayne innocent of any misconduct; however, its report also suggested that he had camped a bit too closely to the enemy. Believing his honor newly assailed, Wayne now demanded a court-martial. Washington again acceded. Wayne defended himself with a lengthy explanation of his intent and actions on the fatal night, and the court acquitted him, observing this time that he had done "everything that could be expected from an active, brave, and vigilant officer."[31]

These various legal proceedings occurred amid a continuing campaign. Howe occupied Philadelphia on September 26 and emplaced a substantial portion of his army 5 miles north of the city at Germantown. Washington wanted to dislodge them if possible, a wish that Wayne avidly shared, his usual aggressiveness amplified by a desire to erase the stain of Paoli. On the evening of October 3, 11,000 American troops in four separate columns began a 16-mile approach march southward, intending to converge on the enemy at Germantown unawares. Wayne's division was part of one of the central corps under Sullivan's command. Before setting out, as was his eve of battle wont, Wayne composed a heroic missive to his wife, melodramatically concluding that "before this reaches you, the Heads of many Worthy fellows will be laid low—dawn is big with the fate of thousands."[32]

Dawn on October 4 found the lead elements of Sullivan's corps driving in British pickets. Sullivan deployed his troops in line of battle, with Wayne assuming the left flank, which since Greene's column had become lost in the dark, was unsupported to its left. The Americans moved steadily forward; a thick fog appeared along with the sun and shielded their advance from British fire, though it made command and control almost impossible. Wayne later recorded that the fog "together with the smoke Occasioned by our Cannon, and Musketry—made it almost as dark as night."[33] Nevertheless, his men drove forward "with great Bravery & Rapidity" for over a mile under a galling enemy fire.[34] Then, with victory seemingly in the Americans' grasp, the fortunes of war switched sides. First, the troops following Wayne's advance got tied down assaulting a large stone house where approximately 120 redcoats had holed up. This slowed the patriots' momentum; additionally, the sound of fire filtering through the fog from their rear agitated some of Wayne's men, who began to wonder if they had somehow been cut off. Then, elements of Greene's lost corps tumbled onto the field to Wayne's left. The two commands, unidentifiable to each other in the thick haze, exchanged shots. That was all it took; the stampede to the rear began and nothing any officer, Wayne included, could do slowed it down. Wayne revealed his disgust at this outcome when he later wrote that "The fog and this mistake [the fratricide between the two patriot forces] prevented us from following a victory that in all Human probability would have put an end to the American War."[35]

Once again, however, Wayne had distinguished himself in defeat. His personal courage had been conspicuous; a horse was killed under him and he sustained wounds himself—"my left foot a little bruised by one of their Cannon shot ... a slight touch on my left hand."[36] These brushes with mortality failed to stifle Wayne's martial ardor; through the closing months of 1777 he urged further offensive action upon Washington, but the commander in chief and the other Continental generals thought better of it, and the army retired to Valley Forge.

Under the highly decentralized warmaking structure established by Congress, the individual states were responsible for providing troops to the Continental army and provisioning them. Hence Wayne, like his fellow generals, busied himself that winter imploring his native state government for adequate supplies and pay for his men. He also found time to socialize with some comely young ladies who resided near his camp. In February 1778 he led a month-long foraging expedition that took him into New Jersey and ultimately saw him ride a complete circle around British-occupied Philadelphia. He clashed with some enemy regiments and amassed a significant herd of livestock on his foray, earning the derisive nickname of "Drover Wayne" from the British. Some of the horses he gathered supplied remounts for Henry Lee's cavalry. In gratitude, Lee gave his friend Wayne a barrel of malt liquor he had liberated on one of his raids.

As spring deepened in Pennsylvania it became evident that the new British commander in America, Henry Clinton, intended to vacate Philadelphia and withdraw to New York City as part of a more defensively oriented strategy. The question facing the American high command was how to respond. Most of Washington's subordinates preferred a cautious approach; predictably, Wayne wanted to fall upon the retreating enemy. Washington adopted the more conservative course. When the British departed Philadelphia on June 18, the Continental Army began to shadow them, but from a safe distance. Clinton had to march through New Jersey, but there were multiple routes available to him. A guessing game ensued, somewhat resembling that of the previous summer when the Americans had to divine where Howe's seaborne force might eventually land. By June 24 Washington had established his headquarters at Hopewell, New Jersey, a dozen miles northwest of Princeton. Intelligence indicated that Clinton's army, to the south below Trenton, was proceeding in a northeasterly direction. Deliberations among Washington's generals revealed another split, with Charles Lee and Henry Knox advising that the Americans should avoid a major engagement, and Wayne, Greene, and the Marquis de Lafayette arguing the opposite. Washington decided to send 1,500 men to harass the enemy's left flank and rear.

Wayne, along with Greene and Lafayette protested vigorously and Washington agreed to increase the size of this force to nearly 5,000, including Wayne's division. Lafayette initially exercised overall command. Then on the 26th, with Clinton resting at Monmouth Court House, Washington sent Charles Lee forward to take charge of this advanced contingent and on the 27th ordered him to attack the British as soon as they began marching out of Monmouth. Lee and his subordinates never formulated a clear plan to accomplish this task. Rather, they pushed forward on the morning of June 28 and reached Monmouth several hours after the British had begun filing out of the village along a road headed north. Lee sent Wayne's 1,000 men to hit the exposed, strung out enemy, deploying the remainder of his troops on each of Wayne's flanks. Wayne encountered a determined enemy rearguard commanded by Lord Cornwallis. While these two forces grappled, the friendly elements on either side of Wayne began to pull back due to a combination of increased enemy pressure and their own growing confusion. Finding himself unsupported, Wayne had to retire also, much to his dismay. In reality, although command and control had largely broken down, it was well that the patriots withdrew, for the bulk of the enemy army had marched to the sound of the guns back to Monmouth and now considerably outnumbered the Americans.

Lee's now-disorganized force leapfrogged back to the west across a series of ravines as the British seized the initiative and began to come on in strength. Washington and the bulk of the army had also made haste to get to the scene of action. The spectacle of Continentals streaming rearward greeted the infuriated Virginian. He encountered Lee and after a brief, stormy interview, dismissed him and took personal command. He ordered Wayne to hold about 2 miles west of Monmouth while the rest of the army established a final defensive position somewhat farther to the rear. Wayne's regiments bought enough time, barely, before the weight of the enemy attack "soon Obliged us after a Severe Conflict to give way."[37] Washington had formed a line anchored on favorable ground and Wayne integrated his men into the center. The enemy struck first at the American left and right wings before trying Wayne's position. Under Wayne's cool supervision his men repelled no fewer than three charges made by elite British grenadiers. This marked the battle's culmination. The British withdrew and the Americans were in no shape to follow, despite Wayne's urging.

This time Wayne could have justifiably claimed to have saved the American army. But as Wayne's star ascended, Charles Lee's dimmed forever. He demanded a court-martial to defend himself from the intimations of disobedience and cowardice that his relief by Washington evoked. The commander in chief obliged him and the hearings persisted for weeks in the high summer of 1778. Wayne was a key witness and his testimony brought no comfort to Lee, who was eventually found guilty and cashiered. By late 1778 the conflict in the north between American and British armies settled into a tense standoff, but that between American generals raged fiercely as ever. Wayne deemed some comments by Lee, which he spied in a newspaper, to be highly derogatory regarding "the Military Character of a Gentleman" and demanded satisfaction from him.[38] Lee, beset by multiple challengers, somehow managed to talk his way out of this particular duel. More concretely, in mid-October, Wayne was forced to relinquish command of his division to a fellow Pennsylvanian with greater seniority. To add insult to injury, the new commander was an officer whom Wayne had long despised, Arthur St. Clair. Wayne briefly and sarcastically threatened "to return to domestic life, & leave the blustering field of Mars to ... gentlemen of more worth," but ultimately thought better of it.[39]

Wayne adamantly refused to serve under St. Clair, however. He cast about for a new post and was rewarded in the spring of 1779 with the command of a special unit recently created by Washington, a light infantry brigade of 1,200 men handpicked from the flower of the army. Another officer who vied for this choice billet was the redoubtable Daniel Morgan who, when passed over in favor of Wayne, manifested an all-too common impulse among Continental officers and resigned in a fit of pique. For his part, Wayne took a furlough back to his home in order to absent himself from the scene of controversy but burned with eagerness to take over his new outfit and lead it to glory on "the field of Mars."[40]

Wayne formally assumed command at West Point in early June, where to his delight he found that Washington already had a plan to commit the light infantry force to battle. The British had recently seized both ends of Kings Ferry, an important Hudson River crossing above British-held New York City and about a dozen miles below West Point. Washington had particular designs on the western terminus at Stony Point and conveyed a great sense of urgency to Wayne, since he desired to strike before the enemy could complete fortifications there. Henry Lee's cavalry had already amassed considerable intelligence on the place, and Wayne and Washington conducted their own personal reconnaissance. Stony Point achieved 150 feet at its highest point and extended for half a mile into the Hudson. Water surrounded it on three sides and the approach from the west was a causeway across a thick swamp. Approximately 500 redcoats manned the defenses, which included abatis and several redoubts.

On the morning of July 15, 1779, Wayne mustered his men. After a detailed inspection, they marched 15 miles to their final assembly area only a mile and a half from Stony Point. Extraordinary precautions were in effect to ensure surprise. Until just before the attack, only a few trusted officers knew the objective. Guards sealed the assembly area to prevent any potential deserter from compromising the operation. Borrowing a page from "no flint Grey," most muskets were unloaded, on pain of death to any unfortunate private who might accidentally discharge one. Even the local dogs had been killed over the preceding days to prevent their barking from alerting the enemy. Wayne composed one of his death or glory missives just before beginning the midnight approach to his target, closing, "I am called to Sup, but where to breakfast, either within the enemy's lines in triumph or in the other World!"[41]

Shrouded in darkness, the Americans split into three elements as they neared the objective. In the center a small party—the only men with loaded weapons—approached the causeway and began a rattle of musketry intended to serve as a diversion. The gambit worked perfectly; the garrison roused itself and charged out to meet this threat. A supporting attack on the patriot left penetrated the British works from the north. Wayne, armed with an espontoon—a type of short spear—accompanied the main effort on the right or south. British fusillades greeted both assaulting parties. Seventeen of the 20 men comprising the lead echelon of the supporting attack were killed or wounded. On the right, a musket ball creased Wayne's skull and four other officers with him were hit. Despite his injury, Wayne remained in command. Once atop the enemy-held hilltop, 15 minutes of ferocious hand-to-hand combat decided the issue. The redcoats en masse threw down their muskets and called for quarter. Wayne had earlier written that "a sanguine God is rather thirsty for Human Gore," but despite this lurid pronouncement, his men showed great restraint.[42] There would be no charges of massacre at Stony Point. American casualties came to 15 dead and 83 wounded. Enemy losses amounted to about 100 killed or wounded, 500 men taken prisoner, and the loss of 15 cannon and valuable stores. In contrast to his normal bombastic style, Wayne sent off a brief, even eloquent note to Washington, "The fort & garrison with Col. Johnston are ours. Our officers & men behaved like men who are determined to be free."[43]

Stony Point represented the crowning moment of Wayne's Revolutionary War career. Congress ordered a special gold medal be struck for him in honor of his victory. After this, the remainder of his war was somewhat anticlimactic and the 18 months immediately following this brilliant stroke were discouraging in the extreme. Wayne's light infantry saw no further action; in fact, it had always been a provisional formation and Washington disbanded it in December 1779. With no troops to command, Wayne took leave of the army and made his way home. Relations with his wife, already cool, became frosty when she learned of his dalliance with a young woman named Mary Vining. While Wayne's wife had tolerated his previous flirtations and infatuations, she correctly suspected something much more serious was afoot here. Indeed, this daughter of a wealthy Wilmington, Delaware society family remained Wayne's *inamorata* until the end of his days. When not courting Miss Vining, Wayne passed the winter carousing with old cronies in Philadelphia and hectoring Pennsylvania's assembly for failing to support the troops adequately.

Despite, or perhaps because of, this relatively placid existence, Wayne hungered to return to the field—so eagerly, that for the campaign of 1780 he even accepted a position as a brigade commander in the Pennsylvania line subordinate to his rival St. Clair. By early September 1780 Wayne became the acting commander of the Pennsylvania division—St. Clair had been given charge of the army's entire right wing—encamped below West Point. Later that month, when Benedict Arnold's traitorous attempt to deliver the vital highland fortress on the Hudson to the enemy was uncovered, Wayne's men made an overnight forced march of 16 miles to help secure the place against a feared British attack. According to Wayne, the commander in chief "received us like a God" and was so relieved that he cried, "'All is safe, & I again am happy.'"[44]

The British refrained from striking at West Point and the opposing armies prepared for another cold winter. And it soon became evident that Arnold was not the only member of the Continental Army whose dissatisfaction would drive him to drastic action. In November the Pennsylvania line went into quarters at Morristown, New Jersey. Of his men Wayne wrote, "They have served their Country for nearly five years with fidelity, poorly clothed, badly fed, & worse paid."[45] In reality, Pennsylvania actually supported its troops somewhat better than the other states. No matter, the troops' condition was wretched and their temper volatile. Perhaps sensing this, Wayne remained with them rather than removing himself to the comforts of home—and Miss Vining—as had been his previous winter habit. The storm broke on New Years Day 1781.

"It is with pain I now inform your Excellency of the general mutiny and defection which suddenly took place in the Penn'a line between nine and ten o'clock last evening."[46] With these words Wayne apprised Washington of the shocking news. Although they had killed one junior officer and injured several others who had attempted to stop them, the mutineers' overall behavior was remarkably restrained. A committee of sergeants emerged to speak for the unhappy soldiers. They pledged not to go over to the enemy; indeed, when the British later sent agents to entice them to do so, the Pennsylvanians contemptuously arrested them. Their grievances centered on arrears pay, inadequate clothing, and the belief of many that their enlistments had expired at the end of 1780. Realizing that most of their officers sympathized with the first two of these, they offered no violence, but maintained that the only way to gain satisfaction was to march on Philadelphia and confront Congress.

Wayne and his officers followed the men—numbering about 1,500—and maintained a dialogue with them. He also notified Congress and the state assembly, and advised them to negotiate. Those two bodies formed a joint commission to treat with the mutineers. Disgruntled soldiers and frightened civil authorities met in Trenton and hammered out an agreement, largely based upon Wayne's advice. The commissioners honored Wayne's promise that the men would all receive amnesty once they came to terms. The eventual compromise granted the soldiers pay warrants and the desired clothing. On the sticky and complex issue of enlistments, Congress created a special board to hear each man's story regarding the terms of his contract; by the end of January over 1,300 men had been released from service. Interestingly, a significant number of them subsequently reenlisted. Finally, the entire Pennsylvania line was furloughed until mid-March. Wayne himself departed for Philadelphia for a rest with the grateful thanks of Washington acknowledging his deft handling of a delicate and explosive situation.

While Wayne and the rest of the American command dealt with rebellious soldiers, the turncoat Benedict Arnold, now fighting for the British, led an expedition of some 1,600 Loyalist troops from New York into Virginia. To counter Arnold's foray, marked by considerable burning and destruction, Washington dispatched a Continental detachment under Lafayette to the Old Dominion. In turn, the British sent additional forces from New York. In early May 1781 Lord Cornwallis arrived from North Carolina to assume overall command of a formidable army that now swelled to more than 7,000. Washington ordered Wayne with 1,000 Pennsylvania Continentals to reinforce Lafayette.

Wayne met the assembled troops in York, Pennsylvania and found embers of the recent mutiny still smoldered. Incidents of insubordination and indiscipline multiplied. Wayne had perhaps exhausted his stock of patience and tact—never high to begin with—during the earlier episode, so he had the suspected ringleaders arrested and in short order executed several of them. This had the desired effect and by the end of May Wayne led his sullen host south after penning another ringing farewell intended for a friend and, no doubt, posterity: "but mark—the ear piercing fife—the Spirit stirring Drum, & all the humble & Glorious Circumstances of War, summons me to haste."[47]

In fact, Wayne's brigade moved at a rather leisurely pace, due largely to some understandable foot-dragging by the soldiers, who had been deprived of powder and ball while on the march by their still suspicious officers. Not until the second week of June did Wayne link up with Lafayette, now his immediate superior, on the Rapidan River. Although still considerably outnumbered, the young Frenchman decided to advance south with his force to challenge Cornwallis who, somewhat inexplicably, began to retreat from Virginia's interior—first back to Richmond, then east down the peninsula. The two armies moved along the north side of the James River; on July 6 Cornwallis gave the impression that he intended to cross over to the south bank near Green Spring Plantation, about 10 miles west of Williamsburg. Lafayette sent Wayne hurrying ahead with an advance guard in hopes of catching the British awkwardly astride the river so that the Americans could destroy a portion of the enemy army.

Cornwallis had actually set an ambush for the Americans; the bulk of his superior force—some 5,000 or so redcoats—lay carefully hidden on the north shore ready to strike the unsuspecting patriots. Late in the afternoon Wayne moved forward with about 900 men and soon bore the brunt of an overwhelming British attack. Seemingly faced with two equally bad choices—retreat and be routed or stand and be crushed—Wayne selected a third, unorthodox, but for him wholly characteristic, option; he attacked with the bayonet. This maneuver, though costly, temporarily threw the enemy off balance and enabled Lafayette and Wayne to retire in good order, aided by swampy ground that hindered a vigorous British pursuit. Wayne lost about 140 men; Cornwallis's casualties totaled 75 or so. While some of Wayne's critics later carped about "Mad Anthony's" unconscionable recklessness, more thoughtful observers agreed that his boldness had saved the day.

The battle and its aftermath also had a tonic effect in improving the Pennsylvania line's *esprit* and morale. Wayne praised them lavishly with the sort of purple rhetoric few could equal. He also did his utmost in waging the never-ending struggle to see them supplied properly. While Cornwallis maneuvered himself into his eventual trap at Yorktown, Wayne bombarded his native state with requests for support and also pressed his demands upon Virginia's government. In early August he went a step further and seized clothing that the state commissary had stockpiled in Richmond. When an official remonstrated to Wayne that he ought to be patient enough at least to await the absent governor's authorization, Wayne sarcastically rejoined, "it may be well to advise Lord Cornwallis to have *patience* 'until the Governor' arrives," while continuing to help himself to the goods.[48] Predictably, when he learned of the unauthorized requisition, Virginia's governor complained loudly to Congress.

This civil–military tempest eventually blew over with Wayne apologizing and returning the confiscated items. In early September, he was shot by nervous pickets while riding into Lafayette's headquarters after dark. The bullets apparently only grazed his lower extremities, though primitive eighteenth-century medical procedures made even the slightest wounds potentially deadly. Happily for Wayne, he recovered over a period of several weeks. He took the misfortune with equanimity, referring to the sentry who loosed the initial shot as a "poor fellow" who made an honest mistake and indulging in black humor by observing that, because American logistics were so poor, a shortage of powder in the musket cartridges had caused a ball to lodge in his body rather than pass cleanly through.[49] Less happily for the ambitious Pennsylvanian, his wounds kept him from much action during the climactic siege at Yorktown. Nevertheless, he was well enough to sit his horse and witness the British surrender on October 19. As Wayne had earlier written, he would not have missed the day under any circumstance, even if it required that he be "borne on the shoulders of my trusty Veterans."[50]

Two long, arduous years of hostilities still lay ahead and the lower south— South Carolina and Georgia—remained an especially vicious cockpit of conflict. Anxious to reinforce the American commander in that contentious region,

Nathanael Greene, Washington dispatched Wayne and a portion of the Pennsylvania line to him almost immediately following Yorktown. Sensing that he would find little major fighting—and because the despised St. Clair was back in overall command of the Pennsylvanians—Wayne traveled separately and made a rather stately procession southward. He arrived at Greene's South Carolina camp in early January 1782 and began angling for an independent assignment. Greene granted this wish by further dispatching him and a small detachment of Continental dragoons and militia to restore order in Georgia, then witness to chaotic fighting between the British with their Loyalist and Indian allies on one side, and a motley collection of patriots on the other.

Wayne entered Georgia on January 19 and wasted little time in making his presence felt. He hammered enemy posts outside of Savannah and soon drove the British back into that town. He also suppressed Loyalist bands through an adroit combination of ruthless campaigning and offers of amnesty. And he fought and won a bloody battle with a war party of Creek Indians who, in an echo of Paoli, fell upon his camp one night. Wayne had a horse killed beneath him as he rallied his men to beat off the surprise raid, killing 18 in return for five of his own dead. In a particularly gruesome denouement, he had an additional dozen Indian captives executed at first light. The British as a matter of policy eventually resolved to evacuate their few remaining garrisons in the former 13 colonies and on July 11, 1782, they left Savannah. Wayne moved in close behind them and assisted the civil authorities in resuming control over the city and the entire state. So grateful was the Georgia Assembly that it voted him—and Greene—adjacent estates upriver from Savannah that had previously belonged to now-departed Loyalists.

Greene now required Wayne's services in South Carolina; Wayne dutifully reported to him outside of Charleston in mid-August. St. Clair was also on hand, so Wayne importuned Greene for a billet that would leave him free from the orders of his fellow Pennsylvanian. Before something could be arranged, Wayne was stricken by a mysterious malady that nearly killed him and that left him with a permanently damaged constitution. He described his illness as a "disorder which I really dread much more than I do the D_l[Devil], a musket and cannon ball." The onset of cooler autumn weather improved his health somewhat and Greene accorded him the signal honor of triumphantly leading American troops into Charleston when the British departed on December 14, 1782. Wayne lingered in the south for another 7 months performing routine duties that included assisting Greene demobilize and ship home various Continental units. Wayne himself embarked for Pennsylvania at the end of July 1783.

Wayne's friends and family gave him a hero's homecoming that gladdened his heart and Congress, rather belatedly, conferred a major general's commission on him in October—a month before he left the army. Soon he hurled himself into politics with the same aggressiveness he displayed on the battlefield and got elected to the Pennsylvania Assembly. There he battled for recognition and reward for the soldiers from those ungrateful citizens "who possessed neither the virtue nor fortitude to meet the enemy in the field" themselves.[51] He also made a series of disastrous financial decisions centered upon turning his new Georgia estate into a viable concern and traveled there several times for extended stays, all without his estranged wife. On one such sojourn in June 1786 he found himself maintaining a deathbed vigil for his neighbor and former commander, Greene. He voted for the new national Constitution in November 1787 as a member of Pennsylvania's ratifying convention before decamping to Georgia for good to duck his creditors and their lawyers. Although not a few Georgians viewed Wayne as a carpetbagger, he won election to the United States Congress from the Peachtree State in 1791, only to be unseated by that body a year latter amid his opponents' complaints of election fraud allegedly perpetrated by his supporters. Though no charges stuck to him personally, Wayne's political career and finances, not to mention his family life, were in shambles. President Washington then threw him a lifeline. Unlike his colleague Henry Lee, who found himself in similar straits after the Revolution, Wayne would enjoy a glorious second act.

American arms had suffered humiliating setbacks at Indian hands in the Northwest Territory—an area comprising more than a quarter of a million square miles that one day would become six new states stretching from Ohio to Minnesota. Two United States armies had been beaten in as many years, including one led by Wayne's *bete noire* St. Clair. Wayne gratefully accepted a recall to active duty to organize and lead a 5,000-man combined infantry–cavalry–artillery force to wrest control of this area from the Indians, as well as their British abettors, who encouraged them from their own frontier posts in Canada and the Old Northwest. Wayne took command at Pittsburgh in June 1792 and applied his proven formula of tough discipline and realistic training for the troops mixed with close attention to their care and welfare. Not even attempts by his second-in-command, the ubiquitous scoundrel James Wilkinson, to sabotage him or his wife's death back east failed to divert Wayne from his passion for soldiering. By the fall of 1793, he had a hard, ready unit that possessed excellent esprit de corps.

He moved west to Cincinnati, then north into the Maumee Valley, building roads and camps while systematically burning Indian towns and fields. The tribes made a stand on the site of modern-day Toledo on August 20, 1794, and the resulting battle of Fallen Timbers broke their power forever in the Old Northwest. Following his overwhelming victory, Wayne dictated harsh terms to the Indian confederacy and forced them to accept a treaty making way for white settlement. The general retained his command, which entailed monitoring Indian compliance with the terms of the agreement and administering a series of outposts. It was at one of these forts, at Presque Isle in northwest Pennsylvania, that the maladies that had lingered ever since the Revolution's southern campaign, along with years of hard living and harder campaigning, caught up to him. After a brief illness, the 51-year-old hero died in his bed on December 15, 1796, and, dressed in his best uniform, was laid to rest in a simple soldier's grave beneath the garrison's flagpole.

Conclusion

Deserving Success

AT THE CONCLUSION of the failed Canadian campaign of 1775–1776, George Washington consoled Benedict Arnold by writing to him, "It is not in the power of any man to command success; but you have done more—you have deserved it."[1] Washington was paraphrasing a line from his favorite play, Joseph Addison's *Cato*, a tragedy about a Roman senator who resists tyranny, first performed on a London stage in 1713. The sentiment expresses the notion that individual merit matters greatly. Even when not sufficient unto itself to ensure victory, no success is possible without it. In some ways this is an old fashioned, maybe even out of fashion, idea. So too, perhaps, is a twin pair of conceits. The first is, borrowing from Ralph Waldo Emerson, that, properly speaking, there is no history, just the biographies of great men. The second is that history can teach us moral lessons. America's revolutionary generation accepted all three of these concepts as self evidently true, however, and the careers of the men examined in *Founding Fighters* illustrate both the prevalence of these convictions over two centuries ago, as well as their general validity in explaining the Revolution's outcome.

These men believed deeply in a stern, Roman type of virtue. Their words and deeds in most instances reflected a high regard for selflessness, sacrifice, and valor. Honor and recognition were vitally important to them. They were very aware not only of the opinions of their contemporaries; they were equally conscious of how posterity might view them. In effect, many of them quite deliberately played to the gallery of generations unborn.

They were hardly perfect. Mingled with their devotion to classical republican ideals were extreme egotism and what, at times, appears an excessive concern for glory and fame. They were extraordinarily sensitive to slights, real or perceived, and about the prerogatives of rank and position. They frequently bickered and feuded with each other and fellow officers, as well as civilian officials. They were not reluctant to express their disgust with Congress and its support of them or the war effort more generally. When denied their wishes, they would sulk, threaten—and, in some instances, carry out—resignation. They lost battles. One committed treason and two others at least flirted with it.

And yet, these 15 men all contributed in important ways to the success of what their generation referred to as the "glorious cause" of American liberty and independence. If there is such a thing as a natural born fighter, then a number of them exemplified this species: Arnold, Clark, Jones, Henry Lee, Marion, Morgan, Pickens, and Wayne. Most began their revolutionary service as idealists, but over time transformed into realists and, in the cases of Charles Lee and Arnold, bitterness and cynicism. They practiced divergent, but in the main, highly effective styles of leadership. Some, such as Montgomery, Pickens, and Marion were quiet. Others—Allen, Arnold, Clark, Morgan, and Sumter come to mind—were charismatic. Gates, Greene, and Knox appeared studious. Their duties and the absence of modern communications technology required them to lead from the front, showing themselves to their men and exposing themselves to the enemy to a degree unthinkable for modern generals. At the same time, the same primitive circumstances of battlefield communications meant they spent a good deal of time writing out orders and instructions by hand.

On balance, their merits significantly outweighed their faults. One can trace the path to victory in our War of Independence through their triumphs and stumbles. Their lives have much to teach us about persistence, endurance, and fortitude in the face of daunting odds and obstacles. And in the end, they not only deserved success, collectively they, in a very real sense, commanded it.

Notes

Introduction

1. J. T. Headley, *Washington and His Generals* (New York: Baker and Scribner, 1847), Vol. I, pp. 2–3.

2. Dave Richard Palmer, *The Way of the Fox: American Strategy in the War for America, 1775–1783* (Westport, CT: Greenwood Press, 1975), p. 3.

3. The literature on American strategy in the Revolution is extensive. As noted in the text, most scholars view it as largely defensive. Russell M. Weigley describes it as a strategy of attrition or, at best, erosion in chapter 1 of his *The American Way of War: A History of United States Military Strategy and Policy* (Bloomington, IN: Indiana University Press, 1977). Similar views are expressed by Robert Middlekauff, *The Glorious Cause: The American Revolution, 1763–1789* (New York: Oxford University Press, 1982) and by Don Higginbotham in his several studies of the Revolution, especially *The War of American Independence: Military Attitudes, Policies, and Practice, 1763–1789* (Boston, MA: Northeastern University Press, 1983). A notable exception to this defensive-oriented view is Palmer, who depicts American strategy as a blend of offense and defense in *Way of the Fox*. Concerning the American Revolution as a "guerilla war," there are too many such pronouncements to cite. Suffice to say, this was a view that entered the popular imagination in the aftermath of Vietnam and the "wars of national liberation" of the 1960s. A typical illustration that came to this author's attention while writing this chapter is from a *New York Times* review of a television documentary on the Revolution. The reviewer quotes the filmmaker as saying that the Americans "had qualities 'very similar' to the Vietcong and Islamic guerillas" and adds knowingly, if rather irrelevantly in the context of the Revolution, "how difficult it is for any occupying force to outlast guerilla warfare and acts of terror." Alessandra Stanley, "British Eyes Look at 1776 and See Less to Approve," *The New York Times*, 23 June 2004, p. B3.

4. As with American strategy, there is an extensive literature on British strategy as well. The discussion here profited from Middlekauff, Palmer, the various chapters on British generals in George A. Billias, ed., *George Washington's Generals and Opponents: Their Exploits and Leadership* (Cambridge, MA: Da Capo Press, 1994), and Ira Gruber's essay, "British Strategy: The Theory and Practice of Eighteenth Century Warfare" in *Reconsiderations on the Revolutionary War: Selected Essays*, ed. Don Higginbotham (Westport, CT: Greenwood Press, 1978).

5. The major generals were Artemus Ward (Massachusetts), Israel Putnam (Connecticut), Charles Lee (Virginia), and Philip Schuyler (New York). The brigadiers were Seth Pomeroy, William Heath, and John Thomas (Massachusetts); David Wooster and Joseph Spencer (Connecticut); Richard Montgomery (New York); John Sullivan (New Hampshire); and Nathanael Greene (Rhode Island). Horatio Gates (Virginia) was named adjutant general.

6. John Adams to Abigail Adams, July 3, 1776, in *Adams Family Correspondence*, ed. L. H. Butterfield, Wendell D. Garrett, and Marjorie E. Sprague (Cambridge, MA: Harvard University Press, 1963), Vol. II, pp. 27–28.

7. David Hackett Fischer, *Washington's Crossing* (New York: Oxford University Press, 2004), p. 104.

8. Thomas Paine, *The American Crisis, Number 1* (1776) in *Thomas Paine: Political Writings*, ed. Bruce Kuklick (Cambridge, UK: Cambridge University Press, 2000), p. 49.

9. Higginbotham, *The War of American Independence*, p. 383.

10. Palmer, *The Way of the Fox*, p. 188.

11. Higginbotham, *The War of American Independence*, p. 414.

Chapter 1

1. Janet Montgomery cited in Michael P. Gabriel, *Major General Richard Montgomery: The Making of an American Hero* (Madison, NJ: Fairleigh Dickinson University Press, 2002), p. 31.

2. Richard Montgomery to Robert R. Livingston, cited in Gabriel, *Major General Richard Montgomery*, p. 73.

3. Richard Montgomery to Robert R. Livingston, cited in Gabriel, *Major General Richard Montgomery*, p. 77.

4. Janet Montgomery cited in Gabriel, *Major General Richard Montgomery*, p. 79.

5. Richard Montgomery to Janet Montgomery, cited in Gabriel, *Major General Richard Montgomery*, p. 100.

6. Richard Montgomery to Philip Schuyler, cited in Gabriel, *Major General Richard Montgomery*, p. 95.

7. Richard Montgomery to Janet Montgomery, cited in Gabriel, *Major General Richard Montgomery*, p. 103.

8. Richard Montgomery to Janet Montgomery, cited in Gabriel, *Major General Richard Montgomery*, p. 112.

9. Richard Montgomery to Robert R. Livingston, cited in Gabriel, *Major General Richard Montgomery*, p. 116.

10. Richard Montgomery to Robert R. Livingston, cited in Hal T. Shelton, *General Richard Montgomery and the American Revolution: From Redcoat to Rebel* (New York: New York University Press, 1994), p. 126.

11. George Washington to Philip Schuyler, cited in Shelton, *General Richard Montgomery*, pp. 124–125.

12. Cited in W. J. Wood, *Battles of the Revolutionary War, 1775–1781* (Chapel Hill, NC: Algonquin Books of Chapel Hill, 1990), p. 47.

13. Inscription cited in Gabriel, *Major General Richard Montgomery*, p. 188.

14. See John Shy's perceptive essay, "Charles Lee: The Soldier as Radical" in *George Washington's Generals and Opponents: Their Exploits and Leadership*, ed. George A. Billias (Cambridge, MA: Da Capo Press, 1994), p. 22, for mention of Lee's tortured psyche.

15. John Adams to Josiah Quincy, cited in Samuel W. Patterson, *Knight Errant of Liberty: The Triumph and Tragedy of General Charles Lee* (New York: Lantern Press, 1958), p. 80.

16. Abigail Adams to Mercy Otis Warren, January ?, 1777, *Adams Family Correspondence*, ed. L. H. Butterfield, Wendell D. Garrett, and Marjorie Sprague. (Cambridge, MA: Harvard University Press, 1963), Vol. II, p. 150.

17. George Washington to John Augustine, cited in John Alden, *Charles Lee, Patriot or Traitor?* (Baton Rouge, LA: Louisiana State University Press, 1951), p. 109.

18. Charles Lee cited in Patterson, *Knight Errant of Liberty*, p. 28.

19. Charles Lee to Sydney Lee, September 16, 1758, *The Lee Papers*, ed. Samuel Osgood (New York: New York Historical Society, 1872), Vol. I, pp. 7, 11–12.

20. Charles Lee to Sydney Lee, March 1, 1766, *The Lee Papers*, Vol. I, p. 43.

21. Charles Lee to Sydney Lee, September 30, 1769, *The Lee Papers*, Vol. I, p. 86.

22. Charles Lee cited in Alden, *Charles Lee, Patriot or Traitor*, p. 40.

23. Charles Lee to Thomas Gage, no date [1774], *The Lee Papers*, Vol. I, 133–134.

24. Charles Lee to Viscount Barrington, June 22, 1775, *The Lee Papers*, I, 186.

25. George Washington cited in Patterson, *Knight Errant of Liberty*, p. 86. Patterson speculates that Lee might have contributed a phrase or two, p. 87.

26. Jeremy Belknap journal cited in Alden, *Charles Lee, Patriot or Traitor*, p. 83.

27. Charles Lee to Robert Morris, cited in Patterson, *Knight Errant of Liberty*, p. 91.

28. Charles Lee to Robert Morris, cited in Patterson, *Knight Errant of Liberty*, pp. 100–101.

29. Charles Lee to George Washington, January 24, 1776, *The Lee Papers*, Vol. I, pp. 259–260.

30. Charles Lee to the Chairman of the New York Committee of Safety [January 1776], *The Lee Papers*, Vol. I, p. 257.

31. Charles Lee to George Washington, February 19, 1776, *The Lee Papers*, Vol. I, p. 309.

32. John Adams to Charles Lee, February 19, 1776, *The Lee Papers*, Vol. I, p. 312.

33. Charles Lee to Richard Henry Lee, July 19, 1776, *The Lee Papers*, ed. Samuel Osgood (New York: New York Historical Society, 1873), Vol. II, p. 146.

34. Charles Lee to Richard Henry Lee, May 10, 1776, *The Lee Papers*, Vol. II, p. 20.

35. Anecdote cited in Alden, *Charles Lee, Patriot or Traitor*, p. 328.

36. Charles Lee to Patrick Henry, July 29, 1776, *The Lee Papers*, Vol. II, p. 177.

37. John Adams to Abigail Adams, October 7, 1776, *Adams Family Correspondence*, Vol. II, p. 139.

38. Charles Lee to Horatio Gates, October 14, 1776, *The Lee Papers*, Vol. II, pp. 261–262.

39. Joseph Reed to Charles Lee, November 21, 1776, *The Lee Papers*, Vol. II, p. 293.

40. Charles Lee to Joseph Reed, November 24, 1776, *The Lee Papers*, Vol. II, p. 305.

41. George Washington to Charles Lee, cited in Alden, *Charles Lee, Patriot or Traitor*, p. 154.

42. Charles Lee to Horatio Gates, December 12–13, 1776, *The Lee Papers*, Vol. II, p. 348.

43. Lee's Plan, dated March 29, 1777, is reproduced in *The Treason of Charles Lee*, ed. George H. Moore (original New York: 1860: reprint New York: Kennikat Press, 1970), pp. 84–90 and also in *The Lee Papers*, Vol. II, pp. 361–366.

44. Moore, who was the librarian of the New York Historical Society, obtained and publicly revealed Lee's letter to Howe in 1858, and wrote a damning indictment of Lee. Patterson takes an extreme opposite approach, contending that Lee was a devoted patriot and attempting to gull Howe, *Knight Errant of Liberty*, pp. 174–178. Alden assumes a middle position and examines all possibilities, finding Lee "guilty, with extenuating circumstances," *Charles Lee, Patriot or Traitor*, pp. 174–179. The most intriguing suggestion comes from Shy, "Charles Lee," pp. 40–41, who raises the possibility that Lee sought "simply to become a participant again instead of a bystander—it would have been perfectly in character for Lee to do such a thing."

45. Charles Lee cited in Alden, *Charles Lee, Patriot or Traitor*, p. 208.

46. Charles Lee and George Washington cited in Alden, *Charles Lee, Patriot or Traitor*, p. 222.

47. Charles Lee to George Washington, June 30, 1778, *The Lee Papers*, Vol. II, p. 437.

48. Lee's will in *The Lee Papers*, ed. Samuel Osgood (New York: New York Historical Society, 1875), Vol. IV, pp. 29–32.

49. Allen Nevins, "Foreword" in Samuel W. Patterson, *Horatio Gates: Defender of American Liberties* (New York: Columbia University Press, 1941), p. vii.

50. Paul David Nelson, *General Horatio Gates: A Biography* (Baton Rouge, LA: Louisiana State University Press, 1976), p. xi.

51. Gates's two principal biographers offer different birthdates. Nelson accepts April 1728, Nelson, *General Horatio Gates*, p. 6. Patterson is more specific in claiming July 26, 1727, Patterson, *Horatio Gates*, p. 4.

52. Charles Lee to Robert Morris, June 16, 1781, *The Lee Papers*, ed. Samuel Osgood (New York: New York Historical Society, 1874), Vol. III, p. 458.

53. Anecdote cited in Patterson, *Horatio Gates*, p. 293.

54. Cited in Nelson, *General Horatio Gates*, p. 34.

55. Horatio Gates to John Winstone, cited in Nelson, *General Horatio Gates*, p. 35.

56. Horatio Gates to Charles Lee, July 1, 1774, *The Lee Papers*, Vol. I, pp. 125–126.

57. Horatio Gates cited in George A. Billias, "Horatio Gates: Professional Soldier" in *George Washington's Generals and Opponents: Their Exploits and Leadership*, ed. George A. Billias (Cambridge, MA: Da Capo Press, 1994), p. 85.

58. Horatio Gates to Robert Morris, cited in Patterson, *Horatio Gates*, p. 53.

59. Charles Lee to Benjamin Rush, October 20, 1775, *The Lee Papers*, Vol. I, p. 214.

60. John Adams to Horatio Gates, cited in Nelson, *General Horatio Gates*, p. 56.

61. Benedict Arnold to Horatio Gates, cited in Nelson, *General Horatio Gates*, p. 56.

62. Matthias Ogden to Aaron Burr and Thomas Hartley to John Sullivan, cited in Nelson, *General Horatio Gates*, p. 66.

63. Horatio Gates to Israel Putnam, cited in Nelson, *General Horatio Gates*, p. 68.

64. William Duer to Phillip Schuyler, cited in Nelson, *General Horatio Gates*, p. 87.

65. Cited in Nelson, *General Horatio Gates*, p. 87.

66. Horatio Gates cited in Nelson, *General Horatio Gates*, p. 111.

67. Cited in Wood, *Battles of the Revolutionary War*, p. 161.

68. Convention cited in Nelson, *General Horatio Gates*, pp. 141–142. Ultimately, Congress refused to honor the agreement, not trusting the British, with some reason, to adhere to the agreement and the nearly 5,800 captured troops ended up being transported to Virginia until the war's end. Burgoyne was allowed to give his parole and return to England in May 1778, where he defended his role in the failed campaign.

69. Horatio Gates to Henry Clinton, cited in Patterson, *Horatio Gates*, pp. 190–191.

70. Horatio Gates to George Washington, cited in Patterson, *Horatio Gates*, p. 287.

71. Horatio Gates to Benjamin Lincoln, cited in Nelson, *General Horatio Gates*, p. 219.

72. Alexander Hamilton cited in Nelson, *General Horatio Gates*, pp. 237–238.

73. Horatio Gates to George Washington, cited in Nelson, *General Horatio Gates*, p. 241.

74. Horatio Gates to Richard Peters, cited in *General Horatio Gates*, Nelson, p. 250.

75. Anecdote cited by Alden, *Charles Lee, Patriot or Traitor*, p. 294.

76. George Washington cited in Don Higginbotham, *The War of American Independence: Military Attitudes, Policies, and Practice, 1763–1789* (Boston, MA: Northeastern University Press, 1983), p. 409.

77. George Washington cited in *The War of American Independence*, Higginbotham, p. 411.

78. Thaddeus Kosciusko to Horatio Gates, cited in Nelson, *General Horatio Gates*, p. 285.

79. Horatio Gates to Samuel Mitchell, cited in Nelson, *General Horatio Gates*, p. 295.

Chapter 2

1. George Washington cited in Noah Brooks, *Henry Knox: A Soldier of the Revolution* (New York: G.P. Putnam's Sons, 1900), p. 34.

2. Henry Knox to George Washington, cited in Brooks, *Henry Knox*, p. 40.

3. Henry Knox to William Knox, cited in Brooks, *Henry Knox*, p. 56.

4. Henry Knox to William Knox, cited in Brooks, *Henry Knox*, p. 68.

5. James Wilkinson, cited in David Hackett Fischer, *Washington's Crossing* (New York: Oxford University Press, 2004), p. 218.

6. Henry Knox to Lucy Knox, cited in Brooks, *Henry Knox*, p. 79.

7. Henry Knox to Lucy Knox, cited in Fischer, *Washington's Crossing*, p. 248.

8. Joseph White, cited in Fischer, *Washington's Crossing*, pp. 306–307.

9. Henry Knox to William Knox, cited in *Henry Knox*, Brooks, p. 70.

10. Henry Knox to Lucy Knox, cited in Brooks, *Henry Knox*, p. 64.

11. Henry Knox to John Hancock, cited in Brooks, *Henry Knox*, p. 90.

12. Henry Knox to Lucy Knox, cited in Brooks, *Henry Knox*, p. 104.

13. Henry Knox cited in Brooks, *Henry Knox*, p. 101.

14. Henry Knox to William Knox, cited in North Callahan, *Henry Knox: General Washington's General* (New York: Rinehart, 1958), p. 143.

15. James Thacher, cited in Callahan, *Henry Knox*, p. 145.

16. Henry Dearborn, cited in Callahan, *Henry Knox*, p. 145.

17. Henry Knox to Lucy Knox, cited in Brooks, *Henry Knox*, pp. 120–121.

18. George Washington, cited in Brooks, *Henry Knox*, p. 124.

19. Henry Knox, cited in Brooks, *Henry Knox*, p. 141.

20. Marquis de Chastellux, cited in Callahan, *Henry Knox*, p. 189.

21. Marquis de Lafayette, cited in Callahan, *Henry Knox*, p. 187.

22. Henry Knox to Alexander McDougall, cited in Brooks, *Henry Knox*, p. 171.

23. George Washington cited in Callahan, *Henry Knox*, p. 208.

24. Washington Irving, cited in Callahan, *Henry Knox*, p. vii.

25. George Washington, cited in Callahan, *Henry Knox*, p. 190.

26. Nathanael Greene cited in Francis V. Greene, *General Greene* (New York: D. Appleton, 1893), p. 5.

27. Nathanael Greene to Catherine Greene, June 2, 1775, *The Papers of General Nathanael Greene*, ed. Richard K. Showman, Margaret Cobb, and Robert E. McCarthy (Chapel Hill, NC: University of North Carolina Press, 1976), Vol. I, p. 83.

28. George Washington, cited in Theodore Thayer, *Nathanael Greene: Strategist of the American Revolution* (New York: Twayne, 1960), p. 67.

29. Nathanael Greene to Samuel Ward, October 16, 1775, *Papers of General Nathanael Greene*, Vol. I, p. 134.

30. Nathanael Greene to Samuel Ward, cited in Greene, *General Greene,* p. 30.

31. Nathanael Greene to Jacob Greene, August 30, 1776, *Papers of General Nathanael Greene*, Vol. I, p. 291.

32. Nathanael Greene to Henry Knox, cited in Brooks, *Henry Knox*, p. 74.

33. Nathanael Greene to Catherine Greene, cited in Thayer, *Nathanael Greene*, p. 146.

34. Nathanael Greene to Nicholas Cooke, January 23, 1777, *The Papers of General Nathanael Greene*, ed. Richard K. Showman, Margaret Cobb, and Robert E.McCarthy (Chapel Hill, NC: University of North Carolina Press, 1980), Vol. II, p. 13.

35. Nathanael Greene to John Hancock, December 21, 1776, *Papers of General Nathanael Greene*, I, 374.

36. Nathanael Greene to John Adams, May 27, 1777, *Papers of General Nathanael Greene*, Vol. II, p. 98.

37. John Adams to Abigail Adams, cited in Thayer, *Nathanael Greene*, p. 163.

38. Nathanael Greene to James Varnum, August 17, 1777, *Papers of General Nathanael Greene*, Vol. II, p. 143.

39. Nathanael Greene to Jacob Greene, August 11, 1777, *Papers of General Nathanael Greene*, II, 138.

40. George Washington, cited in Thayer, *Nathanael Greene*, pp. 196–197.

41. Nathanael Greene to Henry Laurens, January 12, 1778, *Papers of General Nathanael Greene*, Vol. II, pp. 252–253.

42. Nathanael Greene to George Washington, cited in Thayer, *Nathanael Greene*, p. 227.

43. Nathanael Greene, cited in Thayer, *Nathanael Greene*, p. 227.

44. George Washington to Nathanael Greene, cited in Greene, *General Greene*, p. 99.

45. Nathanael Greene to George Washington, cited in Thayer, *Nathanael Greene*, p. 244.

46. George Washington to Nathanael Greene, cited in Greene, *General Greene*, p. 113.

47. Nathanael Greene, cited in Robert Middlekauff, *The Glorious Cause, The American Revolution, 1763–1789* (New York: Oxford University Press, 1982), p. 468.

48. Nathanael Greene to James Varnum, cited in Thayer, *Nathanael Greene*, p. 308.

49. Nathanael Greene, cited in Thayer, *Nathanael Greene*, p. 298.

50. Nathanael Greene, cited in Thayer, *Nathanael Greene*, p. 311.

51. Nathanael Greene to Thomas Jefferson, cited in Thayer, *Nathanael Greene*, p. 326.

52. Nathanael Greene to Chevalier Anne-Cesar de La Luzerne, cited in Thayer, *Nathanael Greene*, p. 348.

53. Nathanael Greene, cited in W. J. Wood, *Battles of the Revolutionary War: 1775–1781* (Chapel Hill, NC: Algonquin Books of Chapel Hill, 1990), p. 246.

54. Nathanael Greene to Baron von Steuben, cited in Middlekauff, *The Glorious Cause*, p. 488.

55. Nathanael Greene to George Washington, March 29, 1781, *The Papers of General Nathanael Greene*, ed. Richard K. Showman, Margaret Cobb, and Robert E. McCarthy (Chapel Hill, NC: University of North Carolina Press, 1994), Vol. VII, p. 481.

56. Nathanael Greene to Henry Knox, cited in Thayer, *Nathanael Greene*, p. 367.

57. Nathanael Greene to Robert Morris, August 18, 1781, *The Papers of General Nathanael Greene*, ed. Dennis M. Conrad (Chapel Hill, NC: University of North Carolina Press, 1997), Vol. IX, p. 250.

58. Nathanael Greene to Board of War. May 2, 1781, *The Papers of General Nathanael Greene*, ed. Dennis M. Conrad. (Chapel Hill, NC: University of North Carolina Press, 1995), Vol. VIII, p. 189.

59. Nathanael Greene, cited in Thayer, *Nathanael Greene*, p. 380.

60. Nathanael Greene, cited in Thayer, *Nathanael Greene*, p. 374.

Chapter 3

1. Arnold was actually born in 1741.

2. Benedict Arnold, cited in James Kirby Martin, *Benedict Arnold, Revolutionary Hero: An American Warrior Reconsidered* (New York: New York University Press, 1997), p. 58.

3. Benedict Arnold, cited in James Thomas Flexner, *The Traitor and the Spy: Benedict Arnold and John Andre* (Boston, MA: Little, Brown and Company, 1975), p. 19.

4. Benedict Arnold, cited in Martin, *Benedict Arnold, Revolutionary Hero*, pp. 85–86.

5. Benedict Arnold, cited in Martin, *Benedict Arnold, Revolutionary Hero*, p. 95.

6. Benedict Arnold, cited in Martin, *Benedict Arnold, Revolutionary Hero*, p. 123.

7. Benedict Arnold to George Washington, cited in Martin, *Benedict Arnold, Revolutionary Hero*, p. 126.

8. Benedict Arnold to George Washington, cited in Martin, *Benedict Arnold, Revolutionary Hero*, p. 135.

9. Simeon Thayer, cited in Martin, *Benedict Arnold, Revolutionary Hero*, p. 139.

10. Benedict Arnold, cited in Martin, *Benedict Arnold, Revolutionary Hero*, p. 145.

11. Benedict Arnold to Hannah Arnold, cited in Martin, *Benedict Arnold, Revolutionary Hero*, p. 174.

12. George Washington, cited in Martin, *Benedict Arnold, Revolutionary Hero*, p. 184.

13. Benedict Arnold, cited in Martin, *Benedict Arnold, Revolutionary Hero*, p. 188.

14. Benedict Arnold, cited in Martin, *Benedict Arnold, Revolutionary Hero*, p. 206.

15. Benedict Arnold, cited in Martin, *Benedict Arnold, Revolutionary Hero*, p. 217.

16. Benedict Arnold, cited in Martin, *Benedict Arnold, Revolutionary Hero*, p. 240.

17. Horatio Gates to John Hancock, cited in Martin, *Benedict Arnold, Revolutionary Hero*, p. 240.

18. Benedict Arnold, cited in Martin, *Benedict Arnold, Revolutionary Hero*, p. 277.

19. Benedict Arnold, cited in Flexner, *The Traitor and the Spy*, p. 111.

20. Benedict Arnold, cited in Martin, *Benedict Arnold, Revolutionary Hero*, p. 303.

21. Benedict Arnold to Horatio Gates, cited in Martin, *Benedict Arnold, Revolutionary Hero*, p. 311.

22. Benedict Arnold, cited in Martin, *Benedict Arnold, Revolutionary Hero*, p. 321.

23. John Adams, cited in Martin, *Benedict Arnold, Revolutionary Hero*, p. 322.

24. Pamphlet cited in Martin, *Benedict Arnold, Revolutionary Hero*, p. 324.

25. Benedict Arnold, cited in Martin, *Benedict Arnold, Revolutionary Hero*, p. 321.

26. Benedict Arnold to John Hancock, cited in Martin, *Benedict Arnold, Revolutionary Hero*, p. 343.

27. Benedict Arnold to Horatio Gates, cited in Martin, *Benedict Arnold, Revolutionary Hero*, p. 364.

28. Enoch Poor and Ebenezer Wakefield, cited in Martin, *Benedict Arnold, Revolutionary Hero*, pp. 379–380.

29. Benedict Arnold to Horatio Gates, cited in Martin, *Benedict Arnold, Revolutionary Hero*, p. 391.

30. Benedict Arnold to George Washington, cited in Martin, *Benedict Arnold, Revolutionary Hero*, p. 417.

31. Benedict Arnold to George Washington, cited in Martin, *Benedict Arnold, Revolutionary Hero*, p. 428.

32. Benedict Arnold, cited in Martin, *Benedict Arnold, Revolutionary Hero*, p. 429.

33. John Paul Jones, cited in Samuel Eliot Morison, *John Paul Jones: A Sailor's Biography* (New York: Time Reading Program Special Edition, 1964), p. 13.

34. John Paul Jones to Benjamin Franklin, cited in Evan Thomas, *John Paul Jones: Sailor, Hero, Father of the American Navy* (New York: Simon & Schuster, 2003), p. 33.

35. John Paul Jones to Benjamin Franklin, cited in Morison, *John Paul Jones*, p. 24.

36. John Paul Jones, cited in Morison, *John Paul Jones*, p. 41.

37. John Paul Jones to Joseph Hewes, cited in Morison, *John Paul Jones*, p. 50.

38. John Paul Jones to Joseph Hewes, cited in Morison, *John Paul Jones*, p. 53.

39. John Paul Jones, cited in Morison, *John Paul Jones*, p. 57.

40. Congress to John Paul Jones, cited in Morison, *John Paul Jones*, p. 59.

41. John Paul Jones to Esek Hopkins, cited in Morison, *John Paul Jones*, p. 61.

42. John Paul Jones, cited in Morison, *John Paul Jones*, p. 79.

43. John Paul Jones, cited in Morison, *John Paul Jones*, p. 104.

44. John Paul Jones, cited in Morison, *John Paul Jones*, p. 113.

45. American commissioners to John Paul Jones, cited in Morison, *John Paul Jones*, p. 125.

46. John Paul Jones to Lady Selkirk, cited in Morison, *John Paul Jones*, p. 149.

47. John Paul Jones, cited in Morison, *John Paul Jones*, p. 158.

48. Cited in Morison, *John Paul Jones*, p. 2.

49. John Paul Jones, cited in Morison, *John Paul Jones*, p. 169.

50. John Paul Jones, cited in Morison, *John Paul Jones*, p. 182.

51. John Paul Jones, cited in Morison, *John Paul Jones*, p. 213.

52. John Paul Jones, cited in Morison, *John Paul Jones*, pp. 219–220.

53. John Paul Jones, cited in Morison, *John Paul Jones*, p. 229.

54. Cited in Thomas, *John Paul Jones*, p. 186.

55. John Paul Jones, cited in Morison, *John Paul Jones*, p. 232.

56. John Paul Jones, cited in Thomas, *John Paul Jones*, p. 192.

57. John Paul Jones, cited in Morison, *John Paul Jones*, p. 290.

Chapter 4

1. Cited in Don Higginbotham, *The War of American Independence: Military Attitudes, Policies, and Practice, 1763–1789* (Boston, MA: Northeastern University Press, 1983), p. 362.

2. Andrew Pickens, cited in Alice Noble Waring, *The Fighting Elder: Andrew Pickens (1739–1817)* (Columbia, SC: University of South Carolina Press, 1962), p. 27.

3. Andrew Pickens to Henry Lee, cited in Waring, *The Fighting Elder*, p. 27.

4. Andrew Pickens, cited in Waring, *The Fighting Elder*, p. 40.

5. Andrew Pickens, cited in Waring, *The Fighting Elder*, p. 46.

6. Andrew Pickens to Henry Lee, cited in Waring, *The Fighting Elder*, p. 49.

7. Andrew Pickens cited in John S. Pancake, *This Destructive War: The British Campaign in the Carolinas, 1780–1782* (Tuscaloosa, AL: The University of Alabama Press, 1985), p. 191.

8. Andrew Pickens to Nathanael Greene, June 7, 1781, *The Papers of General Nathanael Greene*, ed. Dennis M. Conrad (Chapel Hill, NC: University of North Carolina Press, 1995), Vol. VIII, p. 359.

9. Andrew Pickens to Henry Lee, cited in Waring, *The Fighting Elder*, p. 87.

10. Inscription cited in Waring, *The Fighting Elder*, p. 209.

11. Henry Lee, *Memoirs of the War in the Southern Department of the United States* (Philadelphia, PA: 1812: reprint New York: Burt Franklin, 1970), I, 166.

12. Thomas Sumter, cited in Robert D. Bass, *Gamecock: The Life and Campaigns of General Thomas Sumter* (New York: Holt, Rinehart and Winston, 1961), p. 71.

13. Thomas Sumter to Thomas Pinckney, cited in Bass, *Gamecock*, p. 74.

14. Lord Charles Cornwallis to Sir Henry Clinton, cited in Bass, *Gamecock*, p. 85.

15. Nathanael Greene to Thomas Sumter, January 8, 1781, *The Papers of General Nathanael Greene*, ed. Richard K. Showman, Margaret Cobb, and Robert E. McCarthy (Chapel Hill, NC: University of North Carolina Press, 1995), Vol. VII, p. 74.

16. Thomas Sumter, cited in Bass, *Gamecock*, p. 151.

17. Thomas Sumter to Nathanael Greene, April 27, 1781, *The Papers of General Nathanael Greene*, ed. Dennis M. Conrad (Chapel Hill, NC: University of North Carolina Press, 1995), Vol. VIII, pp. 163–164.

18. Nathanael Greene to Joseph Reed, May 4, 1781, *Papers of General Nathanael Greene*, Vol. VIII, p. 200.

19. Thomas Sumter to Nathanael Greene, May 14, 1781, *Papers of General Nathanael Greene*, Vol. VIII, p. 259.

20. Nathanael Greene to Thomas Sumter, May 17, 1781, *Papers of General Nathanael Greene*, Vol. VIII, p. 278.

21. Thomas Sumter to Nathanael Greene, January 2, 1782, *The Papers of General Nathanael Greene*, ed. Dennis M. Conrad (Chapel Hill, NC: University of North Carolina Press, 1998), Vol. X, p. 153.

22. Thomas Sumter, cited in Bass, *Gamecock*, p. 222.

23. Cited in Robert D. Bass, *Swamp Fox: The Life and Campaigns of General Francis Marion* (New York: Henry Holt and Company, 1959), p. 21.

24. Peter Horry, cited in Bass, *Swamp Fox*, p. 22.

25. Peter Horry, cited in Bass, *Swamp Fox*, p. 27.

26. Otho Williams, cited in Bass, *Swamp Fox*, p. 40.

27. Francis Marion to Horatio Gates, cited in Bass, *Swamp Fox*, p. 60.

28. Francis Marion to John Rutledge, cited in Bass, *Swamp Fox*, pp. 78–79.

29. Francis Marion to Horatio Gates, cited in Hugh F. Rankin, *Francis Marion: The Swamp Fox* (New York: Thomas Y. Crowell Company, 1973), p. 92.

30. Banastre Tarleton to Charles Cornwallis, cited in Bass, *Swamp Fox*, p. 82

31. Banastre Tarleton, cited in Bass, *Swamp Fox*, p. 82

32. Francis Marion to Horatio Gates, cited in Bass, *Swamp Fox*, p. 97.

33. Francis Marion to Horatio Gates, cited in Bass, *Swamp Fox*, p. 98.

34. Nathanael Greene to Francis Marion, December 4, 1780, *The Papers of General Nathanael Greene*, ed. Richard K. Showman, Margaret Cobb, and Robert E. McCarthy (Chapel Hill, NC: University of North Carolina Press, 1991), Vol. VI, p. 519.

35. Peter Horry, cited in Bass, *Swamp Fox*, p. 154.

36. John Watson, cited in Bass, *Swamp Fox*, p. 155.

37. Henry Lee to Nathanael Greene, cited in Bass, *Swamp Fox*, p. 175.

38. Nathanael Greene to George Washington, cited in Bass, *Swamp Fox*, p. 175.

39. Nathanael Greene to Francis Marion, May 4, 1781, *Papers of General Nathanael Greene*, Vol. VIII, p. 199.

40. Francis Marion to Nathanael Greene, May 6, 1781, *Papers of General Nathanael Greene*, Vol. VIII, p. 215.

41. Nathanael Greene to Henry Lee, June 24, 1781, *Papers of General Nathanael Greene*, Vol. VIII, p. 452.

42. Francis Marion to Peter Horry, cited in Bass, *Swamp Fox*, p. 217.

43. Francis Marion to Peter Horry, cited in Bass, *Swamp Fox*, p. 229.

Chapter 5

1. Walt Whitman, "Song of Myself," in *Leaves of Grass*, ed. Emory Holloway, Inclusive Edition (Garden City, NY: Doubleday Doran, 1945), p. 75.

2. Ethan Allen cited in Charles A. Jellison, *Ethan Allen: Frontier Rebel* (Syracuse, NY: Syracuse University Press, 1969), p. 62.

3. Ethan Allen, *A Narrative of the Captivity of Col. Ethan Allen* (Albany, NY: Pratt & Clark, 1814), p. 5.

4. Discussion of what Allen may or may not have said in Jellison, *Ethan Allen*, p. 118.

5. Allen, *Narrative*, p. 9.

6. Ethan Allen cited in Jellison, *Ethan Allen*, p. 124.

7. Allen, *Narrative*, p. 18.

8. Ethan Allen cited in Jellison, *Ethan Allen*, p. 156.

9. Allen, *Narrative*, p. 26.

10. Alexander Graydon cited in Christopher Ward, *The War of the Revolution* (New York: McMillan, 1952), Vol. II, pp. 930–931.

11. Allen, *Narrative*, p. 131.

12. George Washington cited in Jellison, *Ethan Allen*, p. 178.

13. Frederick Jackson Turner, "The Significance of the Frontier in American History," in *Frontier and Section: Selected Essays of Frederick Jackson Turner*, ed. Ray Allen Billington (Englewood Cliffs, NJ: Prentice-Hall, 1961), p. 61.

14. George Rogers Clark to Patrick Henry, (no date, but sometime in summer or fall of 1777), *George Rogers Clark Papers 1771–1781*, ed. James Alton James (Springfield, IL: Illinois State Historical Library, 1912), Vol. I, p. 31.

15. Patrick Henry to George Rogers Clark, January 15, 1778, *Clark Papers*, Vol. I, p. 38.

16. George Rogers Clark to Patrick Henry, February 3, 1779, *Clark Papers*, Vol. I, pp. 98–99.

17. Joseph Bowman journal cited in *Clark Papers*, Vol. I, pp. 158–159.

18. Joseph Bowman journal cited in *Clark Papers*, Vol. I, p. 159.

19. George Rogers Clark to Henry Hamilton, February 4, 1779, from Bowman journal, *Clark Papers*, Vol. I, p. 160.

20. Henry Hamilton to George Rogers Clark, February 4, 1779, from Bowman journal, *Clark Papers*, Vol. I, pp. 160–161.

21. George Rogers Clark to R. B. Lernoult, March 16, 1779, *Clark Papers*, Vol. I, pp. 306–307.

22. George Rogers Clark cited in James Alton James, *The Life of George Rogers Clark* (Chicago, IL: The University of Chicago Press, 1928), p. 148.

23. George Washington to Thomas Jefferson cited in James, *The Life of George Rogers Clark*, p. 231.

24. George Rogers Clark to Thomas Jefferson, August 4, 1781 *Clark Papers*, Vol. I, pp. 578.

25. George Rogers Clark to Thomas Nelson, October 1, 1781 *Clark Papers*, Vol. I, pp. 608.

26. Thomas Jefferson to George Rogers Clark, December 4, 1783, *George Rogers Clark Papers 1781–1784*, ed. James Alton James (Springfield, IL: Illinois State Historical Library, 1926), Vol. II, p. 250.

27. George Rogers Clark to Patrick Henry, February 3, 1779, *Clark Papers*, Vol. I, p. 99.

28. Daniel Morgan cited in Don Higginbotham, *Daniel Morgan, Revolutionary Rifleman* (Chapel Hill, NC: The University of North Carolina Press, 1961), p. 18.

29. For instance, the renowned author Kenneth Roberts edited a collection of journals and documents, *March to Quebec* (1940) and published a historically accurate novel on the trek, *Arundel* (1929).

30. Daniel Morgan cited in Higginbotham, *Daniel Morgan, Revolutionary Rifleman*, p. 49.

31. George Washington to John Hancock, cited in Higginbotham, *Daniel Morgan, Revolutionary Rifleman*, p. 55.

32. George Washington to Daniel Morgan, cited in Higginbotham, *Daniel Morgan, Revolutionary Rifleman*, p. 58.

33. George Washington to Daniel Morgan, cited in Higginbotham, *Daniel Morgan, Revolutionary Rifleman*, p. 61.

34. Horatio Gates to George Washington, cited in Higginbotham, *Daniel Morgan, Revolutionary Rifleman*, p. 70.

35. Horatio Gates cited in Higginbotham, *Daniel Morgan, Revolutionary Rifleman*, p. 72.

36. Horatio Gates to John Hancock, cited in Higginbotham, *Daniel Morgan, Revolutionary Rifleman*, p. 76.

37. Daniel Morgan cited in Higginbotham, *Daniel Morgan, Revolutionary Rifleman*, p. 72.

38. Daniel Morgan to Nathanael Greene, December 31, 1780, *The Papers of General Nathanael Greene*, ed. Richard K. Showman, Margaret Cobb, and Robert E. McCarthy (Chapel Hill, NC: University of North Carolina Press, 1994), Vol. VII, p. 190.

39. Daniel Morgan to Horatio Gates, cited in Higginbotham, *Daniel Morgan, Revolutionary Rifleman*, p. 105.

40. Daniel Morgan to Horatio Gates, cited in Higginbotham, *Daniel Morgan, Revolutionary Rifleman*, p. 110.

41. Daniel Morgan to Horatio Gates, cited in Higginbotham, *Daniel Morgan, Revolutionary Rifleman*, p. 116.

42. Nathanael Greene to Daniel Morgan, December 16, 1780, *The Papers of General Nathanael Greene*, ed. Richard K. Showman, Margaret Cobb, and Robert E. McCarthy (Chapel Hill, NC: University of North Carolina Press, 1994), Vol. VI, p. 589.

43. Daniel Morgan to Nathanael Greene, December 31, 1780, *Papers of General Nathanael Greene*, Vol. VII, p. 30.

44. Daniel Morgan to Nathanael Greene, December 31, 1780, *Papers of General Nathanael Greene*, Vol. VII, p. 31.

45. Nathanael Greene to Daniel Morgan, January 13, 1781, *Papers of General Nathanael Greene*, Vol. VII, p. 106.

46. Thomas Young cited in Higginbotham, *Daniel Morgan, Revolutionary Rifleman*, p. 134.

47. Daniel Morgan cited in Higginbotham, *Daniel Morgan, Revolutionary Rifleman*, p. 137.

48. Daniel Morgan cited in Higginbotham, *Daniel Morgan, Revolutionary Rifleman*, p. 139.

49. Daniel Morgan to William Snickers, cited in Higginbotham, *Daniel Morgan, Revolutionary Rifleman*, p. 142.

50. Daniel Morgan to Thomas Jefferson, cited in Higginbotham, *Daniel Morgan, Revolutionary Rifleman*, p. 151.

51. Daniel Morgan cited in Higginbotham, *Daniel Morgan, Revolutionary Rifleman*, p. 174.

52. Daniel Morgan to Otho Williams, cited in Higginbotham, *Daniel Morgan, Revolutionary Rifleman*, p. 181.

53. Nathanael Greene cited in Higginbotham, *Daniel Morgan, Revolutionary Rifleman*, p. 155.

Chapter 6

1. Charles Lee, cited in Charles Royster, *Light-Horse Harry Lee and the Legacy of the American Revolution* (Cambridge, UK: Cambridge University Press, 1982), p. 14.

2. Henry Lee, *Memoirs of the War in the Southern Department of the United States* (Philadelphia, PA: 1812: reprint New York: Burt Franklin, 1970), Vol. II, p. 203.

3. Henry Lee to Charles Lee, cited in Royster, *Light-Horse Harry Lee*, p. 16.

4. Henry Lee, *Memoirs of the War in the Southern Department of the United States* (Philadelphia, PA: 1812: reprint New York: Burt Franklin, 1970), Vol. I, p. 21.

5. Lee, *Memoirs*, Vol. I, p. 48.

6. Henry Lee to George Washington, cited in Royster, *Light-Horse Harry Lee,* p. 25.

7. George Washington to the President of Congress, cited in Royster, *Light-Horse Harry Lee,* p. 21.

8. Henry Lee to Anthony Wayne, cited in Royster, *Light-Horse Harry Lee,* p. 45.

9. Lee, *Memoirs*, I, 251.

10. Francis Marion to Nathanael Greene, cited in Robert D. Bass, *Swamp Fox: The Life and Campaigns of General Francis Marion* (New York: Henry Holt and Company, 1959), p. 137.

11. Lee, *Memoirs*, Vol. I, p. 284.

12. Lee, *Memoirs*, Vol. I, p. 289.

13. Lee, *Memoirs*, Vol. I, p. 344.

14. Lee, *Memoirs*, Vol. I, p. 357.

15. Lee, *Memoirs*, Vol. I, pp. 375–376.

16. Lee, *Memoirs*, Vol. II, p. 51.

17. Lee, *Memoirs*, Vol. II, p. 94.

18. Lee, *Memoirs*, Vol. II, p. 119.

19. Lee, *Memoirs*, Vol. II, p. 283.

20. Lee, *Memoirs*, Vol. II, p. 290.

21. Nathanael Greene to John Hanson, February 18, 1782, *The Papers of General Nathanael Greene*, ed. Dennis M. Conrad (Chapel Hill, NC: University of North Carolina Press, 1998), Vol. X, p. 377.

22. Lee, *Memoirs*, Vol. II, p. 461.

23. Henry Lee, cited in Royster *Light-Horse Harry Lee,* p. 212.

24. Henry Lee, cited in Royster, *Light-Horse Harry Lee* p. 3.

25. Hugh F. Rankin, "Anthony Wayne: Military Romanticist," in *George Washington's Generals and Opponents: Their Exploits and Leadership*, ed. George A. Billias (Cambridge, MA: Da Capo Press, 1994) and Paul David Nelson, *Anthony Wayne: Soldier of the Early Republic* (Bloomington, IN: Indiana University Press, 1985).

26. Isaac Wayne, cited in Nelson, *Anthony Wayne*, p. 8.

27. Anthony Wayne, cited in Nelson, *Anthony Wayne*, p. 25.

28. Anthony Wayne to Benjamin Franklin, cited in Nelson, *Anthony Wayne*, p. 26.

29. Anthony Wayne to Horatio Gates, cited in Nelson, *Anthony Wayne*, p. 33.

30. Anthony Wayne to Richard Peters, cited in Nelson, *Anthony Wayne*, p. 44.

31. Cited in Nelson, *Anthony Wayne*, p. 64.

32. Anthony Wayne to Mary Wayne, cited in Nelson, *Anthony Wayne*, p. 59.

33. Anthony Wayne to Mary Wayne, cited in Nelson, *Anthony Wayne*, p. 60.

34. John Sullivan to Mesech Weare, cited in Nelson, *Anthony Wayne*, p. 60.

35. Anthony Wayne to Mary Wayne, cited in Nelson, *Anthony Wayne*, p. 61.

36. Anthony Wayne to Mary Wayne, cited in Nelson, *Anthony Wayne*, p. 62.

37. Anthony Wayne to Mary Wayne, cited in Nelson, *Anthony Wayne*, p. 81.

38. Anthony Wayne to George Washington, cited in Nelson, *Anthony Wayne*, p. 87.

39. Anthony Wayne, cited in Nelson, *Anthony Wayne*, p. 87.

40. Anthony Wayne to Henry Archer, cited in Nelson, *Anthony Wayne*, p. 93.

41. Anthony Wayne to Sharp Delany, cited in Nelson, *Anthony Wayne*, pp. 97–98.

42. Anthony Wayne to Jack Stewart, cited in Nelson, *Anthony Wayne*, p. 94.

43. Anthony Wayne to George Washington, cited in Charles J. Stille, *Major General Anthony Wayne and the Pennsylvania Line in the Continental Army* (Philadelphia, PA: J.B. Lippincott Company, 1893), p. 196.

44. Anthony Wayne to Hugh Sheel, cited in Nelson, *Anthony Wayne*, p. 114.

45. Anthony Wayne to Joseph Reed, cited in Nelson, *Anthony Wayne*, p. 117.

46. Anthony Wayne to George Washington, cited in Nelson, *Anthony Wayne*, p. 119.

47. Anthony Wayne to Benjamin Fishbourn, cited in Nelson, *Anthony Wayne*, p. 129.

48. Anthony Wayne to William Davies, cited in Nelson, *Anthony Wayne*, p. 139.

49. Anthony Wayne to Mary Wayne, cited in Nelson, *Anthony Wayne*, p. 142.

50. Anthony Wayne to Thomas Burke, cited in Nelson, *Anthony Wayne*, p. 144.

51. Anthony Wayne to William Irvine, cited in Nelson, *Anthony Wayne*, p. 195.

Conclusion

1. George Washington to Benedict Arnold, cited in James Thomas Flexner, *The Traitor and the Spy: Benedict Arnold and John Andre* (Boston, MA: Little, Brown and Company, 1975), p. 100.

Essay on Sources

HERE IS A ROUNDUP of the books found most useful and accessible in the course of researching *Founding Fighters*. While hardly an exhaustive listing, this brief essay constitutes a guide to further reading for those so disposed.

To understand American political culture of the Revolutionary period, see two magisterial works, Bernard Bailyn, *Ideological Origins of the American Revolution* (1967) and Gordon Wood, *The Creation of the American Republic* (1969). On the entire Revolution, to include informed discussion of the military dimension, the best single volume synthesis is by Robert Middlekauff, *The Glorious Cause: The American Revolution, 1763–1789* (1982). Don Higginbotham, *The War of American Independence: Military Attitudes, Policies,and Practice, 1763–1789* (1971), provides a superb analysis of the conflict at all levels from strategic to tactical. The first two chapters of Russell F. Weigley, *The American Way of War: A History of United States Military Policy and Strategy* (1973) offer keen insights into military strategy in the Revolution. Dave R. Palmer, *The Way of the Fox: American Strategy in the War for America 1775–1783* (1975) is a gracefully written and sometimes provocative take on Washington and American strategy. W. J. Wood, *Battles of the Revolutionary War* (1990) thoroughly examines ten key engagements as well as the campaigns that surrounded them. There are several good general reference works that contain overviews of the Revolution's leading personalities and key events. By far the best is Mark M. Boatner III, *Encyclopedia of the American Revolution* (1994). For American military leaders, the collection edited by George A. Billias, *George Washington's Generals and Opponents* (1994) contains scholarly essays on 12 American figures, including eight of the 15 discussed in *Founding Fighters*. Additionally, it paints portraits of ten British military leaders.

Richard Montgomery's martyrdom at Quebec made him an American hero for about half a century, but then he passed from memory. Two superb, recent biographies help rectify that. Hal T. Shelton, *General Richard Montgomery and the American Revolution: From Redcoat to Rebel* (1994) furnishes an excellent military narrative. Michael P. Gabriel, *Major*

General Richard Montgomery: The Making of an American Hero (2002) is especially good, as its subtitle suggests, on Montgomery's "career" as a Revolutionary hero. For Charles Lee the best biography—well documented and mildly sympathetic to its subject—is by John Alden, *Charles Lee: Patriot or Traitor?* (1951). Less scholarly and more emphatically pro-Lee is Samuel W. Patterson, *Knight Errant of Liberty: The Triumph and Tragedy of General Charles Lee* (1958). Indispensable, particularly since the originals have largely disappeared, is a four-volume collection, *The Lee Papers* (1872–1875) edited by the New York Historical Society. Paul David Nelson, *General Horatio Gates: A Biography* (1976) is a thorough study of the victor of Saratoga. An earlier work by Samuel Patterson, *Horatio Gates: Defender of American Liberties* (1941) is too uncritical of its subject, but contains useful information.

The best modern, scholarly biography of Henry Knox is North Callahan, *Henry Knox: General Washington's General* (1958). Two older works, written in hagiographic, nineteenth-century style are useful for the many Knox letters they quote: Francis S. Drake, *Life and Correspondence of Henry Knox* (1873) and Noah Brooks, *Henry Knox: A Soldier of the Revolution* (1900). The best study of Nathanael Greene is Theodore Thayer, *Nathanael Greene; Strategist of the Revolution* (1960). A book by a nineteenth-century soldier-intellectual, Francis V. Greene, *General Greene* (1893) is well written, even literary, in style and contains solid military analysis. *The Papers of General Nathanael Greene* (11 volumes to date, with a 12th and final one projected), edited by Richard K. Showman et al. and published for the Rhode Island Historical Society, represent a treasure trove of documents by an officer whose prolific correspondence was only exceeded by Washington himself.

Authors have subjected Benedict Arnold to many studies. A thoughtful examination of Arnold's pretreason career is James Kirby Martin, *Benedict Arnold, Revolutionary Hero: An American Warrior Reconsidered* (1997). James Thomas Flexner, *The Traitor and the Spy: Benedict Arnold and John Andre* (1975) is an intriguing parallel study of the American general and the British officer whose fates became intertwined. The two best John Paul Jones biographies are Samuel Eliot Morison, *John Paul Jones* (1959) and Evan Thomas, *John Paul Jones: Sailor, Hero, Father of the American Navy* (2003).

An outstanding study of the partisan struggle in the Carolinas is John S. Pancake, *This Destructive War: The British Campaign in the Carolinas* 1780–1782 (1985). Readable and informative biographies of the three great South Carolina partisan leaders include Alice Noble Waring, *The Fighting Elder: Andrew Pickens (1739–1817)* (1962); Robert D. Bass, *Gamecock: The Life and Campaigns of General Thomas Sumter* (1961) and *Swamp Fox: The Life and Campaigns of General Francis Marion* (1959); and Hugh F. Rankin, *Francis Marion: The Swamp Fox* (1973).

Charles Jellison, *Ethan Allen: Frontier Rebel* (1969) is a lively, informative, and balanced study of its fascinating subject. *A Narrative of the Captivity of Col. Ethan Allen*, originally published in 1779 and reprinted many times since, offers Allen's own inimitable account of his Revolutionary service. Lowell H. Harrison, *George Rogers Clark and the War in the West* (1976) is concise, scholarly, and readable. The *George Rogers Clark Papers* (two volumes, 1912, 1926) capture the colorful flavor of the "Conqueror of the Old Northwest." The best Daniel Morgan biography is Don Higginbotham, *Daniel Morgan, Revolutionary Rifleman* (1961).

Charles Royster, *Light-Horse Harry Lee and the Legacy of the American Revolution* (1981) is not, properly speaking, a life of its subject, but rather a fascinating character study, as well as a dazzling discourse on the revolutionary and early republic eras. Lee's own *Memoirs of the War in the Southern Department of the United States* (1812) are indispensable for understanding the man and the war. There are numerous biographies of Anthony Wayne, but the best by far is Paul David Nelson, *Anthony Wayne: Soldier of the Early Republic* (1985).

Index

About the Author

ALAN C. CATE teaches history at University School in Hunting Valley, Ohio. He is a graduate of the US Military Academy at West Point and holds a Masters Degree in American history from Stanford University. He is also a graduate of the *Ecole Superieure de Guerre* in Paris, France, and was a National Security Fellow at Harvard University's John F. Kennedy School of Government. During a twenty-five-year career as an infantry officer, Cate not only commanded at levels ranging from a small Special Forces team to a 1000-soldier battalion, but he also taught history at West Point and served on the faculties of the US Army's Command and General Staff College (Fort Leavenworth, KS) and the Army War College (Carlisle Barracks, PA). He has published numerous articles on American military history.